# JOSEF FRANK

## ARCHITECT

## AND

## DESIGNER

# JOSEF FRANK,

# ARCHITECT AND DESIGNER

An Alternative Vision
of the Modern Home

Leon Botstein
Marianne Lamonaca
Karin Lindegren
Christopher Long
Penny Sparke
Nina Stritzler-Levine
Kristina Wängberg-Eriksson
Christian Witt-Dörring

Nina Stritzler-Levine, Editor

Published for The Bard Graduate Center
for Studies in the Decorative Arts, New York,
by Yale University Press, New Haven and London

This catalogue is published in conjunction with the exhibition "Josef Frank, Architect and Designer: An Alternative Vision of the Modern Home" held at The Bard Graduate Center for Studies in the Decorative Arts from May 9, 1996 to July 21, 1996.

Exhibition Curators: Christopher Long, Nina Stritzler-Levine, Kristina Wängberg-Eriksson, Christian Witt-Dörring
Project Director: Nina Stritzler-Levine
Project Assistant: Lisa Arcomano
Project Editors: Martina D'Alton, New York, and Sally Salvesen, London
Designer: Michael Shroyer

Composition by U.S. Lithograph, typographers, New York
Printed in Italy

Library of Congress Catalog number: 96-083971
ISBN: 0 300 06899 9 (cloth); 0 300 06901 4 (paper)

All designs and products by Josef Frank for Svenskt Tenn are protected by law. © Svenskt Tenn, 1996

On the cover: Josef Frank, Town for 2,000 Families, ca. 1950; pencil and watercolor on paper. Arkitekturmuseet

Frontispiece: Josef Frank, House for Axel and Signhild Cläeson, Falsterbo, Sweden, ca. 1926; ink on tracing paper. Private collection.

Endpapers: Josef Frank, "Gröna Fåglar" (Green Birds), designed 1943–44 ; linen. Svenskt Tenn, Stockholm

Funding for
"Josef Frank, Architect and Designer"
has been generously provided by the
Graham Foundation for Advanced Studies
in the Fine Arts; The Furthermore Program
of The J. M. Kaplan Fund; and the
Kjell and Märta Beijers Foundation.
Additional support has been provided by the
Austrian Cultural Institute, New York; and
the Consulate General of Sweden, New York.

# CONTENTS

# FOREWORD

The Bard Graduate Center is honored to present the first in-depth examination of Josef Frank to be undertaken in the United States. Little known in the English-speaking world, Frank was extraordinarily prolific, making important contributions to twentieth-century architecture and design. This catalogue and the exhibition it accompanies stand as a sweeping survey of Frank's vision. His architecture, textiles, furniture, and glass and metalwork are likely to come as a revelation to most viewers, the discovery of a unique and vital talent.

This is the Center's second collaboration with Yale University Press, an association that is a source of great pleasure. I am grateful to the foundations and corporations that have generously provided funding for this project. The exhibition catalogue has been made possible in part by generous grants from the Graham Foundation for Advanced Studies in the Fine Arts; The Furthermore Program of The J. M. Kaplan Fund; the Kjell and Märta Beijers Foundation; the Austrian Cultural Institute, New York; and the Consulate General of Sweden, New York. Funds for the exhibition have been provided by the Austrian Cultural Institute; the Consulate General of Sweden; Kjell and Märta Beijers Foundation / Svenskt Tenn. In-kind support has been provided by Scandinavian Airline and Ramlösa. I am grateful to Dr. Wolfgang Waldner, Director, and Dr. Ernst Aichinger, Deputy Director, The Austrian Cultural Institute, for presenting this project to the Austrian Government. My thanks also go to Consul General Dag Ahlander and Görel Bogärde, Deputy Consul General of Sweden, for their assistance in securing funds for the exhibition.

This project was conceived by Nina Stritzler-Levine, director of exhibitions at The Bard Graduate Center. It was curated by an international team of scholars who generously shared their knowledge; I am grateful to Christopher Long, Kristina Wängberg-Eriksson, and Christian Witt-Dörring, in addition to Ms Stritzler-Levine, for their cura-

torial efforts in assembling such a fascinating group of works by Frank. Their job was greatly facilitated by the generosity of public and private lenders in Austria, Sweden, and the United States. I want to thank the public institutions and archives that provided loans for the exhibition: The Consulate General of Sweden; Fallingwater, Mill Run, Pennsylvania; Graphische Sammlung, Albertina, Vienna; University of Applied Art, Vienna; Österreichisches Museum für angewandte Kunst (MAK–Museum of Applied Arts), Vienna; Millesgården, Stockholm; Svenskt Tenn and Svenskt Tenn Archive, Stockholm; Swedish Museum of Architecture, Stockholm; Nationalmuseum, Stockholm; and the Technische Universität Wien, Universitätarchiv. My thanks also go to the private lenders including: Ruth Wilson Kalmar; Friedrich Kurrent; Stig Larsson; Camilla Lundberg; Maria Peter; Anna L. Praun; Henning Rydberg; Johannes Spalt; Elisabeth Steiner; and two anonymous lenders.

A special word of thanks goes to Clas Reuterskiöld and Ann Wall who devoted great time and energy to this project in Sweden. Many others assisted with the preparation of loans and with research for the exhibition. I greatly appreciate the work of Richard Bösel, Erika Patka, Christian Witt-Dörring, Elisabeth Schmuttermeier, Angela Völker, Juliane Mikoletzky, Kristina Wängberg-Eriksson, Barbro Hovstadius, and Linda Waggoner.

My thanks to the fine group of scholars who contributed to the catalogue: Leon Botstein, Marianne Lamonaca, Karin Lindegren, Christopher Long, Elisabeth Schmuttermeier, Penny Sparke, Nina Stritzler-Levine, Kristina Wängberg-Eriksson, and Christian Witt-Dörring.

I want to extend my thanks to the catalogue production staff: Martina D'Alton, style editor; Michael Shroyer, designer; Gloria Dougherty, indexer, Roberta Fineman, proofreader, and U.S. Lithograph, typographers. At Yale University Press, John Nicoll, managing director, and Sally Salvesen, project editor, have been supportive from the beginning. Outstanding new photography for the catalogue was taken by Georg Mayer at the MAK, Museum of Applied Arts, Vienna; Gabriel Uggla at Millesgården and Svenskt Tenn; and Bruce White at Svenskt Tenn.

The committed staff of The Bard Graduate Center deserves my thanks for their assistance with this project. Lisa Arcomano, exhibitions coordinator, provided extensive assistance on many aspects of the catalogue and installation; Steve Waterman coordinated the installation and the design; Derek Ostergard, dean, shared his knowledge of twentieth-century design; and Vincent Plescia and Judith Maiorana provided general support and assistance. Linda Hartley, director of development, led the fundraising campaign assisted by Susan Wall and Barat Ellman. Tim Mulligan, director of public relations, coordinated the public relations effort with the exceptional help of Kelly Moody, administrative assistant. Lisa Podos, director of public programs, conceived of a marvelous selection of public events and educational programs, assisted by Jill Gustafson, Lee Bretz, and Amy Henderson. Bobbie Xuereb, chief librarian, and Peter Gammie and Eileen McDonagh,

assistant librarians, were extemely helpful with research. Marcial Lavina, head of the slide library, was especially helpful with photography. Jim Finch, director of finance, attended to all financial matters, assisted by Miao Chen; Stacia Jung and Carolee Goldstein provided logistical assistance; Richard Dominic, facilities manager, attended to the security and maintenance of the galleries with his staff, Alan Crespo, Orlando Diaz, Terence Lyons, Carlton Mitchell, Doru Padure, Dave Rio, Jorge L. SanPablo, Chandler Small, and Kenneth Talley.

Thanks to these collective efforts, "Josef Frank, Architect and Designer: An Alternative Vision of the Modern Home," both the exhibition and this catalogue, takes an important step toward securing Josef Frank's rightful place in the history of twentieth-century architecture and design.

Susan Weber Soros
Director

# PREFACE

Josef Frank once wrote, "It is easy to avoid any tastelessness if you limit yourself to bloodless asceticism and suppress every expression of a temperament. The tasteful becomes drearily boring." These words give us a hint of how he viewed his work and reveal something of his philosophy of life. Frank, an Austrian architect who became a groundbreaking designer in Sweden and helped introduce Swedish Modern design ideas into the United States, liked to provoke and to challenge—always, however, with the intention of encouraging new thought and creativity.

In the 1920s Frank shared the ideas of the architects and designers who wanted to allow air and light into domestic interiors and design. He too championed plain white walls, a position seemingly at odds with his ideas about diversifying interiors through organic forms, patterns, and colors. He was critical of standardization, of the exalted position of the machine, and of tubular furniture ("you can't even burn them!"). Instead Josef Frank embraced the individual, accommodating the needs and taste of the private person. "Mix old and new, colors and forms. Things that you like will all the same melt into a quiet unity. The home does not have to be planned in detail, not artful, just linked together by parts that its occupants enjoy and love."

In our work, we at Svenskt Tenn often return to such quotations. Josef Frank and Svenskt Tenn have been intimately connected since the early 1930s when Frank left Austria to live in Sweden. At the time, he could hardly have anticipated that a collaboration initiated by Estrid Ericson, the founder of the Svenskt Tenn, would be so rewarding and fruitful. He devoted himself almost entirely to developing and designing new furniture and textiles for Svenskt Tenn for almost four decades. Among his earliest work for the firm was the big Liljevalch sofa, seen in this exhibition, which left the Stockholm audience breathless.

Svenskt Tenn and its shop on Strandvägen in Stockholm came to be synonymous with a new kind of

The Swedish stamp issued in 1994 featuring two of Josef Frank's enduring designs: Cabinet on Stand, ca. 1940 (Nationalmuseum, Stockholm) and "Aralia," designed 1928 (Svenskt Tenn, Stockholm).

interior design. Its furnishings and other offerings have become classic, while still in great demand by a wide international clientele. Josef Frank's furniture, made decades ago, has been passed on to new generations and treasured by them or sold as objects of great value at the finest auction houses in Stockholm.

The name of Josef Frank still helps to make Svenskt Tenn a unique company worldwide. Frank-designed furniture, textiles, and lamps are made exclusively for Svenskt Tenn by specially chosen craftsmen. China, glassware, silverware, pewter, and other small objects, some of them designed by Frank, some by talented young Swedish designers, are also offered.

Svenskt Tenn is owned by the Kjell and Märta Beijer Foundation, associated with the Royal Swedish Academy of Sciences. The company's earnings help support the Foundation, and although active in business, Svenskt Tenn has become much more than a commercial venture. Our ambition is to further the ideas of Estrid Ericson and Josef Frank in modern form. The firm organizes lectures and exhibits on modern interior design, decorative arts, and, of course, the work of Josef Frank. The company's archive contains original Frank furniture and textiles and approximately two thousand of his design drawings. In this connection I would like to express my warm gratitude to Kristina Wängberg-Eriksson who, with financial support from the Foundation and Svenskt Tenn, has through her interest and untiring research contributed greatly to our understanding of the work of Estrid Ericson, Svenskt Tenn, and Josef Frank.

It is a true joy for me and special honor for Svenskt Tenn to have The Bard Graduate Center for Studies in the Decorative Arts present this exhibition. The exhibition and this catalogue will enable Frank's work and ideas to reach a widespread audience. Together, they make an essential contribution to the study of Josef Frank, his ideas about architecture, and his philosophy of interior design.

Finally, I must end with more of Frank's words. They shed light on his thinking as well as on the aims that guide us in the task of furthering his achievement: "The room in which you can live and think freely is neither beautiful, nor harmonic. It has come about by coincidence, it will never be completed and it can in itself absorb anything whatsoever to satisfy the changing demands of the owner."

Ann Wall
Director, Svenskt Tenn, Stockholm

# INTRODUCTION

In a startling keynote address, "Was ist modern?" (What is Modern?), delivered at the annual meeting of the Austrian Werkbund in 1930, Josef Frank attacked the functionalist attitudes of the modern movement by calling for abandoning the machine as the paradigm of modernism in architecture and design. Before an audience that included Walter Gropius and Mies van der Rohe, Frank proclaimed that history and the culture of everyday life rather than art and technology were at the center of modernism. While from a contemporary perspective, having lived through the period of Postmodernism, the issue of eliminating the boundaries between high and low culture, and embracing history might appear quite commonplace, in 1930 such views were a radical departure from the modernist discourse of the previous decade. They gave a portentous and rather compelling preview of the future. For Frank "What is Modern?" was the culmination of a long personal campaign against an ideological and dogmatic modernism.

In the years after the First World War, Josef Frank was one of the leading modern architects in Austria and among its most accomplished designers. In 1933, fearing the rise of Fascism, he immigrated to Sweden where he became the chief designer for Svenskt Tenn, the leading Swedish interior design firm, and a founder of Swedish Modern design. Outside Austria and Sweden, however, Frank's unique design philosophy—his alternative vision of the modern home—has been eclipsed, in part by the individuals recognized as the pioneers of the modern movement. Today Josef Frank, a tenacious outspoken critic of modernism, is little known in the English-speaking world. If he is known at all, it is likely to be for his remarkable textile designs. Even then, the full scope of his work in textiles, as well as other areas of the decorative arts and architecture, has been largely overlooked.

*Josef Frank, Architect and Designer: An Alternative Vision of the Modern Home* is intended to bring to the forefront of public attention Frank's extraordinary design achievements by

Josef Frank in Stockholm, ca. 1952.

focusing on his unique vision of the modern home and its furnishings, tracing the development of his career from the formative years in Vienna to his years in exile in Sweden and the United States. The biographical aspects are examined in detail, particularly his Jewish heritage, which, despite claims of Frank's "assimilation," largely dictated the development of his career. His Jewish identity was an underlying issue in the realization of his unique design philosophy.

The ten essays that follow explore the broader themes in Frank's life and work; the full range of his design work is thus represented. Rather than employ the same methodology, each author has developed an individual approach. And for the first time, Frank's achievements as an architect and designer of applied arts are examined in a single volume. This, most likely, is how Frank intended his work to be understood, together as a body. The catalogue section of the book follows a chronological sequence, again so that the many facets of Frank's work will be seen and studied together rather than separated into formal categories.

The idea of organizing a Frank exhibition at The Bard Graduate Center was conceived initially in Stockholm during the summer of 1994 when I learned that Frank would be the focus of two exhibitions there that fall: one at Millesgården examining his work in the applied arts and the other at the Museum of Swedish Architecture focusing on his architectural designs. My first discussions about the exhibition were with Staffan Carlén, director of Milles-gården, who encouraged me to investigate the possibility of a tour for the Stockholm exhibitions. When it was determined that major loans for those exhibitions could not be extended, I proposed that the Center develop its own Frank exhibition to be shown in our New York gallery. I am tremendously grateful to Susan Weber Soros who studied the available materials on Frank and supported my proposal. She has provided considerable encouragement toward the realization of the exhibition and catalogue.

The Frank exhibition is the result of a remarkable collaboration. The research and development was undertaken with astonishing speed and efficiency. Despite the schedule every effort was made to include period pieces of furniture and original textiles. In some cases this was not possible and current production examples were selected to represent a crucial work. Although comparatively few architectural drawings have survived, we agreed that only original drawings, not facsimiles, would be considered.

The selection of loans would not have been possible without the formation of a dedicated curatorial team. Joining me were Kristina Wängberg-Eriksson, an art historian in Stockholm and leading expert on Frank; Christopher Long, visiting professor of architectural history, University of Texas at Austin; and Christian Witt-Dörring, curator of furniture and woodworking at the MAK, Museum of Applied Art, Vienna. The commitment of the curatorial team, their unsurpassed knowledge of Frank, and incredibly hard work were essential to making this exhibition a reality.

I am especially grateful to the catalogue authors for their contributions: Leon Botstein, Marianne Lamonaca, Karin Lindegren, Christopher Long, Penny Sparke, Kristina Wängberg-Eriksson, and Christian Witt-Dörring. I want to express a special note of thanks to the authors whose texts were translated into English. They demonstrated remarkable patience and willingness to work through the difficulties that arise with translations of scholarly texts. In this regard I must acknowledge the superb editorial work of Christopher Long, who assisted with the Swedish texts; Jan Christer Eriksson, who helped navigate through many complex translation questions; and Michael Huey, who was called upon very late to work on the German manuscripts. I also want to thank William Achauer, Charles Fineman, Terry Prince, Roger Tanner, and Irene Zedlacher. At Bard College I want to thank Dorothy Miller for her editorial assistance.

Martina D'Alton, the style editor of the catalogue, was essential to the production of this catalogue. Martina's professionalism and editorial skills are unmatched, and her sense of humor and remarkable capacity to generate calm when deadlines seemed insurmountable have been of great importance. Michael Shroyer provided the marvelous design and attended to all the details of preparing this publication for press in record time. I am tremendously grateful to John Nicoll, managing director, Yale University Press, for believing in this project and presenting it to Yale. Also at Yale University Press, Sally Salvesen gave editorial and production assistance, and I also thank her for the encouragement and support she gave to this project.

Many individuals in Sweden and Austria provided assistance with the research for the exhibition. In Sweden: I am grateful to Ann Wall, director of Svenskt Tenn, who helped in numerous ways logistically and also extended great kindness and hospitality to me and my family. Kristina Wängberg-Eriksson spent many days, even during the cherished Swedish summer, guiding me through the Svenskt Tenn archive and sharing her unsurpassed knowledge of Frank; she has been essential to the success of this project. My thanks go to those at the Swedish Museum of Architecture, Stockholm, especially its director, Jöran Lindvall, who helped raise support for the exhibition. Many people assisted with the photography of Frank material in Sweden. In this regard I want to thank William Wareing at Millesgården and the staff of Svenskt Tenn who put up with my intrusions and seemingly endless requests for assistance. The magnificent photography of work at the Svenskt Tenn archive was taken by Bruce White and Georg Uggla.

A special word of thanks goes to someone in Sweden who has requested to remain anonymous, a "guardian angel" of this project who offered extensive support. I also want to thank The Royal Institute of Technology in Stockholm for providing housing during my research trips and the Department of Chemistry there for the use of its fax machine, an essential tool in completing this catalogue.

In Vienna many people shared their knowledge,

helped with research, and extended hospitality to me during the research for the exhibition. I am especially grateful for the support of Johannes Spalt, Elisabeth Steiner, Ruth Wilson Kalmar, Lea Calice, and Anna Lulia Praun. In addition to Christian Witt-Dörring at the MAK, Museum of Applied Art, Vienna, Elisabeth Schmuttermeier helped organize photography and provided support during long periods away from my family. Angela Völker was always willing to answer questions and helped organize photography of the textile loans. Georg Mayer took the wonderful photographs of the objects in the collection of the MAK, Museum of Applied Art, Vienna. The work of Martina Hoffinger, research assistant to Witt-Dörring in Vienna, was invaluable to the discovery of important loans to the exhibition. Erika Patka, archivist and curator at the University of Applied Art, Vienna, took time away from her many exhibition projects to assist with the viewing of Frank drawings, logistics of object loans, and photography. Richard Bösel, curator of drawings at the Graphische Sammlung Albertina in Vienna, was also tremendously generous with his time, assisting with viewing the Frank drawings and with photography.

I am grateful to the foundations and government agencies that provided generous support for the catalogue and the exhibition. My thanks goes to Lori Schaeffer who was of special help in the fundraising efforts and Lucy Soutter. I want to thank Professor Stanford Anderson and Professor Rosemarie Bletter for their help early on in raising support for the exhibition. In addition Professor Bletter enhanced my knowledge and understanding of the social imperatives of architecture.

At The Bard Graduate Center I have received assistance from many colleagues. A very special word of thanks goes to Derek Ostergard who was present at the beginning of this project in Stockholm, encouraged me to pursue the idea from the start, and has greatly expanded my knowledge of Frank. I am also grateful to Derek for generously sharing his contacts and for providing support on the road when travel and the demands of work seemed overwhelming. In the exhibition department, first and foremost, my thanks go to Lisa Arcomano whose work ethic is unsurpassed. Lisa

assisted with the catalogue production, coordinated loans, and was responsible for overseeing all the shipping arrangements. In addition she coordinated the exhibition graphics. I am also tremendously grateful to Steve Waterman for his consummate professionalism and remarkable work as head preparator and coordinator of installation design. Janet Hawkins has attended brilliantly to the details of object registration and always makes the demands of installations more tolerable. Our installation crew is the finest in New York City. Research and production of the catalogue were greatly facilitated by the slide library and library staff of The Bard Graduate Center. Marcial Lavina was invaluable to the project. I am also grateful for the assistance of Bobbie Xuereb, Peter Gammie, and Eileen McDonagh.

Other colleagues provided assistance and were supportive throughout the development of the exhibition. I want to thank Lisa Podos for her superb organization of the Frank symposium and her overall support of this project; my thanks go to her staff in the public programs office. I am grateful to Linda Hartley, Susan Wall, and Barat Ellman in the development office for the many proposals; Tim Mulligan and Kelly Moody in the press office for attending to the press campaign and many other details pertaining to the public; and the security and maintenance staff of The Bard Graduate Center.

Finally I want to extend a very special thanks to my immediate family who provided constant encouragement and assistance with so many matters surrounding the realization of this catalogue and exhibition. I am especially grateful to my mother, Helen Stritzler, for her editorial, insights and encouragement of my interest in feminist issues.

The most heartfelt word of thanks goes to my marvelous husband, Stuart Stritzler-Levine, who provided endless support, emotional, intellectual, and editorial, during the past year and a half. Stuart's care of me and our child, whose first year and a half of life paralleled this project, ultimately made the undertaking possible.

Nina Stritzler-Levine

# 1. THREE VISIONS OF THE LE CORBUSIER,

Nina Stritzler-Levine

Every human needs a certain degree of sentimentality to be free. This will be taken from him if he is forced to make moral demands of every object, one of which is the aesthetic demand. What we need is variety. . . . Therefore what I suggest are not new rules and forms but a radically different attitude towards art. Away with the universal styles, away with the equalization of industry and art, away with the whole system of thought that has become popular under the name of functionalism.

*Josef Frank*[1]

When Josef Frank wrote these compelling words in 1954 he had almost been forgotten within the history of the modern movement. A leading architect in Vienna, by the end of the 1920s, he had emerged as a harsh critic of many core ideas of the "new architecture." The realization that sentimentality is a pervasive feature of human life and his call for the end of functionalism were among the ideas that were central to his unique vision of the modern home. This vision contrasted sharply with the ideas of progressive architects of the time. A comparison of Frank's aesthetic of interior design and furnishings with that of Le Corbusier and Alvar Aalto demonstrates his importance as a humanizing force within modernism.

The issue of defining an appropriate design philosophy for the modern home has been at the center of modernist discourse since the nineteenth century. After the First World War, however, the discussion intensified as architects were confronted with a new range of challenges: dealing with wartime housing shortages, adapting to new technology, and, most importantly, formulating a definition of the home in a rapidly changing social, economic, and political climate. During the 1920s many progressive architects—most of whom came from France and Germany[2]—tried to consolidate their efforts as a means of gaining public acceptance of the "new architecture." To demonstrate their "solidarity," they organized two events at the end of the 1920s: one, an experimental housing exhibition sponsored by the German Werkbund at Weissenhof under the direction of Mies van der Rohe in 1927[3]; and the other, the first meeting of the International Congress for Modern Architecture (Congress Internationaux d'Architecture Moderne, CIAM)[4], held at the Château La Sarraz in Switzerland in 1928 and essentially dominated by Le Corbusier. Despite the outward appearance of a unified vision of modern architecture during the 1920s, far greater diversity existed within the ranks of the movement than has been suggested by historians both before and after the Second World War[5]. In fact, the historical claim of unity was more myth than reality. The first CIAM conference "was the beginning

# MODERN HOME: JOSEF FRANK, AND ALVAR AALTO

of the great myth of the Modern Movement, which explains and reconstructs events, includes and synthesizes all positions, and finally becomes a historical conjecture with its own beginning and its own linear development, without breaks in continuity."[6] At the heart of the myth was the idea that a select group of "pioneers," among them Le Corbusier, Walter Gropius, and Mies van der Rohe, had, with the machine as their model, created a unified modern aesthetic predicated on functionality of design, standard methods of production and new materials. Moreover, their vision was motivated by a social commitment and the belief that through architecture would come a "new world." While the literature on the movement focused on the "heroic period of modern architecture,"[7] thus supporting this myth, other architects whose ideas did not fit into the established paradigm[8] were largely ignored, if not criticized. This was clearly the case with Josef Frank.

While the standard interpretation of Frank's work has been to establish his position within the legacy of Viennese modernism prior to the First World War, another way of understanding Frank is to consider his vision as it related to central themes and issues and to figures of major concern within the modern movement: specifically, two leading modernist architects, Le Corbusier, who dominated the modern architectural discourse of the 1920s, and Finnish architect Alvar Aalto, who transformed some of the tenets of modernism but clearly remained within its borders.

Le Corbusier, unquestionably among the most outstanding architects of the century, was an exemplar of progressive design in the 1920s, whose architecture and theoretical ideas in many respects epitomized the modernist dogma that Frank resisted. Alvar Aalto emerged as a leading architect during the 1930s when the ideals of the modern

movement had already begun to wane. Although there were important differences between the modernism of Frank and Aalto, there are also clear philosophical parallels in their approach to the modern home, specifically the idea that humankind, rather than functionalist concerns or technology, dictated the design of the modern home.

During the turbulent years that followed the breakup of the Habsburg Empire after the First World War, Josef Frank emerged as one of the leading modern architects in the new nation of Austria. The nascent years of his career developed in response to an earlier generation who had helped shape the course of modernism in fin-de-siècle Vienna, notably Adolf Loos and Josef Hoffmann.[9] Having assimilated the ideas of his mentors into a highly individual design philosophy, by 1927 Frank had attained a prominent position in the Viennese design community and was known throughout Europe as a leading Austrian representative of the modern movement. Frank's rise in stature as an architect occurred while the city of Vienna was in decline as a center of progressive design,[10] a process in part accelerated by the onset of Fascism in the early 1930s. Vienna's cultural decline and the rise of Fascism were particularly relevant to Frank, whose design philosophy, already well defined by the early 1920s, was based on a resistance to all impediments to individual freedom. Ironically his concerns about design restrictions on the modern home would soon take on a far greater personal and perhaps prophetic significance. As a Jewish architect Frank became increasingly isolated professionally in Vienna, and in 1933, fearing that his own freedom was threatened, he chose to leave Austria.

Before the First World War, Frank had demonstrated an early commitment to modernism in his designs for single-family houses, which were the principal focus of his work as an architect. After 1919 he shared in the modernist

Fig. 1-1. Le Corbusier, Pavillon de L'Esprit Nouveau, Paris, 1925; sculpture by Jacques Lipchitz. Courtesy, Fondation Le Corbusier, Paris.

ideal of the social imperative of architecture by taking an active role in the Viennese housing program.[11] Frank joined other progressive architects working to solve Vienna's housing shortage which had reached unprecedented proportions as refugees seeking employment moved from rural areas into the capital of the former monarchy. Yet if Frank was engaged in solving many of the same problems as his contemporaries in the modern movement, his personal design philosophy, specifically his ideas about the modern house, were headed in a distinctly different direction. Throughout the 1920s Frank became increasingly disillusioned with modernist dogma and, between 1927 and 1932, was one of the movement's most outspoken critics.[12] He attacked the modernist claim to universal design principles, the belief that only through a complete break with the past—a severing of all ties with tradition and history—could a modern aesthetic be achieved. He also criticized the privileged position of the machine as well as the influence of contemporary painting and sculpture on design issues.[13] These were

ideals embodied in the Corbusian house and its furnishings.

Frank's views sharply contrasted with those of Le Corbusier, During the 1920s Le Corbusier developed a universal notion of the dwelling designed to meet the needs of a new civilization.[14] The evolution of his theories is evident in several projects: the 1922 project for the Maison Citrohan which was presented at the Paris Salon d'Automne; the 1925 Pavillon de L'Esprit Nouveau at the Exposition International des Arts Décoratifs et Industriels Modernes in Paris; and, finally, the realization of the Five Points of Architecture at the 1927 Weissenhofseidlung in Stuttgart. Governed in part by a strict set of formal dictates derived from Purist painting[15] and from the practical model of the machine—a paradigm of rationalism and standardization—the new dwelling made no reference to the past; it was created from new materials and with new methods of construction. Le Corbusier proposed his version of the mass-produced house as the answer to the problem of the epoch.

As the modern movement's leading polemicist and a master of rhetorical discourse, Le Corbusier disseminated his ideas through the journal *L'Esprit nouveau*[16] and a series of books, published between 1923 and 1925, on the pressing issues for the movement. *Vers une Architecture* (Towards a new architecture)[17] which first appeared in 1923, was especially important in spreading Le Corbusier's vision of the modern house. In one chapter, "Eyes Which Do Not See,"[18] Le Corbusier compared the design of the house to that of an airplane, a machine paradigm, specifying that it was the task of the architect to adhere to universal principles of construction. He also extended the machine metaphor to the internal mechanics of the house by imposing rules on the inhabitants' way of life. The section, "Manual of the Dwelling," was a self-help guide to modern living intended to be "distributed to mothers of families" so they would know how to live in the modern home. Le Corbusier went so far as to establish criteria for modern existence, exhort-ing his readers to "demand a bathroom looking south. . . . demand bare walls in your bedroom, your living room and your dining-room. . . . demand a vacuum cleaner. . . . keep your odds and ends in drawers or cabinets. . . . teach your children that a house is only habitable when it is full of light and air, and when the floors and walls are clear."[19] The inhabitants would need only to follow his rules to achieve an "ordered and rational" way of life.

The first full-scale public demonstration of Corbusian design principles occurred at the Pavillon de L'Esprit Nouveau in 1925. All aspects of the design, its construction, interior, and furnishings adhered to the model of the machine and derived from rational methods of construction and a specific set of universal principles. The plan was conceived as one "cellular-unit" of an *immeuble-villa* (fig. 1-1), an individual apartment in the Plan Voisin, Le Corbusier's urban-planning project for the City of Paris. It was composed of a duplex apartment with the

Fig. 1-2. Le Corbusier, interior of the Pavillon de L'Esprit Nouveau, 1925. Courtesy, Fondation Le Corbusier, Paris.

Fig 1-3. Marcel Breuer, Club Armchair, designed 1925, this example manufactured ca. 1927–28; tubular steel and canvas. Museum of Modern Art, New York, Gift of Herbert Bayer.

second story serving as a cantilevered balcony. The walls were relieved of all superfluous decoration and only paintings by Braque, Léger, and Picasso, among other avantgarde artists, were displayed.

In the conception and selection of furniture Le Corbusier was quite specific; a limited set of behavioral norms should dictate the design. Modern furniture, Le Corbusier argued, "corresponds to constant, daily, regular functions. All men have the same needs, at the same hours, every day, all their lives."[20] Human beings required only a limited vocabulary of furniture forms—"tables for working at and eating, chairs for eating and working, armchairs of different shapes for resting in different ways, and cabinets for storing the objects we use."[21] The furnishings of the Pavillon de L'Esprit Nouveau (fig. 1-2)—Thonet model B9 bentwood chairs, leather upholstered armchairs by Maples and cabinets (*casiers standard*)—represented an initial step toward the realization of standard type furniture, household "equipment" for the new era, designed for specific functions. In Le Corbusier's interiors, "furniture and other objects used in the home were extensions of the human body, equipment that served a precisely defined bodily function, answered a particular human need—nothing more, but also nothing less."[22]

The furnishings Le Corbusier exhibited at the 1925 Paris Exposition were based on the conceptual idea of "type," but their construction in wood was still expressive of the past. A complete program of standard household "*equipement*" would come only with furniture that truly conformed to the Corbusian "house machine" and was produced in a material synonymous with the new era: tubular steel. Introduced at the Bauhaus by Marcel Breuer in his 1925 Club armchair (fig. 1-3), tubular steel furniture was "devoid of reference to the past and partook of the mechanistic imagery that captured the spirit of the period."[23] In 1928, when Charlotte Perriand joined Le Corbusier's rue de Sèvres atelier, they created tubular steel designs (fig. 1-4), among them the *Fauteuil à Dossier Basculant, Grand Confort*, and the *Chaise Longue à Reglage Continu*.[24] This was "type" furniture based on human scale, function, and needs. The emphasis was on the human aspect of design as normative. But this humanness was conceived according to mathematical calculation and rational analysis.[25]

For Frank tubular steel furniture was essentially a novelty, an example of how design had been reduced to a fashion issue. To demand that the inhabitants of the modern home could only purchase "new" furniture—tubular steel furniture—he argued, was to deny them the freedom to assert their own taste. Contradicting the Corbusian premise of rationality, Frank argued that to invent the chair and to standardize its design was nonsense. The chairs in a room, Frank explained must be as different as possible, "to invent 'the' chair and to standardize its design is unnecessary because it serves very different needs, and we want to sit differently at different occasions and at different times of the day. Therefore chairs in a room should be as diverse as possible."[26] He considered furniture that emanated from formal dictates and derived from the same issues and ideas as architecture—new materials, new methods of construction, standardization—as a mere fashion and thought such furniture to be unacceptable. In a statement that clearly distinguished his ideas from those of his modernist contemporaries Frank argued, "Whether or not we use baroque or tubular steel furniture is irrevelant. Out of the modern we can acquire freedom."[27]

During the 1920s Le Corbusier relied on the machine metaphor to construct his vision of the modern home. The machine, mediated through the formal dictates of Purism, was the universal representation of the new epoch. When considering Le Corbusier's ideas within the context of those of Josef Frank, the issue is not who was the better architect/designer but rather who better understood the needs and preferences of the "common man" and the character and quality of everyday life in the modern world. For Le Corbusier the inhabitants of the modern home required instruction to adhere to the rational, ordered model of the machine and thus must follow the "Manual of the Dwelling." For Frank the modern home should encompass a broad spectrum of possibilities and options beyond the rational; the range was potentially as vast as the diversity of humankind.

One of the most striking criticisms of Frank in the

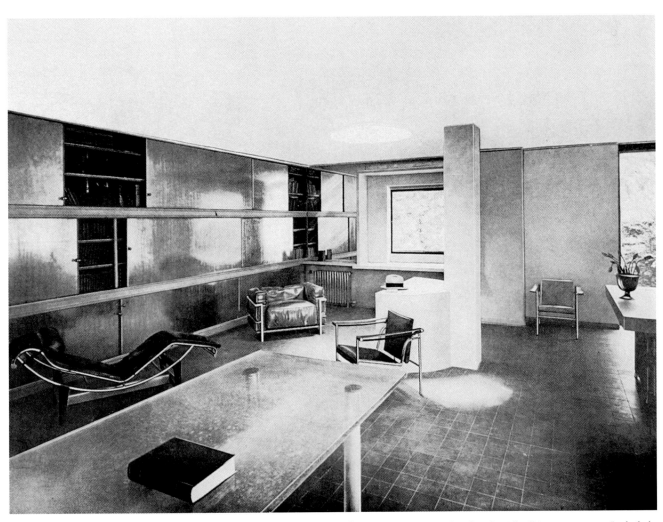

Fig. 1-4. Le Corbusier, Pierre Jeanneret, and Charlotte Perriand, library/living room at the Villa Church, Ville d'Avray, 1928–29. Included are the *Fauteuil à Dossier Basculant*, *Grand Confort*, and *Chaise Longue*, and Built-In Table. Courtesy, Fondation Le Corbusier, Paris.

late 1920s came from those who belittled the "feminine character" of his designs. If the Corbusian house of the 1920s was celebrated for its heroic qualities, the rational, ordered, and disciplined—in other words, its "male qualities"—Frank's designs were criticized for containing the opposite qualities, for exuding a "feminine" character. At the Weissenhofseidlung in 1927, for example, Frank was among a group of architects maligned by Theo van Doesburg for creating "femininely appointed" interiors.[28"] One critic was even more derogatory, describing Frank's interior as a "brothel."[29] While these comments have been cited in other studies of Frank's work, their meaning within the modern movement has not been explored. They are clearly representative of an attitude within the modern movement that was discriminatory toward the "feminine" and are important in terms of modernist attitudes toward home furnishings.

The gender critique of Frank's work[30] derived from the antirational, emotive quality of his interiors, created by the soft contours of fully upholstered furnishings and prominent use of textiles. Before 1927 adherents of the modern movement had dictated either against textiles altogether in the modern home because of their association with the feminine or for textiles that were conceived differently through the use of a more "masculine" objective aesthetic. This hierarchical structuring of design, which placed masculine heroic forms at the top of the pyramid and the more feminine softer ones at the bottom, was most clearly and ironically expressed at the Bauhaus, the mythical place of unity among the arts. One study of the treatment of woman students at the Bauhaus has examined gender discrimination there and the lesser place reserved for the textile arts.[31] This attitude was not necessarily rooted in the curriculum of the Weimar Academy of Arts and Crafts, the institution preceding the Bauhaus under the direction of Henry van de Velde. It appears to have come from Walter Gropius. In 1915 van de Velde was pressured to resign, and Gropius, his future successor, suggested that the impor-

Fig. 1-5. Walter Gropius, dining room of a house for the Weissenhofsiedlung, Stuttgart, 1927. The furniture was designed by Marcel Breuer. Marcel Breuer Collection, George Arent Research Library for Special Collections, Syracuse University.

Fig. 1-6. Josef Frank, part of the living room of the Double House for the Weissenhofsiedlung, Stuttgart, 1927. Stuttgart, Landesbildstelle.

tance of the Academy had diminished during the van de Velde years.[32] As Gropius explained, architecture, the primary element, had been neglected, and what remained had received a somewhat "feminine character." Gropius lamented the fact that the legacy of the Weimar Academy of Arts and Crafts had been the decorative arts, particularly textiles.[33] When Gropius founded the Bauhaus at Weimar in 1919, the curriculum was organized by media, and gender discrimination was evident in the unofficial division of the student body: "All the women students were unofficially [forced] to take the textile workshop . . . and were excluded from the other workshops, including the prestigious architecture department when it was finally introduced in 1926. In this way, the traditional split between high and low art supposedly undermined by the institution was actually maintained in traditionally gendered terms."[34] Within the modern movement architecture came to dominate the discourse of the modern home, while the decorative arts were

assigned to the bottom levels of the hierarchical design structure. Although gender discrimination may not necessarily provide the basis for the divergence of taste and aesthetic within the modern movement, it is pertinent to Frank, who by 1925 had become widely known for the textile designs that were prominent in his interiors. This clearly linked him with the "lowly art" of textile design, the handmaiden of architecture, and his work, among the proponents of the modern movement became "negatively" critiqued as feminine.

Most of the interiors of the houses at the German Werkbund exhibition at Weissenhof (fig. 1-5) adhered to reductive architecture and interiors with planar walls and a lack of ornamentation as common characteristics.[35] Moreover the furniture for the most part throughout the *Siedlung* was consistent both aesthetically and conceptually with the architecture. In this regard, Frank's Double House stood out from the others (fig. 1-6), demonstrating a strik-

Fig. 1-7. Exterior of Haus & Garten on Bösendorferstrasse, early 1930s. Österreichische Nationbibliothek-Bildarchiv.

ing dichotomy between the reductivist appearance of the exterior and comparative richness of the interior. The facade conformed to the overall appearance of the *Siedlung*, but following his principle that called for funishings not defined by the architecture, he used the characteristic white walls on the interior as a framing device, within which he placed fully upholstered chairs, cushions, and pillows. He even used curtains. These were rooms in which people could live freely and at ease in the modern world. As Frank explained, "the modern person who is increasingly more exhausted by his job requires a domicile cozier and more comfortable than those of the past. He has to obtain relaxation in more concentrated ways in a much shorter time. Therefore the domicile has to be the absolute opposite of the workplace. This applies not only to the . . . sitting and resting areas but to every visible object . . . ; ornament and variety create peace and eliminate the pathos of the purely functional."[36]

Two years before the Weissenhofseidlung, Josef Frank and Oskar Wlach opened a retail shop, Haus & Garten, in Vienna (fig. 1-7). Based on the model of the Wiener Werkstätte, which it rivaled during the 1920s, Haus & Garten offered an alternative to the aestheticized design promoted by the Werkstätte, as well as to the dictates of Le Corbusier's "Manual of the Dwelling." As one frequent visitor has recalled, the shop was disheveled, "at times they could not find the right sample books, but there were endless things to choose from."[37] These comments seem to convey the exact feeling that Frank was trying to achieve in his interiors. Haus & Garten was, indeed, a consumer-oriented enterprise, but its products were not mass-market commodites. They represented a vision of the home for the "common man."

In 1932 the Museum of Modern Art in New York City organized "The International Style," an exhibition that served to codify the ideas of the modern movement.[38] Ironically, by that time, Le Corbusier had begun to question the machine aesthetic he had promoted in the 1920s, and it seemed that a less dogmatic functionalism was gaining favor.[39] At the same time another architect, Alvar Aalto, whose work in the 1920s had remained largely unnoticed outside his native Finland, began to receive attention. By the Second World War, Aalto was recognized internationally for his alternative approach to the modern home.

Aalto had emerged in the international community of modern architects in 1929 when he attended the second CIAM meeting,"Existenzminimum," in Frankfurt.[40] This was part of a transition from Nordic classicism to his own distinct interpretation of modern architecture. The most profound influence on Aalto during this time came from Le Corbusier, but a broader constellation of ideas is also apparent in his work. These came from the Bauhaus as well as functionalist architects in Germany. His friendship with Sven Markelius and his awareness of Gunnar Asplund's work, particularly at the Stockhom Exhibition in 1930,[41] made modern architecture in Sweden another factor in Aalto's development.

Unlike Le Corbusier, however, Aalto approached the modern home in a way predicated neither on the dictates of the machine nor on a universal set of design principles. Aalto's design philosophy was distinguished by the role he assigned to nature in architectural conception. There is little connection, however, between Frank and Aalto in this respect since Frank rejected the interpretation of the house as an organic entity.[42]

The connection between the two architects derives from a broader contextual understanding of the modern

Fig. 1-8. Alvar Aalto, Armchair (model no. 41), designed 1930–33; bent plywood, bent laminated birch, solid birch; manufactured by Artek, Helsinki. Artek, Helsinki.

home. What Frank and Aalto did share was a profound concern for humanity and an interest in designing the modern home according to the social and cultural realities of modern life. To achieve this they clearly pursued different paths. Aalto's was through nature, as expressed, for example, in the way he sited his buildings in the landscape and used wood as the primary material in his interiors. He also found inspiration in cubism. Frank, however, embraced all aspects of culture—high and low. In 1931 he explained, ". . . the new architecture will be born of the whole bad taste of our period, of its intricacy, its motleyness, and sentimentality, it will be a product of all that is alive and experienced first hand; at last, an art of the people, for the people."43

The development of Aalto's design philosophy during the 1930s shifted away from the dogmatic functionalism prevalent among progressive architects on the Continent and toward his own personal vision of the modern home.

In 1930 Aalto and his close collaborator and wife Aino Marsio-Aalto participated in the Minimum House exhibition sponsored by the Finnish Society of Arts and Crafts.44 The event, inspired by ideas then under discussion within CIAM, has been recognized as one of the earliest public manifestations of functionalism in Finland. In conjunction with the exhibition Aalto published "The Dwelling as a Problem" which summarized his views about the modern house at that time and was clearly indebted to contemporary ideas in France and Germany.45 By raising the issue of the dwelling as a problem and presenting solutions according to "biodynamic functions," such as work, sleep, and play, Aalto was well within the discourse of the second CIAM meeting at Frankfurt.46 However there were noteworthy differences in his ideas, differences that are telling when compared to Frank's design philosophy. Aalto had expanded the discussion of the social and cultural context of the dwelling and gave little attention to the impor-

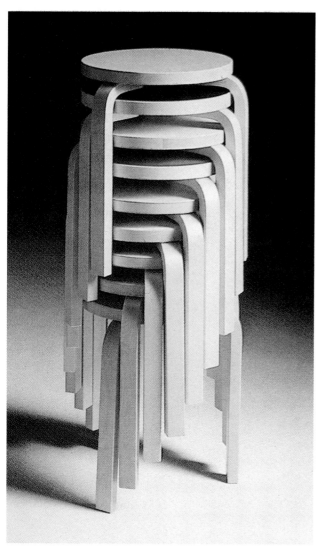

Fig. 1-9. Alvar Aalto, stacking stools (model no. 60), designed 1930–33; solid birch (bent portion laminated) and birch veneer; manufactured by Artek, Helsinki. Artek, Helsinki.

ing attitudes toward the role of women and single-parent families. Nevertheless they did share in the belief that design must address, rather than dictate, the needs, habits, and ways of living in the modern world. They also considered the machine aesthetic a passing "fashion" rather than a lasting response to modern life.

Between 1930 and 1935 Aalto completed two major public commissions—the Paimio Sanitorium and the Viipuri Library—in which he forged his unique design aesthetic.[47] The designs reveal Aalto's complete grasp of a new modern idiom inflected by social and psychological concerns in design, including subtle details that directly affect people and how they "live," whether as patients convalescing in a sanitorium or children reading in a library. For both commissions Aalto designed special furniture. While the armchair for Paimio Sanitorium and the stool for the Viipuri Library represented considerable advancements in bentwood technology, they also demonstrated Aalto's interest in furniture that represented modernity in construction and design while serving basic human needs (figs. 1-8, 1-9).

"Rationalism and Man,"[48] a lecture Aalto delivered before the Svenska Slöjdföreningen (Swedish Society of Craft and Industrial Design) in 1935, showed the development of his ideas since his 1930 essay, "The Dwelling as a Problem." Aalto argued that modernism had "run amuck." The objects that had resulted from a careful analysis of new materials, working methods, and social conditions were completely inadequate. The problem, he explained, was that "the inspiration . . . has not been to any great extent human goals . . . ; the production of form functionalism has been extensive enough to clarify the fact that mutual independence of form and function is not the way in which people will get better and more human things with which to build their surroundings."[49] Aalto explained that the way to create better environments was to expand rational analysis to include psychological and even neurological studies to achieve humane solutions. In a statement reminiscent of Frank, Aalto argued that "A standard article [object] should not be a definitive product; it should on the contrary be made so that the form is completed by man himself according to all the individual laws [personal principles] that involve him."[50] The creation of purely formalist objects, Aalto continued, was highly inhumane because they hindered people from creating an environment for themselves with a living, natural constantly changing character. Ultimately Aalto's furniture designs achieved a harmonious synthesis of formal and humanitarian concerns.

During the 1930s Aalto received several commissions

tance of the machine. His interest focused on societal and cultural issues which in his view had the most significant impact on the modern home. Modern design had to address the changes in social order, the family, and especially the role of women. While Le Corbusier in *Vers une Architecture* had addressed the issue of women, noting that they had preceded the rest of society in adapting to the new technology through changes in fashion, for Aalto, women had influenced domestic changes in a more radical way. Their emancipation and subsequent rise from a subordinate position both in working life and in the home had placed totally new demands on the dwelling.

Clearly Aalto and Frank approached the social needs of architecture from a different perspective, Frank addressing society in a general way as "the people," Aalto being more specific about the details of family life such as chang-

Fig. 1-10. Alvar Aalto, entrance hall looking toward the living room, Villa Mairea, Noormarkku, Finland, ca. 1937–41. From Richard Weston, *Villa Mairea, Alvar Aalto* (London: Phaidon Press, 1992).

for private houses and multiple dwellings, but the consummate expression of his ideas about the modern home came in 1938 with the Villa Mairea,[51] the summer home of Mairea and Harry Gullichsen in Western Finland. For Aalto this was an ideal commission; his wealthy urbane patrons gave him complete jurisdiction over the design. What is most interesting about the house as it relates to the work of Josef Frank are the cultural and social concerns that motivated its design. Aalto distinguished between the notion of the Villa Mairea as a "house," a utopian vision as it was expressed in the Corbusian house machine, and a "home," a place for living in the modern world. In the interior, particularly in the main living areas, Aalto represented many ideas embedded in the Finnish consciousness: an admiration for the vernacular, for the textures of the forest, and the warmth of the sun. Upon entering the Villa Mairea the contact with wood is immediate and continues

throughout the house (fig. 1-10). While the emblematic reinforced concrete and glass houses of the modern movement were uniform and severe, the Villa Mairea displayed a seemingly picturesque sense of variety, a harmony between tradition and modernity.

In contrast to Le Corbusier, Frank did not map out his concept of the modern home in a clear set of points or a universal vision. His philosophy was rooted in a highly personal attitude toward life in the modern world. That was, in fact, his ideology. In this respect Frank's ideas run parallel to Alvar Aalto's humanist, anti-utopian vision centering on the needs of the individual in the modern world. Frank and Aalto were both remarkably versatile designers whose approach transcended the reductivist aesthetic intended to enhance the minimalist character of the modernist architectural environment. While Aalto's objects conform to his interpretation of modern architecture, they also reflect his understanding that the objects we live with everyday derive from more fundamental issues than architecture. Such issues cannot find expression in the limited vocabulary of rationally or mathematically conceived "type" furnishings.

At the end of the millenium, with the new information age upon us and the availability of a technology far exceeding the dreams of the 1920s, there is a merging of public and private space, and public and private life, making the concept of the home increasingly difficult to define. In the next century will it be a place in which to withdraw and escape from the burdens of contemporary life or will its meaning as a safe haven be displaced by a radically new

vision? These questions are particularly relevant to a consideration of Josef Frank's alternative vision of the modern home. During the interwar years Frank dismissed the idea that the new epoch demanded a radical change in the home. His design philosophy embraced the individual—an individual with a personal history, in a collective past, with a vision of the future. While this expansive view of modern life eventually placed Frank at the margins of the modern movement, it is also a more enduring and accurate interpretation of how people live. The desire for comfort, the expression of individual taste, and the presence of objects that evoke our past, present, and future are as vital today as they are likely to be in the future.

1. Josef Frank "Accidentism," *Form* (1958), pp., 161–66, cited in Hermann Czech "A Mode for the Current Interpretation of Josef Frank," *Architecture and Urbanism* 11 (1991), pp. 20–30.

2. Among them Le Corbusier, Walter Gropius, and Mies van der Rohe.

3. See Richard Pommer and Christian F. Otto, *Weissenhof 1927 and the Modern Movement in Architecture* (Chicago: University of Chicago Press, 1991); Deutscher Werkbund, *Bau und Wohnung*, exhib. cat. ( 1927; reprint, Stuttgart: Karl Kramer Verlag, 1992); and Karin Kirsch, *Weissenhofsiedlung: Experimental Housing Built for the Deutscher Werkbund 1927* (Stuttgart: Deutsche Verlags-Anstalt, 1994).

4. See "C.I.A.M. International Congress for Modern Architecture, Congres Internationaux d'Architecture Moderne, 1–2," in O. M. Ungers and Liselotte Ungers, eds., *Documents of Modern Architecture* (Nendeln/Liechtenstein: Kraus Reprint, 1979); and Martin Steinmann, *CIAM Dokumente 1928–1939* (Basel: Birkhäuser Verlag, 1979).

5. See, for example, Nikolaus Pevsner, *Pioneers of Modern Design from William Morris to Walter Gropius* (New York: Museum of Modern Art, 1949); Sigfried Giedion, *Space, Time and Architecture: The Growth of a New Tradition* (Cambridge: Harvard University Press, 1941); Alison M. Smithson and Peter Smithson, *The Heroic Period of Modern Architecture* (New York: Rizzoli, 1981); Henry Russell Hitchcock and Philip Johnson, *The International Style: Architecture Since 1922* (New York: W. W. Norton & Company, 1932).

6. Giorgio Ciucci, "The Invention of the Modern Movement," *Oppositions* 24 (Spring 1981), pp. 68–91.

7. See Smithson and Smithson, *The Heroic Period*.

8. The paradigm was established with the organization of the exhibition, "The International Style." See Hitchcock and Johnson, *The International Style*.

9. See Czech, "A Mode for the Current Interpretation of Josef Frank," pp. 20–30. Czech develops the thesis that Frank represents a synthesis of ideas borrowed from Loos and Hoffmann. Also see Christopher Long, "Josef Frank and the Crisis of Modern Architecture," Ph.D. diss. (University of Texas at Austin, 1993); and chapter 5, below.

10. William H. Johnston, *The Austrian Mind: An Intellectual and Social History, 1848–1938.* (Berkeley, CA: University of California Press, 1983).

11. See Long, "Josef Frank and the Crisis of Modern Architecture"; and Otto Kapfinger, "Josef Frank—Siedlungen und Siedlungsprojekte, 1919–1932" *Um Bau* 10 (August 1986), pp. 39–58.

12. See, for example, Josef Frank, "Der Gschnas fürs G'müt und der Gschnas als Problem," in Deutscher Werkbund, *Bau und Wohnung*, pp. 48–57; and idem, "Das Haus als Weg und Platz" in Johannes Spalt, *Josef Frank, 1885–1967* (Vienna: Hochschule Für Angewandte Kunst, 1981).

13. See, for example, Josef Frank, "Die Moderne Einrichtung des Wohnhauses," in Spalt, *Josef Frank*, pp. 84–87.

14. See Hayward Gallery of Art, London, *Le Corbusier, Architect of the Century*, exhib. cat. (London: Arts Council of Great Britain, 1987).

15. See Christopher Green, "Léger and Purist Paris," exhib. cat. (London: The Tate Gallery, 1970); and idem, "The Architect as Artist," in Hayward Gallery of Art, *Le Corbusier, Architect of the Century*, pp. 110–30.

16. See Kenneth Frampton, "Le Corbusier and *L'Esprit nouveau*," *Oppositions* 15/16 (Winter/Spring 1979), pp. 13–58.

17. Le Corbusier, *Towards a New Architecture* (New York: Holt, Rinehart and Winston, 1982). The French edition, *Vers une Architecture*, appeared in 1923 and the English-language version in 1927.

18. Ibid., pp. 99–119.

19. Ibid., pp. 114–15. "Manual of the Dwelling" was included in the chapter, "Eyes Which Do Not See."

20. Le Corbusier, *Precisions on the Present State of Architecture and City Planning*, trans. Edith Schreiber (Cambridge: MIT Press, 1991), pg. 108.

21. Ibid., p. 108.

22. Quoted from Nancy Troy, *Modernism and the Decorative Arts: Art Nouveau to Le Corbusier* (New Haven: Yale University Press, 1991), p. 216. Troy explains that the "Pavillon de l'Esprit Nouveau called into question the reigning assumption (in France) that only a harmonious ensemble, in which each object would presumably be designed by an artist, could constitute a modern style of decorative art" (ibid., pp. 223–24), which is an interesting comparison to Frank's rejection of the *Gesamtkunstwerk* ideal.

23. Quoted from Christopher Wilk, *Marcel Breuer: Furniture and Interiors* (New York: Museum of Modern Art, 1981), p. 67.

24. See Mary McLeod, "Charlotte Perriand Her First Decade As A Designer," *AA Files* 15 (Summer 1987), pp. 3–13; and Nina Stritzler, "Charlotte Perriand and the Development of the Corbusian Program for *Equipêment de l'Habitation*," M.A. thesis (The Cooper-Hewitt Museum/ Parson's School of Design, New York, 1985).

25. In *L'Art Decoratif d'Aujourd'hui* (1925) Le Corbusier responded to the criticism that he was "killing the individual" stating that any reference to individual needs, or consideration of the character of an individual is irrelevant and contributes to the creation of "sentiment-objects" that "encumber our life and threatens to *kill it*" (Le Corbusier, *The Decorative Art of Today*, trans. James Dummett [Cambridge MA: The MIT Press, 1987], pp. 72–73). It is also interesting to consider that material alone did not provide the required rationality for furniture. Mary McLeod has argued that while tubular steel had become the material of choice among progressive architect/designers of the 1920s, there were distinctions in how it was used for furniture design. Bauhaus furniture represented the most objective (*Sachlich*) approach while other French designers, such as Eileen Gray and Pierre Chareau, were more "subjective and self-consciously artistic." Perriand's designs, although based on a rational analysis of form were distinctly less functionalist in their appearance. It should be added that rationality was at the center of the issue and not absolute functionality. See McLeod, "Charlotte Perriand," p. 10.

26. Josef Frank, "Die moderne Einrichtung des Wohnhauses," in Spalt, *Josef Frank*, pp. 87–94.

27. Ibid., p. 87.

28. See Theo van Doesburg, "Stuttgart-Weissenhof 1927: Die Wohnung" in *Theo van Doesburg On European Architecture: Complete Essays from Het Bouwbedrijf 1924–1931*, trans. Charlotte I. Loeb and Arthur L. Loeb (Boston: Birkhauser Verlag, 1990), pg. 172. The interior was described as "femininely appointed" and under "French influence."

29. See Kirsch, *Weissenhofsiedlung*.

30. For further explanation of the gender critique of modern interiors, see Leslie Kanes Weisman, *Discrimination by Design: A Feminist Critique of the Man-Made Environment* (Urbana: University of Illinois Press, 1992); and Judy Attfield and Pat Kirkham, eds. *A View from the Interior: Feminism, Women and Design* (London: The Women's Press, 1989).

31. Mark Wrigley, "White Out: Fashioning the Modern," in Deborah Fausch, ed., *Architecture: In Fashion* (New York: Princeton University Press, 1994), pp. 148–268.

32. Gropius expressed his views in a letter to Fritz Mackensen, director of the Weimar Academy of Fine Arts. The Belgian van de Velde had been pressured to leave his post due to strong xenophobic attitudes that made him increasingly unwelcome in Germany. See Marcel Franciscono, *The Founding of the Bauhaus in Weimar: Its Artistic Background and First Conception* (Urbana: University of Illinois Press, 1971).

33. For further discussion of Bauhaus textiles, see Magdalena Droste, *Bauhaus, 1919–1933* (Berlin: Bauhaus-Archiv Museum für Gestaltung and Benedikt Taschen, 1990); Sigrid Weltge-Wortmann, *Bauhaus Textiles: Women Artists and the Weaving Workshop* (London: Thames and Hudson, 1993).

34. Quoted from Wrigley, "White Out," p. 215. The passage continues, "After only a year of the school's operation, when women were already in the majority, Gropius—who wrote detailed articles on the way modern architecture actively facilitated the breakdown of the "patriarchal family" and the corresponding emancipation of women, yet who would deny them access to his own workshops—even attempted to have the official policy changed by limiting the overall admission of women and legislating that they be confined to the textile workshop."

35. For further discussion of the *Siedlung* at Weissenhof, see Pommer and Otto, *Weissenhof 1927*; and Kirsch, *Weissenhofsiedlung*.

36. Quoted from Frank, "Die moderne Einrichtung," p.87.

37. Ruth Wilson Kalmar, Vienna, June 1995: personal communication.

38. See Hitchcock and Johnson, *The International Style*.

39. Kenneth Frampton, "The Other Le Corbusier: Primitive Form and the Linear City, 1929–52," in Hayward Gallery of Art, *Le Corbusier, Architect of the Century*.

40. See Steinmann, *CIAM Dokumente*.

41. See Göran Schildt *Alvar Aalto: The Decisive Years* (New York: Rizzoli, 1986); and Richard Weston, *Alvar Aalto* (London: Phaidon, 1995).

42. See Long, "Josef Frank and the Crisis of Modern Architecture"; and chapter 5, below.

43. Quoted from Czech, "A Mode for the Current Interpretation of Josef Frank," p. 23.

44. See Weston, *Alvar Aalto*, pp. 72–74.

45. See Alvar Aalto, "The Dwelling as a Problem," in Göran Schildt, ed., *Sketches* (Cambridge: MIT Press), 1978.

46. Weston, *Alvar Aalto*, p.72.

47. Weston, *Alvar Aalto*; Schildt, *Alvar Aalto: The Decisive Years*.

48. Quoted from Schildt, *Sketches*, pp. 47–51.

49. Ibid., pp. 47–48.

50. Ibid., p. 50.

51. See Weston, *Alvar Aalto*.

# 2. THE CONSEQUENCES OF
# FRANK AND POST-

Leon Botstein

How strange if logic were concerned with an "ideal" language and not with ours![1]

The answers which philosophy gives to our questions must be fundamental to everyday life and science. They must be independent of the experimental findings of science. . . . Philosophy tidies a room and so has to handle things many times. The essence of its procedure is that it starts with a mess; we don't mind being hazy so long as the haze gradually clears.[2]

*Ludwig Wittgenstein*

From the perspective of the end of the twentieth century, Josef Frank's legacy as an architect and designer, and his conceptual approach to design, might appear presciently "postmodern" and even mildly prophetic. But in fact, as Hermann Czech observed, Frank was decidedly an architect "of the modern movement."[3] Although within the history of twentieth-century architecture and design Frank is recognized as a leading Austrian modernist, his critique of modernism, notably at the CIAM meeting in 1928, was intriguingly idiosyncratic. Despite his misgivings about the dominance of functionalism and essentialism in design, Frank shared with Adolf Loos an even deeper hostility to revivalist and stylized design strategies, extending from the historicism characteristic of late-nineteenth-century Vienna, especially to the sentimentalized, provincial, nationalist trends that flourished after 1918.[4] These traditions, insofar as they persisted in postwar architecture, attempted self-consciously to resist and camouflage the imperatives of history that had been made painfully clear by the tragedy of World War I.

Frank's originality—even though it may suggest postmodern aesthetic sensibilities—was rooted in the way in which he mediated the post–World-War-I political and social issues he encountered in Vienna through modernist architecture and design. In the 1920s Frank was forced to reconsider not only the aesthetic principles of architecture and design to which he had formed an allegiance in pre-1914 Vienna, but also the prewar terms of debate concerning the relationship between architecture and society. The 1920s progressive modernism as practiced by Le Corbusier and Mies van der Rohe and the nostalgic, traditionalist, and restorative trends (even in the most refined realizations, such as in the work of Otto Wagner's disciples) failed, in Frank's view, not merely on aesthetic grounds.[5] Their underlying social or political premises—

# CATASTROPHE:JOSEF
# WORLD-WAR-I VIENNA

Fig. 2-1. Perspective drawing of Kundmanngasse, 1926. This drawing of the Wittgenstein House was submitted to the Viennese authorities. It includes a remnant of the pre-1848 perimeter (no longer extant) and reveals Wittgenstein's attempt to emulate its premodern simplicity. Courtesy of the Baupolizei, Vienna.

particularly the continuation of a prewar attraction to the monumental and authoritarian—disturbed him.

During the 1920s, Frank's obsession with the challenges of the postwar world in Austria led him to rethink the process of designing architecture and interiors. As he wrote in *Architektur als Symbol* (1930), in the postwar world one once again had to learn to "open one's eyes." The war had forced humans to confront one another as they really were. Frank argued against the legislation of axiomatic rules and the imposition of abstract closed systems. Rather, by placing the diversity of human beings at the "center of the world," "empirical science and its transformation into organic forms" needed to become the legitimate traditions and procedures of architecture. In Frank's view architecture needed to confront the sufferings faced by individuals in contemporary life by enhancing individual self-realization and the possibilities for humanistic social order, equilibrium, and balance. The war, by virtue of its unanticipated magnitude, had created the possibility of a new beginning as much as it had destroyed all certainties. Therefore, architecture needed to be an instrument of education in the struggle to realize a better world, one in which individual dignity, reason, and a sense of the underlying organic unity of humankind could flourish. The obstacles that architecture faced were that the world was threatened by the machine, uniformity, inequality, economies of scale, superstition, and prejudice.

Frank's attraction to the Classical traditions of Greece and Rome, clearly outlined in *Architektur als Symbol*, was not rooted in a set of aesthetic predispositions. Rather, it mirrored a nineteenth-century tradition of idealizing Classical antiquity common among educated and assimilated Viennese Jews, best exemplified by Theodor Gomperz and Sigmund Freud.[6] In the Greco-Roman polytheistic pre-Christian traditions, rationality and tolerance triumphed over superstition. A cosmopolitan and sophisticated individuality seemed to flourish within Classical culture.[7] Man was "the measure of all things." Antiquity represented a tradition and heritage shared by Jews and non-Jews that proved the possibility of a world in which the modern species of political and cultural prejudice (such as anti-Semitism) did not flourish. Given this view of history, Frank's deep distrust of Christianity and Gothic and Gothic-revival architecture was predictable.[8]

**Observing the Everyday: Josef Frank and Ludwig Wittgenstein.** Frank's postwar re-evaluation of architecture had its other significant root in postwar philosophical speculation. Frank, primarily through his brother Phillip, a physicist, has been linked to Josef Popper-Lynkeus.[9] This extraordinary figure—an engineer, inventor, and idiosyncratic utopian socialist and philosopher—became, at the end of his life in Vienna, a venerated and legendary personality. Like Frank, Popper-Lynkeus never quite fit into any contemporary school or movement. Shortly before his death in 1921, Popper-Lynkeus (who was outspoken as a Jew) showed a particular attachment to his 1910 book *Das Individuum und die Bewertung menschlicher Existenz*, which was reprinted in 1920.[10] The fundamental argument of this philosophical tract was that all individuals, once emancipated from material need, are equal, ethically speaking, and mirror "an infinite greatness." All ideas and actions must be judged by the extent to which they further the "existence of individuals." The key was that each individual and the whole of human kind were linked. Popper-Lynkeus sought to reconcile an ethos of radical individualism—respect for each person's freedom and each person's uniqueness—with a sense of a dynamic totality, an organic wholeness, to which each individual contributed and on which each individual was contingent. It was this notion of organic balance between the whole and its parts, in politics and ethics, that appealed to Frank and seemed especially appropriate to postwar circumstances.[11]

Frank's distinct form of postwar architectural modernism evolved out of his effort to protect and encourage the organic link between individualism and social unity in the face of the matrix of economics, social change, and ideological conflict he encountered in the 1920s and early 1930s in Vienna. Frank's *Architektur als Symbol* opens with a discussion of the cultural consequences of the war and closes with social philosophical claims. Michael Müller has suggested that a key to understanding Frank may lie in the so-called crisis of language of the early twentieth century. A parallel between issues of architecture and language in the context of early-twentieth-century Vienna certainly exists.

But in Frank's case, the pairing is not with the Austrian poet and playwright Hugo von Hofmannsthal and his famous 1902 "Chandos Letter" dealing with issues of poetics and literary self-expression.[12] It is instead with the work of Ludwig Wittgenstein and Wittgenstein's transition during the 1920s from the *Tractatus Logico-Philosophicus* to his later philosophical positions, ultimately articulated in the *Philosophical Investigations*. Even Frank's citation of Friedrich Kürnberger (the nineteenth-century satirist whom Wittgenstein particularly admired) in *Architektur als Symbol* hints at a common ground between Frank and Wittgenstein.[13]

The terms and consequences of the fin-de-siècle Viennese discourse concerning language, culture, and society changed decisively after 1918, particularly for Viennese artists and thinkers of Jewish descent. Wittgenstein found it "almost insuperably difficult to adjust to peacetime conditions"; the war left an "indelible stamp" on him.[14] Like Frank, Wittgenstein spent the interwar years in Austria (where Wittgenstein worked as a schoolteacher) and in Vienna. The experiences spurred him to reconsider his earlier work and set out on a new path. Both Frank and Wittgenstein were of the same generation, one born in 1885 and the other in 1889. Both came of age in Vienna, although Wittgenstein went to school in Linz and Berlin. For both men (who were brought up in affluent circumstances), the war years were utterly transformative. As Wittgenstein wrote to a friend in 1925, "England may not have changed since 1913, but I have."[15]

Both men experienced interesting shifts in profession involving both architecture and philosophy. In the 1920s, Josef Frank attempted to realize his philosophical ambitions; *Architektur als Symbol* was the result of that effort. Wittgenstein turned to architecture in the twenties while living in Vienna. For him the result was also one principal work: a house designed with Paul Engelmann and completed in 1928 (fig. 2-1). Frank and Wittgenstein came into contact during the 1920s within the circle of intellectuals around Moritz Schlick, although Wittgenstein's connection with them was clearly more significant. Both suspected that a significant relationship existed between everyday life, ethics, and epistemological issues on one hand, and language usage and attitudes toward domestic design and spatial organization on the other. Hence Wittgenstein's use of the phrase that science "builds a house" while philosophy "tidies up a room" in which people actually live. The 1920s made both men skeptical of self-referential systems — Wittgenstein of mathematics and Frank of modernist architectural dogma.

A note of caution: Frank's writings bear little overt similarity to Wittgenstein's philosophical style and work (except perhaps for the penchant for suggesting unusual comparisons), and Wittgenstein's quite rigid modernist foray into architecture seems to have little in common with Frank's designs from the same period. The parallels between the two rest in the trajectory within their ideas in their primary fields. They responded to the war years and the events after 1918 with a fundamental reexamination of how humans conduct their everyday lives. Wittgenstein's turn to considering linguistic usage, to a procedure of philosophical inquiry, derived from seeing and listening and, tied to

patterns of making mental pictures that reflected the way language is commonly employed, paralleled Frank's rejection of formalistic modernist credos and his turn to the question of how people actually might live in the modern world, remember their past, and might be able to sustain individual dignity. Wittgenstein's "mess" and the seemingly eclectic character of ordinary life were, for Frank, the proper place to begin to think about designing modern living spaces. Architecture, like philosophy, could "tidy" things up.

Both Frank and Wittgenstein shared an admiration for Adolf Loos suggesting that, despite the profound sense of disorientation and loss that the war had brought, Frank and Wittgenstein rejected conservative postwar philosophies of restoration and irrationalism (e.g. the circle of poet Stefan George) critical of modernity. As Frank observed throughout *Architektur als Symbol*, the war, through its radical overturning of expectations, underscored the capacity to begin anew. The most promising path for architecture was to observe how people wish to live and to determine how best, in the sense of Popper-Lynkeus, to reconcile individuals — as they actually represent themselves — with the whole, revealing their true organic connections. This point of departure informed Frank's focus on single-family houses and his attitude toward the multiple-dwelling projects on which he worked after 1918.[16]

Similarly, in the 1920s Wittgenstein began to think that "the meaning of word lies entirely in its use, and is given in an explanation." Philosophy needed to concern itself with "clearing" up what "can be said about the world."[17] Hence Wittgenstein's interest in writing a dictionary for elementary schools based on the way words are used in a meaningful manner, a project he completed in 1926.[18]

Both Frank and Wittgenstein placed particular emphasis in their postwar work on the act of seeing how people function as the crucial beginning point to knowledge and understanding.[19] But mere observation was only the opening gambit. Then one had to find the rules of the game: how to distinguish sense from nonsense.

In architecture, for Frank, this meant making sense of the chaos of life. The natural condition of chaos was exacerbated as a result of the war. But its consequences were not all bad in that key dimensions of modernity, perhaps only nascent before the war, became clear. The war had brought modernity onto center stage, and with it science, technology, and the machine. There was no turning back. The rules of modern life demanded — in contrast to the work of Josef Hoffmann — confronting machines, modern materi-

als, and mass production and transforming their possibilities, thereby rescuing human beings from the dangers presented by an age of mechanization.[20] Hoffmann may have
rejected dead historical forms and given architecture (as
Frank put it) a sense of lightness and transparency,
but according to Frank he did not transcend the notion
of architecture as mere design. For Frank, the underlying
"rules"—the normative timeless traditions of architecture—were ultimately about the conduct of life.[21]

But most important, for Frank, the postwar era
underscored the dangers and illusions inherent in the allegiance to overarching systems based on metaphysical claims.
The language of "ideals" (on this point Popper-Lynkeus
was particularly clear), the kind that takes the form of
patriotisms and religious doctrines, may actually put forth
dangerous nonsense and untruth. Not all language use (and
therefore not all design) that appears superficially right is
necessarily equal. Wittgenstein saw that the logic of gram-
mar, and therefore meaning, needed to be understood using
a quasiempirical critical procedure. For Frank, therefore, the
claim to have developed a true uniform, international, modern idiom in the 1920s implicit in *Neues Bauen* was wrong on
two accounts. First, its procedure was faulty. It defied the
need to look and listen systematically to how much "more
varied our life has become." It was formalist and abstract.
Second, the Bauhaus was a replay of an attempt to impose
a specific national art, in this case a German style masquerading as internationalism, on the rest of Europe.[22] Yet
Frank argued that modernism was correct in its effort to
find a design vocabulary and approach adequate to contemporary life that acknowledged the irreversible march of history and was consistent with authentic and valid traditions
of human experience.

Frank and Wittgenstein developed a profound skepticism regarding prewar habits of thinking about truth, either
in philosophy or in architecture, particularly the appeal to
static normative concepts. Contemplating the successful
destruction of a seemingly secure and stable world, both
men, in their thirties and early forties, began to think that
the right path lay, rather, in opening one's eyes sympatheti-
cally to the dynamics of life. How did ordinary humans
talk and live? How might they do so, discarding nonsense
and illusion, so that a better life for humankind might be
created? The reason the totally designed environment, the
*Gesamtkunstwerk* strategy (popular in the Vienna Secession),
which sought to render every detail of life coherent and
beautified, was wrong was that it imposed aesthetic values
on individuals. It did not take into account how life actually is and therefore might be lived. Unlike Loos's prewar

attack on this idea, Frank's postwar critique mirrored a
competing social and political vision of the relationship
of the architect to his subject.[23]

In their work from the interwar years, from 1914 to
1939, both Wittgenstein and Frank brought to bear a
common fate, one they shared, particularly in the 1920s,
with Arnold Schoenberg.[24] In postwar Austria, Frank,
Wittgenstein, and Schoenberg were forced to realize that
their status as Jews, no matter how assimilated they were,
assumed a provocative significance in contrast to the patterns and expectations developed in pre-1914 Habsburg
Austria. The rise of populist political anti-Semitism at the
turn of the century in Austria may have offered harbingers
of what was to come after 1918.[25] But the fundamental
break with late-eighteenth century and nineteenth-century
aspirations and experiences among Jews concerning enlight-
enment, assimilation, and integration through the acquisi-
tion of language and culture occurred in the 1920s.[26]
Austria and Vienna of the 1920s led Frank, well before the
Anschluss, to immigrate to Sweden and Wittgenstein to
return to England.

**Austria and Vienna: The Political and Social Context.**[27]
What made Vienna and the Austrian Republic after World
War I distinct in the context of postwar Europe? By the
mid-1920s, the total population of the city had declined
somewhat from the prewar high of over 2 million to just
under 1.9 million. The war and the influenza epidemic of
1918 were the primary causes. However, this did not diminish the impact of terrible postwar economic conditions. In
April 1920, hunger riots and looting broke out in the city.
The aggregate population figures mask the fact that after
the war Vienna's long-standing prewar housing shortage did
not improve. Owing to changes in the distribution of population and the total collapse of new private sector construction, overcrowding and homelessness became a major
problem. In 1920, Austria's economic output was lower than
it had been in 1913. There was a slow and intermittent
recovery to prewar standards by 1929. But the 1929 world
economic crisis and the 1931 collapse of the Credit-Anstalt
Bank in Vienna rapidly brought the economy back down.
The GNP in 1933 was 80 percent of the GNP of 1913. In
Vienna in 1933, industrial production was 40 percent below
the level of 1913. Per-capita income declined between 1918
and 1938. High unemployment became a fact of life that
seemed impervious to change. Between 1922 and 1933, the
unemployment rate in Austria rose from around 10 percent
to over 25 percent. Last but not least, inflation and hyper-
inflation plagued the postwar period.

The legal abolition of the monarchy and aristocracy and the creation of a democracy altered most previous patterns of political life. In Vienna, the existence of squatters and the disenfranchised, including veterans of World War I, presented social problems to a nation and city entirely unaccustomed to government under democratic procedures. In 1925 violence broke out between the police and the unemployed (organized by the communist party) in front of the city hall. The shock of the 1918 defeat spurred the early success of the Pan-German nationalist movement within Austria. The Pan-Germans were determined either to merge Austria with Germany or to generate a sense of nativist conservatism, political values closely linked to those advocated by Austrian Christian Socialism. Both parties offered ideologies protective of the farmer, artisan, shopkeeper, and civil servant. The vitality of right-wing, pre-fascist and fascist politics in Austria and Vienna can be understood in part if one considers that the percentage of the population economically part of the middle class declined steadily during the interwar period.

Christian Socialism and its successor, Austro-Fascism, were the most dynamic postwar forces in the politics of the Austrian Republic (apart from the traditions of socialism and social democracy, particularly in interwar Vienna). Postwar Christian Socialism stemmed from the conservative Christian Socialism of the fin de siècle. This vital, peculiarly Austrian tradition was a provincial, culturally German-centered ideology tied to the Catholic Church and to land and race. Its greatest prewar success was its capture of the mayoralty and the city council of Vienna in the late 1890s under the leadership of the charismatic Karl Lueger, the mayor who was chief patron of the architect Otto Wagner.

A terrifying polarization of politics was visible in the Austrian Republic, especially in Vienna. Between 1919 and 1932, the Social Democrats commanded between 54 and 60 percent of the vote in Vienna. The two right-wing parties polled between 32 and 38 percent in the early 1920s. In 1932, the Nazis received over 17 percent of the vote and the right-wing parties 24 percent.[28] Until the appearance of Austro-fascism and Nazism within Vienna, the Christian Socialists were the Social Democrats' key rivals. At the same time, outside Vienna, right-wing Pan-German nationalism and Christian Socialism flourished at the expense of the Social Democrats. In the national elections, between 1919 and 1930, Christian Socialists, Pan-German Nationalists, and their allies commanded between 54 and 59 percent of the vote.[29] There was, in short, little "middle ground," either in Vienna or in the republic as a whole.

Austria after 1918 faced a problem of self-definition perhaps unique in Central and Eastern Europe. In contrast to Hungary, Poland, and Czechoslovakia, the other new nations that emerged from the Austro-Hungarian Empire, in Austria the dynastic reign of the Habsburgs had not suppressed a seemingly natural nationalism of land and language, which through post-Versailles self-determination, now found itself expressed in a new independent nation state. Left to their own devices, the Austrian German-speaking regions of the Habsburg Empire might have joined Germany and become an Austrian equivalent to Bavaria. The Versailles Treaty made that impossible. The new small republic (which did not contain all German-speaking peoples from the old monarchy) was forced not only to accept democracy and the legal elimination of its most distinct traditions, the monarchy and the aristocracy, but also to fashion a coherent, distinct national identity, an allegiance to something artificial that had never existed in the imaginations of its people: the idea of Austria. The consequence of this was that the 1920s and early 1930s were marked by persistent political instability and violence throughout the country.

Since the mid-nineteenth century, the non-German-speaking subject peoples of the Habsburgs had dreamed of freedom and independence. In contrast, after 1866, when the Habsburgs were defeated by Prussia at Königgrätz, apart from sentiment within Austria for a merger with Germany, there was merely pessimism regarding the prospects for the multinational dynastic Empire. If there was a nationalist sentiment among the German-speaking population before 1914, it was a Pan-German nationalism. As the Galician-born Jewish writer Joseph Roth (who wrote the finest portrayal of the Habsburg era, the 1932 *Radetzkymarsch*) and many of his contemporaries noted with some irony, the only true German-speaking patriots in Habsburg Austria before World War I were Jews.

With the collapse of the monarchy, the Jews of Vienna and Austria found themselves in a new and not altogether welcome political environment. The traditional protection offered by the monarchy was gone. Even though the issue of Austrian national identity was far from resolved among non-Jews, Jews in Austria encountered what their fellow Jews faced in all the new post-1918 nations of Central and Eastern Europe. Modern nation-state building in these regions seemed to require a sharpening of anti-Semitism. Jews emerged as the key minority in the new Poland, Hungary, Lithuania, Czechoslovakia, and Austria. By deepening the rift between Jews and non-Jews, the logic of nationalism in these fledgling states seemed more plausible and convincing.[30]

Fig. 2-2. Jews in a soup kitchen in Vienna, 1920. Courtesy of The YIVO Institute for Jewish Research.

Many Austrian Jews were active in the political left in part because of its inherent mistrust of nationalism. They also were inclined to be sympathetic with a practically non-existent liberal democratic centrism. Some even flirted with conservative Austrian politics and supported the right-wing Heimwehr, a paramilitary group that evolved during the 1920s into a conservative political party. However, given the domination of the right wing in national politics in the later 1920s, and despite the continuing vitality of Marxism and socialism, Jews found themselves excluded, by definition, from a viable political vehicle through which to assert patriotism and national loyalty in the newly founded, ill-defined, and unstable entity, the Republic of Austria. Socialism and communism were, after all, ideologies of internationalism that expressed contempt for precisely the type of patriotic politics that would triumph completely in Germany and Austria in the 1930s.

The Jewish question after the war in Vienna became more acute than it had been before 1914. In the first place, the number of Jews in the city increased from under 9 percent in 1910 to nearly 11 percent in 1923.[31] Jews accounted for three-fifths of all postwar emigrants into Vienna (fig. 2-2).[32] These *Ostjuden* came primarily from the north and east (Poland, Czechoslovakia, and Hungary) and were viewed as unwelcome impoverished foreigners, both by non-Jews and segments of the established, assimilated German-speaking Jewish community who understandably feared the extent to which these Jews fit into stereotypes of anti-Semitic propaganda. In 1922, the Rector of the University of Vienna warned against the influence of these new Jews and recommended a quota system.

Faced with the legal possibility of political participation in the city after 1918, Jews emerged as an explicit political force. A Jewish party fielded candidates in the

Viennese elections. Its presence mirrored the extent to which Zionism had become an increasingly powerful and widespread ideology after the war.[33] But as the economic and social conditions either failed to improve or deteriorated, the scapegoating of Jews became more intense and more plausible. On one hand, Jews were identified with social democracy by the Austrian right, whose most charismatic figure (and compared to others, only mildly anti-Semitic) was a Catholic priest, Ignaz Seipel. He served as chancellor intermittently throughout the 1920s and dominated the politics of the decade. On the other hand, Jews were objects of well-worn anti-Semitic theories of internationalist capitalist exploitation (fig. 2-3). These flourished even within the social democratic party, whose leadership pilloried middle-class Jews who sided with the conservative parties. The prominence of Jews in Vienna—in sheer numbers as a mass of poor people and as eminent individuals in journalism, business, the arts, medicine, and science—only lent credibility to anti-Semitism from both the political left and right.

Viennese Jews did not react to this deteriorating reality in a coherent manner. In 1922, Hugo Bettauer, a controversial and flamboyant writer of Jewish descent, wrote a satire that described an utterly boring and provincial Vienna of the future—one without Jews. *Die Stadt ohne Juden* was wildly successful. In 1925 Bettauer was shot to death in his office by a right-wing fanatic. The trial and the light sentence given to the murderer only underscored the depth of anti-Semitism in Vienna. By the late 1920s and early 1930s, the upper stratum of Jews clung to the hope that the Austrian political right would offer a refuge from the radical left's attack on capitalism and the far more dangerous extreme right represented by Nazism. Other Jews turned to Zionism and slowly detached themselves from any aspirations to become modern Austrian patriots.[34] A substantial portion of the Jewish population remained loyal to social democracy. But most middle-class Jews tried to wish politics away and held on to a vague and unrealistic hope that some sort of paternalistic force—not dissimilar to the benign figure of Franz Josef, who was venerated by the Jews—would protect them from the virulent and violent populist anti-Semitism that had come to dominate Viennese and Austrian politics. The confrontation with the failure of that possibility was, for some, too much to bear, as the suicide of the writer Egon Friedell in 1938 made all too clear.

It was in this environment that Josef Frank worked. In the spring of 1933, the Austrian Werkbund was in the midst of a profound crisis. The great architect and designer

Fig. 2-3. A 1920 Christian Socialist election poster exhorting the citizenry: "Vote Christian Socialist—German Christians—Save Austria!" From Oswald Oberhuber, ed., *Zeitgeist wider den Zeitgeist: Ein Sequenz aus Österreichs Verirrung* (Vienna: Hochschule für angewandte Kunst, 1988), p. 70.

Josef Hoffmann and a key group of associates sought to challenge the leadership of the Werkbund. The target of their attack was Frank, the guiding force of the Werkbund whom Hoffmann characterized as the apostle of a "pedestrian internationalism" (*Allerwelts-Internationalismus*). The Werkbund ultimately broke apart into two groups. Hoffmann's splinter organization, the "Neue Werkbund Österreichs," founded in February 1934, was designed to encourage "healthy and not degenerate" forms of expression; to counter the use of "clever nitpicking and cynical remarks" (*Sptizfindigkeiten und hämischen Bemerkungen*), which "weaken and demoralize" creativity.[35]

Hoffmann's attack on Frank, in both its substance

and timing, fit the political culture of the Austrian Republic of late 1920s and early 1930s perfectly. The rhetoric of the attack echoed familiar fascist claims about what was wrong in Germany and Austria. Fascist propaganda argued that postwar modernism in art and architecture was an abstract, dehumanizing product of modern urban life dominated by rootless cosmopolitan Jews whose insidious capacity for sophistry deflected unwitting and sensitive creative talents from the healthy sources of inspiration: the Christian people of Austria and their artisan and local traditions.

The enemy, whether in art or economics, was not, in this case, the religious traditional Jew or the newcomer, the *Ostjude*, but the highly assimilated Jew—a Josef Frank whose integration into the network of culture and society had first been permitted by the politics of the late nineteenth century. Such Jews also became emblems of the modern city and urban life. After the collapse of the monarchy, their influence seemed to reach a peak. Furthermore, in the wake of the defeat of 1918, the cultural nostalgia (which was well-developed before 1914) for a lost *Alt-Wien*, for the city before its economic and physical transformation in the 1860s and 1870s, became even more powerful. The decline of culture and civility visible in the violence and unrest of the 1920s was tied to the evolution of Vienna after 1866, to an era that coincided with the rapid growth in the Jewish population of Vienna. In 1857 Jews accounted for less than 3 percent of the population. By the end of the century, this had risen to about 10 percent; there were more than 175,000 Jews in Vienna by 1910. Modernization and Jews were inextricably linked in the popular Viennese lore, for better or worse.

In postwar Austria, where a tension between Vienna and the largely rural remainder of the country was severe, another subtle but pervasive link was made: between aesthetic modernism and the foreign international forces that had brought defeat to Habsburg Austria in the war. Anti-Semitism in the interwar years focused on highly intellectual Jews who only appeared superficially like all other Austrians or Germans. These Jews were actually destructive foreign elements masquerading, often under the banner of socialism and communism, as representatives of democracy and a new nation and its people. The reality, however, was that misery and not prosperity was the dominant experience of the Austrian population under democracy. Democracy itself became suspect as something both foreign and Jewish.

In Frank's case, the ironies were severe. Frank attacked German modernism in a manner not dissimilar to that of Hoffmann. He decried the so-called ascetic functionalism

of the international style the Nazis later declared "degenerate." But most important, he worked, in his years in Vienna, to construct public housing projects that sought to realize a utopian vision, not on behalf of the traditional clients of Hoffmann's Wiener Werkstätte—the rich upper classes—but on behalf of the lower classes and poor, who constituted the demographic backbone of postwar modern anti-Semitism.

The Werkbund crisis of 1933–34 paralleled the triumph of Austro-Fascism. In March 1933 the Austrian parliament dissolved, catapulting into power Engelbert Dollfuss, the Christian Social leader, who was Austria's best rival as a homegrown right-wing dictator. However, the German Nazis began a campaign designed to destabilize Dollfuss. That spring the communist party was banned. Concurrent with the creation of the new Werkbund in February of 1934, a brief but bloody civil war took place, leading up to the banning of the Social Democratic Party. By the end of 1934 Dollfuss had been assassinated in an aborted Nazi Putsch and the Nazi Party (despite its popularity in Austria) placed under legal restrictions. Austria's nearly decade and a half ambivalent and painful flirtation with democracy had come to a violent end.

**Politics, Ideology, and Architecture.** Josef Hoffmann's characterization of Frank as excessively clever, analytical, and skeptical was more than a case of a ritual use of anti-Semitic rhetoric. Hoffmann correctly captured one side of Frank's approach to the traditions of the Viennese fin de siècle in which Frank grew up. What Hoffmann missed was the fact that Frank's emphasis on the single-family house and the need to offer the individual the freedom to express uniqueness in the materials and disposition of interiors was driven by the search for an architectural ideology that would transcend the growing rift between Jews and non-Jews, among social classes, between Viennese and rural Austrians, and among adherents of differing political parties characteristic of the 1920s. Frank's architecture sought to decentralize space and render it intimate, in part by connecting it to nature (fig. 2-4). If each individual could gain a sense of his or her worth—and not feel amalgamated into fixed groupings or forced into a particular style of self-representation—then the political currents of the time might be counteracted. In 1929 Frank wrote that "freedom" could stimulate the sense of "cosmopolitanism," emancipating the individual from the "unpleasant dependency on a single point." The individual had to learn that his local place—his roots, so to speak—was not a "closed" ideal, but rather a basis through which "decentralization" could

Fig. 2-4. Bedroom of the A. S. F. Villa with furnishings designed by Frank for Haus & Garten, ca. 1930. The textile pattern is "Primavera." From Johannes Spalt and Otto Kapfinger, *Josef Frank, 1885—1967: Stoffe, Tapeten Teppiche* (Vienna: Hochschule für angewandte Kunst, 1986).

lead to "a sense of unity." Architecture had to spur a habit of "autonomous thinking" that permitted the individual to reach out to others without sacrificing a sense of place and uniqueness.[36]

The last decades of the Habsburg Monarchy, the years of Frank's youth, placed enormous emphasis on art as means of representation, both for the individual (in clothes and interior design) and the State. Even within the competing and overlapping ideological factions of Vienna around 1900 (such as those around Karl Kraus, Adolf Loos, and Arnold Schoenberg on one side and Gustav Klimt, Josef Hoffmann, and Arthur Schnitzler on the other), the terms of debate regarding the nature of art and history—as well as the achievements of the Vienna Secession, of Otto Wagner and the Wiener Werkstätte before 1914—presumed the monarchy and a social and economic structure that was wiped out in the war. Adolf Loos's legendary tirade against ornament, his critique of the Wiener Werkstätte and the Secession, and his celebration of modern materials and manufacture were directed at the prewar

Viennese public and patrons. Likewise, Karl Kraus's pre-1919 attacks on journalism and philistine readers construed aestheticism, the corruption of language, and ethical hypocrisy, as evils. Since the 1860s, public controversy regarding architectural design in Vienna was rooted in issues of taste and fashion whose political consequences were limited to issues of cultural self-image. Culture was politics. Architecture and cultural self-representation went hand in hand. Therefore, the 1910 radicalism of Loos's Michaelerplatz design for Goldman and Salatsch, right across from the Hofburg, was structured within a prewar debate regarding cultural values.[37] The work at once challenged and conceded the limited depoliticized terms of debates about architecture (fig. 2-5).

But after 1918 politics became more than cultural discourse. To an extent far more dramatic than in postwar Germany, the discontinuity between the prewar traditions and the postwar realities in post-1919 Austria was overwhelming. The housing projects Josef Frank undertook in the 1920s constituted an unprecedented challenge. A funda-

Fig. 2-5. Michaelerplatz after construction of the Looshaus, ca. 1912. Courtesy of the Historisches Museum der Stadt Wien.

mental reconsideration of the relationship between issues of design and those of politics was required. The architect Frank, unlike Loos or even Otto Wagner, was building for a social democratic government free of imperial and aristocratic influence; on behalf of individuals in search of a postwar identity, as private persons and citizens. The socialists and their allies worked hard to argue for translations of notions of equality within design. Yet how could one resist the modernist conceit that the simple lines and shapes and anti-ornamentalism—the stress on function—mirrored a superior ideology of life, when, as Frank realized, these views also tended toward mechanization and dehumanization. They argued for a spiritual uniformity at odds with nature dictated from above.

In his dialogue with the postwar modernist ideas of Le Corbusier and the Bauhaus, Frank displayed the special insights that his Viennese circumstance uniquely demanded. He recognized the dissonance between rigid abstract aesthetic principles that limit the possibilities of individual styles of life and the logic of democracy and the overt celebration of diversity. At the same time, Frank asked, how does one further the sense of equality among humans, work against nativism, and honor the irrational collection of fragments of past and present experience that individuals constitute?

In no postwar culture was there such a striking amalgam of seemingly irreconcilable and aimless remnants of history combined with the unfamiliar imperatives of the present than in postwar Vienna. Frank's work confronted the design of the interior and exterior spaces in which a dislocated and disoriented population of the fledgling

Austrian Republic would be living. Frank saw clearly the inadequacy of the debates before 1914. He, unlike Schoenberg, Kraus, or even Loos, did not condemn the bourgeois as an implacable enemy.[38] Frank's objective was not to challenge taste but to permit ordinary people, no matter how insignificant, to improve and sense a link to nature, to others, to one's past, and to one's self. Hence, Frank's active participation in the 1931 Werkbund exhibition, entitled "The Good, Inexpensive Object."

Frank ultimately was suspicious of the idea of progress and a blind embrace of modernity and the machine. He took issue with the modernist focus on monumental structures, no matter how sleek in design (fig. 2-6). The individual once again was dwarfed as he had been by the Ringstrasse. The relationship of design to individuals and their conduct of life altered the meaning of prewar categories such as ornament, structure, and function. Frank's houses from the 1920s reveal a modernist aesthetic because a nearly Neoclassical simplicity permitted individuality. Frank had little use for self-deceptive assertions of radical antitraditionalism. The only question was which tradition was valid.

At the same time, Frank broke with the Viennese habits of the Wiener Werkstätte and the Secession—the overvaluation of the aesthetic dimension, luxury, and artisan handicraft. He mocked all attempts at creating provincial and nationalist aesthetic styles, particularly in the lands formerly part of the Austro-Hungarian Monarchy. Rigid aesthetic ideologies of modernism, which celebrated clean lines and functionalism, were subjected to the same withering attack as nostalgic efforts to re-create the symbols and

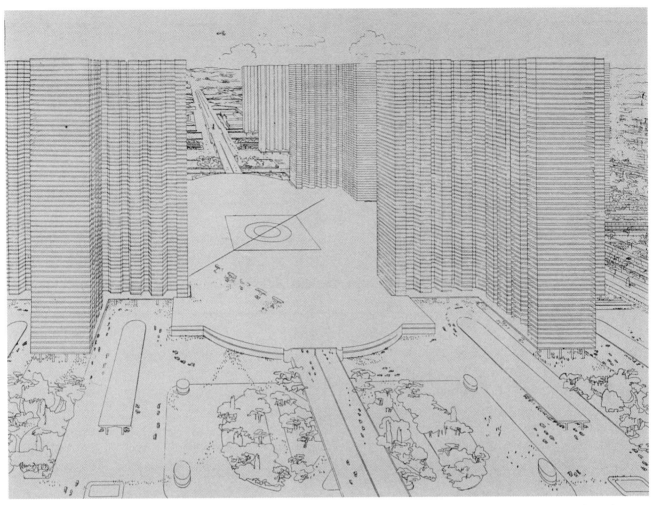

Fig. 2-6. Le Corbusier and Pierre Jeanneret, Plan Voisin, 1925. From Le Corbusier and Jeanneret, *Oeuvre Complète, 1910–1929* (Zurich: Les Editions d'Architecture, 1964).

techniques of the world before World War I, when the modern machine demonstrated its terrifying dominance over contemporary life. For Frank, "only a common tradition can be the basis on which we can make progress, one that is understandable by all people and encourages the highest level of common culture." Frank sought "an art of humanity" in which the arts were more than "the need for luxury on the part of the rich," but were the "possession" of all individuals and reflected their "will" and special character. For each generation, particularly his own, life was a series of "beginnings." In the 1920s, modernism in art and architecture and its opponents made the same fundamental error—one of theoretical and metaphysical systematic absolutism—either in the name of a radical break with history or a return to a mythic past. The leading proponents of modernism found in Frank an unreliable ally; they

saw in him a lack of coherence and clarity with respect to seemingly objective principles of modern design and the imperatives of the historical moment.

Frank's architectural and design work from this period, as well as his realization of the Werkbundsiedlung of 1932, mirrored his philosophy. His houses demonstrated a distinct debt to modernism in line and materials. But in the distribution of space and the disposition of the interiors he realized an original but natural eclecticism. Not surprisingly, then, neither the Marxism nor the Fascism of the 1920s—whether in their German, Soviet, or Austrian forms—appealed to Frank. His art derived from a commitment to a utopian empiricism, at once skeptical and empathetic to the everyday needs of the simple people who, in the end, suffered most from the catastrophe of World War I.

1. Ludwig Wittgenstein, *Philosophical Remarks* (Chicago: University of Chicago Press, 1975) p. 9.

2. Ludwig Wittgenstein, "Lecture B VIII, Lent Term 1931," in Desmond Lee, ed., *Wittgenstein's Lectures Cambridge 1930–1932* (Chicago: University of Chicago Press, 1982), p. 42.

3. Hermann Czech, "Ein Begriffsraster zur aktuellen Interpretation Josef Franks," in Mikael Berquist and Olof Michëlsen, eds., *Josef Frank, Architektur* (Basel: Birkhäuser Verlag, 1994), p. 42.

4. See his 1930 "Adolf Loos" and 1929 "Gesprach under den Werkbund" in Johannes Spalt and Hermann Czech, eds., *Josef Frank 1885–1967* (Vienna: Hochschule für Angewandte Kunst, 1981), pp. 197 and 203.

5. The most prominent example of the influence of Wagner after 1918 was the work Karl Ehn, particularly the Karl-Marx-Hof in the XIX District. See Marco Pozzetto, *Die Schule Otto Wagners, 1894–1912* (Vienna: Schroll, 1980), p. 218; and *Traum und Wirklichkeit Wien 1870–1930*, exhib. cat. (Vienna: Österreichische Akademie der Wissenschaften, 1985), pp. 648–49.

6. On Gomperz (1832–1912), who was an assimilationist and anti-Zionist, see Robert A. Kann, *Theodor Gomperz, Ein Gelehrtenleben im Bürgertum der Franz Josefs-Zeit* (Vienna, 1974).

7. Josef Frank, *Architektur als Symbol: Elemente deutschen neuen Bauens* (Vienna: Anton Schroll, 1931); reprint (Vienna: Löcker, 1981), pp. 39–45.

8. Ibid, pp. 22 and 70–79.

9. Phillip Frank, while he was teaching in Prague, was in contact with Popper-Lynkeus in 1920 and 1921. Frank was also friendly with Ernst Mach and Albert Einstein. See Margit Ornstein and Heinrich Löwy, eds., *Josef Popper-Lynkeus. Gespräche.* (Löwit: Vienna, 1935), p. 50; see also Wilfred Posch, "Josef Frank, eine bedeutende Persönlichkeit des österreichischen Kulturliberaismus," *Um Bau 10* (August 1986), pp. 21–37.

10. Most of the English-language literature on Popper-Lynkeus focuses on the more famous 1899 *Phantasien eines Realisten* (Düsseldorf: Erb, 1980, reprint of 1909) because of its connections to Freud and his work.

11. See Popper-Lynkeus, *Das Individuum* (Dresden, Reissner, 1920), pp. 222–23. The organic elements in Frank's work are particularly visible in the 1932 layout of the Werbundsiedlung (particularly his inclusion of André Lurçat's contribution), the Haus und Garten interiors, and most dramatically in the later work such as the "Town for 2000 Families" and the fantasy houses from 1947; see Spalt and Czech, *Josef Frank*, pp. 218–35, and Berquist and Michëlsen, eds., *Josef Frank*, pp. 45 and 47. Popper-Lynkeus's influence is visible in *Architektur als Symbol*.

12. Michael Müller, "Wie modern war die Avantgarde?" *Um Bau 10* (August 1986), pp. 7–20.

13. Frank, *Architektur*, pp. 5–6. Compare Wittgenstein's use of Kürnberger as the motto for the *Tractatus*. The book was finished in 1918 and first published in 1921.

14. Ray Monk, *Ludwig Wittgenstein: The Duty of Genius* (New York: Free Press, 1990), p. 169.

15. Ludwig Wittgenstein, *Briefe* (Frankfurt: Suhrkamp, 1980), p. 256.

16. See the excellent essay by Friedrich Achleitner, "Josef Frank et l'architecture Viennoise de l'entre-deux guerres," in Jean Clair, ed., *Vienne 1880–1938. L'Apocalypse Joyeuse* (Paris: Centre Pompidou, 1986), pp. 619–25; and Otto Kapfinger, "Josef Frank—Siedlungs und Siedlungsprojekt," *Um Bau 10* (August 1986), pp. 39–58.

17. Lee, ed., *Wittgenstein's Lectures*, pp. 66 and 21–22.

18. Ludwig Wittgenstein, *Wörterbuch für Volksschulen* (Vienna: Pichler-Tempsky, 1926; reprint, 1977).

19. See Monk, *Ludwig Wittgenstein*, pp. 302–303.

20. Both men owed some debt to Goethe on the matter of seeing as knowing. See Frank, *Architektur*, pp. 6–9; 136–37.

21. Similarities exist as well between Frank's postwar views and those of another Jewish Viennese contemporary, the writer Stefan Zweig (1881–1942), who sought to defend humanistic values such as individualism against modernity without rejecting aesthetic modernism. Compare, for example, Frank's views with Zweig's essay "Die Monotisierung der Welt," in *Begegnungen mit Menschen, Büchern Städten* (Vienna/Zurich, 1937).

22. The phrase in German is *"veilformiger unser Leben geworden ist."* Frank's perception contains more truth than he suspected. From the perspective of the post-1945 years, in music, the twelve-tone approach developed by Arnold Schoenberg in the 1920s appeared to be the legitimate modernist path; the true alternative to regressive neoromanticism and the right way of the future. This became the dominant ideology in America and France. Yet, when Schoenberg formulated his system in 1921, he made the now-notorious remark that he had made a discovery that would assure the dominance of German music for the next hundred years. H. H. Stuckenschmidt, *Schönberg: Leben, Umwelt, Werk* (Mainz: Piper-Schutt, 1984), p. 252.

23. See the essays by Christopher Long in this volume and Müller, "Wie modern."

24. On Schoenberg (who had converted to Protestantism) and his encounter with anti-Semitism in Austria in 1921 in Mattsee near Salzburg, see Ernst Hilmar, ed., *Arnold Schoenberg* (Vienna: Universal, 1974), p. 291; and Jelena Hahl-Koch, ed., *Arnold Schoenberg-Wassily Kandinsky* (London: Faber and Faber, 1984), pp. 78–82.

25. Among the many studies of Austrian anti-Semitism, see Bruce F. Pauley, *From Prejudice to Persecution. A History of Austrian Anti-Semitism* (Chapel Hill: University of North Carolina Press, 1992); and Peter Pulzer's classic *The Rise of Anti Semitism in Germany and Austria*, rev. ed. (Cambridge, MA: Harvard University Press, 1988).

26. See Leon Botstein, *Judentum und Modernität: Essays zur Rolle der Juden in der deutschen und österreichischen Kultur 1848–1938* (Vienna: Böhlau, 1991).

27. The material in this section is drawn from Maren Seliger and Karl Ucakar, *Wien: Politische Geschichte*, vol. 2: 1896–1934 (Vienna: Jugend und Volk, 1985), esp. p. 1067.

28. Ibid., p. 1139; see also Erika Weinzierl and Kurt Skalnik, *Österreich 1918–1938: Geschichte der Ersten Republik*, 2 vols. (Graz: Styria, 1983).

29. Data for this section also comes from Ernst Hanisch, *Der lange Schatten des Staates: Öesterreichische Gesellschaftsgeschichte im 20. Jahrhundert* (Vienna: Überreuter, 1994), p. 127.

30. See Ezra Mendelsohn, *The Jews of East Central Europe Between the World Wars* (Bloomington: Indiana University Press, 1983).

31. One way to put the significance of the Jews in Vienna into perspective when considering Josef Frank is to consider the percentage of Jews in the k.k. Staatsoberrealschule and the Technische Hochschule in Vienna when Frank attended them. In the Oberrealschule, out of 535 students in 1896, 178 were Jewish and 35 were Protestants. In 1897, in the Technische Hochschule out of 1,706 students, 473 were Jewish. Another 113 were Protestant. The precentage of Jews was, at a minimum, 33. Since a high proportion of the Protestants were probably of Jewish descent and considered by anti-Semites as Jews (conversion to Protestantism as opposed

to Catholicism was considered a more palatable option among those Jews considering conversion), the percentage of Jews was even higher. In 1902 the numbers were 702 Jews, 208 Protestants, out of 2,525 students. In 1906, there were 819 Jews, and 240 Protestants, out of 2,983 students. In 1924, the percentage had gone down, with only 723 Jews out of 3,677, probably the result of restrictive admissions policies. In any event, in the context of the total population, the percentage of Jews in this leading educational institution was striking. *Statistisches Jahrbuch der Stadt* (Vienna, 1896), pp. 358−59; *Statistisches Jahrbuch der Stadt* (Vienna, 1901), p. 445; *Statistisches Jahrbuch der Stadt* (1906), p. 379; Leo Goldhammer, *Die Juden Wiens: Eine statistische Studie* (Vienna: Löwit, 1927), p. 41.

32. See Goldhammer, *Die Juden Wiens*; Klaus Hödl, *Als Bettler in die Leopoldstadt* (Vienna: Böhlau, 1994), pp. 283−317; and Michael John and Albert Lichtblau, *Schmelztiegel Wien: Einst und Jetzt zur Geschichte und Gegenwart von Zuwanderung und Minderheiten* (Vienna: Böhlau, 1990), pp. 208−10.

33. See George E. Berkeley, *Vienna and Its Jews 1880−1980s* (Cambridge: Abt, 1988), pp. 149−161; and Bruno Frei, *Jüdisches Elend in Wien* (Vienna: Löwit, 1920).

34. Among Viennese Jews who turned to Zionism between 1918 and 1933 were Felix Salten (who wrote *Bambi*), Richard Beer-Hofmann, Arnold Schoenberg, Popper-Lynkeus, Wittgenstein's architectural collaborator Paul Engelmann, and to some degree Arthur Schnitzler.

35. Astrid Gmeiner and Gottfried Pirhofer, eds., *Der Österreichische Werkbund* (Salzburg: Residenz Verlag, 1985), pp. 182−87; see also Eduard F. Sekler, *Josef Hoffmann: Das architektonische Werk* (Salzburg: Residenz Verlag, 1982), pp. 207−14.

36. Spalt and Czech, *Josef Frank*, p. 203.

37. See Burkhardt Rukschcio and Roland Schachel, *Adolf Loos Leben und Werk* (Salzburg: Residenz Verlag, 1982), pp. 147−60 and 461.

38. Consider, for example, Frank's work in the 1920s with Schoenberg's creation of the exclusive Society for Private Performances, which sought to protect modernism from the tastes of the public.

Christopher Long

Although Joseph Frank spent nearly half of his adult life in exile, mostly in Sweden, his personality and work were deeply etched by his upbringing during the Viennese fin de siècle. For much of his working life, even after he left Austria in 1933, Frank struggled to come to terms with the legacy left by Otto Wagner, Josef Maria Olbrich, Josef Hoffmann, Adolf Loos, and the other architects and designers of the early Viennese modern movement. In many respects, Frank carried on and even broadened the revolution they inaugurated in the 1890s. Yet if Frank continued to bear the torch of Viennese modernism well after most of its original leaders had passed from the scene, he also called into question many of its core convictions. Indeed, much like Loos, he adopted a course that not only often ran counter to the mainstream of Viennese architecture and design, but also stood in opposition to the wider modern movement. While he never completely shed the cultural and intellectual assumptions of the Vienna of his youth, in the end he charted his own direction, one that led to a unique, complex, and personal vision of the modern.

Josef Frank was born on July 15, 1885. His father Ignaz Frank was a well-to-do Jewish textile manufacturer and wholesaler, who had moved to Vienna in the 1860s from Heves, a small market town in eastern Hungary; his mother Jenney née Feilendorf was the daughter of a wealthy Viennese industrialist family originally from Slovakia. Josef, the second of the couple's four children, was born in the picturesque little spa town of Baden, some nineteen miles (30 km) south of Vienna, where the Franks often spent the summer months.[1]

The Franks were in many ways typical of the ascendant Jewish middle class living in Central Europe on the cusp of the new century—assimilated, worldly, cultured, interested in the newest trends and ideas. As for many assimilated families of the "Mosaic persuasion," religion for the Franks was little more than a formality; though the specter of anti-Semitism was never far from the surface, the family's Jewishness caused them little inconvenience. While some barriers to advancement for Jews remained, especially in the army and civil service, the marginalization and social dislocation that they later experienced was not yet in evidence. Indeed, the years between 1860 and 1890 marked the heyday for assimilated Jews in Austria; the emancipation decree of 1867 and the rise of liberal politics in Austria opened new vistas of opportunity, allowing many to make the extraordinary climb from peddlers and artisans to jurists, professors, businessmen, and politicians. Frank's family exemplified this new social mobility: his father struggled up from modest circumstances to become a man of some means; one of his maternal uncles rose to become a high official with the Austrian State Railways; and

another uncle was an engineer who oversaw the construction of the *Riesenrad*, the city's great Ferris wheel, and later
became a successful manufacturer of car batteries.[2]

From 1895 to 1903, Frank attended the k. k. Staatsoberrealschule (higher secondary school) in the city's first
district. Although he showed a marked talent for drawing
and for history, on the whole he was a rather desultory
student: his grades were average or just below, and he was
forced to repeat the fifth form after failing English and
mathematics. Despite his less than stellar record, Frank
passed his final examinations in June 1903, and the following
October he enrolled in the architecture faculty at the Vienna
Technische Hochschule, or Polytechnic Institute (fig. 3-1).

Compared with the nearby Kunstgewerbeschule
(School of Arts and Crafts), whose faculty included many
of the leading Secessionists, among them Josef Hoffmann
and Kolo Moser, or the Academy of Fine Arts, where Otto
Wagner and Friedrich Ohmann conducted the two special
architecture classes, the Technische Hochschule remained a
conservative bastion. Most of the professors were representatives of the late Viennese historicist school—the
generation that followed after the great builders of the
Ringstrasse—and many were openly hostile to the cause of
architectural reform.

Of Frank's professors at the Technische Hochschule it
was Carl König, holder of the chair for Classical and
Renaissance architecture, who had the most lasting influence on him.[3] König was very much an architect of the old
school, who remained convinced that a new architectural
expression could only come out of the historical tradition.
But to his credit, König, unlike many of his contemporaries,
did not view the architecture of the past merely as an inven-
tory of forms that could be applied to any building project
regardless of their original purpose or meaning. In his lec-

Fig. 3-1. Josef Frank, ca. 1903. Universitätsarchiv, Technische
Universität, Vienna.

tures he emphasized not only the value of learning the visual language of Classicism, but also of understanding the
process through which the basic forms of antique building
had been derived. The purpose of studying historical
motifs, König stressed, was not to learn how to imitate
them, but to understand how they had been created; only
when armed with this knowledge could the architect rework
these qualities in a new spirit.

Fig. 3-5. Room 12, Ostasiatiches Museum, Cologne, 1912–13. Rheinisches Bildarchiv, Cologne.

*Gesamtkunstwerk* (total work of art) ideals that Hoffmann, Olbrich, and the other Secessionists had long championed. At the same time it also engendered a stylelessness, a look that was unquestionably modern but was lacking specific rules. "A room like the salon in the Tedesco apartment," Wlach wrote in an essay on Frank's early work, "in which a Persian rug, an English table, a Chinese lamp, and a Swedish blanket, etc., form a resonant harmony . . . cannot be damaged, one can add what one will. It remains mutable and lives along with the life of its owners."[14]

This new eclecticism that Frank displayed in the Tedesco interiors was also strikingly evident in his designs for the Schwedische Turnschule Strömberg-Palm (Strömberg-Palm Swedish Gymnastics School, 1910–11; fig. 3-4) in Vienna and the Ostasiatiches Museum (East Asian Art Museum, 1912–13; fig. 3-5) in Cologne. In both works Frank drew on historical forms—Swedish folk motifs in the case of the former; traditional Chinese

design, the latter—but he simplified and altered them, combining them with other influences to create an idiom that both harkened back to the past and was still unmistakably new.

While working on the commission for the Strömberg-Palm school, Frank met a Swedish woman, Anna Sebenius, who was teaching there.[15] They were married two years later in Cologne, while Frank was putting the final touches on the Asian Art Museum; with her, Frank made numerous trips to Sweden over the next two decades, establishing connections that eventually brought him there permanently in the 1930s.

In 1913 and 1914 Frank designed and built several innovative villas in and around Vienna in collaboration with Strnad and Wlach, including the Scholl and Strauss houses (fig. 3-6). Although the works still manifested faint historical references, their clarity of line and striking simplicity posed a direct challenge to the more standard architecture of the day, and they established Frank at the forefront of those in search of a new architecture. After the outbreak of the war in 1914, however, he was forced to suspend his work. At the end of January 1915, Frank was called up for military service and assigned to the Imperial army's railroad engineering regiment; he spent much of the remainder of the war planning and overseeing the construction of various strategic rail lines and roads in the Balkans.[16]

In 1919 Frank and Wlach resumed their joint practice; Strnad, however, withdrew from the partnership to devote himself to teaching and to concentrate on his first love, stage design. The severe postwar inflation in Austria, however, precluded any possibility of finding private commissions, so Frank, with support from Strnad and Hoffmann, applied for and was granted a teaching position at the Kunstgewerbeschule. The post provided a modest but steady source of income that allowed Frank to support himself during 1919 and the early 1920s when private building had come to almost a complete halt.

Aside from his teaching duties Frank spent much of his time and energy searching for solutions to Vienna's severe postwar housing shortage. The disastrous economic

Fig. 3-6. Villa for Oskar and Hanny Strauss, Vienna, 1913–14. From *Wasmuths Monatshefte für Baukunst* 6 (1921).

Fig. 3-7. Workers' Housing Settlement, Ortmann, Lower Austria, 1919–20. From *Deutsche Kunst und Dekoration* 48 (1921).

Fig. 3-8. Wiedenhofer-Hof Housing Project, 1923–24. Historisches Museum der Stadt Wien.

Fig. 3-9. Haus & Garten showroom, ca. 1926. From *Innen-Dekoration* 37 (1926).

situation in Austria and a huge influx of German-speaking refugees from the outlying provinces during and after the war had combined to further exacerbate the city's chronic housing problem. During the war, squatters' camps had begun to appear on the town's edge and in open areas, and by 1919 entire makeshift villages had sprung up all over the city.[17]

In response to the mounting crisis, Frank, who was sympathetic to the new Socialist administration,[18] proposed several innovative solutions, including a plan for poured concrete housing projects using prefabricated forms.[19] Most of the schemes were based on simply constructed, low-density row house developments, which pro-

vided the occupants with small plots of land so that they could grow their own food.[20] From 1921 to 1924, Frank worked as an adviser to the *Österreichischer Verband für Siedlungs- und Kleingartenwesen* (Austrian Union of Settlers and Small Gardeners), an umbrella organization for the many grassroots housing cooperatives formed after the war, which was headed up by Frank's close friend Otto Neurath.[21] Frank gave lectures on building techniques and planning to many of these groups and helped them to plan future developments. But in the end he was able to realize only two housing settlements, one for the municipality and another for the workers at his cousin Hugo Bunzl's paper mill in Ortmann (fig. 3-7).

By 1923 the economy had improved sufficiently to allow the Socialist-dominated Viennese city government to undertake a five-year program to build 5,000 housing units. To the surprise of nearly everyone, the plan was fulfilled the first year, and in 1924 the city authorities launched a second five-year program to build an additional 25,000 apartments. Frank, though opposed to the construction of the sort of high-density blocks that the Socialist authorities favored (arguing that they were not cheaper nor did they provide a higher standard of living than lower-density row housing), nevertheless designed several of these large apartment projects, including the Wiedenhofer-Hof (1923–24; fig. 3-8) and the Winarsky-Hof (1923–25), the latter produced jointly with Behrens, Hoffmann, Strnad, and Wlach.

Frank continued to design housing blocks for the municipal housing authority through the early 1930s, but after 1924 he once again turned his attentions to the single-family home and its furnishings. Encouraged by the country's newly found, if still somewhat shaky, prosperity, Frank and Wlach launched a home furnishings business, which they named Haus & Garten. Frank assumed the duties of principal designer, while Wlach concentrated on overseeing the business. The new store, which opened in 1925 on the Bösendorferstrasse just a block from the Opera, was loosely patterned after the Wiener Werkstätte. Like the Werkstätte, it featured well-designed, carefully crafted items for the home, ranging from furniture, textiles, and carpets to complete remodeling jobs, or even, if a client so desired, an entire house. Pieces could be purchased individually, or en suite from the showroom floor (fig. 3-9), or custom ordered.[22]

In many respects Frank's designs for Haus & Garten extended and refined the "styleless" eclecticism of his prewar work (fig. 3-10). The basis of Haus & Garten was, critic Leopold Greiner observed, the belief that "applied forms do not necessarily have to be thoroughly 'new.'" For Frank and Wlach, he noted, contemporary forms "do not have to be free of every connection with the inheritance of past cultures"; past forms do not have to be rejected "as long as [they are] creatively alive."[23] Frank's emphasis was on comfort and coziness, which he argued should not be sacrificed for mere "appearance." "The goal . . . in designing an interior," he wrote in an essay in 1927, "is not to make it as luxurious as possible or as simple as possible, but rather to make it as comfortable as possible . . . . The most comfortable interiors have always been those that the occupant himself has put together over the course of time which betray no sense of intention or plan."[24]

In addition to his work for Haus & Garten, Frank

Fig. 3-10. Bedroom, house for A. S. F., Vienna, ca. 1932. From *Innen-Dekoration* 44 (1933).

also worked sporadically on various architectural projects. During the early 1920s, he had produced several buildings for private clients, including a kindergarten for the Ortmann housing development (1921) and a house for Theo Herzberg-Fraenkel, manager of the Ortmann paper factory (1923), as well as unrealized designs for a school in Tiberias, Palestine (1922), a synagogue in Antwerp (1922–23), and an apartment house for the Skoda-Wetzler Company (1923). After 1924, Frank began to focus once more on designing private residences, and over the course of the next five years he conceived of a number of single-family homes, including a remarkable series of works that explored different means of breaking up and rearranging the interior spaces (fig. 3-11). This new "volumetric" planning, which was similar in some respects to Loos's *Raumplan* (space-plan) idea of stacked and interlocking spaces, was as startlingly innovative as the works of any of his modernist contemporaries. But because of their radical nature and the uncertainty of the times, only a few of these houses were realized.

Despite Frank's relatively meager output, the years between 1927 and 1930 marked the pinnacle of his prestige and influence. Photographs of his buildings and projects, accompanied by his own statements, appeared in many of the leading architectural journals of the time, including

WOHNHAUS für WIEN XIII

Fig. 3-11. House for Vienna XIII, ca. 1926. From *Moderne Bauformen* 26 (1927).

*Wasmuths Monatshefte für Baukunst, Deutsche Kunst und Dekoration,* and *Der Baumeister,* and a broad spectrum of critics praised his work. An article in the May 1927 issue of *Moderne Bauformen,* which devoted a large section to Frank's work, called him "a born representative of the '*Neue Sachlichkeit*'" (New Objectivity) adding that "Modern architecture cannot be more purely or more significantly advanced than through this, one of its leaders."[25] Similarly, Bruno Taut, writing in 1929, called Frank the "most sensitive" and "most clear-headed" of the modernists in Austria, and described his buildings as "the most sympathetic examples of present-day architecture."[26] And the same year Henry-Russell Hitchcock lauded Frank's "delicate and individual post-eclectic touch."[27]

The most visible sign of Frank's rising stature within the modernist ranks was an invitation from Ludwig Mies van der Rohe to take part in the German Werkbund exhibition planned for the Stuttgart suburb of Weissenhof in 1927. Frank, assigned to create two single-family units,

responded with a rectangular, two-story structure, in which the upper story was set back to form a continuous terrace on the street side (fig. 3-12). Intended as party wall units, the houses could be built singly or in pairs, or could serve as a basic prototype for row houses, which could be combined to form a larger grouping.[28]

In keeping with the exhibition's emphasis on technology, Frank incorporated a number of new construction techniques, including a demonstration of special insulating blocks developed by German engineer Albert Feifel for the building's outer walls, and the use of a system of horizontal gypsum boards held in place by steel stud frames for the interior. But while the structure generally earned praise for its simple massing and clear and practical plan, Frank came under attack from a number of critics for the interiors (fig. 3-13), which featured his usual range of upholstered chairs and colorful fabrics and rugs. Théo van Doesburg, for example, charged that while Mies, Mart Stam, and the other functionalists had aimed for "maximal neutralization

Fig. 3-12. Double house, Weissenhofsiedlung Exhibition, Stuttgart, 1927. Private collection.

Fig. 3-13. Living Room, double house, Weissenhofsiedlung Exhibition, Stuttgart, 1927. From *Innen-Dekoration* 38 (1927).

Fig. 3-14. Delegates at the first CIAM conference, La Sarraz, Switzerland, June 1928. Standing (*from left*): Richard Dupierre, Mart Stam, Pierre Chareau, Victor Bourgeois, Max Haefeli, Pierre Jeanneret, Gerrit Rietveld, Rudolf Steiger, Ernst May (partially hidden), Alberto Sartoris, Gabriel Guevrékian, Hans Schmidt, Hugo Häring, Zavala, Lucienne Florentin, Le Corbusier, Paul Artaria, Hélène de Mandrot, Friedrich Gubler, P. Rochat, André Lurçat, Henri Robert von der Mühll, Gino Maggioni, Huib Hoste, Sigfried Giedion, Werner Moser, Josef Frank. Seated (*from left*): Fernando Garcia Mercadal, Molly Weber, Tadevossian. CIAM-Archiv, Eidgenössische Technische Hochschule, Zurich.

and austerity in the dwelling," Frank (along with Taut, Behrens, and J. J. P. Oud) had created "femininely appointed interiors" which were "obtrusive" and "middle class."[29] Werner Gräff, the press relations chief for the exhibition, went even further, remarking that to him Frank's furnishings seemed "almost provocatively conservative."[30] But the most devastating verdict came from Paul Meller, J. J. P. Oud's assistant, who referred to the interiors in a letter as "Frank's bordello."[31]

Frank responded to the criticisms in an article—bearing the curious title, "Der Gschnas fürs G'mut und der Gschnas als Problem" (Frippery as comfort and frippery as

a problem)—which appeared in one of the exhibition's official publications. To the charge that his interiors were bourgeois and old-fashioned, Frank replied that the stripped-down, "functional" style of the radical modernists simply did not respond to most people's needs. "Every person has a certain amount of sentimentality, which he must satisfy."[32] "Frippery" (*Gschnas*), far from being unnecessary, provided many people with a sense of comfort and well-being. The arts and crafts had only become a "problem," Frank argued, because of the determination of a small clique of radicals to forge a wholly new style stripped of decoration. To those who claimed that the machine demanded a radically new design approach, Frank countered that it was "nothing more than a tool, which can produce anything"; it did not dictate a particular formal program.[33] Echoing Loos's earlier critique of the Werkbund,[34] he argued that forms evolved gradually in response to everyday concerns and disappeared when they no longer had relevance. For an architect or designer to make a self-conscious effort to create a new expression was futile. Although industrialization had brought myriad changes, many old forms retained their usefulness; modern life, he argued, was rich enough to take over many of the things from former times: "One can use everything, which still can be used."[35]

In 1928 Frank accepted an invitation to join the newly formed Congrés Internationaux d'Architecture Moderne (CIAM). He attended the group's inaugural meeting in La Sarraz, Switzerland (fig. 3-14), but already during the first day's discussions found himself becoming increasingly alarmed by the insistence of the radical—mostly German-speaking—architects on equating architecture with technology. Indeed, Frank was so disturbed by the tenor of the discussions that he considered not signing the group's joint declaration, and it was only after some persuasion from Sigfried Giedion, one of the organization's co-founders, that he agreed to add his name. After attending the CIAM's second meeting held in Frankfurt the following year, Frank wrote to Giedion announcing his resignation. In his letter, he cited what he called "the climate of intrigues" that pervaded the meetings and what he viewed as the increasingly dogmatic stance of the radical functionalists.[36]

Underlying Frank's sense of discomfort with the CIAM was his conviction that the cause of modern architecture was being undermined by a growing emphasis on an empty formalism that merely paid lip service to considerations of rationality, economy, and constructional requirements. Instead of responding to the real needs of people, too many architects, he believed, merely sought to create the appearance of a functional solution, and as a result modernism was rapidly devolving into another style, little different from the earlier historic revival styles.

Frank returned to these themes in the keynote address he delivered at the 1930 Werkbund Congress, which met in Vienna. With Gropius and Mies seated on either side of him on the speaker's podium, Frank launched into a blistering attack on many of modern arcitecture's most cherished ideals. Responding to the notion that architects should reject the past and begin anew, Frank asserted that it was senseless to disregard the rich legacy of history; instead, he argued, architects and designers "should use

Fig. 3-15. Flyer for a Vienna Circle lecture series, 1929. Carnap Papers in the Archives of Scientific Philosophy, University of Pittsburgh Libraries, University of Pittsburgh.

everything available to them."[37] Moreover, Frank asserted that the attempt to find a single modern style was tragically misguided. The modern world, he declared, was too multi-faceted and modern life too diverse to be encompassed by a single style: "The striving for complete simplicity is pathetic, it is pathetic to want to make everything the same, so that variations are no longer possible, to want to organize everything to force all people into a large homogeneous mass."[38] For Frank, this attempt to codify and thereby limit the modernist revolution was driven by a new irrationalism, what Paul Westheim, the influential editor of *Das Kunstblatt*, called a "new romanticism of the engineer and the machine."[39] Rather than subscribing to this new "pathos," Frank asserted, architects should instead move beyond it to a new "scientific" world view, one based on reason rather than dogma.

Frank had made this same plea for a reasonable and dispassionate approach to modern design in a lecture he presented in April 1929, under the auspices of the Vienna Circle (or the *Verein Ernst Mach*, as it was officially known; fig. 3-15)—a group of like-minded scientists and philosophers that included Frank's older brother Philipp, a physi-

Fig. 3-16. Vienna Werkbundsiedlung (aerial view), 1932. Bildarchiv der Österreichischen Nationalbibliothek, Vienna.

cist, and Frank's close friend Otto Neurath.[40] This plea for a new undogmatic rationalism also resounded in many of his other writings of the period.[41] On one hand, he repeatedly assailed what he saw as the naively progressivist functionalism of German modernists like Walter Gropius and Hans Schmidt, who he argued were more interested in making superficial gestures than addressing the real technical and aesthetic issues of the "new architecture."[42] But he also rejected the penchant that many of his fellow Austrians (especially Hoffmann) showed for a new ornamentalism and nationalism, which Frank claimed were borne of a similar sort of "unscientific" thinking.

In the wake of the 1930 Werkbund meeting, Frank began to work on an even more extensive critique of the modern movement, which he published at the end of the year in book form under the title *Architektur als Symbol: Elemente deutschen neuen Bauens* (Architecture as symbol: elements of German modern architecture).[43] The ostensible theme of the book, as its title suggests, was the role of symbolic language in architecture. At its most fundamental level, Frank asserted, architecture is "a symbol of our lives

and our times." Every age has had its own architectural expression, its own symbolic language. The "collective appearance" of these symbols "constitutes the style of a [particular] epoch." As previous epochs had their own symbolic language, so too the modern era had its own, which was derived from the new machine age.[44]

But at the core of the book was a withering attack on the radical functionalists, particularly those in Germany, who Frank accused of confusing the notion of "usefulness" (*Nützlichkeit*) with "function" (*Funktion*). The true "function" of modern architecture, Frank charged, should not be to create an image of practicality, but to respond to the people's genuine needs, including such concerns as sentimentality and comfort.[45]

As one might expect, the reaction to the book in avant-garde circles was generally negative. One critic, Fritz Roh, reviewing the book in *Das Neue Frankfurt*, accused Frank of "undervaluing every advance of modern architecture," and of being "a classicist in disguise."[46] Wolfgang Hermann, writing in *Kunst und Künstler*, questioned how it was possible for someone of Frank's modernist background to produce a book so fraught with "the dangers of eclecticism."[47]

Frank, dismayed but unbowed by the reactions, focused his attentions on the Austrian Werkbund[48] and its plans to mount a large housing exhibition in the summer of 1932. The exhibit, patterned after the 1927 Weissenhofsiedlung, had originally been timed to coincide with the annual Werkbund Congress in Vienna in the summer of 1930, but problems with financing and with the original site selection had forced the exhibit's postponement for two years.[49] Frank, who was placed in charge of the overall planning and construction of the project, saw in the Vienna exhibit a chance to pose an alternative to the Weissenhofsiedlung, and by extension to the ideas of the radicals. In drawing up the list of participants, he avoided most of the best-known modernists, inviting instead only those architects whom he felt had views similar to his own. Indeed, none of those who had taken part in the Weissenhofsiedlung, aside from Frank himself, was included. The only German architect Frank asked to participate was Hugo

Häring, whose idiosyncratic ideas of organic form made him something of an outsider.[50] The other foreigners invited, Gerrit Rietveld from the Netherlands and André Lurçat and Gabriel Guevrékian from France, had reputations as moderates. All of the remaining participants were Austrians, most of them either older, established figures like Hoffmann, Strnad, Wlach, and Clemens Holzmeister or members of the younger, postwar generation of Viennese modernists, including Karl A. Bieber, Anton Brenner, Oswald Haerdtl, Walter Loos, Grete Schütte-Lihotzky, Ernst Plischke, and Hans Vetter, whose work had been influenced by Frank. Only two names stood out from the list: Richard Neutra, who had emigrated to America a decade before; and Adolf Loos, whom Frank had convinced to take part in spite of his long-standing antipathy toward the Werkbund.[51]

In what amounted to a direct challenge to Weissenhofsiedlung's emphasis on the technical aspects of the new architecture, Frank stressed the importance of creating a livable, comfortable environment (figs. 3-16 and 3-17). His

Fig. 3-17. House 12, Vienna Werkbundsiedlung, 1932. Bildarchiv der Österreichischen Nationalbibliothek, Vienna.

plan for the Vienna *Siedlung* was modeled after the traditional village, and he sought to create the impression of assemblage that had grown up over time rather than one that had been planned.[52] To avoid the sort of monumental effect that the mostly white buildings at the Weissenhofsiedlung had engendered, Frank adopted a color scheme proposed by the artist László Gábor, which called for randomly painting the houses in a variety of bright pastel hues—yellow, blue, green, pink, and off-white. The effect, as Frank had hoped, was light and cheerful, the overall appearance of the grounds strikingly different from the pristine look of the Weissenhofsiedlung.[53]

Although a few critics, among them Hugo Häring,[54] commended Frank's efforts, the international architectural press on the whole was quite critical.[55] In the wake of the exhibit, Frank also found himself under attack at home. Even before the show had opened there had been signs of mounting tension between Frank and Hoffmann, and between the members of their respective circles.[56] On the surface the conflict centered on the organization and running of the Werkbund. [57] But underneath there were unmistakable signs that the rising tide of anti-Semitism was fueling the split. In early 1933, a number of right-wing members, protesting what they called the "Semitization" (*Verjudung*) of the organization, resigned, and the president, Hermann Neubacher (at the time a secret member of the illegal Nazi party and later first mayor of Vienna after the Anschluss), stepped down, claiming to be "occupationally overburdened." In the following weeks Hoffmann and his assistant Oswald Haerdtl also officially left the organization.[58]

Frank made several last-ditch efforts to reconcile the opposing factions, but his attempts only postponed the inevitable. By the end of 1933 the Austrian Werkbund had formally broken into two separate organizations, one, almost exclusively Socialist and Jewish, centered around Frank and Strnad, and another "New Werkbund," conservative and Catholic, led by Hoffmann and Clemens Holzmeister.[59] In the wake of the breakup of the Werkbund, Frank was disheartened and fearful that the growing tide of Nazism would soon spill over into Austria. He decided to accept an offer from Estrid Ericson to work as chief designer for her interior design shop Svenskt Tenn in Stockholm. In December he and his wife Anna immigrated to Sweden.

Frank returned to Austria periodically over the course of the next few years, visiting friends and relatives and consulting on the running of Haus & Garten (which Wlach continued to operate in his absence). But the Nazi takeover of Austria in 1938 put an end to these trips, and after the death of his mother in 1941, he severed his last ties with Vienna. In the years after the Second World War, he made a few brief visits, but by then only a spiritual bond still connected him with the city of his youth.

1. In addition to Josef, the Frank children included Philipp (1884–1966), who became a noted physicist and philosopher of science, Hedwig (1887–1966), and Rudolf (1890–1942?). For details of Frank's biography, see Christopher Long, "Josef Frank and the Crisis of Modern Architecture" (Ph.D. diss., University of Texas at Austin, 1993); Wilfried Posch, "Josef Frank, eine bedeutende Persönlichkeit des österreichischen Kulturliberalismus," *Um Bau* 10 (1986), pp. 21–38; and Kristina Wängberg-Eriksson, *Josef Frank: Livsträd i krigens skugga* (Lund, Sweden: Signum, 1994).

2. Anni Feilendorf (Frank's cousin), December 30, 1993: personal communication.

3. On Karl König's life and work, see Renate Wagner-Rieger, "Karl König," in *Österreichisches Biographisches Lexikon 1815–1950* (Vienna: Böhlau Verlag, 1969), pp. 36–37; *Bauten und Entwürfe von Carl König herausgegeben von seinen Schülern* (Vienna: Gerlach & Wiedling, [1910]), pp. 5–6; and "Karl König," in Ulrich Thieme and Felix Becker, eds., *Allgemeines Lexikon der bildenden Künstler von der Antike bis zur Gegenwart* (Leipzig: E. A. Seemann, 1935), vol. 21, pp. 157–58.

4. J. P. Hodin, *Oskar Kokoschka: The Artist and His Time* (London: Cory, Adams & Mackay, 1966), p. 76.

5. Marco Pozzetto, *Max Fabiani: Ein Architekt der Monarchie* (Vienna: Edition Tusch, 1983), p. 18.

6. Although Frank had a deep admiration for Wagner and his work, he evidently never applied for admission to Wagner's Master Class at the Academy of Fine Arts, a route several of his fellow students from Technische Hochschule took, among them Rudolf Schindler, Oskar Laske, and Emil Pirchan. The anti-Semitic atmosphere of the school was no doubt one reason for this, but probably even more important was the strong attraction that König—himself an assimilated Jew—had for young Jews like Frank, who saw in him a model for the dream of com-

plete emancipation. While perhaps as many as one-third of the students in the architecture program of the Technische Hochschule were Jewish—among them Strnad, Wlach, and Richard Neutra—apparently only 1 of the 190 students who studied in the Wagnerschule between 1894 and 1914—Ernst Lichtblau—came from a Jewish background. The two schools were also characterized by a marked difference in approach. Though a strict adherent of late historicism in his own work, König showed a remarkable tolerance for other approaches. By contrast, Wagner, although his own work was at the cutting edge of developments at the time, was much less open to other styles and methods. One of the ironies of this situation is that it was König's students, who, despite their much more conservative education, found it relatively easy to cast off the teachings of their master and were typically at the forefront of modernist developments in the 1920s and 1930s, while Wagner's students, who remained more or less faithful to his ideas, formed the conservative guard in interwar Vienna—a fact that also led to increasing tensions between the two groups in the early 1930s. See Marco Pozzetto, "Karl König und die Architekten der Wiener Technischen Hochschule," in Maria Marchetti, ed., *Wien um 1900: Kunst und Kultur* (Vienna and Munich: Christian Brandstätter Verlag, 1985), pp. 305–6; and Ursula Prokop, *Wien: Aufbruch zur Metropole: Geschäfts- und Wohnhäuser der Innenstadt 1910 bis 1914* (Vienna, Cologne and Weimar: Böhlau Verlag, 1994), p. 65.

7. On Bruno Möhring's life and work, see Ines Gesine Wagemann, *Der Architekt Bruno Möhring 1863–1929*, Beiträge zur Kunstgeschichte 8 (Bonn/Witterslick: Wehle, 1992).

8. Lewerentz worked in Möhring's office from the summer of 1908 through February 1909, when he left to take up an apprenticeship in the office of Theodor Fischer in Munich. See Janne Ahlin, *Sigurd Lewerentz, Architect 1885–1975* (Cambridge, Mass.: MIT Press, 1987), p. 14.

9. Josef Frank, "Über die urspüngliche Gestalt der kirchlichen Bauten des Leone Battista Alberti" (Ph.D. diss., Technische Hochschule, Vienna, 1910).

10. Oskar Strnad (1879–1935) was born in Vienna, the son of an estate manager. After graduating from the Technische Hochschule in 1904, he worked for Friedrich Ohmann and theater specialists Ferdinand Fellner and Hermann Helmer. In 1909, Hoffmann recommended him for a vacant post at the Kunstgewerbeschule where for many years he taught the school's basic design course. After World War I he devoted himself largely to theater design. On Strnad's life and work, see Max Eisler, "Oskar Strnad zum 50. Geburtstag," *Deutsche Kunst und Dekoration*, 33 (January 1930), pp. 253–68; idem, *Oskar Strnad* (Vienna: Gerlach & Weidling, 1936); Joseph Gregor, *Rede auf Oskar Strnad* (Vienna: Herbert Reicher Verlag, 1936); Otto Niedermoser, *Oskar Strnad 1879–1935* (Vienna: Bergland Verlag, 1935); and Johannes Spalt, ed., *Der Architekt Oskar Strnad: Zum hundersten Geburtstag am 26. Oktober 1979*, exhib. cat., (Vienna: Hochschule für angewandte Kunst, 1979).

Oskar Wlach (1881–1963) was born in Vienna and entered the Technische Hochschule in 1898. While still a student he designed the governor's palace in Trieste. He and Frank collaborated until the 1930s. After the Anschluss in 1938, he immigrated to New York where he worked for various architects and construction companies, including the interior design firm Hopeman Brothers, until he retired in 1958. See Herbert A. Strauss et al., *International Biographical Dictionary of Central European Emigrés, 1933–1945*, 3 vols. (Munich, New York, London and Paris: K. G. Saur, 1983), vol. 2, p. 1255.

11. On the role of Jewish patrons in Viennese modernist culture, see for example, Jane Kallir, *Viennese Design and the Wiener Werkstätte* (New York: Galerie St. Etienne/George Braziller, 1986), pp. 33–34; and Steven Beller, *Vienna and the Jews 1867–1938: A Cultural History* (Cambridge, Eng.: Cambridge University Press, 1989), esp. chaps. 3, 4, and 5.

12. Oskar Wlach, "Professional Career of Dr. Oskar Wlach," typescript dated April 1958 (copy in possession of the author).

13. Josef Frank, "Die Einrichtung des Wohnzimmers," *Innen-Dekoration* 30 (1919), p. 417.

14. Oskar Wlach, "Zu den Arbeiten von Josef Frank," *Das Interieur* 13 (1912), p. 45.

15. Stephanie Feilendorf (Frank's cousin), July 14, 1987: personal communication.

16. Josef Frank, military service records (Österreichisches Staatsarchiv-Kriegsarchiv, Vienna).

17. On the history of Vienna's housing problems, see Hans and Rudolf Hautmann, *Die Gemeindebauten des Roten Wien, 1919–1934* (Vienna: Schönbrunn-Verlag, 1980); Peter Marcuse, "The Housing Policy of Social Democracy: Determinants and Consequences" in *The Austrian Socialist Experiment: Social Democracy and Austromarxism, 1918–1934*, Anson Rabinbach, ed. (Boulder, Colo., and London: Westview Press, 1985), pp. 201–22; Manfredo Tafuri, *Vienna Rosa: La politica residenziale nella Vienna socialista, 1919–1933* (Milan: Electa editrice, 1980); and Helmut Weihsmann, *Sozialdemokratische Architektur und Kommunalpolitik, 1919–1934* (Vienna: Promedia, 1985).

18. The exact nature of Frank's relationship with the Austrian Socialist Party is unclear. Frank's one-time assistant, Ernst A. Plischke, has asserted that Frank was an active party member (August 25, 1986: personal communication), but it is not possible to confirm this because the membership records have been lost. Certainly Frank had close connections with leading figures in the Socialist Party heirarchy, among them Otto Neurath, who belonged to his intimate circle of friends.

19. See Josef Frank, Hugo Fuchs, and Franz Zettinig, "Wohnhäuser aus Gußbeton: Ein Vorschlag zur Lösung der Wohnungsfrage," *Der Architekt* 22 (1919), pp. 33–37.

20. See Otto Kapfinger, "Josef Frank—Siedlungen und Siedlungsprojekte, 1919–1932," *Um Bau* 10 (1986), pp. 39–58.

21. Otto Neurath (1882–1945) was one of the most remarkable intellectual figures in Austria during the period between the two world wars, a polymath whose contributions ranged from optics and economics to philosophy of science and mathematics. The son of a university professor, he studied mathematics and ancient languages in Vienna and Berlin, and later economics and sociology in Heidelberg. In 1919, he occupied a post in the central planning office of the short-lived Bavarian Soviet Republic. After its fall, he fled to Vienna and became active in the settlers' movement. Under Neurath's energetic leadership, the *Verband für Siedlungs- und Kleingartenwesen* developed into a formidable organization, effectively pressuring the city and federal governments for land, building supplies, and financial support. Frank and Neurath, who had been friends since their student years, also later collaborated on the design for Neurath's Wirtschafts- und Gesellschaftsmuseum (Social and Economic Museum) in Vienna, which was established to inform the public about the Socialist Party's programs. On Neurath's life and work, see Marie Neurath and Robert S. Cohen, eds., *Otto Neurath: Empiricism and Sociology* (Dordrecht, Holland, and Boston: D. Reidel Publishing Company, 1973); Karola Fleck, "Otto Neurath: Eine biographische und systematische Untersuchung," Ph.D. diss. (Karl-Franzens–Universität Graz, 1979); and Friedrich Stadler, ed., *Arbeiterbildung in der Zwischenkriegszeit: Otto Neurath–Gerd Arntz*, exhib. cat. (Vienna and Munich: Österreichisches Gesellschafts- und Wirtschaftsmuseum/Löcker Verlag, 1982).

22. Monika Platzer, "Einrichtungshaus 'Haus & Garten,' Josef Frank," unpublished essay (Vienna, 1986), pp. 4–5.

23. Leopold Greiner, "Möbel und Einrichtung der Neuzeit. Arbeiten der Werkstätten 'Haus & Garten'-Wien," *Innen-Dekoration* 37 (1926), p. 351.

24. Josef Frank, "Fassade und Interieur," *Deutsche Kunst und Dekoration* 31 (June 1928), p. 187.

25. "Josef Frank," *Moderne Bauformen* 26 (1927), pp. 172–73.

26. Bruno Taut, *Modern Architecture* (London: The Studio; New York: Albert & Charles Boni, Inc., [1929]), p. 54.

27. Henry-Russell Hitchcock, *Modern Architecture: Romanticism and Reintegration* (New York: Payson & Clark, Ltd., 1929), p. 197.

28. On Frank's participation in the Weissenhofsiedlung, see Richard Pommer and Christian F. Otto, *Weissenhof 1927 and the Modern Movement in Architecture* (Chicago and London: University of Chicago Press, 1991), esp. pp. 99–100; and Karin Kirsch, *Die Weissenhofsiedlung: Werkbund Ausstellung "Die Wohnung"—Stuttgart 1927* (Stuttgart: Deutsche Verlags-Anstalt, 1987), English ed., *The Weissenhofsiedlung: Experimental Housing Built for the Deutscher Werkbund, Stuttgart, 1927*, trans. David Britt (New York: Rizzoli, 1987), pp. 164–67.

29. "Die Wohnung," (1927; reprint in Théo van Doesburg, *On European Architecture: Complete Essays from Het Bouwbedrijf 1924–1931*, trans. Charlotte I. Loeb and Arthur L. Loeb [Basel, Berlin, and Boston: Birkhäuser Verlag, 1990]), p. 172.

30. Werner Gräff, "Hinter den Kulissen der Weissenhofsiedlung," Werner-Gräff-Archiv, Mülheim, quoted in Kirsch, *The Weissenhofsiedlung*, p. 166.

31. Letter, Paul Meller to J. J. P. Oud, August 31, 1927, Oud Archive, Rotterdam, quoted in Kirsch, *The Weissenhofsiedlung*, p. 166.

32. Josef Frank, "Der Gschnas fürs G'müt und der Gschnas als Problem," in Deutscher Werkbund, *Bau und Wohnung*, exhib. cat. (Stuttgart: Akademischer Verlag Dr. Fr. Wedekind & Co., 1927), p. 49.

33. Ibid., p. 55.

34. Adolf Loos, "Die überflüssigen (Deutscher werkbund)" (1908; reprint in *Trotzdem 1900–1930* [Vienna: Georg Prachner Verlag, 1982]), pp. 71–74.

35. Frank, "Der Gschnas," p. 55; see also idem, "Drei Behauptungen und ihre Folgen," *Die Form* 2 (1927), pp. 289–91.

36. Letter, Josef Frank to Sigfried Giedion, November 5, 1929, CIAM-Archiv, Institut für Geschichte und Theorie der Architektur, Eidgenössische Technische Hochschule, Zurich. On Frank and the CIAM, see Armand Brulhart, "Josef Frank und die CIAM bis zum Bruch, 1928–1929," *Bauwelt* 26 (July 12, 1985), pp. 1058–60.

37. Josef Frank, "Was ist Modern?" *Die Form* 5 (August 1, 1930), p. 199ff; reprinted in *Der Baumeister* 28 (1930), pp. 388–411.

38. Ibid., p. 400.

39. Paul Westheim, "Architektur-Entwicklung," *Die Glocke* 10 (1924), p. 181ff. Frank's sentiments were echoed by Walter Müller-Wulckow, author of the Blauen Bücher series of books on modern architecture, who argued that the new architectural style "is characterized by a passionate desire for pure forms, a desire which penetrates deeper into the idea and essence of reality than a mere love of ornament ever could. Strange as it may sound, these logically planned and constructed buildings embody a metaphysical yearning. These creations of the machine age reflect a new phantasy of the spirit and a new mysticism of the soul." *Bauten der Arbeit*, 10 (Königstein im Taunus and Leipzig: K. R. Langewiesche, 1929), quoted in Barbara Miller Lane, *Architecture and Politics in Germany, 1918–1945* (Cambridge, Mass.: Harvard University Press, 1968), p. 132.

40. Frank in fact was listed in a Vienna Circle official publication as one of its "allied authors" ("*Dem Wiener Kreise nahstehende Autoren*"), and he apparently took part in some of its activities (Hans Hahn, Otto Neurath, and Rudolf Carnap, *Wissenschaftliche Weltauffassung: Der Wiener Kreis* [Vienna: Verein Ernst Mach/Artur Wolf Verlag, 1929], pp. 48–49). On Frank's connections with the Vienna Circle, see Peter Galison, "Aufbau/Bauhaus: Logical Positivism and Architectural Modernism," *Critical Inquiry* 16 (Summer 1990), pp. 720–25.

41. See Josef Frank, "Vom neuen Stil: Einige Fragen und Antworten," *Innen-Dekoration* 39 (1928), p. 103; idem, "Gespräch über den Werkbund," in *Österreichischer Werkbund* (Vienna, 1929), pp. 3–13; and idem and Otto Neurath, "Hannes Meyer," *Der Klassenkampf: Sozialistische Politik und Wirtschaft* 3 (1930), pp. 573–75.

42. Letter, Frank to Giedion, November 5, 1929, CIAM-Archiv.

43. Josef Frank, *Architektur als Symbol: Elemente deutschen neuen Bauens* (1931; reprint ed., Vienna: Löcker Verlag, 1981).

44. Ibid., p. 16.

45. Ibid., p. 135.

46. [Fritz] Roh, review of *Architektur als Symbol*, in *Das Neue Frankfurt* 5 (1931), p. 59.

47. Wolfgang Hermann, review of *Architektur als Symbol*, in *Kunst und Künstler* 29 (1931), p. 464.

48. Frank served as vice president of the Austrian Werkbund from 1928 through the early 1930s and was largely responsible for the burst of activity the organization experienced during that period. Working in close collaboration with Oswald Haerdtl, Walter Sobotka, and others, he organized a regular series of lectures and radio broadcasts, featuring speakers such as Hugo Häring, Ernst May, and German film director Hans Richter. He also helped to mount several exhibitions, including the 1929 "New Architecture" (*Neues Bauen*) and the 1930 "Film and Photo" (*Film und Foto*) shows. See Astrid Gmeiner and Gottfried Pirhofer, *Der Österreichische Werkbund: Alternative zur klassischen Moderne in Architektur, Raum- und Produktgestaltung* (Salzburg and Vienna: Residenz Verlag, 1985), pp. 123–28.

49. On the genesis and construction of the Vienna Werkbundsiedlung see Josef Frank, ed., *Die internationale Werkbundsiedlung Wien 1932*, exhib. cat. (Vienna: Verlag von Anton Schroll & Co., 1932); Wolfdieter Dreibholz, "Die internationale Werkbundsiedlung, Wien, 1932," *Bauforum* 10, no. 61 (1977): 19–22; Adolf Krischanitz and Otto Kapfinger, *Die Wiener Werkbundsiedlung: Dokumentation einer Erneuerung* (Vienna: Compress Verlag, 1985); and Jan Tabor, "Die erneuerte Vision: Die Wiener Werkbundsiedlung, 1924–1984," in *Reflexionen und Aphorismen zur österreichischen Architektur*, Viktor Hufnagl, ed. (Vienna: Georg Prachner, 1984), pp. 346–52.

50. Häring and Frank were in many respects kindred spirits and carried on a lively and interesting correspondence during the late 1920s and early 1930s. Some of Frank's letters to Häring have been preserved in his papers in the archive of the Akademie der Künste, Berlin. See also Maria Welzig, "Die Wiener Internationalität des Josef Frank: Das Werk des Architekten bis 1938" (Ph.D. diss., Universität Wien, 1994), pp. 219–26.

51. Otto Kapfinger, "Positionen einer liberalen Moderne: Die Wiener Werkbundsiedlung—1932," in Gmeiner and Pirhofer, *Der Österreichische Werkbund*, pp. 155–78.

52. Frank, *Die internationale Werkbundsiedlung Wien 1932*, p. 8.

53. Kapfinger, "Positionen einer liberalen Moderne," p. 159.

54. Hugo Häring, "Bermerkungen zur Werkbundsiedlung Wien-Lainz 1932," *Die Form* (July 15, 1932), pp. 204—8.

55. For some critical responses, see Guido Harbers, "'Moderne Linie', Wohnkultur und Stagnation: Abschliessende Randbemerkungen zur Werkbundsiedlung," *Der Baumeister* 30 (October 1932), pp. 367—73; and Wilhelm Lotz, "Die Wiener Werkbundsiedlung," *Die Form* 7 (July 15, 1932), pp. 201—4.

56. Although they were never particularly close, Frank and Hoffmann had nevertheless enjoyed a good rapport for many years, and on several occasions Hoffmann evidently recommended Frank for commissions. Their relationship began to deteriorate in the late 1920s and early 1930s because of deep-seated ideological differences and competition for clients. See Eduard F. Sekler, *Josef Hoffmann: Das architektonische Werk—*

*Monographie und Werkverzeichnis* (Salzburg and Vienna: Residenz Verlag, 1982), pp. 208—9; and Giovanni Fanelli and Ezio Godoli, *La Vienna di Hoffmann, architetto della qualitá* (Rome: Editori Laterza, 1981), p. 401ff.

57. On the growing tensions within the Austrian Werkbund in the wake of the Vienna exhibition, see Astrid Gmeiner and Gottfried Pirhofer, *Der Österreichische Werkbund*, pp. 179—86.

58. Friedrich Achleitner, "Der Österreichische Werkbund und seine Beziehungen zum Deutschen Werkbund," *Bauforum* 10 (1977), p. 17.

59. On the sources of the split within the Werkbund, see Eduard F. Sekler, "The Architectural Reaction in Austria," *Journal of the Society of Architectural Historians* 24 (March 1965), pp. 67—70.

# 4. LIFE IN EXILE: JOSEF FRANK IN 1933–

Kristina Wängberg-Eriksson

In 1933 Josef Frank and his wife emigrated from Austria to Sweden. Very early on, long before the Nazi takeover in Germany, Frank had sensed that the volatile political situation in Central Europe would only end in disaster. In October 1930 in a letter to Hannes Meyer, then recently dismissed as director of the Bauhaus, he wrote: "As to fascism, it is a phenomenon of our time that cannot be checked. In our country it has grown strong, and the prospects for the future are bleak, especially since we are surrounded by reactionary states."[1] Frank, however, remained in Austria for another three years, despite increasingly harsh attacks on him both professionally and personally from the political right.[2] Then after the Austrian Werkbund formally split and a "New Werkbund," which was overtly anti-Semitic, was organized in December 1933,[3] he decided that the time to leave had arrived.

Frank's connection to Sweden stretched back many years. In the 1920s he and his Swedish wife Anna had spent their summers in Falsterbo, on the country's southern coast (fig. 4-1). In addition to Anna's two sisters, Signhild and Wendela, and their families, a number of well-known Swedish cultural figures belonged to their circle of friends there, among them the poet, Anders Österling, who for many years served as permanent secretary of Svenska Akademien (the Swedish Academy).[4] While storm clouds of war were gathering over Europe, the Franks enjoyed the idyllic seaside setting, and the experience no doubt influenced their decision to leave Vienna and settle in Sweden.

It was in fact on the sandy moors of the Falsterbo peninsula that Frank designed and built some of the earliest functionalist houses in Sweden. The first of these, the Claëson House, for Signhild and her husband Axel Claëson, was constructed in 1927; in the following years three more houses bearing his unique signature were built. They still stand today; with their decks and "gunwales," they resemble ships that have run aground. Although Frank later developed a reputation in Sweden as the master of floral cretonnes and elegant cabinets, few realized that he was the architect behind these early modern houses, and it was not until 1994 that his architectural work was finally exhibited in Sweden.[5]

Frank's decision to move to Sweden was also influenced by an offer from Estrid Ericson to work as chief designer in her interior design shop, Svenskt Tenn, in Stockholm which she had founded in 1924. Originally the firm had specialized in pewter ware—hence its name, which means "Swedish pewter"—but after the landmark Stockholm Exhibition of 1930 (Stockholmsutställningen 1930 av konstindustri, konsthandverk och hemslöjd), which introduced functionalist architecture and design in Sweden, she branched out to include furnishings and carpets. During the early 1930s Ericson worked with a number of leading Swedish design-

# SWEDEN AND THE UNITED STATES, 1967

Fig. 4-1. The Franks in Falsterbo, Sweden. Svenskt Tenn Archive, Stockholm.

ers, including architect Uno Åhrén and the young artist, Björn Trägårdh.[6]

Ericson had become aware of Frank's work as early as 1921, when she happened to see some dining-room furniture he had designed for acquaintances living in Djursholm, a fashionable suburb to the north of Stockholm. In subsequent years she followed the progress of his work in *Innen-Dekoration*, *The Studio*, and other journals.[7] In 1932, with an eye toward expanding the range of furnishings offered by Svenskt Tenn, she wrote to Frank and asked him to send her

Fig. 4-2. Frank's designs featured in the Svenskt Tenn installation at the 1934 exhibition of decorative art held at the Liljevalchs Konsthall, Stockholm.

some designs for furniture, which he did, inaugurating a long and very successful partnership that was to span more than three decades. Soon afterward Ericson offered Frank a permanent position at Svenskt Tenn, thus removing the final obstacle to his move to Stockholm.

The Franks arrived in Sweden just before Christmas 1933 and moved into a small apartment in a newly constructed modern apartment house on Rindögatan in Stockholm. Several years later, at the time of the Anschluss in March 1938, Frank applied for and was eventually granted Swedish citizenship.[8]

Despite Frank's earlier architectural projects at Falsterbo, he virtually abandoned his practice soon after moving to Sweden, devoting his energies instead to his work for Svenskt Tenn. Reflecting on the decision years later, he wrote: "I established myself as an architect in Sweden in 1924 . . . but soon after moving there I gave up architecture, the principal reason being that it was much

too complicated; indeed, much of the work consists merely of dealing with customers, suppliers, and authorities."[9] In fact Frank had little interest in the more mundane tasks involved in either architecture or design work, preferring instead to concentrate on "creative" endeavors. In Vienna Oskar Wlach, his partner at Haus & Garten, had overseen the day-to-day running of the business; in Stockholm Ericson saw to the job of producing and selling Frank's designs, freeing him to concentrate on doing what he loved most. The arrangement with Svenskt Tenn proved to be so comfortable for Frank that he had little incentive for continuing his architectural practice. This in part explains why he never attempted to establish contacts with Swedish architects or building contractors—which at any rate would have been problematic for a Jewish immigrant at the time. Moreover he thought little of contemporary Swedish architecture and preferred to keep his distance.[10] At Svenskt Tenn Frank had every opportunity to refine the furniture and textile designs and expand on ideas about interior decoration that he had developed in Vienna. Nevertheless it was not without a certain degree of bitterness that he turned his back on architecture, and in his later years he occasionally voiced his regrets about the decision.

The first public manifestation of Frank's work under the aegis of Svenskt Tenn took place in 1934 at an exhibition of contemporary Swedish decorative art held at Liljevalchs Konsthall in Stockholm; also included was the work of Carl Malmsten, Elsa Gullberg, Märta Måås-Fjetterström, David Blomberg, and the young Nils Ahrbom.[11] In place of the refined simplicity that had marked Svenskt Tenn's furnishings in the early 1930s, Frank substituted a new design vocabulary—colorful, spirited, and altogether novel (fig. 4-2). Instead of birch and elm, which were favored by Swedish designers, Frank employed

teak and mahogany, adding to the ensemble travertine and green marble to provide a vaguely "Roman" accent. But even more notable were the extravagantly curved lines of the sofa Frank exhibited, which made a striking contrast to the light and graceful "Viennese" dining chairs. The furnishings, with their "provocatively" sinuous lines, seemed to fly in the face of the "straight-edged" reductivist aesthetic promulgated by the Bauhaus. But Frank also appears to have intended the flamboyant designs as an announcement of his arrival in Sweden and a powerful protest against what he termed "the tedium of the Svenska Slöjdföreningen [Swedish Society of Craft and Industrial Design]."

The Liljevalchs exhibition marked the beginning of a long artistic collaboration between Frank and Ericson (fig. 4-3). Although the two came from very different backgrounds and had different temperaments, they shared a rich

Fig. 4-3. Josef Frank and Estrid Ericson in 1964, toward the end of their long collaboration at Svenskt Tenn. Svenskt Tenn Archive, Stockholm.

imagination and similar tastes. Perhaps more importantly, Ericson acted as a sort of muse for Frank, helping him to realize and embellish his ideas. The journalist Eva von Zweigbergk, a good friend of Ericson's for many years, wrote that Ericson "approved of everything that Frank designed, and he, in turn, fulfilled every request she made."[12]

Frank's designs for Svenskt Tenn built upon his earlier Viennese work, but there were also signs that he was moving in new directions. He gave voice to his evolving ideas of design in an article entitled "Rum och inredning" (Room and interior decoration), published in 1934, in which he laid out a series of basic guidelines for interior design. In large measure these principles were based on the ideas Frank and Oskar Strnad had developed together in the 1910s. But there are also less than subtle signs of Frank's growing impatience with the functionalist aesthetic. Although he emphasized the importance of creating a sense

of purity—asserting, for example, that rooms should generally have white walls—Frank cautioned against confusing architecture with interior design: "We should take care to avoid making architecture with furniture, and thereby disturbing the clarity of the room. To create a comfortable impression, the room itself, with all of its boundary lines, should be readily grasped."[13] Frank, however, fulminated against those like Gerrit Rietveld or Marcel Breuer who applied the "prismatic" lines of the new architecture to furniture design: "Without taking a dogmatic approach to design, who would hit upon the idea of forcing a prismatic form onto a chair and making its surfaces rectangular? A chair's form must be adapted to the shape of the human body (the negative of which it should constitute), which resists all geometry."[14] Similarly Frank rejected the notion of a new "*sachlich*" minimalism, arguing that it would only end in banality: "We can easily avoid every touch of tastelessness if we restrict ourselves to a bloodless aestheticism

Fig. 4-4. One of Frank's lecture slides demonstrating a "bad" design solution. From *Innen-Dekoration* 31 (1928), p. 354.

Fig. 4-5. Tables designed by Frank for Svenskt Tenn. Drawing by Kerstin Österman. Svenskt Tenn Archive, Stockholm.

and suppress all expression of sentiment. But then what is tasteful will become hopelessly boring."[15]

Frank's own attempts to overcome this growing sense of monotony resulted in an extraordinary outpouring of design ideas. Over the course of his career, he produced close to two thousand different pieces of furniture—an average of nearly one per week during the four decades from the end of World War I until his retirement in the 1960s. In addition, Frank also designed textiles, floor coverings, lamps, and other decorative objects, and he continued to explore alternative approaches to modern architecture in unrealized projects even after giving up his practice in the mid-1930s. When one considers that for long periods of his life external conditions—during and between the two world wars—were not particularly favorable to work, his achievement becomes all the more impressive.

Frank's remarkable fecundity grew in part from his continual attempts to improve on his earlier designs. "While I am planning a chair," he once remarked, "I always think it will be my best because I am aware of what mistakes I made before. Afterward, when the chair is finished, I discover new mistakes, so I am most pleased with those chairs I have not yet created."[16]

As a designer Frank drew on his considerable knowledge of furniture history, and he very consciously incorporated those aspects of past examples which he thought were particularly successful. At times, much like Adolf Loos, he

more or less faithfully reproduced pieces from antiquity, as evidenced by his oft-used Egyptian footstool. His design philosophy was grounded in basic principles of historical design, such as the simple, undecorated forms of Biedermeier and Shaker work or the gracefully curving lines characteristic of Georgian furniture.[17] In his frequent lectures on interior decoration Frank often showed slides, carefully noting what he thought constituted "good" and "bad" solutions (fig. 4-4).[18] He preferred seat furniture that was lightweight with an open back or pierced splat, which thus did not disrupt the room by "framing extra walls"; for this reason he was particularly fond of Windsor chairs, and over the years he produced a number of different variations of the original Windsor chair form.

During his years at Svenskt Tenn, Frank incorporated a remarkable variety of materials in his furniture designs. He showed a particular penchant for light, natural materials, such as cane or rattan—because they reduce the weight of the furniture, making it more movable and because they create an open appearance. He often employed these materials in headboards, chair backs, splats, and stiles, and the like. This choice of materials also derived from East Asian furniture, especially Chinese. But Frank also made use of animal skins, various types of stone, and occasionally even semiprecious jewels. His tables (fig. 4-5) were embellished with grained veneers of tropical and other rare woods—especially root because of its rich patterning—or incorpo-

Fig. 4-6. Svenskt Tenn's installation at the 1939 World's Fair in New York. Svenskt Tenn Archive, Stockholm.

rated polished stone, such as granite, marble, travertine, or limestone. He lavished particular attention on the legs of his tables and chairs, which generally have attractive, gently curving lines, and stylized "English" feet.

The eclectic modern idiom that Frank introduced at Svenskt Tenn had a decisive influence on the emergence of what became known as Swedish Modern design. Although many of the forms and ideas Frank incorporated in his works for Svenskt Tenn stemmed from his Viennese days, ironically by the end of the 1930s they were becoming increasingly recognized abroad as an expression of a new, specifically Swedish, design aesthetic. The Swedish Pavilion at the 1937 Exposition Internationale in Paris, at which Frank and Ericson exhibited a garden terrace, had first brought Swedish Modern to international attention, and the success of their installation at the 1939 New York World's Fair only confirmed its growing popularity.[19]

The Swedish pavilion in New York, designed by Sven Markelius, proved to be among the most popular exhibits at the fair. One critic writing for *Architectural Review* praised its "elegant charm," "restraint," and "rich variety of invention."[20] The casual informality of the structure was also reflected in the displays of modern furniture and applied arts, which included five model rooms arranged by some of the country's leading designers: Frank, G. A. Berg, Axel Larsson, Carl Malmsten, and Elias Svedberg.[21]

The studio Frank and Ericson showed at the fair (fig. 4-6), with its kidney-shaped teakwood writing desk and a low sofa, clearly anticipated what was to become a standard look for Scandinavian design in the 1950s. Yet several of the pieces, including the Biedermeier-inspired chair in the forefront, still showed heavy traces of Frank's earlier Haus & Garten design aesthetic.

The combination of Frank's furniture design and

Ericson's *esprit d'arrangement* delighted visitors and critics alike, and the exhibit marked the breakthrough of Frank's own individual design style. Nevertheless it was Ericson—and not Frank—who received much of the attention. Interviews and feature stories, one anointing her the "Mistress of Modern,"[22] appeared in a number of popular and professional journals, while Frank's role in fostering the new look was largely overlooked. American recognition of Swedish Modern design was further enhanced by the press attention given to Frank's design for the Svenskt Tenn installation at the Golden Gate exhibition in San Francisco later in 1939.

Although Frank devoted most of his energies to Svenskt Tenn during the later 1930s, he retained his interest in Haus & Garten in Vienna, which he and Oskar Wlach continued to operate until 1938. Between 1933 and 1938 Frank made several return visits to Vienna, including one in the summer of 1935 when he celebrated his fiftieth birth-

day among friends and colleagues (fig. 4-7), and he continued to collaborate with Wlach on various commissions, occasionally designing new works. After the Anschluss in 1938 when laws were issued prohibiting Jews from holding property, he and Wlach managed at the eleventh hour to sell the business to a gentile friend, Julius Kalmár, the owner of a factory that manufactured the ingenious brass lamps designed by Frank. (Kalmár's niece, Lea Calice, and architect Anna-Lülja Praun ran the company until the 1950s when they were forced to close in the face of declining sales and problems with an embezzling accountant.[23])

During the late 1930s, Anna and Josef Frank's apartment on Rindögatan in Stockholm became a favored gathering place for their wide circle of friends. Many of those who spent time there were Austrians or Germans fleeing Nazism, among them Bertolt Brecht and composer Ernst Krenek (fig. 4-8). Clearly Frank felt at home surrounded by remembrances of Vienna, and for many refugees the Franks'

Fig. 4-7. Josef Frank (*front row*) at his fiftieth birthday celebration in Vienna, 1935. Courtesy of Otto Kapfinger.

Fig. 4-8. Josef Frank (*left*) and Ernst Krenek, Stockholm, 1938.
Svenskt Tenn Archive, Stockholm.

tiny, three-room apartment became, as Elsa Björkman-Goldschmidt recounted afterward, "a space to breathe," an "oasis in the desert journey."[24] Visitors came and went as they pleased, often sitting and talking for hours, and as several of them later recalled, the apartment took on the atmosphere of a lively Viennese coffeehouse.

Frank, living in neutral Sweden, was initially little concerned about his own safety, but after the German occupations of Denmark and Norway in 1940 and growing rumors of a possible Nazi coup d'etat in Sweden, he began to investigate the prospect of taking refuge in the United States. In 1941, with the assistance of his brother Philipp who was teaching at Harvard University at the time, Frank received an invitation to lecture at the New School for Social Research in New York, which allowed him and Anna to obtain the requisite papers. Late in the fall of the same year, after a good deal of hesitation, they decided to make

the dangerous wartime crossing of the North Atlantic, arriving in New York aboard the S.S. *Santa Rosa*, on December 18, shortly after the U.S. entry into the war.

At the New School Frank joined an illustrious faculty that included other expatriates from wartorn Europe. Between February 1942 and the winter of 1944, Frank gave several lecture series on themes such as "The Future of Art and Decoration," "Postwar Problems of Art," and "The Appreciation of Architecture," all of which focused on the recent history of art and design and their prospects in the immediate future. Because of the war, however, the lectures proved to be poorly attended, and Frank turned instead to writing. During his earlier years he had occasionally written short essays and other pieces, including a collection of poems reflecting the political antagonisms in Austria in the 1920s and early 1930s. But with little else to occupy his attentions, he spent much of his time sitting at his desk in a small two-room apartment on Park Terrace on the Upper West Side of Manhattan churning out several novels and plays. His first novel, *The Peace Conference*, which completed in 1942, was a wicked satire poking fun at the naiveté of the American belief in progress and opportunity (which Frank later came to appreciate). Another novel, *Das Leben des Malers Lucien Sanders* (The life of the painter Lucien Sanders) was a biting commentary on modern art, in which the protagonist, the founder of an artistic movement called "sublimism," is quickly eclipsed after his death, and his works—like those of Brancusi, Kandinsky, Léger, Míro, and others who had resolutely turned their backs on the past—were consigned to museum storerooms.

These manuscripts were never published, however, and Frank found little satisfaction in his life as a writer and lecturer. After the winter 1943–44 term, he resigned from his teaching post at the New School and focused his interest once more on textile design. By May 1944, as he wrote to Estrid Ericson, he had completed twenty-three new patterns; and by late summer of the same year he finished twenty-seven more, sending the entire collection of fifty as a gift to Ericson, who celebrated her fiftieth birthday in September. The "birthday patterns" have formed the core of Svenskt Tenn's textile offerings ever since, and although some of them have never been printed, most are still in production and remain among the best-selling items at the shop.

During this period Frank also attempted to find an outlet for his textile designs in the United States, in part as an attempt to ease his and Anna's strained financial circumstances.[25] He designed several patterns for F. Schumacher & Co., but was never completely satisfied with the quality of printing, and in the end his efforts came to little.[26] During his years in New York he also created a few designs for proposed architectural projects, including a slum clearance project commissioned by the Metropolitan Gas Company for the Lower East Side, and in 1943 he mounted a small exhibition of his earlier architectural works at the New School's building on West 12th Street.[27]

After the war the Franks' return to Sweden was delayed by a shortage of passenger ships until the end of February 1946. Once in Stockholm they took up residence again on Rindögatan,[28] and Frank resumed his work for Svenskt Tenn. During the early postwar years, he was often invited to lecture on "The American Home," comparing American and European styles of living.[29] But for the most part he concentrated on Svenskt Tenn, and in the late 1940s and early 1950s he produced some of his most important designs, including interiors for Swedish embassies and consulates, such as the Swedish General Consulate in New York, and a host of notable clients, among them sculptor Carl Milles.

In 1951 Frank and Ericson mounted an exhibition at Kaufmann's Department Store in Pittsburgh, arranged by one of Frank's former colleagues from Vienna, László Gábor, who was the store's art director. The displays, which consisted of five model rooms—a living room, dining room, garden room, study, and bedroom (fig. 4-9)—featured a wide range of Frank's designs for Svenskt Tenn, including a new chest of drawers laminated with prints from an old book of Swedish flora. The piece, with its simple, elegant proportions,[30] light mahogany, and contrasting colors, was typical of Frank's postwar works for Svenskt Tenn—colorful, with an echo of the past, but still unmistakably modern.

Although the Kaufmann displays, as well as a series of later exhibitions of Svenskt Tenn furnishings in Sweden, presented Frank's design ideas to a wide public, most of his work was in private homes, a fact that makes it difficult to fully analyze his work as an interior designer. Two interiors from the 1950s,[31] however, one the home of an anonymous client and the other Anne's House at Millesgården, reveal the qualities of timelessness, elegance, and variety of invention that characterize Frank's design. They represent

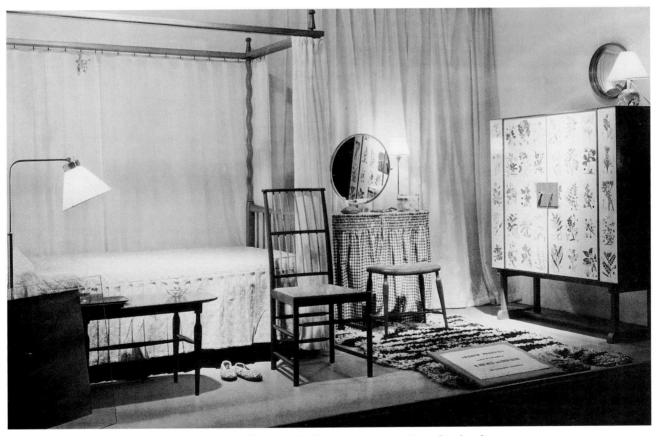

Fig. 4-9. Frank's installation at Kauffman's Department Store, Pittsburgh, 1951.

Fig. 4-10. Josef Frank in his Stockholm apartment, photographed by Hans Hammarskiöld in 1958. Svenskt Tenn Archive, Stockholm.

the full maturity of his work at Svenskt Tenn. Both interiors are framed with white walls, and the rooms are fully furnished with upholstered armchairs and sofas, as well as chairs and sofas with distinctive rattan backs, and small stools and tables. The floors are either covered with simple floor coverings or Oriental rugs.

A poignant example of Frank's approach to interior design is his own apartment in Stockholm, documented in a series of photographs by Hans Hammarskiöld from 1958 (fig. 4-10). Frank lived as he advocated, unpretentiously and simply, but with his own distinctive personal style. The interiors, slightly worn yet manifestly comfortable, evince his strong interest in juxtaposing contrasting patterns, colors, and ideas; the emphasis, as everywhere in Frank's work, is on fostering an amiable and humane environment.

These same themes were on display in a large retro-

spective exhibition of his work for Svenskt Tenn held at the National Museum in Stockholm in 1952. The exhibit brought together for the first time the full breadth of Frank's design production, from small articles such as candlesticks, serving glasses, and tobacco jars, to large pieces such as secretaries, sofas, and vitrines. Overall the designs not only provided further evidence of Frank's extraordinary versatility, but raised the question of Frank's role in the rise of Swedish—and by extension Scandinavian—modern design.[32] When Estrid Ericson posed this same question to Frank in 1950, he replied with uncharacteristic immodesty: "I am building on a cultivated tradition. I have saved all of Swedish decoration and created the Scandinavian style. Before me, the Bauhaus was the only source of inspiration."[33]

While Frank's answer blithely ignored the contributions of the Swedes such as G. A. Berg, Carl Malmsten, Bruno Mathsson, and Elias Svedberg to the creation of modern Swedish design, or the role of the Danes, Kaare Klint, Mogens Koch, and Hans Wegner in the development of Scandinavian design,[34] it nevertheless contained a grain of truth. More than anyone else in the early 1930s, Frank had pointed the way to a softer, more humane, alternative modernism; his work had been important to the formation of a new design direction. And yet he had sedulously kept his distance from the mainstream of Scandinavian developments, and his work remained personal and distinctive. Indeed as the 1950s wore on, his designs and ideas became more and more idiosyncratic.

In connection with an anniversary exhibition at Svenskt Tenn in 1958—*Josef Frank 25 år i Sverige* (Josef Frank 25 years in Sweden)—Frank was invited to write on a subject of his choosing in the journal *Form*, and he responded with one of his most important essays, "Accidentism." The piece was accompanied by an editorial disclaimer to the effect that the author's views differed significantly from those of the Svenska Slöjdföreningen, publisher of the journal and the leading organization advocating the cause of Scandinavian modern design. The essay began with what for Frank was a typically grandiose, though rather pessimistic, view of the role of art in the machine age:

> In our time of scientific thinking bit by bit our traditions are being lost. There is no longer any reason to acknowledge laws that cannot be rigorously proven. Art and beauty have thus become suspicious concepts because they cannot be precisely defined. The exact sciences, on the other hand, with their ties to technology and the business world are strong enough to speed up the devastation of the art.[35]

Frank went on to express his strong aversion to everything related to standardization, taking the living room as his point of departure for a general discussion of architectural and design principles:

> The living room, where one can live and think freely, is neither attractive nor harmonic nor photogenic; it came about as the result of accidental events, will never be finished, and by itself can absorb anything whatsoever to satisfy the owner's varying expectations.[36]

Drawing on the idea of the necessity of inexactitude spawned by physicist Werner Heisenberg's "uncertainty principle" and other new advances in theoretical physics (with which Frank was intimately familiar through discussions with his brother Philipp, a follower of Einstein[37]), Frank argued against rigorous planning and standardization "that leaves nothing to chance." Instead, Frank asserted,

Fig. 4-11. A page from Frank's Provence sketchbook. Svenskt Tenn Archive, Stockholm.

Fig. 4-12. One of Frank's watercolor of the Provence landscape. Svenskt Tenn Archive, Stockholm.

the environment should be shaped "accidentally"—as if it had happened without any guiding hand, thus reflecting the role unpredictable events often play. At various times in the 1950s he even experimented with designing a number of "accidental houses," working through his ideas in elaborately rendered drawings and watercolors. These projects can be understood as essays on an alternative modernism and they gave form to his theoretical discourse.

During the 1950s Frank made annual summer pilgrimages to Provence, to the home of his close friend Trude Waehner.[38] He spent much of his time outdoors—gardening, sketching, or painting (figs. 4-11, 4-12). Some of the landscapes attest to Frank's technical proficiency as a

Fig. 4-13. A living-room installation at Svenskt Tenn, arranged by Estrid Ericson in 1968, a year after Frank's death. Svenskt Tenn Archive, Stockholm.

watercolorist, but they generally lack the power and sensuality of his textile designs. Obviously the liberation from the geometric repetition of textile designs did not succeed to his satisfaction. "I started to paint at age 68," he reported in a magazine interview. "But age 68 is too late, far too late, you lack the technique, but it's nice."39

In 1957 Anna Frank died, and for the remainder of his life Frank lived with Anna's cousin Dagmar Grill, surrounded as always by a coterie of women friends and admirers, his "harem," as one of his relatives once described it. Despite his growing physical problems, Frank remained vivacious and active. He continued to design new works for Svenskt Tenn, often stopping by the showrooms to check on the progress of various projects, and he kept up a lively correspondence with his family and many friends. In 1960, he was awarded the City of Vienna's Prize for artistic accomplishment, and in 1965 the Austrian government bestowed on him the State Prize for Architecture. His contribution to modernism in Vienna had finally been

acknowledged in full. Frank, however, was too weak to travel to Vienna to accept the award, and he died in Stockholm on January 8, 1967. At the funeral ceremony interior designer Sixten Wohlin praised Frank's "consummate" professionalism, adding, "What gripped us most was his warm humanity, which we realized acutely had been the guiding principle of his life."40

In April 1968, the National Museum in Stockholm mounted a commemorative exhibition of Frank's work, featuring a suite of furnishings covered with the light-colored root veneers that Frank so prized. At the same time, Estrid Ericson arranged a display at Svenskt Tenn, a living room (fig. 4-13), which she intended as a summation of her long collaboration with Frank. A guiding principle of his later years—that the environment "should be arranged as if it had come about by chance"—seems at first glance to be the foundation of the design. In fact everything in the room—as in all of Svenskt Tenn's interiors—was minutely planned and arranged by Ericson. Frank provided her with designs that she carefully wove together into a refined whole. The cabinet displayed in the right rear of the living room, which Frank designed in 1957, with its drawers of different sizes and shapes, exemplified his "accidentist" ideas and his rich sense of imagination, as well as desire to foster a sense of ambiguity and mystery. Indeed, the entire ensemble, with its richness of forms and patterns, echoed Frank's wish to blur the boundaries of time and space.

Despite the wide recognition Frank's work for Svenskt Tenn earned him in Sweden after the Second World War, he was largely forgotten outside Scandinavia, and his name was rarely mentioned in avant-garde architectural and design circles in the 1940s. Frank himself was acutely aware of his situation. In a letter to Trude Waehner in 1948, he wrote of his deep dissatisfaction with his work up to that time: "It is not what I had imagined and what I wanted and would have been able to do, but rather only what I was able to accomplish under the circumstances. When I look back it makes me very sad."

Ironically Frank's rediscovery began in Vienna, the city in which he once remarked "that he could never breathe freely," because of the *Dorftrottelfaschismus* ("village idiot Fascism") that had once reigned there.[41] In the late 1950s a number of younger Austrian architects and critics, including Friedrich Kurrent and Johannes Spalt, started to examine Frank's architectural works and writings, and since the 1960s Spalt, Kurrent, Hermann Czech, and others have

arranged several exhibitions of Frank's works, including a major retrospective in 1981 held at the Österreichisches Museum für Angewandte Kunst (Austrian Museum for Applied Art) in Vienna.

Much of the recent focus on Frank has been centered on his connections with the other leading representatives of the Viennese modernism—Otto Wagner, Josef Hoffmann, and especially Adolf Loos.[42] More than that, however, Frank's work and ideas are influencing a new generation of European architects, who see in him a link with the past. Yet what is perhaps most remarkable about Frank is not his specific contributions to Viennese modernism and Scandinavian design, but his deeper message about the importance of forging an environment that is rooted in our cultural and historical traditions and responds to the real needs of people. With his cultivated humanist approach Frank was both behind and ahead of his time. While most of his modernist contemporaries sought to break free of the past—believing that the future lay in a wholly new approach to design—Frank continued to advocate a recourse to tradition as the best way to find solutions for his time. This, however, did not prevent him from creating his own uniquely personal expression, both in his architecture and his interior design. Through his ties to the past, he also ensured for himself the admiration and respect of future generations including the present.

1. Letter, Josef Frank to Hannes Meyer, October 7, 1930, Bauhaus Correspondence, Archives of the History of Art, Getty Center for the History of Art and the Humanities, Santa Monica. Although Frank was a major critic of the Bauhaus, he publicly defended Meyer when he was dismissed as director of the Bauhaus in 1930 and was a strong advocate of Meyer's approach to architecture and pedagogy; see Christopher Long, "Josef Frank and the Crisis of Modern Architecture," Ph. D. diss. (University of Texas at Austin, 1993).

2. See Wilfried Posch, "Josef Frank, eine bedeutende Persönlichkeit des österreichischen Kulturliberalismus," *Um Bau* 10 (1986), pp. 34–35.

3. Astrid Gmeiner and Gottfried Pirhofer, *Der Österreichische Werkbund: Alternative zur klassischen Moderne in Architektur, Raum- und Produktgestaltung* (Salzburg and Vienna: Residenz Verlag, 1985), pp. 179–90.

4. As permanent secretary of the Swedish Academy, Österling had much to say about the awarding of the Nobel Prize in Literature. In 1935 Frank designed a "poet's lair" for Österling's summer house in Falsterbo. It was a low wooden building with a brick foundation containing a single large room and adjoining bath.

5. The exhibition, "Josef Frank arkitektur," at the Swedish Museum of Architecture, Stockholm, in the autumn of 1994; see Mikael Bergquist and Olof Michélsen, eds., *Josef Frank arkitektur* (Stockholm: Arkitektur-museet, 1994).

6. For more information on Uno Åhrén and Björn Trägärdh, see Monica Boman, ed., *An Orchid in Winter: The Story of Estrid Ericson* (Stockholm: Carlsson Bohförlag, 1989).

7. See, for example, Leopold Greiner, "Möbel und Einrichtung der Neuzeit. Arbeiten der Werkstätten Haus & Garten, Wien," *Innen-Dekoration* 37 (1926), pp. 348–84; Max Eisler, "Neu-Wiener Innenräume," *Moderne Bauformen* 26 (1927), pp. 388–409; idem, "Neue Bauten und Innenräume von Josef Frank, Oskar Wlach ('Haus und Garten') — Arnold Karplus Wohnhaus auf der Hohen Warte in Wien," *Moderne Bauformen* 39 (1930): 429–48; "Werkstätten 'Haus & Garten' in Wien," *Innen-Dekoration* 41 (November 1930), pp. 402–34; Wolfgang Born, "Neue Innenräume von Haus & Garten," *Innen-Dekoration* 44 (June 1933), pp. 184–210; "Neue Wohnungen von 'Haus und Garten,'" *Innen-Dekoration*

Fig. 5-2. Summer house for Hugo Bunzl, Ortmann, Lower Austria, 1913–14. Graphische Sammlung Albertina, Vienna.

Fig. 5-3. Villa for Dr. Emil and Agnes Scholl, Vienna, 1913–14. From Max Eisler, *Österreichische Werkkultur* (Vienna, 1916).

Fig. 5-4. Adolf Loos, Scheu House, Vienna, 1912–13; rear facade. From Heinrich Kulka, *Adolf Loos: Das Werk des Architekten* (Vienna, 1931).

windows and doors; an interest in linking together the various spaces with a carefully arranged network of pathways; and an attempt to break up the interior spaces by means of free and open planning.

Another work Frank designed around the same time, the Scholl House (1913–14; fig. 5-3), went even further in its rejection of historical precedent. Aside from the narrow string courses and abstracted corner pilasters, the structure was devoid of decoration. Indeed, with its spare, cubic form, it strongly resembled Loos's famed residences of the same years, especially his 1912 Scheu House (fig. 5-4). The similarities, in fact, went even deeper. Like Loos, Frank began the process of design from the inside, developing the interior volumes first and then wrapping them in a tight, outer "container." The windows and doors were placed to serve the needs of the inner spaces, so that the complex plan is revealed in the idiosyncratic arrangement of the facade.

But what set Frank's houses apart was their strong emphasis on what he often referred to as *Wohnlichkeit*—coziness and livability. He rejected the traditional planning concepts of axiality and symmetry, seeking instead to reproduce the rambling effect he so admired in the English country house.[5] By breaking down the old architectonic codes in this way, he created an environment in which the furnishings could be placed without regard to any hierarchical scheme or controlling idea. There is no conception of unity, no *Gesamtkunstwerk* ideal which can be undermined or violated. The various components of the houses, whether "fixed" or "movable," exist more or less individually, and could be altered without fundamentally changing the nature of the whole.

The various housing settlements, including the Hoffingergasse Housing Project of 1921–24 (fig. 5-5), which Frank designed in the period just after the First World War, returned to these themes, albeit on a much less

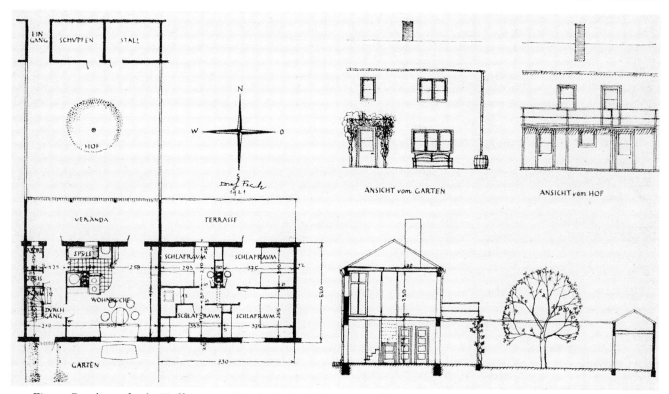

Fig. 5-5. Row house for the Hoffingergasse Housing Project, Vienna, 1921; plans, section, and elevations. From *Der Neubau* 6 (1924).

ambitious scale. Most of the projects featured unadorned, matter-of-fact structures, with pitched roofs and simple materials and detailing. But while greatly reduced in terms of size, the houses showed Frank's interest in fostering a sense of variety and comfort. Indeed, much as in his prewar houses, Frank emphasized the appealing and affective space. The windows and perceptive axes were generally arranged to make for pleasing vistas; the interiors were configured to give the greatest possible impression of diversity; and the use of terraces and verandas, where possible, provided access to the outdoors and served to make the living space seem larger than it was. However, in marked contrast to many of the other modernists of the time—such as Le Corbusier, Mart Stam, and Hannes Meyer—who sought to impose their own ideas of "how one should live," Frank based his designs on the real, everyday needs of the working-class inhabitants. Rejecting the use of a bourgeois "salon" or living room, which he asserted was inappropriate for such houses, he provided instead a large combination sitting area and kitchen or *Wohnküche*, common to traditional vernacular housing in Austria.

Stylistically, the settlement projects prior to 1923 display a pared-down vernacular idiom strongly reminiscent of Heinrich Tessenow's houses for the prewar garden-city settlement at Hellerau. But by 1923, Frank once more began to explore the use of a more expressly "modern" look. The projects for the Klosterneuburg Housing Settlement or the Main Square for the Pernitz Settlement, both designed that year, have flat roofs and crisp, unadorned facades, reflecting the new emphasis on purism emerging in the works of the avant-garde.

Yet while Frank's works began to evince the outward image of the *Neue Sachlichkeit* (New Objectivity) aesthetic, his desire to furnish "livable" and "interesting" space remained at the forefront of his design efforts. Even in the series of large housing blocks he designed for the Vienna municipal authorities between the mid-1920s and the early 1930s, Frank took pains to ensure that the apartments would be comfortable, conveniently planned, and well ventilated. The goal of the new housing projects, Frank wrote in 1926, should be to elevate the level of the *Wohnkultur* (literally, "living culture"), while at the same time providing a maximum of "light, air, space, sun, etc."[6] In the Wiedenhofer-Hof Housing Project of 1923–24 (fig. 5-6), for example, which was among the first of these large housing blocks, Frank opened up the building mass by arranging the structure around two large central courtyards. Most of the apartments had rooms facing both the street and courtyard sides, which ensured that they were sunny and well ventilated. The building offered a wide variety of floor plans, ranging from small one-room efficiencies to comparatively spacious two-bedroom units. Though neither the apartments nor the individual rooms were large, they were considerably more comfortable and better arranged than the typical prewar tenements. In his later housing projects, such as the Leopoldine Glöckel-Hof (1931–32) or the Simmeringer Hauptstrasse Housing Project (1931–32), Frank developed these ideas further, increasing the size both of the apartments and the courtyards, while decreasing the overall percentage of the site covered by the structure.[7]

However, in contrast to other well-known modernist architects of the time—such as Gropius, Bruno Taut, and Ernst May—who were urging the construction of such large housing blocks as a solution to the "housing prob-lem," Frank continued to advocate the cause of the small single-family house. The large apartment building, Frank insisted, was at best a "compromise." He also called into question the conventional view that size alone was a determinant of housing quality: the best living space, he argued, "does not consist of the number or size of the rooms, but the quality of life that they enable."[8]

By the mid-1920s, the economic situation in Austria had improved sufficiently for Frank to focus once more on the single-family home. Between 1924 and 1930, he designed a series of houses that further developed the spatial and planning ideas he had first explored in his prewar villas. In the end, only a few of these houses were actually realized, but the surviving projects represent one of the most important and sustained investigations of the problems of space and living of this century, an achievement in many respects on a par with Le Corbusier's contemporary Stein and Savoye villas or Loos's Moller House.

Among the earliest of these works—and one of the few which was actually constructed—was a summer house for Frank's sister- and brother-in-law, Signhild and Axel Claëson, in the southern Swedish resort town of Falsterbo.

Fig. 5-6. Wiedenhofer-Hof Housing Project, Vienna, 1923–24; plan of the second floor. From *Die Wohnhausanlage der Gemeinde Wien, Wiedenhofer-Hof im XVII. Bezirk* (Vienna, 1926).

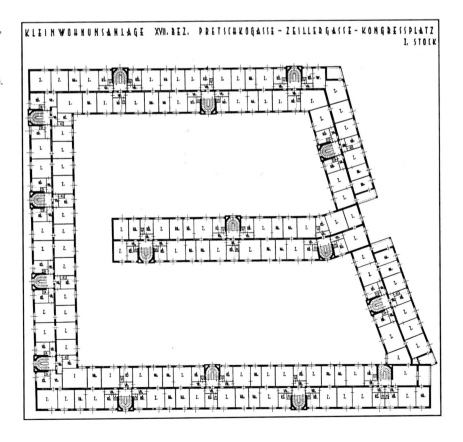

Fig. 5-7. House for Axel and Signhild Claëson, Falsterbo, Sweden, 1924–27. Arkitekturmuseet, Stockholm.

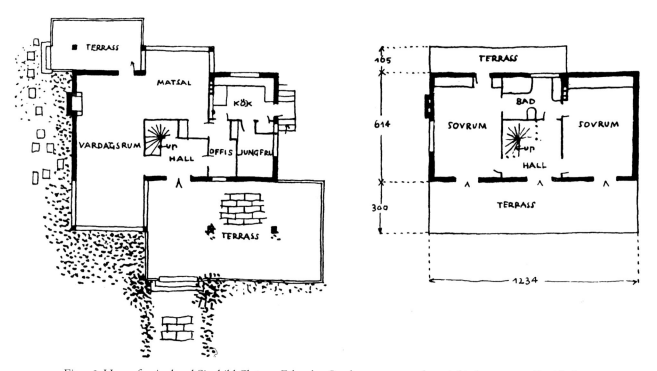

Fig. 5-8. House for Axel and Signhild Claëson, Falsterbo, Sweden, 1924–27; plans. Arkitekturmuseet, Stockholm.

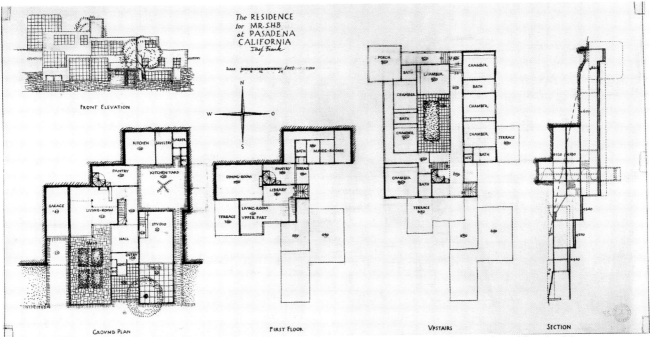

Fig. 5-9. Project for a residence for Mr. S. H. B., Pasadena, California, 1927. Graphische Sammlung Albertina, Vienna.

Fig. 5-10. House for Julius and Margarete Beer, Vienna, 1929–30. Hochschule für angewandte Kunst-Archiv, Vienna.

Fig. 5-11. Ludwig Mies van der Rohe, Tugendhat House, Brno, 1928–30; view from the garden. Museum of Modern Art, New York.

Frank began work on the house in 1924, though it was not actually completed until 1927. With its spare, unadorned facades, blocky massing, and nautical railings, the three-story brick house (fig. 5-7) was, in fact, Frank's first executed work to which the stylistic term *modern* may truly apply. (It was also the first "functionalist" building constructed in Sweden.9) The house featured a generally open plan, with a large L-shaped living and dining area serving as the compositional focus (fig. 5-8). Much as in Mies van der Rohe's houses of the early 1920s, the spaces were oriented toward the garden or the open landscape beyond. No single axis dominated; instead, one was encouraged to move about at will, to choose whatever position seemed appropriate.10

Yet although Frank eschewed a rigid, hierarchical layout, the rooms themselves and the areas linking them were still largely static. While he was at work on the Claëson House, however, Frank began to experiment with various ways to introduce a stronger sense of movement and fluidi-

ty into his work. In his unrealized residence and dance school for a Mr. Ornstein in Tel Aviv (1926), for example, he broke up the regular horizontal layering of floors, placing the various spaces on different levels, which were linked together by a central stair. The individual rooms themselves became stopping points along several carefully conceived routes of penetration leading from the entry to the dance studio at the rear or to the upper living areas. In his house in Salzburg and the house for Dagmar Grill in Skärgården of the same period Frank explored this idea more fully, further breaking up the interiors and providing even more varied and complex routes through and around the houses. Even more ambitious in this respect was the unrealized residence for Mr. S. H. B. in Pasadena, California (fig. 5-9), which Frank also evidently designed around 1927.11 Arrayed along a gently sloping hillside, it is fragmented into a number of separate volumes of different sizes and heights. These distinct parts in turn are shaped and disposed by a series of circulation patterns, which connect the main living areas, and the whole assemblage is combined into a network of tightly interlocking volumes.

The effect of the Pasadena floor plan was not unlike Loos's *Raumplan* or "space-plan" idea, which he developed in a number of villas designed in the same years.[12] But while Loos was very much concerned with economies of space, Frank was principally interested in ways to foster new spatial sensations. And while Loos focused on how to establish discrete rooms that were proper and efficient, Frank emphasized instead effects which were psychologically effective and would provide the best possible backdrop for living.

Frank elaborated on these ideas in the large villa he designed for the wealthy industrialist Julius Beer and his wife Margarete in Vienna. Completed in 1930 the Beer House (fig. 5-10) was one of Frank's most sophisticated essays in spatial planning; indeed it represents one of the landmarks of modern architecture, an accomplishment equal to Mies's Tugendhat House (fig. 5-11) and Loos's Villa Müller (fig. 5-12), both finished the same year. Like Frank's earlier residential projects, it was arranged on a series of different levels connected by a carefully conceived "archi-

tectural promenade." The main body of the house was three-and-a-half stories, with a large entresol or mezzanine positioned between the ground floor and second story (fig. 5-13). The central feature and dramatic focus of the house was the main staircase (fig. 5-14), which led past the raised living room to the entresol where a small library and music room were located (fig. 5-15), and from there to bedrooms on the upper floors.

In his 1931 essay "Das Haus als Weg und Platz" (The house as path and place), Frank explained that he had conceived of the Beer House as a city in miniature, with traffic patterns designed for specific activities. "A well-organized house," he wrote, "should be laid out like a city, with streets and alleys that lead inevitably to places which are cut off from traffic, so that one can rest there. . . . It is of the utmost importance that this path is not marked by some obvious means or decorative scheme, so that the visitor will never have the idea that he is being led around. A well-laid-out house is comparable to one of those beautiful old cities, in which even a stranger immediately knows his way around and can find the city hall and the market square without having to ask."[13]

But if the guiding principle underlying the house's

Fig. 5-12. Adolf Loos, Villa Müller, Prague, 1928–30; view from the southeast. Graphische Sammlung Albertina, Vienna.

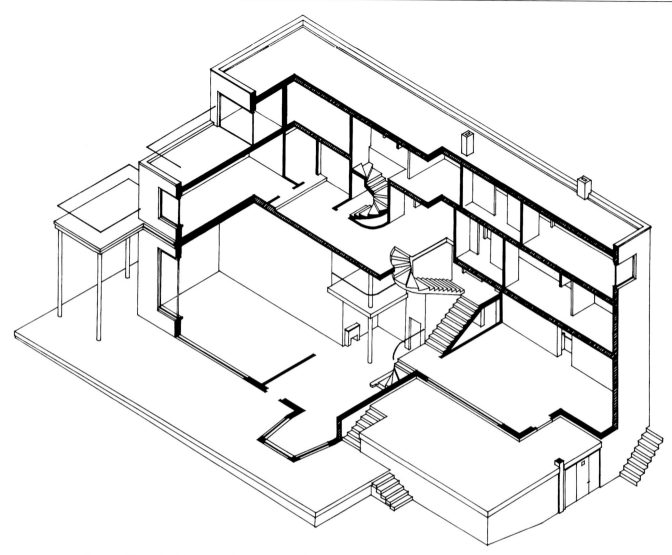

Fig. 5-13. House for Julius and Margarete Beer, Vienna, 1929–30; axonometric view. Drawing by Ivan Tkachenko.

design was concerned with creating a tension between zones of movement and repose, the essence of the house—as indeed in all of Frank's houses—was an attempt to engender a sense of freedom and ease. The rooms were intended as more or less neutral backdrops, in which the inhabitants could choose to place whatever furnishings they wished—and to arrange them however they deemed fit. For Frank, the house was a private place, the intimate preserve of the individual and family. Unlike Le Corbusier, who saw the house as a place of action, Frank viewed the home as a refuge, if an illusory one; it was not an extension of the modern world, but a haven from it, a place where one could escape the rigors of life in the machine age. Indeed, if the exterior of the Beer House, with its taut white surfaces and crisp massing, was unmistakably modern, its interior reflected Frank's belief that houses should serve the needs

and pleasures of the body and the spirit.[14] While most of his modernist contemporaries sought to create an aesthetic purged of the past, Frank sought to foster an environment where all things had a place, the old and the new, the Spartan and the luxurious, the simple and the complex. Rejecting the notion of the dwelling as machine, he argued that the modern house should not be modeled on the steamship or train, but on the garret: "The bohemian garret, condemned by authorities and modern architects as unhygienic . . . contains all that . . . which we seek in vain in rationally planned homes: vitality, large spaces, large windows, multiple corners, angled walls, steps and height differences, pillars and beams, in short all those things that we seek . . . in order to avoid the desolate wasteland of the square room. . . . The task of the architect is to arrange all of the elements . . . into a house."[15]

Even while the Beer House was still under construction, Frank was looking for alternative ways to produce this feeling of architectural play. In the first version of his unrealized project for the house for M. S. in Los Angeles of 1930 (fig. 5-16), for example, he explored the possibilities of using spatial displacements and discontinuities to break out of the rigid constraints of the regular four-cornered room. Although the overall outline of the house was still based on a grid, Frank introduced several "disruptions"—a serpentine patio area, curved dining and tea rooms, and walls set at slightly oblique angles at several locations—to undermine its basic rectangularity. As in his other houses of the period, the sense of interruption was further accentuated by changes in level; the numerous shifts in height served to break the grid not only horizontally but vertically as well.

By the mid-1930s Frank was also experimenting with the use of free or irregular spaces as a means to further undermine the right-angled room. As early as 1931 in his essay "The House as Path and Place," he had discussed the possibility of abandoning conventional planning in favor of a new, less regular form of ordering: "The square room," he asserted, "is the most unsuitable for living; it is practical as a storehouse for furniture, but is not good for anything else. I believe that a polygon drawn by chance, whether with right or obtuse angles, is much better than a regular four-cornered room."[16]

Fig. 5-14. House for Julius and Margarete Beer, Vienna, 1929–30; view of the stair looking toward the dining room. From *Der Baumeister* 29 (1931).

Fig. 5-15. House for Julius and Margarete Beer, Vienna, 1929–30; music room. From *Der Baumeister* 29 (1931).

These freely formed spaces first appear in Frank's house for Walter Wehtje, which he designed and built between 1935 and 1936 in Falsterbo only a short distance from the Claëson House. While portions of the rambling, mostly one-story structure preserved the standard gridlike arrangement of straight lines and right-angled rooms, Frank set a number of the walls at oblique angles or gently bent them into soft curvilinear shapes. The resulting irregularly shaped rooms and passageways served to generate a highly complex spatial experience, giving the impression of being at once free, flowing, and plastic. Although most of the spatial play was confined to a single, uniform level, the combination of regular and irregular rooms, differences in lighting effects, and the house's large, open two-story hall engendered a remarkable sense of spatial variety and complexity.

In 1938, Frank designed another house for Wehtje, this time in the Stockholm suburb of Djursholm, that pushed even further in the direction of completely irregular planning. Aside from the kitchen, bathrooms, and an upstairs maid's room, none of the spaces was a regular rectangle. Instead, each of the rooms was more or less freely developed, its form determined by Frank's own sense of what would be most "emotionally effective."

Although it was never realized, the second Wehtje House represents perhaps the most complete expression of Frank's notion of the house as a series of paths and places. The entire ensemble of rooms was intended as a spatial continuum through which the occupant could wander at will, in the expectation that each movement or turn would offer a new spatial sensation. By "breaking the box" in this way, Frank had fostered a new kind of spatial ordering, one that departed radically from conventional architecture practice. The old, solid structural order was fragmented and reconstituted to create a sense of almost continuous movement through space. To the conventional notion of architecture as a three-dimensional spatial art, Frank added a fourth dimension, the experience of time-space.

Frank's attempts to find an alternative to traditional planning has obvious parallels in the works of architects

Fig. 5-16. House for M. S., Los Angeles, 1930; plan. From *Der Baumeister* 29 (1931).

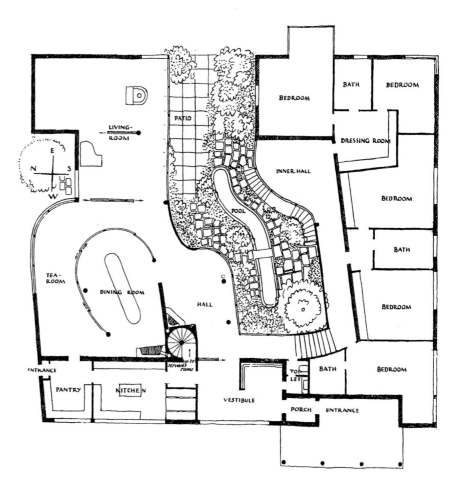

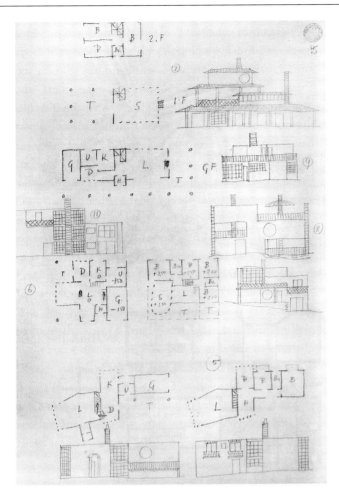

Fig. 5-17. Thirteen Houses for Dagmar Grill, 1947; houses 1, 2, 3, 4, plans and elevations. Graphische Sammlung Albertina, Vienna.

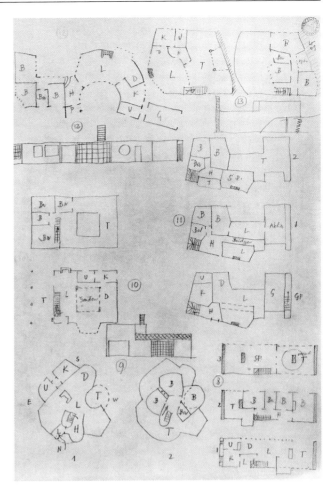

Fig. 5-18. Thirteen Houses for Dagmar Grill, 1947; houses 5, 6, 7, 8, 9, plans and elevations. Graphische Sammlung Albertina, Vienna.

such as Frank Lloyd Wright, Alvar Aalto, Hugo Häring, and Hans Scharoun. But while his works manifest certain outward similarities with some of their designs, his underlying rationale was in fact quite different. Rejecting the label of "organic" architecture, Frank insisted that the curvilinear shapes were not based on "natural forms." Indeed, he explicitly rejected nature as a model for architecture: "The architect fashions different forms from those of nature; in fact, we could define architecture as being an ordering of nature, with its own individual forms; the further the forms of architecture are from those of nature the better they will be—that is the great lesson of classical art."[17] Frank similarly rejected the charge of formalism, responding that his irregular forms were simply an attempt to adjust to the living needs of the inhabitants: the unusual spaces, he claimed, proceeded from a "functional" point of view; their purpose was to provide the greatest possible sense of comfort and freedom.[18]

Although Frank abandoned his architectural practice in the late 1930s to devote himself to his work for Svenskt Tenn, he continued to reflect on the problem of the modern home. In 1947, in a series of letters to his wife's cousin, Dagmar Grill, he discussed the possibility of creating a new kind of architecture, one based loosely on random or chance ordering.[19] He illustrated the letters with sketches of thirteen different houses (figs. 5-17, 5-18, and 5-19), intended to demonstrate what this radical new form of planning might yield.

While the projects varied considerably in structure and character, they repeated many of the themes of Frank's houses of the late 1920s and 1930s, including the use of changes in level, the architectural promenade, and the irregular arrangement of spaces—all aimed to produce an impression of spatial variety and complexity. But their overall composition is even more idiosyncratic—one is tempted to say mannered—than Frank's earlier works. The

# 6. ARCHITEKTUR ALS SYMBOL:

## Karin Lindegren

Editor's note: This chapter, which explores some of the major arguments Frank presented in his polemical treatise *Architektur als Symbol: Elemente deutschen Neues Bauens* (Architecture as symbol: elements of German modern architecture), has been adapted from the preface to the Swedish translation of Frank's book (*Arkitektur som Symbol*, translated and with a preface by Karin Lindegren [Lund, Sweden: ellerströms, 1995]). English-speaking scholars of Frank and the modern movement have long been at a disadvantage. *Architektur als Symbol*, published in Vienna in 1931, stands at the center of Frank's criticism of modernism, yet it has never been translated into English. The inclusion in this catalogue of Karin Lindegren's analysis of the book and its contents is an attempt to bridge the gap at least temporarily until such a translation is available. Most of the sources used in preparing this text will be found in the bibliography.

dolf Loos—architect, reformer, and cultural commentator—turned sixty in 1930. The event was officially ignored in Austria, but leading figures from the European art world wrote essays and tributes which were collected in a *Festschrift*. Josef Frank was one of the contributors; he wrote:

> Adolf Loos has given us the cultural axioms of modern architecture, but these are not confined to the modern architecture of our time: they are so great and comprehensive that they were valid in the past and will retain their value in future.
>
> We will not, however, conceal the fact that many today who ostensibly follow these rules are only trying to use and restrict them for something momentary and fashionable. Not until the failure of these attempts has been everywhere realized will the struggle waged by Adolf Loos for the reversion to a modern mentality and architecture have succeeded.

"Reversion to a modern mentality" is a remarkable turn of phrase, but the polemical tone of the statement suits Loos and probably has the same import as Karl Kraus's celebrated criticism of his contemporaries who were incapable of distinguishing "an urn from a chamberpot."

**Between the Wars.** That same year, 1930, Frank had signed a contract with the Viennese publisher Anton Schroll for a book about *"Traditionen deutschen neuen Bauens."* For two years, beginning in 1929, he had lectured throughout Austria, arguing the case for modernism and warning against authoritarianism in any form. His book, published in 1931, was entitled *Architektur als Symbol: Elemente deutschen Neuen Bauens* (Architecture as symbol: elements of German modern architecture). *"Neues Bauen"* in Germany was one of the names for what came to be known as Functionalism in Sweden and elsewhere.

Overall it is an unpleasant book, full of unnecessary sideswipes, excoriating sarcasms, ardent hatred of things German, and conservative (if mistaken) forecasts, but it also includes intelligent analyses, acute observations, breathtaking prophesies, and valid truths. It is really

Fig. 6-1. Josef Frank, Entry hall, Nursery School (*Kinderheim*) in Ortmann, Lower Austria, ca. 1921. From Alexander Koch, *Farbige Wohnräume der Neuzeit* (Darmstadt: Verlagsanstalt Alexander Koch, 1926), p. 60.

a critique of culture, with architecture as its barometer. Frank, unquestionably, follows in the footsteps of Loos, but whereas Loos, fifteen years his senior, had the advantage of campaigning against an outdated nineteenth-century eclecticism and a phony, false-fronted architecture, which meant that he was moving forward in time, Frank waged a war on two fronts, against both the past and the present. Europe had changed since the First World War. "Mankind with modern nerves," as Loos had observed in his time, was threatened by such a degree of restlessness and aggression that it needed pacifying. Frank's methodology in *Architektur als Symbol* is not so much linear as circular, his thoughts describing a long, undulating Ariadne's thread which does not always lead to the exit anticipated by the reader—to be precise, it does not lead to an exit at all but to a number of possibilities.

*Architektur als Symbol* was written at a time when one disaster had only just been overcome and a new one was in the offing. The intermittently choleric tone, presumably, is connected with the author's possession of a sensitive, seismographic instrument for detecting cultural oscillations that are manifestations of political ones. He does not explode, like Loos, in direct confrontation with a specific event, but gathers circumstantial evidence. It is symptomatic that the book opens with a wrathful commentary on the First World War as a ghastly communion between nations, a kind of *Völkerverständigung* (international rapprochement) in reverse.

**A Viennese Tradition.** Josef Frank was no more a philosopher than were Adolf Loos and Karl Kraus, his elder contemporaries and in part his role models as cultural commentators. But they share the same spirit: they are personal truth-tellers who allow themselves the liberty of flouting objectivity in the realization that only their own truth is absolute, and in doing so they too make use of irony, satire, parody, and travesty as stylistic vehicles. Since 1899 Kraus had been the editor of *Die Fackel* (The Torch), a political journal, in which he ruthlessly showered his contempt over everything that was false and opportunistic in his view. In 1919 Kraus's *Die letzten Tage der Menschheit* (The last days of mankind), an epic drama, was published; in it the First World War was used as a backdrop for the cataclysm, the doomsday of Austria and Europe. In 1921 Adolf Loos's *Ins Leere gesprochen* (Spoken into the void), a selection of his early critical articles, was published (but in France!). The second compilation of his essays, *Trotzdem* (Notwithstanding), did not appear until 1931. Frank was presumably acquainted with these works, especially the articles by Loos, which had

previously been published in newspapers and magazines. During the later 1920s, traditionalism came to play an increasingly important part in the work of both Loos and Frank.

There is, however, another name to be mentioned in connection with *Architektur als Symbol*: Egon Friedell, writer, dramatist, actor, translator, satirist, and philosopher. The first two parts of his *Kulturgeschichte der Neuzeit* (Cultural history of the modern age) were published in 1927 and 1928. This is an elegantly written exposé—witty, original, personal, erudite, but completely unscholarly. It was immensely popular and can hardly have escaped Frank's notice.

For *Architektur als Symbol* not only contains contemporary criticism, but also includes a historical review of ideas concerning art and its interpretation in Western civilization, sometimes in direct opposition to accepted academic theories. As mentioned, Frank's train of thought is not linear; his review of the course of history is interspersed with references to his own time, and conversely, criticism of his own time includes criticism of the course of history. Unlike Frank, Friedell, a Jew who had converted to Evangelical-Lutheranism, represents a Christian, German-idealist viewpoint in his book. In Frank's book the presence of elements from Oswald Spengler's *Der Untergang des Abendlandes* (The Decline of the West; 1918–22)—the development and decline of different civilizations at different times—is perhaps merely an example of the cultural philosophy that was in vogue at the time. Frank's way of using analogy as a method and analyzing "the formal language of history" as a means of probing the future further suggests a reading of Spengler. The only historian Frank mentions by name is Renaissance scholar Jacob Burckhardt, but this is hardly surprising since Frank's own doctoral dissertation had been about the Renaissance architect Leon Battista Alberti.

Architect and theorist Gottfried Semper, whose evolutionary theory of architecture parallels Darwin's origin of species, may have had a profound influence on Otto Wagner and Adolf Loos, but Frank considered Semper's theories to be based too much on construction materials. Frank's view of the art of earlier periods falls somewhere between Alois Riegl's interpretation of form as a criterion of a will to art (*Kunstwollen*) and Max Dvořák's interpretation of art history in the light of cultural psychology. The latter belonged to a Viennese school of art scholarship which, at the end of the nineteenth century and in the early decades of the twentieth, was as renowned as other "Viennese schools." When Dvořák died in 1921, Loos designed a mausoleum, a cubic structure with a stepped roof which was never built. Although never built, it shows how much Dvořák meant to Loos and his circle.

From the viewpoint of style, some parts of Frank's book resemble journalist Joseph Roth's widely read critical impressions of such topics as visits to various German cities, which were published in periodicals in the 1920s. Roth and Frank had a mutual friend in the writer Soma Morgenstern, also an Austrian Jew, who later immigrated to New York.

**Neues Bauen and the German Mentality.** At the Frank symposium in Vienna in 1985 Swiss architectural historian Martin Steinmann described *Architektur als Symbol* as a "sloppy book," but it is in fact anything but sloppy. It is not just a number of essays or articles that are loosely linked and can be read separately. Despite its chapter divisions, the book is actually a single essay, but on the grand scale. The first eight sections of text are a kind of exposition of current themes. These are then intertwined with historical motifs into a fugue which demands concentration from the reader. As a menacing *cantus firmus* is Frank's warning against the "German mentality"—nationalism, extremism, uniformity, standardization: intellectual arrogance shaded by metaphysics and mysticism. Considering what happened in Germany after 1933, there is an uncanny psychological perceptiveness about Frank's attack.

The Bauhaus and its educational and ideological program, which sometimes took on scriptural overtones, were the principal targets for Frank's barbs. He labels its professors—who were great artists and architects such as Walter Gropius, Marcel Breuer, Josef Albers, Paul Klee, and Theo van Doesburg—"handicraft supervisors" or simply instructors. Frank also criticizes the Bauhaus for its way of generating finance by putting the school's products on the market, which he dubbed "art in the service of the shopkeeper." In his chapter entitled "German Outfit," he finds fault with the distinctive Bauhaus typography. Elsewhere, tubular steel furniture is the target of castigation.

By 1930/31 the survival of the Bauhaus was being threatened by internal dissension and Nazi control of the Dessau city council. Mies van der Rohe, who had recently been appointed director, tried to save the school, but his efforts failed, and in 1933, after a year-long interlude in Berlin, the Bauhaus closed. Frank, therefore, writing in 1931 in a critical vein is perhaps flogging a dead horse.

Toward the end of the 1920s *Neues Bauen* was criticized for being forced by the economic and social crises of the 1920s into an increasingly rigid standardization and thus exercising a new Big Brotherism underpinned by ideological

explanations. Buildings were no longer adapted to human beings. If anything, the presence of human beings was an unruly disruption. This theme was argued, for example, by Adolf Behne, one of the most prominent German-speaking architectural critics of the time, who in 1929 in his magazine *Das Neue Berlin*, also passed judgment on a new superficiality. "The poster has replaced the problem; . . . the street, the shop window, the facade became the true sensations of the city, the places of art experience for the masses—the commercialization of art." It is likely that Frank read Behne's articles; he deals with exactly the same theme.

In his use of the word "German," Frank sometimes oscillates between indicating "German-speaking" or those of the German nation, on one hand, and "German" in the sense of belonging to the German state or being *"Reichsdeutsch,"* a term sometimes used in Austria at that time, on the other hand.

In the chapter *"Heimatkunst"* (regionalist art), however, Frank speaks out clearly, heaping contempt on Vienna where he views everything about the new architecture as the fruit of coincidence and carelessness, and where everything has remained as it was. Neither the alpine villa architecture of the Vienna *Vororte* nor the "apartment palaces" for workers in the *Vorstädte*—*"Die Ringstrasse des Proletariats"*—outside the city's old (Patrician) Ring found favor in Frank's eyes. The facades of various buildings—Reumann-Hof, Sandleiten-Hof, Karl-Marx-Hof—built by pupils of Otto Wagner, employed a gentrified symbolism and vocabulary which was in no way matched on the interior by the comfort of the apartments.

**An Amazing History of Art.** In the book's "historical" chapter dealing with prehistoric and medieval times, Frank displays absolutely no understanding of the twentieth-century interest in the "primitive." Despite his own occasional use of folkloric or Egyptian motifs and forms, overall he found Nordic dragon ornamentation (which he calls "serpentine ornament") as repulsive as Egyptian or Near-Eastern deities in its anthropo/zoomorphism. He dismissed Egyptian art as "lifeless"; because much of Egyptian art is made for the cult of death, it is thus unchangeable. And from their very inception, for Frank, the Romanesque churches with their clumsy sculptures resemble nothing so much as heaps of rubble.

Frank's fiercest criticism is reserved for the Gothic design idiom as the climax of a Christian hypocrisy, the mystical combination of scholasticism and inverted architectural construction. Frank compares it to two people trying to climb out of a well, back to back and with their feet against the wall. This chapter is as unfair as it is brilliant. It demonstrates Frank's complete skepticism of a metaphysical mentality. Mysticism is the determination to stop thinking. Here one senses both the seminars of Moritz Schlick—visited, not without opposition, by Ludwig Wittgenstein—and Frank's Jewish cultural background: God is to be parlayed with directly.

The author's attempted hatchet job on Albrecht Dürer, however, fails in a way that is nothing short of comic. Frank chose an excerpt from *Unterweysung der messung mit dem zirckel* (1525), a perfectly ordinary textbook of geometry and proportion. Toward the end of the book, Dürer, "with the German mentality in mind" according to Frank, and with irony intended, describes the making of a victory monument to a defeated peasant in the form of a drunkard and a beer barrel. While Dürer's position in the so-called Peasant War in the early years of the Reformation has never been fully clarified, the text and its grotesque accompanying illustration seem to be intended as a sharp warning against ridiculously allegorical statues. Frank uses this text, which he arbitrarily abridged, as evidence that the German Renaissance was never anything but *Kleinkunst* (minor arts), an overburdened handicraft subsequently elevated to a national style. He applies this argument to his own age, in opposition to the modern German view of architecture.

In Frank's view, there is no doubt about the identity of the true European tradition: it is Classical antiquity. He does not regard it as an ideal period from a social point of view, but he sees its buildings as the only tenable framework for variation and change. "If today one constructs a building in the Roman style ['style' in the most popular sense]—that is, with all the details such as columns, moldings and so on—no eyebrows will be raised and it will not even look old-fashioned." On the other hand, every single Gothic building with pointed arches and so on will announce to the beholder: "This is a Gothic building." Time has proven him right. Regularity also saves the Italian Renaissance from being merely the fruit of new technical inventions, endowing it with a universal and ever-serviceable beauty.

One recurrent theme in Frank's text is his definition of the "living" as that which is first destroyed, then preserved as a ferment, and is finally transformed into something new. This notion, also to be found in Spengler, is arguable, making the concept of "timeless" an ambiguous one.

In the central chapter of *Architektur als Symbol*, "Hellas and Ourselves," Frank subscribes to the Classical concept of harmony: "Anyone who has ever trodden the colonnades of the Parthenon will know that this happy state of total harmony, achieved here on a single occasion, can be nothing else but the sole ideal of architecture."

**Mechanical Man.** One theme that had been discussed since the turn of the nineteenth century in Central Europe and even longer in England was the relationship between craft and the mechanized production of furnishings. Apart from the influence of the English Arts and Crafts movement on Austrian design, Loos and Frank both realized that the machine could not be ignored, but both of them took an ambivalent attitude toward its use. Frank expands the realm of discussion to include the armaments industry, mass production, the cult of the machine, and thus dehumanization. He warns against the machine, which was becoming humanity's master instead of its servant. He paints a picture of the new human robot with the same ruthless humor that Chaplin later employed in *Modern Times*. Frank was no champion of "honest toil" as a moral principle, and he mocks the notion of the distance between two points being reduced because the time spent traveling between them is lessened by new technologies while at the same time people feel that we have less and less time to spare. Today, substituting the words *electronics*, *computers*, *the Internet*, and *virtual reality*, and pondering the possibility of endless communication with neither physical motion nor the necessity of meeting a single human being in reality, we can understand what Frank was arguing.

Frank lampooned modern culture, but he had no understanding whatsoever for modernism in painting and sculpture and he completely rejected mass media and the big-city entertainment industry. In his view expressionism, cubism, futurism, dadaism, and constructivism are caricatures; photography and film are a form of artistic charlatanism; jazz is an inferno.

Ostensibly the reason for Frank's apparent lack of sympathy with modernism came from his view of civilization, namely that humanity was not made for authoritarianism. He argued that in the long run we cannot tolerate extremes but are psychologically impaired by them. We need a measure of calm, comfort, and stability. The golden mean suits us best. Frank finds the antithesis of the fidgety, hurried, amusement-hungry, news-thirsty, changeable, short-sighted contemporary European in the East Asian.

**The Wisdom of the Chinese.** Frank takes a romantic view of the "slow" civilization of the Chinese and Japanese. Like a lyrical storyteller, he describes the simple Asian artifact that has had the same form and same production process for centuries. It is continuity and variation that count, neither invention of new forms nor changes in fashion. It is not linear but cyclical time that prevails. He pronounces that for Asians all things in nature are interrelated through reincarnation, constantly exchanging shapes with one another in successive lives. In the Japanese tea ceremony, the participants attain absolute classlessness in a ritual admiration of the beauty of the artifacts used in the ceremony. Even in 1930, Frank's description was no longer entirely valid. But this does not matter, for the chapters about East Asia contain his second confession of identity.

The contemplation of nature and artifacts provides a means of escape from Frank's view of the European dilemma, a faltering guide leading away from modern technology, economic speculation, and the class struggle over status symbols, an emancipation from the unnecessary caprices of style. Otherwise the only thing one has to go by is proportion—the harmony of the parts with each other and with the whole—which according to Frank is the ancient criterion of good architecture. The vexing nineteenth-century question, "in which style are we to build?" can, Frank tells us, be safely forgotten. Instead he advises: "Our time is the whole of the historical time known to us." This is a remarkable thesis.

Frank never fully experienced what in Sweden was known as the Million Homes Program. This project, which was mirrored in other countries around the globe, was a social housing program of the 1960s and 1970s that fostered the building of huge boxlike apartment blocks, with government funds, on the outskirts of major cities. Most of the residents were from underprivileged backgrounds, and these projects, often with an inferior infrastructure, many times became nothing more than new ghettos. It was exactly this kind of "functionalism," without alternative, private initiatives, that Frank feared would come out of a govern-

ment-regulated housing program. Those areas (such as the Banlieu outside Paris) "have come to symbolize segregation, tedium, and potentially violent teenagers." They are today a great social problem in Europe, and Frank was prophetic by having early premonitions about the drawbacks to this type of public housing. The home, to him, was the great building issue of the twentieth century. His declarations that the aircraft, on the whole, was a worthless trinket and that the tower block an archaism were to be disproved by events, but his protest against Eurocentrism and his protectionist attitude toward nature versus industrial overuse were farsighted in 1930.

In 1941 Frank left a Sweden threatened by Nazis, having been invited to lecture at the New School for Social Research in New York. While in New York he had *Architektur als Symbol* translated by his Austrian friend Trude Waehner, who was also living in New York, but the publisher Alfred Knopf did not believe it would interest American readers and it was never published. This is hardly surprising. The International Style had been launched in America largely under the auspices of the Museum of Modern Art in New York while at the same time it was suppressed in Germany by the Nazis. In addition its principal exponents—Gropius, Mies van der Rohe, Breuer, and other former Bauhaus professors—were now living and working in the States. These circumstances meant that it was not a popular target of criticism in the United States at the time.

*Architektur als Symbol* is not a scientifically based book. It is subjective and tendentious. It is entertaining and incites resistance. Sometimes it is hard to take seriously, but it should be taken seriously. Architecture has always been, *par excellence*, the outward and visible sign of ideologies, classes, and economies.

# 7. "STEEL IS NOT A RAW MATERIAL; THE EARLY FURNITURE DESIGNS

Christian Witt-Dörring

> Forms are symbols of will and attitude.
> *Josef Frank*[1]

This is the first American exhibition to give an in-depth examination to furniture designed by Josef Frank. That this should occur so late in the century makes one wonder at its relevance. How can Frank's long absence from the study of the history of modern furniture be explained?

Part of the answer lies in the American values that have long influenced the field of furniture history. I would argue that twentieth-century modern furniture is judged in the U.S. according to two main factors. In the first place, France is viewed as the great model for the production of high-style luxury furniture; and secondly, "modern" furniture—that which was designed during the period from the 1920s to the 1950s—is evaluated almost exclusively on the basis of criteria introduced in American beginning in the 1930s through the teachings and work of Mies van der Rohe, Walter Gropius, and László Moholy-Nagy.[2] Josef Frank's furniture eludes both categories: it belongs neither to the conservative nor the "progressive," modern camp. Its quality lies in its unspectacular design; these are personal rather than art objects. Much like the furniture of Adolf Loos, it is, therefore, ill-suited to the "masterpiece presentation" typically displayed in American museum collections.

Removed from its cultural and personal context, it raises more questions than it answers. Those who know Frank's furniture and interiors only from black-and-white illustrations in period publications[3]—today often the only means of introduction—do not realize his very conscious use of color contrast and evocative materials. But this additional information is needed to complete the two-dimensional form, to breathe life into it and give it shape. Finally, Frank's theoretical text, *Architektur als Symbol*,[4] one of the most important keys to understanding his oeuvre, has not been translated into English, making it inaccessible to many in the English-speaking world.

Frank's ideas for furniture and their subsequent realization were the direct result of his reassessment of Vienna's fin-de-siècle architectural opposites of the day: Adolf Loos and Josef Hoffmann. Frank was nonetheless a member of the next generation of architects, one that primarily saw itself confronted with the new political, social, and economic realities of the tiny remains of an empire that had become the new Austrian state after the First World War.[5] By this time furniture was no longer regarded as a means of expressing wealth and status, but rather

# STEEL IS A *WELTANSCHAUUNG*":
# OF JOSEF FRANK, 1910–1933

Fig. 7-1. Exhibition of Swedish Folk Art and Cottage Industries at the Österreichisches Museum für angewandte Kunst, Vienna, 1910. The exhibition mainly featured textiles, whose patterns and colors served as sources of inspiration for Frank's ornamental details in the Swedish Gymnasium, the Austrian Applied Arts Exhibition of 1911/12, and the Tedesco apartment textiles.
MAK, Museum of Applied Arts, Vienna, model
collection, inv. no. 7754)

Fig. 7-2. Dining room of the Tedesco Apartment, Vienna, 1910. The clear horizontal alignment of the room, achieved by isolating floor, wall, and ceiling (as well as through the horizontal line of the pictures and the low height of the case pieces), is reminiscent of Biedermeier interiors. "The use of many pure, unbroken colors allows each newly added color to achieve its full effect without detracting from those already there. . . . [T]hus, for example . . . blue and green are used for the ceiling, the tablecloth [is] a splendid red, the carpet black and blue" (Oskar Wlach, "Zu den Arbeiten Josef Frank," *Das Interieur* 13 [1912], p. 43). (Photograph from Max Eisler, *Österr. Werkkultur* [Vienna, 1916], p. 89)

Fig. 7-3. Ladies' drawing room from the Tedesco Apartment, Vienna, 1910. Commenting on the Tedesco apartment, Oskar Wlach wrote, "The only fixed things in the living room are its boundaries: ceiling, walls, and floor. All the objects in the room have to appear to be mobile, regardless of whether they are its inhabitants or its furniture. The walls are boundaries within which all things are subject to the changing needs and moods of the human [inhabitant]. Such things must not resist serving free human desires and chance needs for the sake of a rigid principle of superficial architectural composition" (Oskar Wlach, "Zu den Arbeiten Josef Frank," *Das Interieur* 13 [1912], p. 43). (Photograph from Max Eisler, *Österr. Werkkultur* (Vienna, 1916), p. 87)

Fig. 7-4. Dining room chairs from the Tedesco Apartment, Vienna, 1910. "The cupboards for clothing or linen, the buffets, sideboards, bookcases, etc. must have different designs which are not arbitrary, but logical extensions of their various requirements. The same goes for furniture, which is only used for the same purpose and in the same shape in the dining room" (Oskar Wlach, "Zu den Arbeiten Josef Frank," *Das Interieur* 13 [1912], p. 43 and pl. 45).

it was viewed as an end unto itself. And so humankind became central to Frank's design work. It was his profound belief that a person's everyday environment should not be constrained by furniture ensembles and severe geometric shapes. Rather, according to Frank, the interior should be furnished with so-called "organic" forms that gave the impression of having come into existence as part of the process of living, of having evolved naturally.[6] His insistence on these two points is what most clearly distinguishes his furniture designs from those of his contemporaries.

As early as 1910, four years before the outbreak of World War I, Frank's first interior design commission foreshadows important elements of his later development. In the apartment he furnished for his sister Hedwig and her husband Carl Tedesco,[7] he broke with the kind of unified interior décor so typical of the period. The concept of the *Gesamtkunstwerk*, which unites fixed and mobile furnishings in one decorative system, was championed especially by Josef Hoffmann in his work with the Wiener Werkstätte. The same concept was vehemently criticized by Adolf Loos from the time of its inception in 1903. Loos regarded the

*Gesamtkunstwerk* in architectural and interior work as an unacceptable appropriation of the rights of the individual.[8] But Frank went even further than Loos. He not only released the free-standing furnishings and eliminated the connection between the architecture and interior decoration, but he gave the various elements, especially the furniture, individual traits.[9]

While the furnishings for Carl Tedesco's own room were all finished in the same wood-grained veneer, elsewhere, for example in the dining room, furniture of varying styles and material qualities was used. Frank combined Neoclassical and folk-art motifs in the case pieces—buffet, silver cabinet, and sideboard. The high-backed chairs were a direct interpretation of Italian Renaissance models, and the dining table owed its form to Viennese modernism. The result was like a stroll through the cultural history of mankind. Supported by the knowledge he acquired while an architecture student at the Vienna Technische Hochschule, Frank was able to design freely and cite sources with self-assurance.[10]

Concurrent with Frank's interest in historical forms,

Fig. 7-5. View into Room 2 of the Austrian Applied Arts Exhibition at the Österreichischen Museums für Kunst und Industrie (Austrian Museum for Art and Industry), Vienna, 1911/12. In the catalogue for the Applied Arts Exhibition the room is listed as the collaborative effort of architects Josef Frank, Hugo Gorge, Victor Lurje, and Oskar Strnad. With the exception of Gorge, all had studied at the Vienna Technische Hochschule. Within their circle— broadened by the addition of Oscar Wlach—ideas for a new kind of Viennese interior were born in the period between the wars. This view of the space shows painted and metal-laminated furniture designed by Frank and positioned in front of a simple white wall which makes the room appear larger and also serves as a neutral background that shows off the forms and colors of the furniture. The dark-colored ceiling contrasts with the wall, creating a reduced, more human scale. (Photograph, MAK, Museum of Applied Arts, Vienna, model collection, inv. no. 7826/10)

beginning in 1905 there was a general renewal of interest in period furniture in Vienna.[11] This in part formed the foundation for Frank's subsequent subjective, occasionally contradictory approach to the course of history. In *Architectur als Symbol* he makes reference to history over and over again to support his theories: ". . . but history is not there to be understood correctly; it must act as a raw material for science and the arts, from which they may take what they require."[12] Nevertheless, this call for a generous evaluation of history is quickly contrasted with an equally impassioned demand for precise historical consciousness: "But how shall we recognize them [traditional forms] if we consider tradition the unconscious affinity for form—form here understood as a way of thinking—and the use this form necessitates?"[13]

Like Loos, Frank rejected the search for new forms for novelty's sake alone. If humankind in the course of its cultural history had developed certain tried-and-true solu-

tions, then there could be no reason to replace them simply because of their age.[14] "Perfection leaves us no room for collaboration, and this makes it difficult to bear. Thus we feel the easily explicable desire to create new things our of a void, although we [must] recognize that in doing so we go down the same path three times over, a path which breaks off at ever the same spot."[15]

The dining room chairs of the Tedesco apartment must be understood as an outgrowth of this conviction no matter how historically obsequious they may at first appear. The typical high-backed shape of the dining room chair here adopted the appearance of a Renaissance chair; it has been slightly altered, "redesigned" as it were, by toning down its monumentality through a reduction in the cross-section of the legs and back. At the same time, the leather upholstery has been made more comfortable to the sitter. Instead of being tightly stretched over all four sides of the apron, the leather strip is only stretched over its lateral

Fig. 7-6. Josef Frank, "Living Hall of a Country House," Room 13 of the Frühjahrsausstellung (Spring Exhibition), Österreichischen Museums für Kunst und Industrie, Vienna, 1912. With the exception of an inlaid oak bookcase by J. Müller, all the furnishings in the room were done in cherry wood. Their forms were influenced by English models like those made by Sidney and Ernest Barnsley and Ernest Gimson in the Cotswolds at the turn of the century. This applies, in particular, to the reuse of the ladderback chair, a type of seating furniture from the seventeenth century. (Photograph, MAK, Museum of Applied Arts, Vienna, model collection, inv. no. 7835)

sides, which are rounded off at the top. In this way the leather has enough latitude to adjust to the human form; the rounded apron also prevents it from breaking too easily. Solutions such as these, which owe their existence to the creative use of historical information, caused conservatives and progressive alike to be suspicious of Frank: he defied definitive categorization.

In the Tedesco interior the unifying introduction of a "horizon"—in the form of a wall covering—represented a final attempt to integrate the wall into the interior. In contrast the walls and furnishings of a residential hall, shown at the Frühjahrsausstellung (Spring Exhibition), of the Österreichischen Museums für Kunst und Industrie in 1912 were distinctly independent of each other. Frank moved farther way from a rigid spatial concept, liberating even the floor plan. He was the only exhibitor to rotate his installation out of the axis of the enfilade of displays, thus forcing viewers to experience actively, rather than unconsciously consume his "living hall."[16] Frank took a completely new approach in its furnishings as well, and, in so doing, made a final break with the tradition of Viennese modernism. All the decorative and stereometric details of Viennese modernism which had persisted in the furniture he designed for the Tedesco residence disappeared. Entirely different aspects of the original, most important inspirational source of Viennese modernism—Anglo-Saxon culture—had gained significance.

Frank discovered the simple Puritan element of English colonial furniture and the world of Scandinavian interiors.[17] Accordingly, his furniture bears the strong influence of contemporary English work, such as Ernest Gimson, who, in turn, had borrowed heavily from the eighteenth century in his designs. In addition, Frank hung watercolors by Swedish painter Carl Larsson on the walls of the exhibition space.[18] (Around 1910 Larsson's depictions of interiors were the subject of illustrated publications and

Fig. 7-10. Josef Frank, Living Room of the Bunzl House, Ortmann/Lower Austria, 1914. The interior of this log house, designed and furnished by Frank, once again shows the strong influence of English interior design ideas. In 1919 Frank himself commented on this photograph, "The apartment of a person lacking feeling—an apartment into which an architect has imported the loveliest objects and tastefully and symmetrically arranged or hung them—will always remain cold and austere, even if these lovely things are always returned to the very same positions. The living room is never unfinished, just as it is never finished; it lives along with its human inhabitants" (Josef Frank, "Die Einrichtung des Wohnzimmers," *Innen-Dekoration* 30 (1919), p. 417 and photograph p. 413).

"The house . . . is an end unto itself and, through its existence, brings people happiness; each of its parts must contribute to their pleasure"[32]; or, "The architectural idea of our time! Where is the idea revealing the incredible diversity of desires, revealing the will of the individual—who has concealed it as mere purpose? With the help of historical hindsight we will see that only a building without purpose—a building which is an end unto itself—is capable of expressing it. Any purpose destroys the idea and replaces it with money."[33] Frank extricated himself from the constraints of an overemphasis on structural and material (artisan) values in order to place the artistic, creative process in the foreground.[34]

He devoted large portions of *Architektur als Symbol* to this conviction.[35] Frank's studies of Leone Battista Alberti and his internship with Bruno Möhring in Berlin were certainly influential in this regard.[36] And it was in this spirit during the early 1920s—after his collaborative effort with Oskar Strnad ended in 1919[37]—that Frank developed the unique furniture forms to which he remained true until the end of his life. His explanation in *Architektur als Symbol* takes a cultural historical detour: "The will to achieve the necessary form was primary, the material served this will."[38] Ultimately, however, it leads to the question, at the conclusion of the book, "who can discern whether or not all that we construct is influenced by the formal tradition within these rules [of the Semper School]?"[39] With this question Frank reestablished the Rieglian notion of *Kunstwollen*, which the ideal of the "living, organic form"[40] evolved,

over function and material. Neither the ornament nor formalism can affect his ideal since "the ornament has always destroyed the form."[41] By taking this standpoint Frank took the next logical step after the accomplishments of the Ver Sacrum group. He countered the design of furniture based on cubes and stereometric shapes and its call for integrity of materials, with a seat shaped to fit the human body and the "blasphemous" though deliberate use of ersatz materials.[42] The freedom he gained by doing so added to his furniture designs: seating furniture or lamps, for examples, whose organic, "living forms" became spatial ornaments; or a table whose top consisted of a slab of cross-cut wood with a free-edge; or a case piece whose surface was covered with glued-on engravings or fabric. His various designs for canopy beds, the complicated, profiled surfaces of his chests, and the variety of his designs for seating furniture in combination with fanciful textiles, all must have appeared anachronistic to his modern contemporaries.

To make his furniture and interior design ideas available to a larger public, Josef Frank founded the furnishings and accessories firm "Haus und Garten & Co."[43] in 1925 together with Oskar Wlach and Walter Sobotka. (Although his own designs were sold in Vienna, production was farmed out to individual artisans.) A year later, on January 22, 1926, the firm was renamed "Haus & Garten, Frank & Wlach" after Walter Sobotka's departure. Haus & Garten fostered an eclectic modernism encouraging customers to arrange their interiors piecemeal using modern furnishings

Fig. 7-11. Josef Frank, dressing table and small chest of drawers with a wall mirror. These furniture designs were among nine illustrating Frank's programmatic essay "Einzelmöbel und Kunsthandwerk" (The individual piece of furniture and artistic handicrafts), in which he refers in particular to the independent and exemplary English furniture tradition—a tradition lacking in the Austrian culture. Once again Frank drew from English ideas which he felt allowed the expression of forms that had evolved naturally. (Photograph from *Innen-Dekoration* 34 [1923], p. 342)

Fig. 7-12. Josef Frank, bedroom, H. and M. Blitz Apartment, Vienna, 1928. According to Ernst A. Plischke, one of the leading Austrian architects in the years between the wars, the Blitz apartment, which was in a nineteenth-century Ringstrasse building, was considered one of the most striking of Frank's interiors. Plischke worked in the Frank atelier in in the late twenties; he compared Frank's work with that of Josef Hoffmann and Dagobert Peche: "Frank's designs were, in contrast, light, transparent, sometimes even playful. Furniture, for example, was situated randomly in the living room, as though by chance. There was neither axis or symmetry. As curtains, the colorful cretonnes of his design further livened up the room, just as they did the individual furnishings when used as fabrics for upholstery" (Johannes Spalt and Hermann Czech, eds., *Josef Frank, 1885–1967*, exhib. cat. (Vienna: Hochschule für angewandte Kunst, 1981). (Photograph from *Innen-Dekoration* 39 (1928), p. 466)

Fig. 7-13. Josef Frank, living room of the Beer House, Vienna, 1930. Criticizing the large immovable wardrobe, which he characterized as a "room within a room," Frank wrote, "When the 'room within a room' disappears, the entire [concept of an] 'interior layout' with 'furniture' disappears with it. For otherwise only movable 'tables' and 'chairs' remain, and they have no influence on things, since their positions are arbitrary—they have no fixed place. This is why each of these pieces must be independent of the rest, obstructing nothing and only giving the impression of belonging together as a 'group' in this particular context. We no longer need 'sets' consisting of two inseparable easy chairs, a couch, and a table" (Josef Frank, "Einzelmöbel und Kunsthandwerk," *Innen-Dekoration* 34 [1923], p.338). (Photograph from *Innen-Dekoration* 42 [1931], p. 375)

Fig. 7-14. Josef Frank, living room of the A. W. House, Vienna, ca. 1933/34. Describing the qualities of this space, Heinrich Ritter wrote: "the various woods—walnut, mahogany, Swedish birch—and with them the fabrics, bring color to the space, just as the large windows give it light (which is regulated with the help of translucent curtains). The flowered upholstery of the chairs stands out against the tranquillity of the floors and walls; gridlike or woven chair backs and slender furniture supports allow the room to be taken in as a whole, and give it an impression of lightness. The furniture on the whole is kept to a medium height, which allows the human inhabitant to appear as 'master' of the space. This room not only pleases the eye—it provides intellectual satisfaction" (Heinrich Ritter, "Neue Wohnungen von 'Haus und Garten'," *Innen-Dekoration* 45 [1934], p. 375 and photograph p. 330)

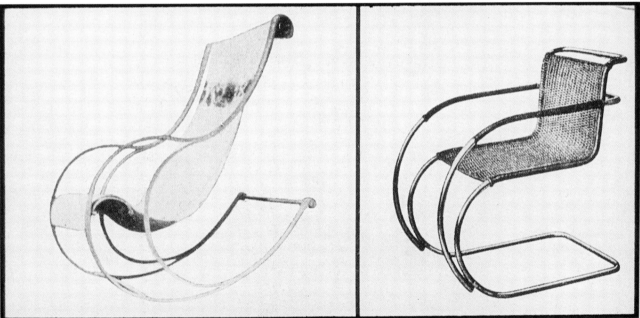

Fig. 7-15. Slides to Josef Frank's lectures: comparison of English easy chairs (*top*) with tubular steel Chair MR 34 by Mies van der Rohe (1927; *bottom right*) and an English rocking chair in iron (second half of the 19th century; *bottom left*). "Without in any way wishing to deny the virtues of the metal chair, which have certainly been amply demonstrated over the course of two thousand years of its use, one might nonetheless add that the comfort provided by a chair has nothing to do with the material of its frame, but is, instead, a result of its dimensions. Its natural shape, therefore, [should be] the same in metal as in wood" (Josef Frank, *Architektur als Symbol*, p. 130). (Photographs, Architekturmuseet Stockholm; inv. no. 1968-102-88 and 81)

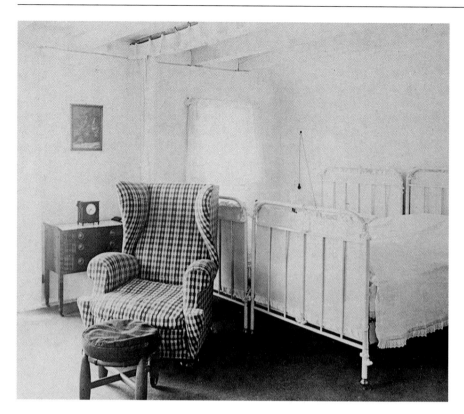

Fig. 7-16. Slides to Josef Frank's lectures: comparison of the bedroom of the Bunzl House, Ortmann/Lower Austria (1914; *left*) and an unidentified English example (*below*) from the turn of the century. Frank wrote, "If the English place a Windsor or Adam chair in a room, no one will take notice. But when we use a piece of furniture from the same period, it looks like an antique: it may seem stylish or cozy or pleasant, but it certainly will not seem self-evident" ("Einzenmöbel und Kunsthandwerk," *Innen-Dekoration* 34 [1923], p. 337). (Photographs, Architekturmuseet Stockholm; inv. no. 1968-102-74 and 44)

chosen and matched at will—something that had been, until then, acceptable only with antiques. The customer was no longer forced into a one-time purchase of a dining-room, living-room, or bedroom suite. Frank may have been inspired to this undertaking by the Wiener Werkstätte which was in business at the same time, but their philosophies were different. The Wiener Werkstätte did not promote individual pieces of furniture. Frank became familiar

with the product philosophy of the Werkstätte when he worked there as an occasional collaborator between 1916 and 1919. Fabric patterns, metal objects, and furniture mounts are known to have been designed by him during these years.[44] The end of his collaboration with the Wiener Werkstätte is also marked by the publication of an article outlining his program: "The Furnishing of the Living Room."[45] In it he promotes the design of a living

Fig. 7-17. Slide to Josef Frank's lectures: an unidentified English or American living room from the turn of the century. "There are yet today (without passing judgment on the value of these things) enough people who have certain attachments to the old forms. America has proven to us that any house, even the most comfortable one, can be built in any given style without forfeiting even a bit of its comfort" (Josef Frank, *Architektur als Symbol*, p. 135). (Photograph, Architekturmuseet Stockholm; inv. no. 1968-102-72)

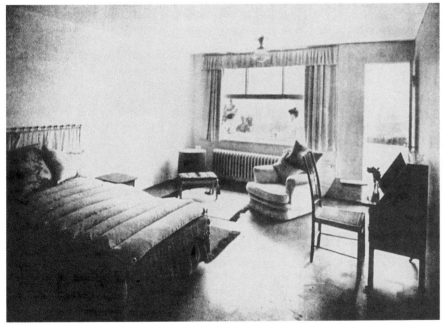

Fig. 7-18. Slide to Josef Frank's lectures: living room in Josef Frank's house in the Weissenhofsiedlung in Stuttgart, 1927. While the architectural concept of Frank's "settlement houses" in the Stuttgart exhibition met with the approval of the "moderns," the interiors he designed for them were criticized as being too "feminine" or bourgeois. Frank justified his mixture of industrial and hand-crafted furnishings, writing: "No one can live the high life at all times; everyone possesses a certain measure of sentimentality which must be satisfied" (Josef Frank, "Der Gschnas fürs G'müt und der Gschnas als Problem," *Bau und Wohnung* [1927], p. 48). (Photograph, Architekturmuseet Stockholm; inv. no. 1968-102-32)

room that develops and is furnished over time, through use, as opposed to the kind of unified interior an architect might have designed.[46] Frank took a clear stand against the treacherous attempt to create a unity between, or a transition to, inherited furnishings[47] from the reality of industrial products in the form of objects made by artisans after architect designs.

Given his mistrust of architect-designed environments, why did Frank nonetheless design furniture for his clients and go so far as to found his own firm to sell and distribute furnishings? Frank offers purely practical reasons:

"That an architect should be forced to design the furniture for a given purpose is simply a further indication of just how little unified today's formal approach is."[48] (The formal approach was once "superficially" unified by the concept of the furniture "en suite"; a conceptual unity stressing the value of individual pieces did not yet exist in the marketplace. Thus, an architect who favored the use of individual pieces had to design his own if they were to work together.) Furthermore, Frank was in no way threatened by the machine as a means of production. It only became a threat, he claimed, when the worker allowed himself to be governed by it and stopped thinking about what it was actually there for: to relieve the artisan of the "worthless" part of the work.[49] Frank thus acknowledges the industrial reality of the twentieth century. The so-called old-fashioned atmosphere quality of the artisan-produced pieces, with their French-polished surfaces, elaborately curved arms, and lovingly rounded edges, owes its existence to the possibilities introduced by the machine dovetail (*Maschinensinke*), as well as razor-cut veneer and laminated or plywood board.

In his work Frank always addressed the questions of his time. Whether his furniture conforms to our understanding of modernity or not is irrelevant. He tried to convince his public by means of the unspectacular or, as he called it, the "meaningless banality"[50] of daily life which transcends fashion; in so doing he hoped to allow a new culture of tradition in furniture to grow. The political events of 1934 and 1938 left him too little time.[51] And so that tradition grew elsewhere—in Scandinavia, its humanist homeland.

Editor's note: There are no in-text figure references in this chapter; the captions to the illustrations constitute a parallel text. The Frank quotation in the chapter title includes the word *Weltanschauung*, which loosely translates to mean "world view," "philosophy of life," or "ideology"; for the source of the quotation, see below, n. 26.

1. Josef Frank, "Gespräch über den Werkbund," in *Österreichischer Werkbund 1929* (Vienna: Verlag der Österreichischer Werkbund, 1929), p. 12.

2. Frank himself comments on this in a letter written from New York: "thus I take little pleasure in things produced 'in the spirit of our time,' be they local fashions or Bauhaus, which, by the way, has enjoyed an unbelievable success here. [Its proponents] have occupied all the teaching positions in the schools and, by these means, the entire artistic ideology here (inasmuch as such a thing exists). Their profound speculations are now being used in the realm of fashion" (Frank, letter to Mr. Lampl, December 28, 1946, Handschriftensammlung der Österreichischen Nationalbibliothek, Vienna).

3. See, especially, the German-language magazines: *Deutsche Kunst und Dekoration, Innen-Dekoration, Das Interieur,* and *Moderne Bauformen.*

4. Josef Frank, *Architektur als Symbol: Elemente deutschen neuen Bauens* (Vienna: Anton Schroll, 1931); reprint (Vienna: Löcker, 1981); translated into Swedish in 1995.

5. Frank began *Architektur als Symbol* with a chapter entitled "Nach Kriegen" (After wars).

6. ". . . but instead a striving toward the organic fashioning of inanimate matter; as long as man is the measure of all things, this tradition must continue to govern our culture" (Frank, *Architektur* [reprint, 1981], p. 22).

7. Hedwig Frank (1887–1966) married the industrialist Carl Tedesco on November 6, 1910.

8. See, for example, "Die Geschichte vom armen reichen Mann," in Adolf Loos, *Ins Locre gesprochen* (Vienna: Herold, 1962), pp. 201–207.

9. Oskar Wlach, "Zu den Arbeiten Josef Franks," *Das Interieur* 13 (1912), pp. 40–45. Frank, *Architektur,* p. 166: "The delusion of the uniformity of form, the eternal ensemble, the dictates of outdated decorative arts as a closed system are unchanged, and [the decorative artist] cannot seem to grasp the fact of how much more varied our lives have become, how everything that exists much subordinate itself to this way of living; our time is the whole of the historical time known to us"; and "I will choose an example from the jumble of the modern endeavor to archaicize . . . the *Gesamtkunstwerk* . . . was the attempt to lower art to the level of the decorative arts."

10. Maria Welzig, "Die Wiener Internationalität des Josef Frank: Das

Werk des Architekten bis 1938," Ph.D. diss. (University of Vienna, 1994), pp. 12–20.

11. Christopher Long, "Josef Frank and the Crisis of Modern Architecture," Ph.D. diss. (University of Texas at Austin, 1993), p. 36.

12. Frank, *Architektur,* p. 172.

13. Ibid., p. 184

14. Ibid., p. 31: "This is the eternal endeavor of mankind: to invent new things before even having comprehended existing ones."

15. Ibid., p. 181.

16. In the Beer House (1929–31), built in Vienna's 13th district (Wenzgasse 13), this spatial demand achieves its ultimate realization. On its completion Frank published an essay on the subject: "Das Haus als Weg und Platz," *Der Baumeister* 29 (1931), p. 316–23.

17. The slides to Frank's lectures, now in the Museum of Architecture, Stockholm, include a large number of English and American examples.

18. Benotto, "Frühjahrausstellung im Österreichischen Museum," *Das Interieur* 13 (1912), p. 60.

19. Carl Larsson, *Lasst Licht hineln: Ein Buch von Wohnzimmern, von Kindern, von Dir, von Blumen, von Allern* (Stockholm and Leipzig: Albert Bonnier, 1911).

20. In 1910 the Austrian Museum for Art and Industry presented an exhibition on Swedish folk art and home industry. See Long, "Josef Frank," pp. 43–44; and Welzig, "Die Wiener Internationalität des Josef Frank," pp. 62–65.

21. Frank, *Architektur,* p. 52: "Let it here be said that our tradition is in no way based on forms, as the folk artist and his antipode, the worshiper of the machine, believe. Rather, our tradition goes back to the early conceps and fundamental ideas of Classical architecture, which places the human being at the center of the world." And see above, n. 5.

22. Time and again Frank refers to historical developments to explain the state of things. He tries to arrive at a cultural consciousness for Austria by understanding one's own history. Among other things, he wrote, "If by tradition one means continuity of thought and the renunciation of patently fashionable sensations, then we are certainly for it." See Frank, "Gespräch," p. 3.

23. Frank, *Architektur,* p. 20.

24. *Innen-Dekoration* 34 (1923), p. 337ff.

25. He describes this as "systemzatized taste" (Frank, *Architektur,* p. 171f) and "upswing" (ibid., p. 125–28); he also wrote, "Today it is impossible to invent a kind of national art. The attempt—hidden in the guise of

striving for internationalism—to help German art along to victory by basing it on absolute ethics (which are unknown elsewhere) cannot succeed" (ibid., p. 175).

26. "What good is the tubular steel chair to us as long as our way of living is still founded on furniture 'ensembles'? . . . Steel is not a raw material; it's a *Weltanschauung*. These chairs were actually thought up to serve as seats for reparations commissioners, to show them the solemn seriousness of the German endeavor" (ibid., p. 131.ff).

27. "[Savonarola] was naturally ill-disposed toward any assertion of joy in life, as he espoused an absolute Puritanical ideal unbearable to humansin the long run. Again today this Puritanical ideal is often cited, as it offers the opportunity to postulate something absolute which can not only be explained with words, but, moreover, can be proven; this gives its disciples a moral stronghold from which they may disdainfully reject anything which is different" (ibid., p. 89).

28. Ibid., pp. 133ff.

29. "Luther, the Renaissance man, tried to mediate, and he succeeded in rescuing one side of religion. He failed with the arts, however; they withered next to the thriving religious idea which one dared not form into a likeness" (ibid., p. 90). Elsewhere Frank wrote, "A: Don't you think, though, that we overestimate form? B: . . . forms are symbols of will and attitude. Don't underestimate that. And clarity and harmony are goals worth working toward. Consider how easily one is irritated merely by a room with poor proportions and the wrong color. To give as much happiness as possible to as many people as possible is, after all, a beautiful goal, even if we are only involved in one part of the task" (Frank, "Gespräch," p. 12).

30. "But indifference toward unimportant things, the knowledge of the plurality of our world, the recognition of our entirely justified emotional values is part of the foundation of modern life and its symbols, of modern architecture. There are yet today (without passing judgment on the value of these things) enough people who have certain attachments to the old forms. For form and content have little to do with one another. America has proven to us that any house, even the most comfortable one, can be built in any given style without forfeiting even a bit of its comfort. The secure and clear lifestyle of their occupants makes such houses far superior to our formal trifles (Frank, *Architektur*, p. 135).

31. In the waning years of eclecticism Otto Wagner (1841–1918), the father of the Ver Sacrum movement at the turn of the century, defined the style of the upcoming age as the future use-oriented style. In his programmatic book, *Moderne Architektur* (Vienna: Schroll, 1895; fourth edition, 1913) he discribed the path leading to this goal. He thus created the theoretical and formal requisites for the making of modern applied arts in the twentieth century. Wagner lists four points, not unlike a recipe: "I. Painstakingly detailed understanding and perfect fulfillment of the purpose . . . / II. Correct choice of material (ergo easily available, easy to work with, durable, economical. / III. Simple and economical construction and, only after taking these three main points into consideration, / IV. The development of the form from these premises (practically draws itself and is always readily comprehensible)" (p. 135ff).

32. Frank, *Architektur*, p. 174.

33. Ibid., p. 173.

34. "The pecular thing about any type of classical art is that, from the moment it overcomes primitivism it no longer thinks in terms of material (which can only be an obstacle to its expressivity). It seeks organic expression and starts with the form, a fact many architects nowadays are ashamed to admit. . ." (ibid., p. 47).

35. The chapters, "Der Mensch das Mass aller Dinge" (The human being as the measure of all things) and "A und O" are expecially worth mention.

36. According to Alberti, "the plans are not bound to matter; they are conceived in spirit, without regard to the material" (cited in Welzig, "Die Wiener Internationalität des Josef Frank," p. 21, n. 1); Möhring wrote, "A process has been repeated here analagous to that artisan view which, unfortunately, has yet to be overcome—it attempts to explain art through technical analysis, and is, nonetheless, able to muster but a marginal interest in that secondary side of artistic creation which may be acquired through study" (cited in ibid., p. 26).

37. Oskar Strnad (1879–1935), who was somewhat older than Frank, must be seen as one of the spiritual leaders of the renewal of Viennese modernism around 1910. See ibid., pp. 37–47.

38. Frank, *Architektur*, p. 26.

39. Ibid., p. 184. For further reading on Gottfried Semper and this problem, see Otto Wagner, "Die Baukunst unserer Zeit," p. 58. Werner Oechslin, *Stilhülse und Kern: Otto Wagner, Adolf Loos und der evolutionäre Weg zur modernen Architektur* (Zurich, Ernst & Sohn, 1994).

40. "Regard the artist; without even once looking up, he draws his flourishes and ith dull fantasy and infinite diligence, and without knowing that there is something else. . . . The work of a man, leading to no result, since he's looking for things that already exist, namely the organic form" (ibid., p. 28).

41. Ibid., p. 27.

42. Ibid., p. 132ff.

43. Central registration archives of the city of Vienna (MA 63); commercial law recording, June 6, 1925; professional registration, July 29, 1925 at Bösendorferstrasse 5, Vienna I.

44. Frank's first work for the WW was the fabric design "Schöpfung" (Creation); see Angela Völker, *Die Stoffe der Wiener Werkstätte, 1910-1932* (Vienna: Brandstätter Verlag, 1987), p. 217. Further designs for fabrics, bowls, boxes with lids, and a bread board with knife are in the drawing collection of the Österreichisches Museum für angewandte Kunst, Vienna.

45. Josef Frank, "Die Einrichtung des Wohnzimmers," *Innen-Dekoration* 30 (1919), pp. 416ff.

46. "The living room is never unfinished, just as it is never finished; it lives together with those who dwell in it" (ibid.); with these words Frank assumes a position formerly taken by Adolf Loos. See Adolf Loos, *Ins Leere gesprochen* (Vienna: Herold, 1962), p. 56.

47. The writing desk for the living room of Frank's sister Hedwig is interesting in this context. In essence it is a Viennese Josefinian piece dating to the end of the eighteenth century; Frank redesigned its body, marquetry, and mounts, work which was accomplished by the cabinetmaker and restorer, Franz Krejei, at Gusshausstrasse 16, Vienna IV (*Das Interieur* 13 [1912], pl. 43).

48. Josef Frank, "Das neuzeitliche Landhaus," *Innen-Dekoration* 30 (1919), p. 415.

49. Frank, *Architektur*, p. 110ff.

50. Ernst A. Plischke, "Josef Frank, wie ich ihn kannte," in *Josef Frank, 1885–1967*, ed. J. Spalt and Hermann Czech (Vienna, 1981), p. 8.

51. Civil war in Austria began in 1934, just after Frank's immigration to Sweden. In 1938 Austria was annexed by Hitler's Germany.

# 8. "CONVENIENCE AND
# AND THE SWEDISH MODERN

Penny Sparke

I n 1939 Estrid Ericson, owner of Svenskt Tenn in Stockholm's Strandvägen, which was renowned at the time for its innovative interior furnishings, outlined her criteria for successful interior decoration, concluding that ". . . the modern home, therefore, will be a mixture of items, some more expensive than others, and they do not have to match. . . . Convenience and pleasantness, quite simply, are the main considerations."[1] A year earlier Swedish furniture designer G. A. Berg had used similar words in an attempt to define the concept of "Swedish Modern," a term used in the late 1930s to denote Sweden's unique contribution to the modern movement in design. "Interiors of today," Berg had explained, "are characterized with sun, air, flowers and color, with harmony, simplicity, comfort and pleasantness, cleanliness and purity."[2]

Berg's statement makes interesting reading in the context of modern architecture and design as it was then understood.[3] Rooted in propositions put forward by, among others, Le Corbusier, Walter Gropius, Mies van der Rohe, and numerous other practitioners in Europe and the United States, the ideologues of modernism could have aligned themselves with some of Berg's claims without reservation, with, for example, the importance of "sun," "air," "simplicity," and "cleanliness and purity." They likely would have felt less happy, however, with Berg's inclusion of other features of the Swedish Modern phenomenon. "Flowers and colour," "harmony," and "comfort and pleasantness" were undoubtedly less central to these architects' program of radical reform. They were more concerned with the utilitarian and rationalizing aspects of architecture than its aesthetic, psychological, and symbolic functions.

For Berg, therefore, Swedish Modern was a hybrid philosophy of design, embracing some of the tenets of modernism but also containing its own clear agenda, rooted in an alternative set of propositions. Ericson's statement, which paralleled Berg's so closely, provides a clue to Sweden's unique contribution to modern design beginning in the 1930s. She had taken many of her ideas from the Viennese architect and designer, Josef Frank, whom she had since 1934 as chief designer for Svenskt Tenn in Stockholm, producing furniture and textiles. Much of his work originated in designs he had created for his interior design firm, Haus & Garten, in Vienna. Many of the printed textile patterns such as "Aralia," "Primavera," "Mirakel," and others that came to be familiar Svenskt Tenn products, as well as a large number of furnishings, had been designed by Frank in the 1920s. Some of them were to re-emerge in various guises throughout his long working life.

What was clearly seen at the time as an indigenous Swedish design movement was thus significantly indebted to a foreign contributor. When Frank was honored with an exhibition at Stockholm's National Museum in 1952, both Gotthard Johansson and Gustaf Näsström,[4] writing in the catalogue, paid homage to the designer as a key participant in Sweden's national achievement in design. "It [the work of Frank]," wrote Näsström, "radiates repose, harmony and refinement and conveys the purest fragrance of the style epoch which has been dubbed 'Swedish Modern.'"[5] Clearly by 1952 there was a consensus of opinion within Sweden about the nature of the country's contribution to modernism and Frank's important role within it. It was also clear at that time that the idea of Swedish Modern was based on apparent contradictions and ambiguities, a fact that Berg had already exposed. Johansson, for example, talked of the style "with its one and the same time strict and playful, sober and lovably florid ethos,"[6] reiterating the double-edged nature of this compelling movement which softened, humanized, and thereby made acceptable to a wide public the otherwise harsh and uncompromising face of modern design.

Frank's contribution to Swedish Modern lay in the unique approach to modern design that he brought with him from Austria to Sweden and the unique formulation that resulted from his collaboration with Ericson in the context of the domestic interior over a period of years. It was the negotiation and resulting tensions of both of these special circumstances with Sweden's internal program of design reform that resulted in the "structure of feeling,"[7] recognized internationally as Sweden's contribution to modern material culture in the mid-twentieth century.

In 1934, the year of the first public exhibition of Frank's work in Sweden, he outlined his ideas about interior decoration in an article entitled "Rum och inredning" (Room and furnishings) which was published in *Form*,[8] the mouthpiece of the Svenska Slöjdföreningen (Swedish Society of Craft and Industrial Design). In it he set out a number of propositions, many of which had been developed over many years, beginning in his early career as an architect and interior designer. His design philosophy was manifest in, among other examples, a small "niche" interior exhibited by Haus & Garten in the 1925 Paris Exposition des Arts Décoratifs et Industriels Modernes and in the comfortable interior furnishings of the duplex housing that he designed in 1927 for the Weissenhofsiedlung in Stuttgart.

For Frank, interior decoration had to incorporate white walls with case pieces raised from the floor on legs to allow the intersection of planes—the "twelve boundaries"—in the room to be revealed. Furnishings did not have to be designed en suite but could be combined and moved around as necessary. In his designs for interiors Frank applied pattern and color in various ways. As he explained, "The monochromed surface has an unsettling effect, the patterned surface is a calming one because the beholder is involuntarily affected by the slow, calm mode of production."[9] Embellishment on furniture, such as marquetry, inlay, and decorative hardware, was considered necessary to provide a calming effect on the eyes. Lighting was to be provided by floor and desk lamps, not from a central ceiling fixture (the latter belonged to the age of gas, not electric lighting, claimed Frank). Frank valued the importance of a sense of harmony in an interior space, created not by a *Gesamtkunstwerk* but by strict attention to proportions, based on the golden section.[10] Above all he was committed to the idea that an interior could be lived in comfortably and agreeably.

Frank arrived in Sweden armed with a sophisticated philosophy of the interior which derived from a combination of ideas, aesthetic preferences, and experiences. Key to his theories were a love of the comfort and harmony inherent in the Austrian Biedermeier (fig. 8-1), an idiom well known to him from his childhood years, and his knowledge

Fig. 8-1. A typical Biedermeier interior depicted in Carl Wilhelm Gropius's *Das Wohnzimmer des Künstlers* (The sitting room of the artists), ca. 1830.

of the ideas and work of the early twentieth-century Viennese protagonists of modern architecture and design, prominent among them Adolf Loos and Josef Hoffmann. They had treated the interior as an essentially modern space, but one which nevertheless retained a sense of continuity with the past by using pattern and materials in a highly decorative manner. For Loos and Hoffmann, as for Frank, the nineteenth-century "bourgeois" idea of the interior as a site of luxury and refinement, expressed through materials and decoration—often traditional or tradition-inspired in nature—was fundamental.[11] By the 1920s proponents of the modern movement considered this approach to design anathema. Le Corbusier, for example, conceived of a domestic interior as an extension of the architectural shell; his interiors included built-in furnishings and expressed modernity through the use of new materials—reinforced concrete and tubular steel among others.

Frank's deep commitment to the past also singled him out as emanating from an alternative tradition to that of the hard-line functionalists who, although indebted to Classicism, avoided historicism at all costs. He brought with him to Sweden an understanding of Asian design, especially Chinese (in contrast to modernism's debt to Japanese design, as mediated through the work of Frank Lloyd Wright). He had a passion for the Italian Renaissance (having written his doctoral thesis at the Technische Hochschule in Vienna on the churches of Alberti). He greatly admired eighteenth-century English furniture, notably the work of Chippendale and Sheraton,

and was sensitive to folk culture, especially its Central European manifestations.

On the face of it this last source of inspiration brought Frank close to the overtly nationalistic preoccupations of the indigenous Swedish Modern movement. Swedish folk culture found expression in the craft-oriented furniture of Carl Malmsten, the simple, woven textiles of Astrid Sampe, the folk-inspired ceramics of Wilhelm Kåge and Stig Lindberg for Gustavsberg, and the lyrical, decorative glass of Simon Gate and Edward Hald for Orrefors.[12] At first glance there seems to be a formal and iconographic similarity between Frank's textile patterns and Swedish folk embroidery. This might suggest that he was aligning himself with other Swedish Modern designers of the interwar years whose nationally oriented quest for a modern style led them to their indigenous folk roots. It is much more likely, however, that Frank's sources came from outside Sweden, from, for example, his knowledge of the Österreichisches Museum für Volkskunde (Museum of Folk Culture) in Vienna where embroidery closely resembling Swedish examples could easily be found. For Frank this was part of his "natural" eclecticism rather than a nationalistic effort. This possible misreading of Frank's relationship with the indigenous Swedish Modern movement can also apply to his repeated designs for beds either set in alcoves or surrounded by hangings. The "built-in" bed played a key role within the folk cultures of both Sweden and Central Europe, as did painted furniture which also played an important part in Frank's oeuvre. While many of his interests appeared to blend seamlessly with those of contemporary Swedish designers, unlike them Frank was not motivated by nationalistic zeal. In fact Frank never strictly followed any nationalistic or ideological agenda. And his status as a Jewish immigrant was likely to have isolated him further from his Swedish contemporaries.

The eighteenth century played key roles within both the indigenous Swedish Modern movement and Frank's work. For the Swedes it was the simplicity of their own eighteenth-century Gustavian style[13] that appealed to their need to discover a national idiom predating the "vulgar" historicism and eclecticism of mass-produced furniture of the nineteenth century. Frank's eighteenth-century inspiration was, in contrast, essentially English in origin, although for his textile patterns he might have drawn upon luxury French silks and tapestries. His many designs for furniture with elegant tapering legs and claw feet, in addition to his frequent reworking of the more popular Windsor chair (fig. 8-2), bore witness to this source of inspiration. It was from the eighteenth century that he also acquired his appreciation for "Chinoiserie," yet another of the decorative idioms that helped form his own highly eclectic taste. The same French source that might have inspired Frank in the twentieth century had permeated Swedish achievements in the eighteenth century; French craftsmen, for example, had decorated the Royal Palace in Stockholm. As a result of these shared impulses, it is difficult to disentangle the influences on Frank's work from those of the more nationalistic promoters of Swedish Modern design.

Frank was inherently eclectic in his tastes and relied upon a wide range of stimuli for his formulation of the modern interior. Other sources for his highly heterogeneous work included ancient art, particularly Egyptian, as expressed in the little "Tutankhamun" stool that he designed in 1941. The work of the American Shakers also inspired him. The unifying factor behind this heterogeneity was the unique sensibility and eye of a man who took in everything around him as a possible source but who instinctively edited as he did so, with the result that seemingly disparate items in a Frank interior could be seen to work together. This was apparent in the public and private interiors he created with Ericson, beginning with the four rooms in the 1934 exhibition in the Liljevalchs Gallery, to the countless installations at Svenskt Tenn from that year onward and the interiors of the Ericson's weekend residence, Tolvekarna (Twelve Oaks, completed 1942; fig. 8-3).

If the absence of a nationalistic program distanced Frank from proponents of historicism within the Swedish Modern movement as it reached its peak in the late 1930s, he had even less in common with that manifestation of the movement that centered on the reforming efforts of the Svenska Slöjdföreningen. Formed in 1845 in an attempt to maintain design standards in the face of rampant industrialization and the abolition of the guild system, the society was motivated by a strong social program. Inspired by the work of William Morris (as indeed was Frank, although probably for different reasons) it sought to combine an interest in design standards with a commitment to social democracy. The ideas of the Svenska Slöjdföreningen were conveyed in an exhibition held in 1917 at the Liljevalchs Gallery in Stockholm. Dedicated to "The Home," the show consisted of a series of very simple room settings for one- and two-room apartments intended for working people on low incomes. A strong folk-cultural flavor was present in 1917, demonstrated by Wilhelm Kåge's earthenware tableware manufactured by Gustavsberg and called the "Workers" service. Its strongly rustic appearance provided a direction for the Swedish Modern movement at a very early date.

Fig. 8-2. Bedroom in the guest cottage of industrialist Hjalmar Olson. The furnishings by Svenskt Tenn in 1935 included a Windsor chair design.

The next contribution of the Svenska Slöjdföreningen to the development of Swedish Modern design was the 1919 publication of *Vackrare Vardagsvara* (More beautiful things for everyday use) by Gregor Paulsson who would soon become the society's director. In this book, Paulsson stressed the need for beauty to enter the everyday lives of ordinary people and for design to take on that challenge.[14] Frank's social housing in Vienna of this period was conceived within the same spirit and, indeed, his 1925 "niche" installation at the Paris Exposition was also devoted to the cause—the desire, that is, to produce utility furniture which could be manufactured relatively simply. At the same time, however, Frank's architectural and design work—holiday villas in Falsterbo in the 1920s and those he worked on for clients through Haus & Garten in Vienna—displayed a conceptual dichotomy. It was clear that, while, on one level, he could relate to the social program of architecture and design, in the end he was committed to a notion of the "individual" and to the ideas of comfort, pleasantness, and "civilized" values that could be achieved through an understanding of the interior as ultimately a symbolic rather than utilitarian space. Although his interiors were distinquished by white walls and clean lines, they were never severe, featuring as they always did comfy sofas, floral textiles, patterned rugs, and the all-important fireplace. The odd piece of exotica such as a fake tiger-skin rug, an extravagance often attributed to Estrid Ericson, was another device used.

The main aim of the Slöjdföreningen was to introduce designers to industry so that collaborative efforts might result in the actual realization of "more beautiful everyday things." It was a program that did not reap instant results; the most notable Swedish designs to emerge in the 1920s and receive international acclaim were unique handcrafted objects such as the engraved glass designed by Simon Gate and Edward Hald for Orrefors. Stylistically Swedish design in the 1920s was dominated by Neoclassicism, but at the end of the decade, in response to the influence of Germany and the 1927 Weissenhofsiedlung, Swedish architects and to some extent designers as well revisited the social program of a decade earlier and developed their own version of architectural functionalism.

The Slöjdföreningen welcomed this development and became prime movers in planning the Stockholm

Exhibition of 1930 (Stockholmsutställningen 1930 av konstindustri, konsthantverk och hemslöjd; fig. 8-4) at which Swedish functionalist architecture and social reform joined hands. Characterized by its white modernist buildings and its commitment to a modern age predicated upon rationalism and the advent of the "machine," the exhibition provided an opportunity for the two ends of the spectrum of Swedish modern architecture and design to meet each other in head-on conflict. The battle that raged in the press between the "Funkis" and the "Tradis"[15] represented a clash between the supporters of nationalism and modernism; between those who favored a reworking of the past in the present and those who wanted to abandon history altogether; between those who worked on the basis of the craft process and those who openly supported standardization and mechanization. In some ways it was a battle between the architects and the decorative artists who sought different ways of encountering the "new." An exception to the traditionalist approach of the decorative industries, however, was that of Gustavsberg, which with the help of Wilhelm Kåge, experimented with functional ceramics, producing in 1933 a radically different table service called

Fig. 8-3. The living room at Tolvekarna, ca. 1942. Svenskt Tenn Archive, Stockholm.

Fig. 8-4. The Stockholm Exhibition of 1930.

"Praktika" (fig. 8-5). A commercial failure, however, it was rapidly replaced by "Pyro," an earthy, organically shaped design that combined tradition and innovation in a much more acceptable way within the Swedish market. The schizophrenia that characterized modern Swedish design at this time—the spectrum of possibilities, that is, that spanned radical functionalism to vernacular design—was still apparent in 1948 when Åke H. Huldt and Eva Benedicks noted that "two distinct trends are evident in Sweden today—one building on tradition and adapting the inherited forms to modern surroundings, the other concentrating singlemindedly on forging pleasant new shapes from functional necessities."[16]

Frank stood outside both of these trends, neither responding to specifically Swedish traditions nor aligning himself with the more progressive, rational face of modernism. His was a third path, rooted in another set of modern compulsions which were neither those of the functionalist extremes of the modern movement nor of traditionalism, but which combined an internationalist approach with a respect for tradition albeit reworked in a modern manner. As such Frank did not belong specifically to the Swedish program. Ironically, however, by the late 1930s he had come to encapsulate the idea of Swedish Modern

design to the outside world. The Svenska Slöjdföreningen was compelled to accept this and to use Frank as representative of what was happening in Sweden at a number of international venues.

The Svenska Slöjdföreningen sustained its efforts through the 1930s, supporting links between designers and manufacturing industries and promoting modern Swedish design whenever and wherever possible. The coming of the Social Democrats to power in Sweden in 1932 reinforced the society's social program. As noted, Frank's introduction to the Swedish design community in 1934 was acknowledged by the society in the publication of his influential article in Form, but in many ways the Austrian architect and designer remained very much on the periphery of the high-minded Swedish reforming zeal that surrounded him. Frank remained in contact with many of his Austrian colleagues and friends after his departure from Vienna in 1933, but he stood outside the Swedish architectural community, despite the fact that leading architects such as Gunnar Asplund and Sven Markelius were working in Sweden at that time. Not surprisingly he received no architectural commissions in Sweden after settling there. He was at odds with the nationalistic flavor of the more historicist face of Swedish craft and design manufacture and was ambivalent about

Fig. 8-5. Wilhelm Kåge, "Praktika" table service, 1933.

the program of social reform that underpinned so much contemporary Swedish design practice. As such, although his work was well received by the middle-class sector of the market that visited Svenskt Tenn, he remained very much on the periphery of the activities of the Svenska Slöjdföreningen.

A sense of marginalization was strongly reinforced by Frank's alliance with Estrid Ericson and his relationship with Svenskt Tenn. The eclecticism, historicism, and strong sense of individualism, elitism, and luxury that emanated from the shop forcefully mitigated against Frank being accepted by the Svenska Slöjdföreningen. Svenskt Tenn's reputation had been established before Frank had arrived. Ericson's special approach to interior decoration had much in common with ideas that had been developed in the early twentieth century in the United States by the pioneer interior decorator, Elsie de Wolfe, who had favored a "soft" response to the world of modernity. Trained as a pattern designer Ericson had as many ideas as Frank about what an interior should look like and the success of Svenskt Tenn was largely the result of their collaboration. While Frank designed the interior objects Ericson "arranged" them, transforming furnishings into elements of interior decor and, more significantly, into the components of a "home." The shop was divided into a number of "lived-in" interior installations complete with books in shelves, knick-knacks in display cabinets, ornaments on mantelpieces, coffee cups on coffee-tables, flowers in vases, and cushions on sofas. Frank and Ericson complemented each other perfectly: furnishings and arrangements formed a complete whole.

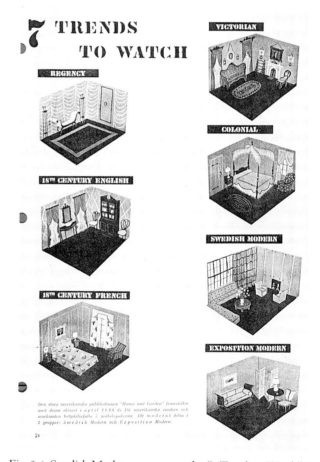

Fig. 8-6. Swedish Modern was among the "7 Trends to Watch" in American interior design. From *Form* 6 (1938), p. 165.

Fig. 8-7. Furnishings by Josef Frank featured in Svenskt Tenn's installation at the Paris Exposition of 1937. Svenskt Tenn Archive, Stockholm.

When Svenskt Tenn responded to a commission—such as the one from Carl Milles to design the interior of a new building at Millesgården, which came to be known as Anne's House (1947–51)—the combined forces of Frank's furnishings with Ericson's arrangement were such that the result constituted a complete language of interior decoration, one whose elements were flexible enough to respond to change and to the addition of the client's own treasured possessions, but a complete language nonetheless. It was at odds, however, with the much more nationally and socially oriented voice of the Svenska Slöjdföreningen. As a result, while Frank was not totally ignored by the Swedish design mainstream in the 1930s, he was positioned, nonetheless, firmly on its margins.

Given this ambivalent relationship between Frank and the Swedish design mainstream, and the formation of so many of his ideas outside the boundaries of Sweden, it is surprising that he was so seminal in the formation of the concept of Swedish Modern as it came to be understood outside Sweden from the 1930s to the 1950s, especially in the United States. In 1938 an article appeared in the April edition of the American magazine, *House and Garden*, entitled "Trends to Watch" (fig. 8-6). "Swedish Modern" was given as one option among an eclectic group of other possibilities, including "Regency, eighteenth-century English, eighteenth-century French, Victorian, Colonial and Exposition Modern." Swedish Modern was, therefore, one of the two modern trends to watch for in the United States in 1938. In *The Group*, a story of four Vassar graduates written in 1936, novelist Mary McCarthy had already observed that young New Yorkers recognized the fashionable nature of the new Swedish style: "Pure white walls and wood-

work . . . . The latest model of stove, sink and ice-box . . . . Every stick of furniture was the latest thing: blond Swedish chairs and folding table . . . ,"[17] she wrote, in describing the contents of a protagonist's smart new apartment.

It was at the Paris Exhibition of 1937, however, that Frank and Ericson came to be linked directly with the idea of "Swedish Modern." Asked by the Svenska Slöjdföreningen to participate in the Swedish pavilion, they contributed a paved, open-air terrace with rattan garden chairs by Frank, trees in pots, and a fountain designed by him (fig. 8-7). It had a lightness and humanity that appealed to visitors from many countries. As a writer in a 1938 article in the English *Architectural Review* explained,

> When the bright boys from the US snooped round the Paris exhibition looking for furnishing ideas last year they all agreed that the snip of the decade was the Swedish exhibit. They hurried back to America with masses of photographs and drawings, got in touch with their suppliers and announced with a typhoon of advertising that Swedish Modern has been selling in America. It has been selling in Europe too. It is selling in Britain today.[18]

Thus was consolidated a concept of Swedish Modern design that was reinforced two years later at the New York World's Fair of 1939. Once again, Frank and Ericson were asked to present a room setting in the Swedish pavilion, which was designed by Sven Markelius and contained a number of interiors and displays of decorative art objects, among them one by Carl Malmsten. While the Svenska Slöjdföreningen may have had some reservations about Svenskt Tenn in terms of its lack of a politically oriented program of reform, as part of the need to create international trade links and to convey a national image in an international marketplace, the huge popularity of Svenskt Tenn with foreign customers made it a first choice as an ambassador of Swedish Modern. The 1937 exhibit had inspired one writer to coin the expression "Swedish Modern—a movement towards sanity and design," a phrase that was reiterated in the U.S. in the context of the 1939 pavilion and its contents.[19]

The dominant idiom of the New York exposition was that of "streamlining"—an aggressively modernistic style expressed through objects of transportation and consumer machines made in evocatively curved metal and plastics with no hint of continuity with the past. The American industrial designers of the day—Walter Dorwin Teague, Norman Bel Geddes, and Raymond Loewy, among them—left little room for other countries to make their mark. In quiet contrast the Swedish pavilion represented a moment of "sanity" in which older values combined with new ones to suggest a more gentle response to the modern age. Svenskt Tenn's interior, with furniture designed exclusively by Frank, had a strikingly abstract black and white checkerboard floor and sofa with a pattern of triangles and squares which contrasted with the softer floral upholstery on the fireside chair, the kidney-shaped desk that curved around the user's body, and the small round table that stood on the fireside mat. Many of the pieces were "old favorites," reworked in a new setting. Estrid Ericson had "arranged" them in her usual manner, adding books to the bookshelves and putting knick-knacks in the display cabinets. The total effect was novel, but its novelty respected the scale of human beings and their participation in the space on view. Once again, this time for a vast international audience, Frank and Ericson had succeeded in speaking a new language for the domestic interior which had reverberations for large numbers of onlookers.

In the same year the American public had yet another taste of this new domestic aesthetic which seemed to offer a new and dynamic approach to interior design. At the 1939 Golden Gate Exhibition in San Francisco, Frank and Ericson presented an interior made up of familiar elements, among them: the lady's dressing table with three round mirrors, a design that originated at Haus & Garten; a bed that was separated from the main room by a partition which, like the adjacent walls, was covered in floral motifs; an easy chair, and a flexible floor lamp. Furniture themes, originated by Frank in Vienna, now formed the basis of what an American audience recognized as "Swedish Modern." At the end of the 1930s that idiom was complete and fully

expressed by Frank's work as it was seen in New York and San Francisco.

The Second World War created a moment of stasis. Sweden closed its frontiers and Frank went to live in the U.S. for four years, returning to Stockholm in early 1946. The 1940s saw a consolidation of prewar developments and an enthusiastic flowering of the values that had been emerging at that time. Frank's fifty new fabric designs, sent from New York City in 1944 at the time of Estrid Ericson's fiftieth birthday, formed the basis of a new period of energetic activity for Svenskt Tenn, and numerous commissions after the war provided the opportunity for Frank and Ericson to continue their collaboration within a climate that was highly supportive of their work and attitudes.

The art critic Dag Widman described the 1940s in Sweden as a period of "idyllic retrospection and decorative formalism."[20] Within this ambiance Frank and Ericson found the ideal environment in which to work and an audience that was highly receptive to their ideas. So strong, in fact, was the impact of their vision of domesticity that their view began to permeate Swedish culture in a visible way. The modern Swedish home became, in fact, the basis for cultural reconstruction in general, the starting point for a re-emergence of a set of values which came to underpin Swedish society as a whole. As Huldt and Benedicks, writing in *Design in Sweden Today* (1948), explained:

> After clothes home furnishings reveal most clearly the aesthetic and cultural status of nations as of individuals. Today's Swedish home is a friendly place, light both to the eye and to the mind, functionally furnished in a natural and unconventional manner. The light woods of the delicately scaled furniture give it a self-effacing quality against the light-colored walls—the personal touch being supplied by fresh cut flowers, small decorative objects, paintings, and textiles in clean, clear colors.[21]

They could have been talking about a Svenskt Tenn interior. No longer was individualism seen as elitist or personal choices as antidemocratic. A compromise had occurred between the collectivist idealism of the interwar years and the vision of the home that was expressed by Frank and Ericson, thought at the time to be exclusive and nondemocratic.

The Slöjdföreningen responded vigorously with a new, highly rational program aimed at quantifying the needs of the Swedish home, the optimum size of its case pieces, the ideal length of a bed, and so on. In 1955 it held a major exhibition in Hälsinborg to revive and celebrate the ideals that had underpinned the Stockholm Exhibition of 1930. Svenskt Tenn was notable by its absence from Hälsinborg '55, another instance of the rationalist, collectivist end of the Swedish Modern spectrum trying to deny the importance of Frank to that movement. (Interestingly this recurred at the Liljevalchs Gallery's 1995 exhibition "Formens rörelse" [The Movement of Form] which was organized by the Svensk Form, as the Slöjdföreningen is now known.) The exhibition at the National Museum in 1952, however, had established his significance in a way which could not be overlooked so easily. Gotthard Johannson dubbed Frank at the time, "the foremost exponent of Swedish Modern."[22] In spite of his own rationalist leanings the writer was drawn to what he saw as the contradictions within Frank, the combination of simplicity with compexity, the richness with the purity. As he wrote, "Perhaps, when all is said and done, it is this union of abundant detailing and the purity of the room which endows these interiors with their special atmospheres and makes them rooms one wants to live in."[23] In the end

Swedish Modern was neither a style nor an ideology nor a movement in any fully fledged sense of the term. It was instead a "way of life," a set of strategies for moving gently from one world view to another, from one in which servants had looked after the middle classes to one in which the serving trollies and the liquor cabinets designed by Frank make it easy to serve oneself. The small coffee tables, soft chairs, curved desks, and calming textiles that Frank provided made it easy to live in the modern world without having to sacrifice the comfort, convenience, and pleasantness that had hitherto made the home the cultural center of things. This, ultimately, was Frank's unique contribution to architecture and design culture in the twentieth century. It made him crucial to the concept of Swedish Modern, that internationally influential mid-century "way of life" that allowed one world to become transformed into another without anybody really noticing, and without anyone suffering the trauma that comes with a sudden, painful transition.

1. Quoted in M. Lindahl-Åkerman, "A Working Life," in Monica Boman, ed., *Estrid Ericson: Founder of Svenskt Tenn* (Stockholm, 1989), p. 42.

2. Quoted in Helena Dahlbeck-Lutteman, "Scandinavia: Democracy and Design" (manuscript, 1984). A copy is in the possession of the author. For further information on G. A. Berg, see Monica Boman, ed., *Svenska Möbler* (Lund, Sweden: Signum 1991).

3. A dissemination of the concept of modernism in architecture occurred at the exhibition, "The International Style," at the Museum of Modern Art, New York, held in 1932. It was curated by H. R. Hitchcock and Philip Johnson and served to consolidate and provide a rationale for many of the achievements of the previous decade.

4. Gotthard Johansson (1891–1968) was a writer and critic who served as chairman of the Svenska Slöjdföreningen from 1951 to 1960. Gustaf Näsström (1899–1979) was also a writer and art critic. He was employed by one of Stockholm's newpapers, *Stockhomstidningen*, beginning in 1932.

5. Lindahl-Åkerman, "A Working Life," p. 48.

6. Ibid.

7. The phrase *structure of feeling* was coined by the English cultural theorist Raymond Williams in the 1950s in an attempt to explain that many seminal moments in culture are represented by sets of powerful, shared feelings that cannot be described in a rational or reductive manner. See Raymond Williams, *Culture & Society, 1780–1950* (London: Penguin Books, 1958).

8. See Josef Frank, "Rum och inredning," *Form* 30 (1934), pp. 217–25.

9. Quoted in *Josef Frank: Inredning*, exhib. cat. (Stockholm: Millesgården, 1994), p. 70.

10. The golden section is the division of a line or the set of proportions of a geometrical figure in which the smaller dimension relates to the larger dimension with the same ratio as the larger dimension relates to the whole.

11. This is especially apparent in Loos's Müller House in which marble is used to great sensuous effect in the interior. Later modernists such as Mies van der Rohe used marble, although to quite different ends.

12. See David McFadden, *Scandinavian Modern Design, 1880–1980* (New York: Harry N. Abrams, 1982); Boman, ed., *Svenska Möbler*;

13. The Gustavian style is associated with the period from approximately 1770 to 1810. See, for example, Hakan Groth, *Neoclassicism in the North: Swedish Furniture and Interiors* (New York: Rizzoli, 1990); and Erik Andren, *Möbelstilarna: den svenska möbel och inrednings konstens historia* (Stockholm: Nordiska Museet, 1981).

14. See David R. McFadden, ed., *Scandinavian Modern Design, 1880–1980* (New York: Harry N. Abrams, 1983).

15. "Funkis" and "Tradis," abbreviated names for the Functionalists and Traditionalists, were terms used in Sweden by the contemporary press.

16. Å. H. Huldt and E. Benedicks, *Design In Sweden Today* (Stockholm: Swedish Institute, 1948), p. 11.

17. Mary McCarthy, *The Group* (London: Penguin, 1968), pp. 89–90.

18. Quoted in Kristina Wängberg-Eriksson, "Svenskt Tenn: Josef Frank och Estrid Ericson, en konsthistorisk studie," master's thesis (Stockholm University, 1985).

19. Ibid.

20. Quoted in McFadden, ed., *Scandinavian Modern Design*, p. 134.

21. Huldt and Benedicks, *Design*, p. 39.

22. G. Johansson quoted in Lindahl-Åkerman, "A Working Life," p. 48.

23. Ibid., p. 51.

# 9. JOSEF FRANK AND GIO PONTI: AND THE "GARDEN,"

**Marianne Lamonaca**

The cities of Milan and Vienna have had a long, close relationship, its roots going back to the eighteenth century when the region of Lombardy was under the rule of the Habsburg Empire and Northern Italians looked to Austria for their cultural sustenance. Vienna's design initiatives continued to have repercussions in Milan into the twentieth century. One manifestation of this can be seen in a surprising design relationship: the influence of Josef Frank's furniture and interior designs on the work of the Milanese architect Gio Ponti (1891–1979; fig. 9-1). Ponti had a deep affection for Vienna. According to his daughter Lisa, "there was a kind of affinity, an affinity that lay more in a way of thinking than in form."[1]

Ponti was the founder and editor of *Domus*, the most influential interior design magazine in Italy during the 1920s and 1930s. He promoted a modern, Italian aesthetic in architecture and design, through his writings, his active involvement with the Biennale di Monza (later the Triennale di Milano), and the example of his own work. Mostly he used his influence to champion the reform of decorative arts production in Italy. While he recognized the need for large-scale manufacture (and encouraged its development), Ponti maintained the conviction that craft production was the best expression of quality Italian products.

Many of Josef Frank's design ideals were shared by Ponti. Both men were deeply committed to developing a modern design idiom that reflected human civility. Both rooted their work in the styles of the past. And both celebrated traditional methods of craftsmanship. While their experiences intersect, this story unfolds in an improvisational rather than ordered manner.

In the March 1937 issue of *Domus*, Ponti introduced "a small interesting collection of objects . . . by 'Casa e Giardino', a Milanese initiative in the field of home furnishings."[2] The collection encompassed a range of objects, including handsome textiles, a bed pillow, fireplace implements, and chairs (fig. 9-2). The company's director was architect Lio Carminati,[3] but Ponti seems to have played a meaningful role both as promoter and as a designer—four of the nine illustrations in the brief *Domus* article were of objects designed by Ponti.

Exactly a year earlier Ponti had published an article in *Domus* about the Viennese firm of the same name, Haus & Garten, which had been established in 1925 by Josef Frank and his partner Oskar Wlach.[4] More than forty illustrations depicting interiors, fabrics, and chairs accompanied the text (fig. 9-3). The most obvious association between the two firms, of course, is the name, but they shared a great deal more than that. Both firms produced and sold high-quality objects for the home, including furniture, lighting, and textiles. Each one promoted the work of local artisans, and they reflected similar design philosophies.

# REFLECTIONS ON THE "HOUSE"

# A VIEW FROM ITALY

Ponti's 1936 article in *Domus* serves as a guide to understanding the relationship between the two firms— Haus & Garten, Casa e Giardino—and Ponti's own design idiom. The language he used emphasized his strong affinity for Frank's distinctive approach to design for the home. He wrote:

> We demonstrate . . . some interiors and some furnishings by these two Viennese masters [Frank and Wlach]. They are the character of modern simplicity, without excluding grace, or color, or the softness of fabrics, and create a neat and comfortable atmosphere in which to live. . . . Readers note the many interesting and typical details: the recessed panels (so useful and so elegant) by the handles of the armoires; the great variety of chairs and tables; beds abundant with drapery; wall-mounted night lamps, with skirts; and the use of gaily printed cotton draperies. . . .[5]

Frank's interiors were furnished in a style that preserved tradition and comfort. He believed that "ornament and complexity create peacefulness and get rid of the disturbing aspect of pure functional form."[6] Ponti's own programmatic text for modern Italian architecture and interior design—"La Casa all'Italiana" (The Italian-style house)— also stressed "comfort" and "simplicity."[7] In the first issue of *Domus* in 1928, Ponti had identified the Italian-style house as a place in which to "enjoy life." He wrote: "[the house] is not only a 'machine à habiter'. . . its comfort is in something superior . . . in the invitation that the Italian-style house offers to our spirit to enjoy itself."[8]

Why were Ponti and Carminati looking at Frank's designs, which had matured almost a decade earlier? In fact by 1937 Frank had already moved to Stockholm where he was actively designing for Svenskt Tenn, although he continued to be involved with Haus & Garten until the

Fig. 9-1. Gio Ponti, 1923. From L. L. Ponti, *Gio Ponti*, p. 16.

129

Fig. 9-2. Casa e Giardino products. From *Domus* (March 1937),
p. 26.

Fig. 9-3. A Haus & Garten interior by Josef Frank and Oskar
Wlach. From *Domus* (March 1936).

Anschluss in 1938. Ponti provided the most cogent answer to the question when he wrote: "From the architecture and decorative arts of Germany, Austria, Denmark and Sweden we have taken the lesson of energy, ingenuity, organized production, perfect execution, virtuosity."[9]

Like Haus & Garten, Casa e Giardino offered designs created by its director, Lio Carminati. They also sold objects by notable Italian artisans, such as enameled metalwork by Paolo de Poli and glassware by the Seguso firm. Championing fine craftwork was part of the programs of both firms. In Italy the revival of the small crafts industries was an important step toward creating a modern design idiom. Frank's furnishings embodied the craft principles of simplicity, practicality, and the rational use of materials. Ponti valued the sanity of Frank's designs, which were marked by their "skillful handicraft, right proportions . . . and unpretending [*sic*] elegance."[10] Moreover, Italy's Fascist government encouraged the growth of craft industries as a means of boosting Italy's economy. According to a government-sponsored publication, "In Italy more than in any other country, the small artistic manufactures for the decorative arts can boast glorious traditions of superiority" that have developed from the Middle Ages to the present day.[11]

An allegiance to a classical design idiom was another feature shared by Frank and Ponti and a distinctive aspect of their work. When discussing furnishings by the two designers, the term *classical* could be understood as classicism, a canon of absolute formal values (form, proportion, linear simplicity) or as classic, a work of art that transcends its own and every time. Ponti was particularly fond of the contemporary home furnishings produced in Vienna and the Scandinavian countries, examples of which were displayed at the Paris Exposition des Arts Décoratifs et Industriels Modernes in 1925. An Italian art critic reviewing the exhibits wrote: "the objects of the most stable and persuasive character to our eyes are those that take their inspiration most directly from neo-classicism."[12] Josef Frank was cited, along with Carl Malmsten from Sweden and Jacques-Emile Ruhlmann from France, as exemplifying this tendency.

At the Paris exposition, Haus & Garten was represented by a refined and understated installation designed by Frank (fig. 9-4). The wood furnishings reflected the Arts and Crafts underpinnings of his work. The furniture forms, which were firmly rooted in the past, ranged from a vernacular stool with a rush seat to a drop-front desk of eighteenth-century derivation. Such blending of vernacular and classical idioms was often practiced by Italian designers, for whom classicism was a native tradition, and thus

Frank's interpretations had particular relevance. In both Austria and Italy the clean lines and elegant forms of classicism appealed to the upper-middle-class consumer. *Domus* reported in 1931 that Frank had arrived at this conclusion in *Architektur als Symbol*: "that our unique and continuous tradition is the classical tradition."[13]

Significantly the Haus & Garten installation, unlike the French exhibits, was not arranged as a unified ensemble. Instead, Frank and Wlach presented a collection of individual furnishings that could complement any interior. Several years earlier Frank had criticized the modern, homogeneous interior, the kind of room that "constitutes a definite whole," adding that "in such a room each object newly added certainly would be considered bothersome."[14] Frank's solution was to create a tranquil interior with white walls that allowed for the inclusion of personal objects. He asserted that "our personal relationship to many objects is and shall be of much greater importance to us than any aesthetic consideration," arguing that "living rooms . . . should not be regarded as works of art" but "should serve as the background . . . for its inhabitants allowing for continuously changing and developing ideas."[15]

Frank's words resonate with the lessons taught by Viennese architect Adolf Loos. In both word and deed Loos fought against the tyranny of modern architects who, in their desire to create a *Gesamtkunstwerk* (total work of art), cleansed interiors of any objects that would reflect the personal history of their occupants. Ponti conceived of the house as an "uncomplicated" structure that could accommodate furnishings and beautiful works of art in an ordered and uncrowded manner.[16]

Ponti had first-hand knowledge of Frank's work through publications and exhibitions. He attended the 1925 Paris exposition in his role as artistic director for Richard-Ginori, the Italian ceramics manufacturer. The products he conceived for Ginori were "modern" objects that would "harmonize" with Italian "customs and everyday environment."[17] The majority of Ponti's designs for this centuries-old company reflect the Italian classical tradition and were produced in series by hand, but many of them also reveal the influence of the Wiener Werkstätte, in particular the designs of Josef Hoffmann and Dagobert Peche.

Progressive Viennese art and architecture were popular in Northern Italy in the first two decades of the century. Significantly, many of the Viennese designers whose ideas found fertile ground in Italy asserted that modern design would emerge from a careful study of traditional forms. The most influential of them, Otto Wagner, Adolf Loos, and Josef Hoffmann, firmly based their architectural

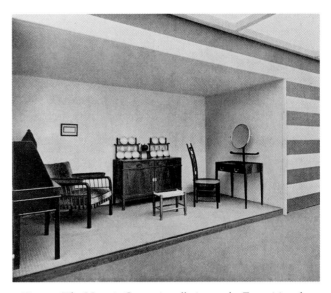

Fig. 9-4. The Haus & Garten installation at the Exposition des Arts Décoratifs et Industriels Modernes, Paris, 1925. From *Moderne Bauformen* (1925), p. 276.

and design aesthetics on classicism. Gustav Klimt and Hoffmann participated in the Biennale di Venezia as well as exhibitions in Rome.[18] Years later Ponti wrote that he "got to know the Vienna of the Secession, of Klimt, Loos, Max Reinhardt," and he praised their work as "examples of modern perfection of expression."[19]

Haus & Garten participated in the Fourth (1930), Fifth (1933), and Sixth (1936) Triennale exhibitions in Milan. In addition, Frank promoted his program for the single-family house at the Weissenhofsiedlung in Stuttgart in 1927 and the Vienna Werkbund exhibition in 1932. All of the major Italian publications reported on these important international events. Italian design books such as *Mobili Tipici Moderni* (Typical modern furniture; 1933) and *L'Arredamento Moderno* (Modern interior design; 1934 and 1939) presented images of Haus & Garten designs.[20]

In the mid-1930s Ponti worked on a project in Vienna: he arranged the interiors for the Fürstenberg Palace, which was being used as the Italian Cultural Institute. Ponti acknowledged his contact with Hoffmann, Frank, Wlach, Oskar Strnad, and Oswald Haerdtl and was most strongly impressed by the Kunstgewerbeschule (School of Arts and Crafts).[21] He perceived the "splendid fragility" of Viennese culture, "ennobled by the presence of a lofty nostalgia and that touch of melancholy that makes things human."[22]

The political and economic realities of Italy in the 1930s may also have influenced Ponti's allegiance to Frank's

Fig. 9-5. Lio Carminati, printed textile, 1936. From *Domus* (July 1936), p. 23.

Fig. 9-6. Lio Carminati, printed textile, 1936. From *Domus* (July 1936), p. 23.

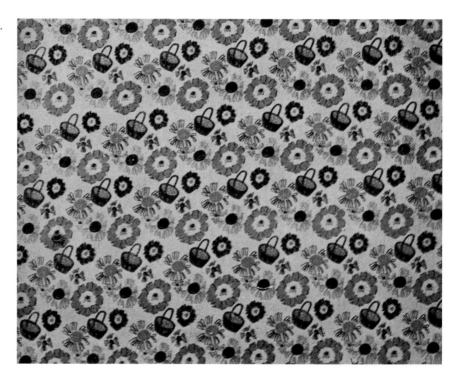

design philosophy. There is a strange irony in the fact that Frank was forced to flee Austria because of the rising threat of Fascism at this exact time. Politics also meant that Italy was experiencing strict economic sanctions imposed by the League of Nations in response to Mussolini's invasion of Abyssinia (Ethiopia). As a result, Italian craftsmen and manufacturers had access to few commodities. Only natural resources from Italy and its colonies were available.

The furnishings Ponti designed during this period were made from a very limited range of materials: native woods from nut and fruit trees such as walnut, chestnut, pear, and cherry; wicker harvested from Italy's abundant willow trees; agricultural products, such as flax and hemp, which were used for textiles; glass and glass products; metals, especially aluminum and new products developed from aluminum, such as Xantal (bronzed aluminum); and natural materials, such as parchment made from animal skins.

The Fascist government sponsored many initiatives

Fig. 9-7. Gio Ponti, "Demonstrative Dwelling" at the Sixth Triennale, Milan, 1936. From *Domus* (July 1936), p. 15.

to promote the use of native resources. Organizations such as the Lanificio e Canapaficio Nazionale (National Flax and Hemp Producers Association) were set up to oversee the production of materials or, in the case of E.N.A.P.I. (a national association for artisans and small industries), to promote crafts production. In addition, both national and regional exhibitions were held to promote various aspects of the self-sufficiency campaign.

Interestingly in 1936, just four months after the Frank/Wlach article by Ponti appeared in *Domus*, the journal ran a review of printed textiles by Lio Carminati (figs. 9-5 and 9-6). The caption reads: "We have been lacking for furniture a modern and original Italian printed fabric. This lacuna is filled by Artela textiles exhibited by De Angeli Frua at the Triennale."[23] Carminati's designs imitated many of Frank's printed floral patterns. Frank's fabrics must have appealed to the Italian middle class during this period of economic austerity. They provided a moderately priced means to redecorate and enliven a home during wartime. Indeed, the only prior example of Carminati's work that has come to light was a brief mention of him in *Domus* as an exhibitor at the Fifth Triennale in 1933. It noted "the textiles of Texilar alias Lio Carminati . . . hand-printed textiles with patterns by Lucas, Cesare Monti and by Carminati himself."[24]

Many comparisons may be drawn between Haus & Garten's furniture and interior designs published in *Domus* in 1936 and two of Ponti's most important domestic projects of the mid-1930s: the "Demonstrative Dwelling" at the Sixth Triennale (1936; fig. 9-7) and his own house, known as Casa Laporte (1936; fig. 9-8), where Ponti put his "demonstration" to work.[25]

The architecture of Casa Laporte bears a striking

Fig. 9-8. Gio Ponti, interior, Casa Laporte, Milan, 1936. From *Domus* (March 1937), p. 6.

Fig. 9-9. Josef Frank, interior, Beer House, Vienna, 1931. From *Moderne Bauformen* (1932), p. 93.

Fig. 9-10. Gio Ponti, armoire, 1936. From *Domus* (July 1936), p. 20.

resemblance to Frank's Beer House in Vienna (1930; fig. 9-9). Significantly, Ponti published two articles on the Beer House in *Domus*, soon after the project was completed.[26] The articles were written by *Domus*'s Viennese correspondent, Carmela Haerdtl, the wife of architect Oswald Haerdtl. For Casa Laporte, Ponti borrowed Frank's use of the double-height living room with a staircase leading to the second floor and culminating in an interior balcony; the roof garden and terrace; and the large round window. Ponti's daughter, who grew up in the house, characterized it as a meeting between the "Mediterranean and Vienna."[27]

In addition to the similarities between Frank's and Carminati's textiles, which were used by Ponti in both projects, many of the furniture forms were similar to Haus & Garten designs. Ponti used built-in armoires. He even copied from Frank the detail of door handles set within

Fig. 9-11. Josef Frank, interior. From
*Domus* (July 1931), p. 48.

recessed panels (fig. 9-10), which he had earlier praised in
*Domus* in his Haus & Garten article. Ponti also used a variety of tables, including a low round dining table, small
round service tables, and a large drop-leaf extension table.
Window treatments, bed coverings, and an assortment of
upholstered seat furniture, including dining chairs, a divan,
and a puff, were embellished with attractive combinations
of gaily printed textiles. And like Frank (fig. 9-11), Ponti
always included raised cabinets and built-in bookcases in
his interiors.

A side chair designed by Ponti was included in both
the "Demonstrative Dwelling" (fig. 9-12) and Casa Laporte.
Its overall form reflects both the austerity and restrained

frivolity of nineteenth-century Biedermeier furniture. The
Biedermeier style was a nineteenth-century expression of
Neoclassicism. Its severe yet comfortable forms appealed to
the burgeoning Viennese middle class. Both the classically
derived Biedermeier and vernacular styles served as potent
precedents for progressive Viennese designers at the beginning of the twentieth century such as Hoffmann and Peche.

Many of Ponti's furniture pieces which were illustrated in *Domus* throughout the 1930s were produced and sold
by Casa e Giardino over the next decade. Moreover, Lio
Carminati absorbed the lessons of Frank and Ponti and
designed furnishings and interiors that were comfortable
and elegant, as the illustrations of his own apartment

Fig. 9-12. Gio Ponti, "Demonstrative Dwelling" at the Sixth Triennale, Milan, 1936. From *Domus* (July 1936), p. 22.

Fig. 9-13. Lio Carminati, interior. From *Domus* (June 1937), p. 4.

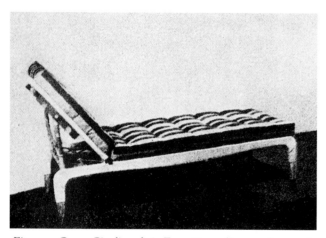

Fig. 9-14. Casa e Giardino chair. From *Domus* (June 1937), p. xxxi.

demonstrate (fig. 9-13). "The modern person who is increasingly more stressed and exhausted by his job," Frank wrote, "requires an apartment cozier and more comfortable than those of the past."[28] Similarly Ponti conceived of the house to "serve our material life. . .[it] accompanies our life, it is the vase of our good and bad hours, and is the temple of our most noble thoughts, it should not be fashionable."[29]

Casa e Giardino also made and sold furnishings for the garden or terrace, an area of major concern to Frank as well. These designs rested predominantly on vernacular forms. An article written by Carminati entitled "Vivere all'aperto" (Living outdoors) was devoted to providing good examples for local craftsmen to create. He wrote that outdoor living demanded "lightweight furnishings that were easily transportable; a few simple, pleasing, and useful objects."[29] Ponti created a suite of simple, yet sophisticated pieces for the terrace which he embellished by wrapping willow around portions of the plain wood structure (fig. 9-14). In Ponti's vision of the modern, Italian-style home, the outdoors melded into the interior by means of terraces, kitchen gardens, courtyards, and roof terraces.[30]

Articles and advertisements for Casa e Giardino consistently appeared in *Domus* and other Italian periodicals

Fig. 9-15. Casa e Giardino chair. From *Stile* (December 1943), p. 48.

such as *Stile* and *Cellini* from 1937 through the end of the war.[31] In addition to its own shops in Milan, Casa e Giardino also maintained an outlet at the fashionable Milanese department store, La Rinascente, located in the Piazza del Duomo. Elsewhere its products were sold in Florence and Rome at Gallenga (a textile showroom) and in Genoa. The December 1943 issue of *Stile* presented a large assortment of illustrations of Casa e Giardino's products, including Ponti's dining table and chairs from the "Demonstrative Dwelling," designed seven years earlier. Also shown were a variety of awkward-looking chairs based on a traditional ladder-back form (fig. 9-15), as well as some practical furnishings such as folding tables, carts, and flower stands.[32]

While scant information has come to light about Casa e Giardino, the company provides an interesting link between the design culture of Vienna and Milan in the 1930s. Casa e Giardino created up-to-date furnishings for the modern Italian home in a period of economic constraint. The company sold the type of products that would appeal to the bourgeois consumer despite the scarcity of extravagant materials. Ponti and Carminati, following Frank's example (fig. 9-16), met the needs of the Italian

Fig. 9-16. Josef Frank, chair. From *Domus* (March 1936), p. 14.

Fig. 10-3. "Tulipan," designed ca. 1925, printed ca. 1930; linen. Private collection.

Fig. 10-4. Bedroom furnishings designed by Frank for Haus & Garten, ca. 1925. From *Innen-Dekoration* 37 (1926), p. 368.

densely ramified tree of life with birds of paradise and exotic flowers, was probably modeled after Persian or Indian designs (fig. 10-2) and also shows a certain affinity with Roman mosaics.[8]

The most telling difference, however, between Frank's conception of textiles and that of most other Wiener Werkstätte artists was in the vision Frank had of the role textiles might play in the modern interior. While designers such as Hoffmann and Moser had sought to create a unified design scheme, in which everything in a room—right down to the hostess's dress—repeated the same pattern or basic motif, Frank took a much freer, more eclectic approach. Rejecting the *Gesamtkunstwerk* ideal that had been so much a part of the fin-de-siècle Viennese design ethos, he envisioned an aesthetic framework that allowed the furnishings to be assembled piecemeal. He was especially fond of mixing seemingly discordant patterns or employing uncommon color combinations, which provides a sense of richness and vibrancy to his interiors.

Yet, despite such conceptual differences, Frank's textiles—even in his later years—evince strong links with prewar Viennese design. This is apparent in the "Tulipan" pattern (fig. 10-3; later redesigned at Svenskt Tenn under the name "Mille Fleurs"), especially when it is printed on cotton chintz and made into a long gown in typical Wiener Werkstätte fashion. Frank's insistence on the finest quality materials and his love for lavish color and pattern also relate his textiles to those of the Werkstätte. Perhaps even more importantly, Frank's printed textiles were products of a shared belief in the importance of championing material pleasure and the gratification of the senses that distinguished turn-of-the-century Viennese aesthetics.

Frank also remained deeply indebted to English models. A bedroom with a four-poster bed and patterned bed curtains, which he designed for Haus & Garten around 1925 (fig. 10-4), exhibits striking similarities to the traditional arrangements of the English interior decoration firm Heal & Sons, which frequently used cretonnes based on older Persian and Indian calicos featuring brightly colored trees of life and birds of paradise. Such fabrics had arrived in Europe in the seventeenth century and were widely imitated by English, French, and Swiss manufacturers.[9]

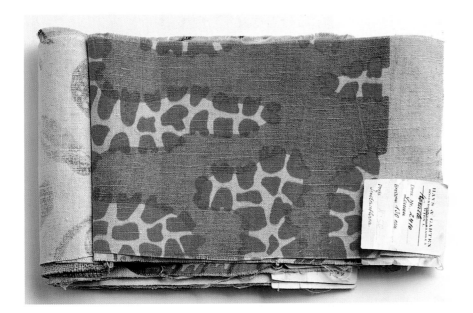

Fig. 10-5. Swatch of "Koralle" in the Haus & Garten samplebook. Svenskt Tenn Archive, Stockholm.

Fig. 10-6. Swatch of "Tang" in the Haus & Garten samplebook. Later, at Svenskt Tenn, it was renamed "Aristidia." Svenskt Tenn Archive, Stockholm.

During the 1910s Frank conceived of his own patterns based on Oriental models. In the 1920s he broadened his vocabulary further and experimented widely until he had achieved his own distinctive idiom. By the time of the founding of Haus & Garten in 1925,[10] he had become an accomplished textile designer, and the store sold a large number of his patterns. The only extant samplebook from Haus & Garten (now in the archives of Svenskt Tenn and thought to have been brought to Stockholm by Frank) includes seventeen different patterns, among them "Primavera," "Mirakel," "Koralle" (fig. 10-5), and "Tang" (fig. 10-6)."[11] Many of the Frank interiors published in contemporary periodicals such as *Innen-Dekoration* illustrate the use of these designs for upholstery and curtains. Frank's textiles were also quite popular with other designers in Vienna in the period between the world wars. Felix Augenfeld, Walter Sobotka, and others preferred to use Frank cretonnes in their interiors.

Frank's early textile designs for Haus & Garten were block-printed by several different Austrian firms. The laborious process involved cutting the pattern in relief in blocks of linden or pear wood, one for each color. The color was then transferred from the block face to the cloth by striking the back of the block with a mallet. Most of the patterns were printed on Bohemian or Irish linen, sometimes heavy and unbleached, sometimes thinner and sheerer, with a silk-like luster. Around 1930, Frank began having the fabrics printed in England by the firm G. P. and J. Baker,[12] which also supplied traditional English cretonnes for his interior designs, and after Frank moved to Sweden in 1933, he con-

Fig. 10-7. Interior designed by Frank for the 1932 Werkbundsiedlung; it features the textile "Karma." Österreichische Nationalbibliothek.

tinued to have his patterns printed there until the beginning of the 1940s. About printed textiles Frank wrote, "Woven patterned textiles with lasting and durable qualities are now being replaced by printed cretonnes which we prefer to use, not just because they are cheaper but because we like them better."[13]

During the 1920s Frank also turned his attentions to carpets. Unlike his other textiles, his carpets were based on "paving patterns" or abstract motifs vaguely reminiscent of the form language of Jóan Miró and Paul Klee. In contrast to his patterned cretonnes, which he often gave exotic-sounding names, the carpets remained anonymous, because he viewed them as having merely an ordinary decorative function. The deep-pile carpets were hand-knotted by J. Backhausen & Söhne in Vienna, but they found little acceptance with customers. Even during Frank's later years in Sweden, the carpets were never particularly popular.[14] Today, however, more than a half-century later, they seem all the more desirable.

Frank's use of colorful, patterned cretonnes (fig. 10-7), which were so much a part of his interiors beginning in the 1920s, derived from his conviction that complex patterns bring a sense of calm to a room. In a 1934 essay he wrote that ". . . ornamentation subdivides the surface and thus reduces it in size. The monochrome surface seems restless, the patterned one calming. . . . The richness of the ornament cannot be fathomed immediately, whereas the plain surface can be grasped instantaneously and thus ceases to be of interest."[15] Frank adhered to this notion by using his own designs and often specifying Oriental rugs for his houses and apartments.[16] But he nevertheless insisted on plain white walls for his interiors: "The modern living room has white walls; that is the only possibility to preserve the freedom of introducing into a room whatever one wants without being hindered by colored decorations."[17] Such freedom allowed him to mix together different patterns and colors on upholstery, bed curtains, drapes, and cushions. He took special care, however, to avoid allowing a

Fig. 10-8. The William Morris exhibition held at Svenskt Tenn in 1938. Svenskt Tenn Archive, Stockholm.

single favorite color to dominate, which he thought was "primitive" and "too tiring." One design ethos he especially cherished was, "we should not build cages but rather open up worlds."[18]

When Frank moved to Sweden in 1933 and became associated with Svenskt Tenn, he brought with him many of his patterns from Haus & Garten. But although Estrid Ericson, the founder and director of the firm, promoted the fabrics, it was several years before his designs began to be accepted by the shop's clientele. The breakthrough came in 1938, when a major exhibition of William Morris's patterned fabrics and wallpapers was shown at Svenskt Tenn (fig. 10-8).

At the opening of the exhibition, Frank delivered a lecture entitled "Morris and Our Time," examining Morris's ideas and discussing their relevance for the twentieth century.[19] Frank's own approach to design revealed many similarities to Morris's, including a shared predilection for subjects derived from nature, a strong interest in historical tradition, and a genuine appreciation for craft production. But although Frank was sympathetic to Morris's socialist ideals, he had little patience for the British designer's love of the Gothic and rejection of the Renaissance, preferring instead the clarity of reason and of classicism.[20] Moreover, Frank's own pattern designs were much freer, featuring billowing lines and an absence of apparent repetitive symmetry. Indeed he seemed to follow Morris's advice not to ". . . copy any style at all. Yet you must study the history of your art, or you will be nose-led by the first bad copyist of it that you come across."[21]

During the 1930s several of Frank's Haus & Garten patterns were block-printed for Svenskt Tenn by Baker's. But he also designed a number of new patterns in the period prior to the outbreak of the Second World War, including "Catleya" (sic), "Svenska vårblommor" (Swedish spring flowers), "Tolvekarna" (Twelve Oaks; fig. 10-9), and "Tre öar i Svarta Havet" (Three islands in the Black Sea). The inspiration for these textiles came from diverse sources including books on flora and art history publications. Occasionally it was Estrid Ericson who took the initiative and made suggestions. The genesis of "Anakreon" is illuminating in this regard.[22] While glancing through Arthur Evans's The Palace of Minos at Knossos, Ericson noticed the image of a blue dove among the palace frescos which had been discovered a decade earlier.[23] She showed it to Frank who, enthused by its decorative possibilities, transformed the composition into a textile pattern. In his original watercolor for "Anakreon," he reproduced the wild Cretan roses, crocuses, and narcissi of the fresco but made the sky bluer and included a nest with speckled eggs. He also added ivy, the symbol of the Bacchantes which is associated with Anachreon, the Greek poet of love and drinking songs. Frank's subtle alterations and skillful adaptation to an elusive geometric format gave the design his personal stamp. Thus while "Anakreon" is in essence a copy of the bluebird fresco, it is nevertheless an independent work of art, possessing a powerful and timeless quality.

By the late 1930s, Frank's work began to influence the distinct aesthetic associated with Swedish Modern design. The bright, bold colors of the cretonnes, in particular,

Fig. 10-9. Drawing for "Tolvekarna" (Twelve Oaks), ca. 1940; pencil, watercolor and gouache on paper. Svenskt Tenn Archive, Stockholm.

found increasing favor with other designers in Sweden, who often reproduced their spirit without necessarily copying their distinctive appearance. An article on Swedish textiles in a 1943 issue of *Svenska Hem*, one of the leading Swedish design magazines, praised Frank's patterns for their high quality and subtlety, adding that they "belong to a class of their own."[24] Frank, however, as he revealed in an interview in 1951, viewed his patterned fabrics as a continuation of a long and widespread tradition, which he had merely introduced to Sweden: "When I moved to Stockholm close to twenty years ago, I introduced a new 'style.' I went back to American Colonial and English eighteenth-century furniture, especially Chippendale and Queen Anne. And I introduced printed cretonnes with floral patterns which were already popular in England, France, India, China, indeed everywhere, but, strangely enough, not in Sweden. What Sweden has in abundance is good taste and unpretentiousness."[25] Indeed the Swedes were more accustomed to woven textiles with a strong textural quality and an aesthetic that was very different from printed cretonnes.

But it was in New York City, and not Sweden, that Frank produced his most innovative and significant body of

Fig. 10-10. The series of American field guides that served as inspiration for Frank's textile designs. Private collection.

Fig. 10-11. Drawing for "Butterfly," one of the patterns inspired by American field guides. Svenskt Tenn Archive, Stockholm.

textile designs. During the winter of 1943/44, after giving his final lectures at the New School for Social Research, he began work on the first of fifty patterns intended as a gift for Estrid Ericson on her fiftieth birthday in September 1944. Reinterpreting pictures he found in American field manuals of trees, plants, birds, and insects (fig. 10-10), he produced a remarkable range of patterns, most of which are referential to his American experience. Some of the textiles, such as "U S Tree," which has leaves of the linden, magnolia, overcup oak, sugar maple, sycamore, tulip tree, and several other species, all with their Latin names printed in red, are naturalistic depictions of North American flora. Others, such as "Vegetable Tree" and "Hawaii," are "trees of life" based as much on imagination as reality. Often different varieties of plants "grow" on the same branches; the

forms are stylized and the colors heightened to achieve maximal decorative effect. This blending of the natural and the fantastic amplifies the effects, creating a potent visual tension.

Frank refashioned the illustrations found in two small field guides—*Butterflies of America* and *Insects of America*—into a pattern he called "Butterfly" (fig. 10-11), which features butterflies, as well as a range of insects, and animals, from dragonflies and beetles to earthworms, snails, and even a tadpole. *The Green Book of Birds* inspired Frank to design "Gröna Fåglar" (Green Birds) which displays birds on a mangrovelike tree of paradise. The tree's cone-shaped flowers resemble those of bindweed (*Convolvulus*), a favorite motif that dates to Frank's early years in Vienna (fig. 10-12).

A small surviving notebook, in which Frank recorded

Fig. 10-12. "Sweet," designed, ca. 1920–25, printed ca. 1925–30; cotton chintz. Österreichisches Museum für angewandte Kunst, Vienna

Fig. 10-13. Frank's preliminary sketch for "Gröna Fåglar" (Green Birds). Svenskt Tenn Archive, Stockholm.

ideas for patterns, gives a suggestion of his working method; he often made several preliminary pencil drawings before executing a final pattern design in watercolor and gouache. In the case of "Gröna Fåglar," he began with a sketch of the tree and the starlings (fig. 10-13), which he then adapted and stylized. In a similar manner he made a series of drawings using the mountains of southern China for inspiration. Little by little, the mountains were rendered more distinctly, and, finally, to increase the tension in the picture and for the sake of the graphic effect, he added figs

and fig leaves in a totally different scale, eventually dubbing the design "Rox and Fix"—rocks and figs.

Frank in fact attached great importance to the names of his patterns. Some names, such as "Rox and Fix," are plays on words. Others are intended to evoke a certain time, place, or mood. "Arras," "Tournai," and "Mille Fleurs" suggest medieval tapestries; "Baranquilla," "Brazil," "Jungle," and "La Plata" conjure up images of exotic, tropical locales and themes. Still other names, such as "Drinks," "Honey," "Italian Dinner," "Poisons," "Vitamins," "Citrus," and "Herbs" are simply descriptive.

Frank regarded his American textile patterns, with their unruly lines and vibrant energy—which "could not be fitted into any totalitarian system"— an antidote to the rigid straight-edged design approach that was coming more and more to define modernism. In his apartment on the eighth floor of Park Terrace Gardens on Manhattan's Upper West Side, he sat day after day drawing his intricate, almost willful patterns, as if by such an act alone he could overcome the evils of his time. The variety in nature, he believed, could inspire a feeling of freedom and affirmation, even indoors in closed spaces, and at the same time could provide a refuge from the pressures of life in the technological age.

Shortly after the end of the Second World War, production of Frank's New York designs started up under the skillful direction of master printer Erik Ljungberg.[26] A few years later, Ljungberg founded Ljungbergs Textiltryck AB in Floda outside of Göteborg. There, he employed the film-printing method, an American invention dating from 1907, in which the pattern was photographically transferred to a metal (in later years nylon) screen, one for each color. The framed screens were then placed over the fabric by hand and the colors applied successively. In skilled hands, the technique could achieve a higher level of quality than the traditional block-printing method, and Frank, who was quite demanding, was satisfied with this method of production.

The "American patterns" met with approval, and Svenskt Tenn received a large number of orders, many from prestigious clients, including Sweden's consulates and embassies. Around 1950 Swedish sculptor Carl Milles commissioned Svenskt Tenn to furnish a small house on his estate at Millesgården for his secretary Anne Hedmark. The music room of the house (fig. 10-14), now preserved as a museum and one of Frank's best-known interiors, exemplifies the power and grace of his later textiles.[27]

Frank's success as a pattern designer was based not only on his artistic ability and early training in ornamental

Fig. 10-14. Carl and Olga Milles in the music room of Anne's House, Millesgården. The textile is Frank's "La Plata" pattern which replaced the "Drinks" pattern that Frank had originally chosen for this interior.

design, but also on his understanding of the aesthetic effects of patterns and their psychological function. He sought to foster a sense of "natural variation" (figs. 10-15, 10-16, and 10-17) in his designs, which he believed to be essential to a pleasing and comfortable environment. He often made use of a centered rectangular composition, which results when vertical rows of the basic repeat unit are shifted in relation to one another. For many of his patterns, however, it takes a while to comprehend how Frank has organized his design so that in principle the pattern can

cover any size surface. He handled the geometrical element with great deftness, leaving the viewer with an impression of continual flow rather than constraint. In fact, within a fairly narrow geometric framework, he was able to draw in a remarkably free and unfettered fashion.

During his later years, Frank's patterns grew larger while he maintained the same richness of detail, so that it becomes even more difficult to discern the basic repetition. "Himalaya," for example (fig. 10-18), which was probably his last textile pattern, is exceptionally large; the width of the

Fig. 10-15. "Seegras," designed ca. 1925-30, printed ca. 1930; cotton chintz. Victoria and Albert Museum, London.

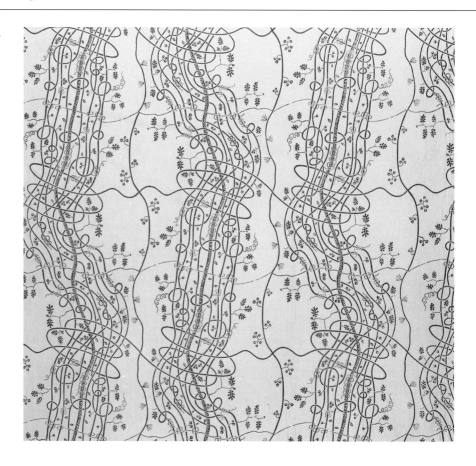

Fig. 10-16. "Parnassius Apollo," printed ca. 1994 by Ljungbergs Textiltryck for Svenskt Tenn; linen. Svenskt Tenn, Stockholm

repeat pattern is the same as the customary width of the fabric. And in "Hawaii," another large pattern, the height of the repeat unit is 74 inches (188 cm)—nearly life size—which seems to be a response to Morris's dictum not to be "afraid of large patterns; if properly designed they are more restful to the eye than small ones."[28]

Some of the patterns, such as "Anakreon," "Drinks," and "Parnassius Apollo," contain meandering, cloud-shaped areas or "islands" depicted against a white or black background that produces a dynamic, intensifying effect. For others, including "Mirakel," "Seegras," and "La Plata," Frank used a rather different approach, one closely tied to the block-printing technique, involving a sinuous and intricate play of lines. In both types, many areas are left blank, so that the white or black background occupies a remarkably large portion of the total surface area, a device that only serves to heighten the effect of the pattern.

On many designs, including "Vegetable Tree" and "Catleya," colored surfaces are subdivided by thin lines or tiny dots, which are shaded to convey liveliness and depth, a technique vaguely similar to the one often used in Oriental rug patterns. And, as in Oriental designs, Frank also chose to stylize flowers and birds, although not as strongly as did Morris and Voysey. Nonetheless, it is still difficult to determine the species or type with certainty, making the patterns all the more intriguing to the the viewer.

Fig. 10-17. "La Plata," designed 1943–44; printed ca. 1947 by Ljungbergs Textiltryck for Svenskt Tenn; linen. Svenskt Tenn, Stockholm.

Fig. 10-18. Drawing for "Himalaya," ca. 1950; pencil, watercolor, and gouache on paper. Svenskt Tenn Archive, Stockholm.

Fig. 10-19. Josef Frank at home in Stockholm, 1956.

Like Morris, Frank synthesized an interest in past traditions with a freshness of vision and a love of the natural world, lending his textiles their singular quality. But although he was clearly influenced by Morris, Frank charted his own course, eventually finding his own distinctive style. His achievement as a textile designer goes beyond the individual works. The extraordinary sense of joy and wonderment he conveys through his patterns is an expression of a larger vision, a belief that the modern movement would bring forth a more balanced view of the world, with humanity firmly positioned at its center. At the same time, he sought a new, harmonious relationship between man and nature, one that would provide the greatest measure of freedom without obliterating a link to the past.

Frank fought against the notions of adapting to the machine and the new geometric style advanced by the Bauhaus. By drawing his inspiration from nature and by experimenting to find his own particular idiom, he ultimately freed himself from the constraints of "fashion," and timelessness came within reach. The idea of a comfortable, human-centered design based on the natural world is still strongly echoed by contemporary Swedish interior decoration. Reverberations of Frank's design ideas can be seen in a surprisingly large number of products sold by IKEA and other Scandinavian interior furnishings firms, which now export their products to countries around the globe.

Frank would undoubtedly be pleased with the fruits of his works, as delighted and satisfied as he appears in a photograph taken in his own apartment (fig. 10-19) which shows him at age seventy-one, resting on a divan surrounded by his own textile flora and fauna. He had succeeded in lending "rest to our eyes and refreshment to our minds," and that was precisely what he wanted to achieve.

1. See Wilfried Posch, "Josef Frank, eine bedeutende Persönlichkeit des österreichischen Kulturliberalismus," *Um Bau* 10 (August 1986), p. 21; and Kristina Wängberg-Eriksson, *Josef Frank—Livsträd i krigens skugga* (Lund, Sweden: Signum, 1994), p. 11.

2. In 1905 the Wiener Werkstätte, the crafts collective founded by Hoffmann, Moser, and industrialist Fritz Wärndorfer in 1903, first began printing its own fabrics. By 1909 or 1910 a complete textile division was in operation. Over the course of the next two decades—until its closing in 1932—the Wiener Werkstätte textile department produced some eighteen hundred different designs by more than eighty different artists. See Angela Völker, *Die Stoffe der Wiener Werkstätte, 1910–1932* (Vienna: Brandstätter Verlag, 1987); Werner J. Schweiger, *Wiener Werkstätte: Design in Vienna, 1903–1932* (New York: Abbeville Press, 1984), pp. 220–22; and Jane Kallir, *Viennese Design and the Wiener Werkstätte* (New York: Galerie St. Etienne/George Braziller, 1986), pp. 99–102.

3. In the fall of 1901 Charles Rennie MacIntosh and a group of Scottish artists were invited to install a room at the eighth exhibition of the Secession; see, for example, *Die Kunst* 2, supplement no, 4 (1901), pp. 171–73.

4. *The Studio* was in fact available in many Viennese cafés, particularly those frequented by artists, architects, and designers. See Amelia S. Levetus, "The European Influence of the Studio," *The Studio* 105 (1933), pp. 257–58.

5. See, for example, Kallir, *Viennese Design*, p. 22.

6. Völker, *Die Stoffe*, p. 217.

7. The original watercolor rendering for "Tropenzauber" is in the collection of Johannes Spalt in Vienna. It shows a canceled number (665) which corresponds with the numbering system of the Wiener Werkstätte. The drawing for "Pax," numbered 714, was recently discovered in the Wiener Werkstätte archive at the Österreichisches Museum für angewandte Kunst in Vienna. "Schöpfung," which was produced, was numbered 634.

8. Karin Lindegren, "Arkitektur som symbol, illustrerad," lecture given at the Academy of Fine Arts, Stockholm (September 1995). The mosaics mentioned were those of the Church of Santa Costanza in Rome.

9. J. Persoz, *Traité théorique et pratique de l'impression des tissues* (Paris 1846).

10. In the official registration records preserved in the Zentralregister-archiv in Vienna, Walter Sobotka (1888–1972), another noted architect and designer and friend of Frank's, was listed as one of the partners of Haus & Garten when the firm was founded in July 1925. However, he resigned his partnership in January 1926, and thereafter the firm was offi-cally registered as "Haus & Garten—Frank & Wlach" and went by that name until the Anschluss in 1938 (Christian Witt-Dörring, October 1995: personal communication).

11. Several of the patterns in the sample book, including "Primavera," one of Frank's most popular designs, are still being produced by Svenskt Tenn.

12. G. P. and J. Baker, Ltd., London, was founded by the brothers George Percival and James Baker in 1884. George was a noted collector of his-toric textiles—especially Persian and Indian—and many of the designs in his collection were adapted for block-printing.

13. Josef Frank, "Zum Formproblem," Der gute billige Gegenstand, exhib. cat. (Vienna: Österreichisches Museum für Kunst und Industrie, 1931/32), p. 12.

14. One client, for whom Frank designed a carpet in 1938, was displeased with the final product and accepted it only with great reservations after some persuasion by Estrid Ericson. In 1985, while preparations were underway for a centenary exhibition on Frank at Svenskt Tenn, the family contacted the company, offering its rug—which had in the mean-time become a valued family heirloom—for the exhibition. After it was exhibited, the pattern became so popular that it was put back into pro-duction. Also see Sarah B. Sherrill, Carpets and Rugs of Europe and America (New York: Abbeville Press, 1995).

15. Josef Frank, "Rum och inredning," Form 30 (1934), p. 217.

16. Frank also wrote: "Someone who sits on a Persian carpet grows calm, while a person who has to run through rooms with such carpets on the floors will develop a feeling of uncertainty because it will always seem to him that he has left behind something that has not been fully appre-hended" (ibid).

17. Ibid.

18. Oskar Strnad, "Neue Wege in der Wohnraumeinrichtung," Innen-Dekoration 33 (1922), p. 323.

19. Frank generally did not write out his lectures, preferring to improvise in order to make them more lively. Yet it may be assumed that he had studied Morris's "Some Hints on Pattern Designing" lecture given at the Working Men's College in London in 1881. See William Morris, News from Nowhere and Other Writings (London: Penguin Books, 1993), pp. 257–83.

20. Of Gothic architecture, Frank wrote: "For the first time a yearning for the infinite and the noncomprehensible took shape. Its symbol was the tower, which in the narrow alley is lost with its spires lost in the gray mist, and the arch whose ribs disappear into twilight and incense. But our sobriety returns again when our bright sun intrudes through open windows. How poor the construction's much extolled truth seems to us then." Josef Frank, Architektur als Symbol : Elemente deutschen neuen Bauens (Vienna: Verlag Anton Schroll, 1931), Swedish trans. Arkitektur som symbol, translated by Karin Lindegren (Lund: ellerströms, 1995), p. 55.

21. Morris, News from Nowhere, p. 279.

22. Eva von Zweigbergk, "Josef Frank," Form 63 (1967), p. 180.

23. See Arthur Evans, The Palace of Minos at Knossos (London: Macmillan & Co., 1928), vol. 2, p. 454.

24. "Above all other pattern compositions, Josef Frank's fabrics for Svenskt Tenn should be mentioned. . . .they are not just beautiful in terms of color and printing, they also possess a high objective value as patterns. With their subtle and complex composition, they are a feast for the eye." Tyra Lundgren, "Den moderna blommigheten," Svenska Hem 4 (1943), p. 92.

25. Josef Frank, interview in the Pittsburgh Post-Gazette, February 6, 1951.

26. Ericson showed some thirty patterns that had been test printed by Ljungberg to Prince Eugen, who "considered them above even the classic William Morris." Clippings files, Estrid Ericson archive, National Museum, Stockholm.

27. The sofa and chair in the room were originally covered in the "Drinks" pattern, but Milles found the strong colors too bold. He had them recovered in the calmer and cooler "La Plata" pattern in white and blue, imagining that Hedmark "would live there as if on a white wisp of cloud in a blue sky."

28. William Morris, quoted in Michel Thomas, Christine Minguy, and Sophie Pommier, Textile Art , trans. André Marling (Geneva, Switz.: Skira; London, Weidenfeld & Nicolson, 1985), p. 187.

# CATALOGUE
# OF THE
# EXHIBITION

Christopher Long (CL)

Elisabeth Schmuttermeier (ES)

Nina Stritzler-Levine (NS-L)

Kristina Wängberg-Eriksson (KW-E)

Christian Witt-Dörring (CW-D)

The development of Frank's alternative vision of the modern home is the main theme explored in the catalogue section. It begins with works created during his formative years in Vienna from 1910 to 1933 and continues through the years in exile from 1934 to 1967, the year of Frank's death. Frank's most important architectural commissions and the furnishings and textiles he created for Haus & Garten are examined in the first part of this section, while the second part considers his work for Svenskt Tenn, his touchstone public commissions in Sweden, the unique textiles he designed in New York City, and the postwar architectural projects that mark his last attempt at an individual expression of modernism in the later years of his life. Each part encompasses the full range of Frank's design work, from architectural and design drawings to furniture, textiles, metalwork and glass. The date of the design rather than of execution has determined placement in the catalogue.

Editor's note: In the text that follows, dimensions are given with height preceding width preceding depth. The following abbreviations are used where necessary: H. (height); W. (width); L. (length); and Diam. (diameter). Dimensions of some of the chairs include the seat height because the measurement from the floor to the seat sometimes changed in early and late versions of the same design. Dimensions of the textiles include both the size of the repeat and, wherever possible, the size of the piece shown. Svenska Slöjdföreningen has been translated as "Swedish Society of Craft and Industrial Design," thereby emphasizing its comitment to industrial production and the notion of design relating specifically to industry. At the end of each entry, initials identify the author. Source references are cited in shortened form; full citations will be found in the bibliography.

## 1. Santa Maria Novella, Florence

ca. 1910
Pencil, pen and ink, watercolor on paper
19⅞ x 19⅛ in. (50.5 x 48.5 cm)

Front elevation
Inscription: "Von der Kirche S. Maria Novella im Florenz; Vorderansicht der Kirche im Masstab 1:81"

Technische Universität Wien, Universitätsarchiv

These two drawings, part of a set of twenty preserved in the archives of the Vienna Technische Universität (formerly the Technische Hochschule), are the only known original graphic works to have survived from Frank's student years. Frank produced the renderings to illustrate his dissertation, a study of the ecclesiastical works of the Florentine Renaissance architect Leon Battista Alberti, which he prepared under the supervision of his mentor Karl König between 1909 and 1910.

Frank's interest in Alberti no doubt was fired by König, who was himself deeply enamored of Alberti and the architecture of the Quattrocento. But while König stressed Alberti's role in reviving and expanding the classical tradition, Frank seems to have been equally interested in Alberti's sensitivity and almost puritanical restraint. Years later, Frank, no doubt with the architecture of the early Florentine Renaissance in mind, wrote in *Architektur als Symbol* that the "modern style" had "originated in the year 1420."

The drawings are not dated but were most likely executed during a trip Frank made to Italy in the summer and fall of 1909, or they were prepared from sketches shortly after his return to Vienna in late 1909 or early 1910. They depict Frank's

reconstructions of the original appearance of many of Alberti's best known works, including the churches of Santa Maria Novella and Santa Annunziata in Florence, San Sebastiano in Mantua, and San Francesco in Rimini. Particularly striking is the attention that Frank pays to Alberti's polychromatic decorative patterning, which seems to presage the richly colored and complex ornamental schemes of his mature work. Also noteworthy is the rather stiff academic character of the renderings — typical of late Viennese historicism — which contrasts sharply with the casual, freehand drawing style that Frank adopted in his later years. CL

References: Frank, "Über die ursprüngliche Gestalt" (1910); Long, "Josef Frank and the Crisis of Modern Architecture" (1993), pp. 33–34, 264–67; Welzig, "Die Wiener Internationalität des Josef Frank" (1994), pp. 20–21.

## 2. San Sebastiano, Mantua

ca. 1910
Pencil, pen and ink, watercolor on paper
15½ x 15⅜ in. (39.5 x 39 cm)

Elevation
Inscription: "Von der Kirche S. Sebastiano in Mantua; Hauptansicht der Kirche im Masstab 1:72"

Technische Universität Wien, Universitätsarchiv

### 3. "Florens"

Designed 1909, printed ca. 1920
Cotton; fragment
7 x 37½ in. (17.8 x 95 cm)

Blockprinted in Austria

Svenskt Tenn Archive, Stockholm

*Florens* was Josef Frank's first printed textile pattern, dating to his sojourn in northern Italy in 1909. The pattern, known only from this small fragment (in which the repeat is incomplete), is less conventional and more personal than his designs from a decade later. Frank has freely distributed his motifs: a Renaissance facade; roses, daisies, and tulips; a butterfly; and a figure, presumably Venus, draperies notwithstanding, newly born from the ocean's foam. The tiny flowers strewn in the background may relate to Flora, the goddess of flowers, as do those in Sandro Botticelli's allegorical painting *Primavera*, a theme Frank pursued in his Haus & Garten period. Throughout his fifty years as a textile designer, Frank continued to come up with variants of the rose, daisy, and tulip, his favorite flowers. In his last pattern, "Himalaya" (1950), they appear together with mountains and parrots.

Frank's studies in northern Italy fostered a lifelong appreciation for the region, especially Florence and the hills of Tuscany. A copperplate engraving of the walled city of Florence as it appeared in the sixteenth century was always prominent in his home. This small strip, with a label bearing his nickname—"Pepi's first print in Vienna"—was presented to Svenskt Tenn by Frank's wife's cousin Dagmar Grill after Frank's death in 1967. KW-E

## 4. Vitrine

1910

Rosewood veneer; black-stained ball feet, glass
72⅞ x 37⅝ x 21⅛ in. (185 x 95.5 x 53.7 cm)

Maker: Franz Krejci, Vienna

Private collection, Switzerland

This vitrine, one of Frank's earliest furniture designs, was originally made for the living room of his sister Hedwig Tedesco's apartment in Vienna; its stereometric details are still firmly rooted in the aesthetic propagated by the Wiener Werkstätte. (By 1920 orthogonal lines had disappeared from Frank's vocabulary altogether, replaced by rounded edges and curvilinear silhouettes.) Frank's approach to form is never straightforward but rather elicits a tenuous harmony which gradually reveals itself to the viewer. The two rectangular vitrines are structured with a square grid pattern; the sharp-edged bottom feet correspond to the ball feet of the upper section. Finally, the transparent volume of the upper vitrine terminates in a solid, blocklike roof. The vitrine first appears for domestic use in Austrian furniture during the Biedermeier period as does the gable-shaped vitrine.
CW-D

References: *Das Interieur* 13 (1912), pl. 44; Eisler, *Österreichische Werkkultur* (1916), p. 87.

### 5. Silver Cabinet

1910
Oak and walnut veneer, marquetry of different woods; turned black-stained wood; ivory
52¾ x 37¾ x 19⅝ in. (134 x 96 x 50 cm)

Private collection, Switzerland

Frank designed this silver cabinet and a complementary sideboard which had a gablelike top but different marquetry decoration, as part of the dining room furnishings for the Tedesco apartment. The fact that Frank placed two pieces of furniture with identical outlines but differing surface ornamentation in the same room signals a conscious break with the Viennese tradition of unified and symmetrical interiors. These two pieces, therefore, both chronologically and pragmatically, represent the beginning of Frank's redefinition of interior design to favor a more flexible, eclectic, humanizing approach. The cabinet's marquetry, however, with its repeating checkerboard-like pattern and Neoclassical wreath with bow motif, still bears a strong resemblance to contemporaneous traditional Viennese design influenced by French Neoclassical forms of the Louis XVI period.

Frank may have been introduced to the extremely unusual gable form as an architectural student; it is found on Egyptian, Greek, and Etruscan sarcophagi, as well as medieval chests and cupboards. The gable form contributes to the cabinet's appearance of being a "free-standing" piece, but here again, the design is ambiguous—although the back is veneered, it lacks marquetry and is therefore clearly not meant to be seen. Even the scale of the cabinet is oddly difficult to read; in photographs it looks as though it might be small enough to be placed on another piece of furniture.
CW-D

References: Richter, *Furniture of the Greeks* (1966); Windisch-Graetz, *Möbel Europas* (1982).

## 6. Sideboard

1912

Solid cherry and cherry veneer, brass hardware

35 x 62¼ x 22½ in. (88.5 x 157.5 x 54 cm)

Maker: J. Müller, Vienna

Private collection, Vienna

This sideboard was part of the furnishings for the "Living Hall of a Country House," installation that Frank designed for the 1912 Spring Exhibition at the Austrian Museum of Art and Industry. In writing of the exhibition in *Kunst und Kunsthandwerk*, Hartwig Fischel made special note of the "strong emphasis on construction" in the furniture on display. This was achieved by the medieval-type front post construction and the visible mortise joints which also served a decorative function. Here Frank was not so much returning to the medieval "plank style" of the Secessionists of the late 1890s, whose furniture in this style was executed almost exclusively in softwood such as pine, as he was extracting elements from the furniture of the English designer Ernest Gimson. Frank's debt to Gimson is especially evident in the hardwood plank construction, shaping of the wooden drawer pulls, and structuring of the two doors by means of horizontal, protruding groin moldings that are cut off at an angle at the end. After the exhibition, Frank incorporated this sideboard into the living/music room of his apartment at Wiedner Haustrasse 64, Vienna IV.

Frank made another interpretation of a Gimson design (cat. fig. 6a). This type of ladderback armchair is a recurring theme in his work. Though the simple rush-seated chair was widely used throughout Austria during the eighteenth century, Frank's version revived a tradition generally associated with English or Dutch furniture. (During the Arts and Crafts Movement in England this tradition had also returned to the Continent.) One of the most well-known examples of this chair form is the so-called Sussex chair by Morris & Company; the typical structure of its armrests is also to be found in Frank's drawing (the conical armrest supports, which narrow to a point, are directed via the chairframe into the stretcher). Ernest Gimson arrives at very similar solutions in his "turned chairs" from the same period.

CW-D

References: Österr. Museum für Kunst und Industrie *Frühjahresausstellung* (1912), p. 73, cat. no. 590; *Kunst and Kunsthandwerk* 15 (1912), p. 348 and photograph p. 352; *Innen-Dekoration*, 30 (1919), p. 416; Lethaby, Powell, and Griggs, *Ernest Gimson* (1924); Leicestershire Museums, *Ernest Gimson and the Cotswold Group of Craftsmen* (1978).

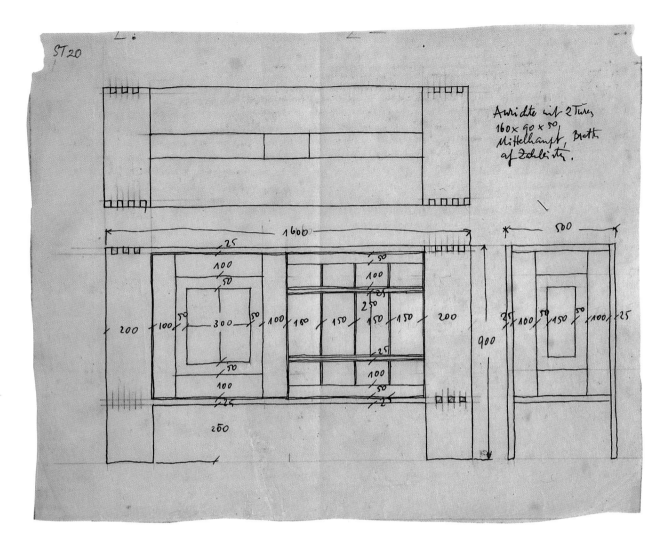

## 7. Drawing for Sideboard

ca. 1910

Ink and pencil on tracing paper

8¼ x 10⅜ in. (21 x 26.4 cm)

Private Collection, Vienna

This drawing, which shows two alternatives for the door construction, most likely depicts the sideboard Frank designed for the 1912 Spring Exhibition at the Austrian Museum of Art and Industry. Unlike the drawing, however, the finished piece has two drawers; otherwise it varies only slightly in its dimensions. Interestingly the mortise joint in the design is limited only to the juncture of the front post and bottom and top surfaces, its placement motivated entirely by construction issues. The decorative structure and construction of the top and lateral sides of the sideboard were likewise altered in the course of execution. CW-D

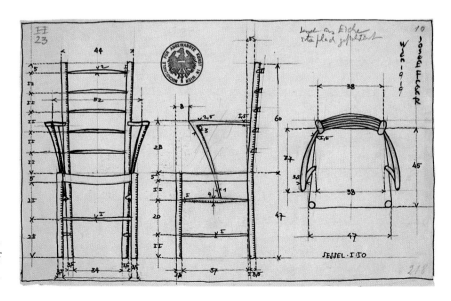

**Fig. 6a.** Design for ladderback armchair, ca. 1919; ink on paper. University of Applied Arts, Vienna, inv. no. 365.

### 8. Summer House for Hugo Bunzl, Ortmann bei Pernitz, Lower Austria

ca. 1913
Pencil, pen and ink on tracing paper
17⅜ x 24 in. (44 x 61 cm)

Elevations, plans, sections, 1:100

University of Applied Arts, Vienna
Inv. no. 1219

### 9. Summer House for Hugo Bunzl, Ortmann bei Pernitz, Lower Austria

ca. 1913
Pencil, pen and ink on tracing paper
17½ x 22¼ in. (44.5 x 56.6 cm)

Facades 1:100

University of Applied Arts, Vienna
Inv. no. 1216
Not in exhibition

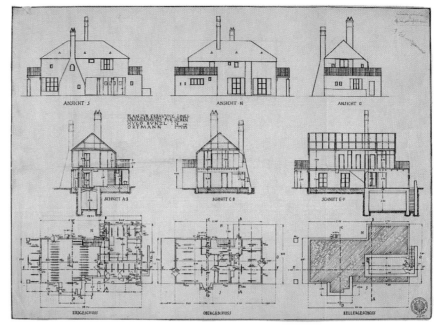

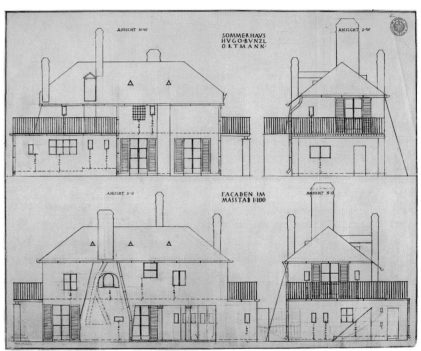

Frank designed this house for industrialist Hugo Bunzl to whom he was related both on his maternal side and through his sister's husband. Bunzl owned a large paper factory in the Piesting valley near the town of Pernitz, approximately 25 miles southwest of Vienna. Around 1913 Bunzl asked Frank to design a house for him not far from the factory complex that would serve as a summer residence.

Frank began work on the project the same year, and construction was evidently completed in 1914. The site chosen was a clearing atop a small wooded hill which afforded sweeping views in all directions. Although the two-story, hipped-roofed house appears at first glance to be a conventional block and stucco structure, it is in fact built entirely of wood, except for the foundation, fireplace, and chimney. The walls are constructed of large squared logs, about 6 inches thick, with dovetail joints at the corners, and the floors are supported with massive rough-hewn beams.

The plan is typical of Frank's early houses: clearly laid-out, yet informal, with a strong emphasis on comfort and coziness. As befits a summer house, the rooms are open and airy. "It was my intention," Frank wrote in a short article in *Innen-Dekoration*, "to link the living rooms of the ground floor with the garden by means of large glass doors, and to open the bedrooms on the upper floor to all sides with added-on balconies." Frank further underscored this sense of lightness by painting most of the interior walls and ceilings white and using simple unadorned furnishings. "The few furnishings are placed independently of the space," Frank noted. "To avoid any sense of heaviness, they are made of the most diverse materials. But the wood is neither stained nor painted, so that none of the freshness and natural character of the wood is lost. Similarly, the curtains on the windows and the lampshades are white so that the light can fall into the room in its natural color. . . . The fabrics and carpets are multicolored, like the gardens outside the windows, but are mostly red and yellow, and thus provide a warm-toned contrast to the broad expanses of sky and forest on all sides of the house."

The house is still in the hands of the Bunzl family. Most of the original furnishings have been removed, but it has otherwise survived in good condition. CL

References: *Innen-Dekoration* 30 (December 1919), pp. 410–15; Long, "Josef Frank and the Crisis of Modern Architecture" (1993), pp. 44–48, 270–71; Welzig, "Die Wiener Internationalität des Josef Frank" (1994), pp. 80–85.

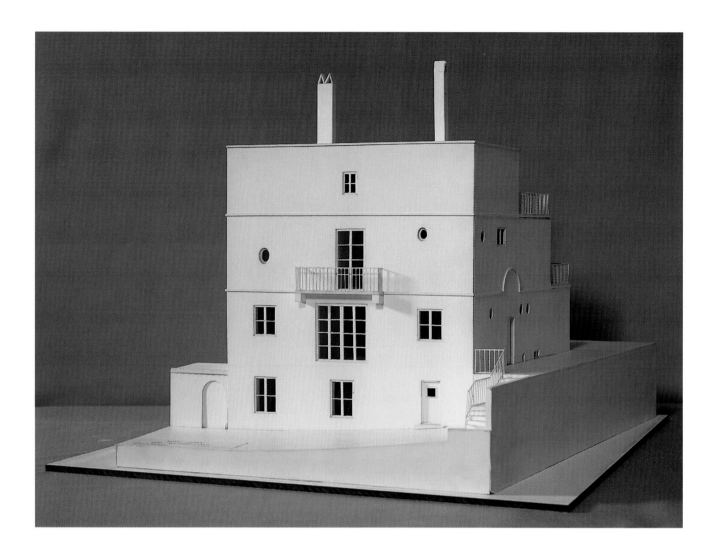

## 10. House for Emil and Agnes Scholl (model)

1913–14; model, ca. 1985
Cardboard (covered with plexiglass)
10⅝ x 18½ x 24⅝ in. (27 x 47 x 62.5 cm)

Graphische Sammlung Albertina, Vienna
Architekturmodelle, FJ01

After returning from Cologne in the fall of 1913, Frank apparently began work on this large, three-story house for the writer Emil Scholl and his wife Agnes. A lantern slide of a perspective sketch, probably from the same year, found among Frank's papers after his death shows an early version of the structure along with three similar houses arrayed in a row, suggesting that it was originally conceived as part of a small villa colony (similar to Josef Hoffmann's nearby Kaasgraben Colony). The two houses at either end of the row, the Scholl House (Wilbrandtgasse 3) and the Strauss House (Wilbrandtgasse 11), were built the following year; the other two were never realized.

The house is located in what was then a largely unbuilt area on the city's western edge. It sits on a long ridge extending between the Pötzleinsdorf and Sievering valleys, with a view of the Grinzing valley to the north. The site slopes sharply toward the street so that the basement story, visible from the front, is below grade at the rear.

With its simple blocklike massing, the house bears a marked resemblance to Adolf Loos's villas of the same period. In contrast to Loos, however, Frank included several pared-down classical decorative elements—pilasters, string courses, and window and door surrounds—on the facades, which give the house a vaguely neo-Biedermeier guise, somewhat like the Villa Wassermann, which Frank's partner Oskar Strnad designed at about the same time. The street (north) facade has rather small openings—designed, as Frank explained, to protect the house from the cold winter winds—while the rear (south) facade, which faced a small formal rose garden, is more open, with large windows and doors.

The construction of the house was somewhat unusual for Vienna at the time. Frank employed a structural system of brick load-bearing walls (originally left unpainted), with a flat, poured concrete roof. The upper floor is supported by a reinforced concrete beam extending lengthwise through the house's center, providing a long open span for the main living areas.

The configuration of the interior spaces was similarly unconventional. In what would become Frank's standard practice, the plan is irregularly arranged, with the emphasis on fostering an impression of spatial diversity and complexity. To promote the sort of rambling feeling he admired in English houses, Frank avoided any axial planning or symmetrical arrangement. He largely dispensed with hallways, so that most of the rooms open directly into one another, and he reduced the size of the service areas and anteroom on the first floor, thereby increasing the amount of "living space." To further underscore the sense of spatial play, he used windows of varying sizes and shapes and made the entire structure slightly pie-shaped, with the walls splaying outward toward the rear, paralleling the property lines. As a result the outer rooms of the house have both acute and obtuse corners, making them seem larger than they are.

The main entrance is through a small, inconspicuous door on the northwest side. It opens into a small vestibule that provides access to the kitchen and the main living areas of the first floor. On one side of the vestibule is a service stairway leading up to the second and third floors and down into the basement. The center of the main floor is dominated by a large living area (*Halle*), which extends the width of the house, while the eastern end of the ground floor is taken up by a small winter sun room and a study. The southwest corner contains the dining room.

From the east side of the living room another stairway leads to the second floor. The southern portion of the second floor is taken up by a children's room and the master bedroom, which opens out onto a balcony facing the rear garden. On the north side are a bathroom and servant's room. The third floor, set back to form a continuous terrace, is occupied by two stor-

age rooms and a space for drying clothes.

The interior has been altered somewhat in recent years and the brick has been painted, but the house otherwise remains in good condition. CL

References: *Wasmuths Monatshefte für Baukunst 2* (1915/16), pp. 522–24; Eisler, *Österreichische Werkkultur* [1916], pp. 83–84; *Innen-Dekoration 30* (1919), pp. 241–43; Gmeiner and Pirhofer, *Der Österreichische Werkbund* (1985), p. 112; Moravánszky, *Die Architektur der Donaumonarchie* (1988), pp. 171, 174; Long, "Josef Frank and the Crisis of Modern Architecture" (1993), pp. 47–49, 272–73; Welzig, "Die Wiener Internationalität des Josef Frank" (1994), pp. 72–80.

**Fig. 10a.** Scholl House, Wilbrandtgasse 3, Vienna, 1913–14. Courtesy Swedish Museum of Architecture, Stockholm.

### 11. Table Lamp

1919
Brass, silk
29 x 20½ in. (73.5 x 51 cm)

Wiener Werkstätte, model number "M 2997"

MAK-Austrian Museum of Applied Arts,
Vienna
Inv. no. [Me] 912

In 1919, the year Josef Frank started his tenure as professor at the Vienna School of Arts and Crafts (Kunstgewerbeschule), he also began to create designs for the Wiener Werkstätte. The company's order book lists twelve designs by Frank for table centerpieces, fruit bowls, boxes, table lamps, standing lamps, a tray, small case, and mirror. Of these designs, however, only five were actually executed: a centerpiece for serving candies, a fruit bowl, and three different lamp models, including the one shown here; it was also the most popular Frank model. Twelve examples of this lamp were produced, each with a different fabric pattern for the lampshades.

Frank's design work for the Wiener Werkstätte was soon forgotten. He worked there for a very short period, a mere two years (1919–20), and few of his designs were executed. As a consequence, this table lamp has been wrongly attributed to Dagobert Peche, another Wiener Werkstätte artist, perhaps because it was photographed atop a desk by Peche. The spiral motif that Frank used in the arms can also be found in other designs by Peche and Josef Hoffmann, as well as in some of the lamps that Frank later designed for Svenskt Tenn. ES

References: Eisler, *Dagobert Peche* (1925), pl. 21; *Wien 1900: Kunst & Design* (1991), p. 79, no. 190.

## 12. "Pax"

ca. 1919
Watercolor and pencil on paper
23⅞ x 27¼ in. (60.7 x 69.2 cm)

MAK-Austrian Museum of Applied Arts,
Vienna
Wiener Werkstätte Archive No. 3103
Inv. no. 11820/1

In *Architektur als Symbol* Frank wrote, "The great experience [of World War I] was understanding that nothing had to be the way it is and that everything can be different: that there does not need to be bread, that money has no set value and that we could feel comfortable in a situation that until then would have been unimaginable. We were shaken from security and everyday occupations, away from our plans for the future, and for four years we lived a passive life—which did not bring us nearer to our goals. We got to know people of whose existences we would formerly only have had a vague idea, and thereby [we also got to know] a bigger world; that has always been the result of every war. . . . Sacrosanct concepts such as emperor, kingdom, life, and property were shattered; now we seek a fixed point."

"Pax" (Peace), with its radiance, reflects Frank's search for a fixed point and his joy over the end of World War I. As a design it is linked to European calicoes that were first printed in France during the latter half of the seventeenth century, inspired by much-admired Indian and Persian models.

Dazzling, whimsical flowers sprout from shimmering blue mounds. The stamens and pistils have been greatly enlarged and are themselves almost flowers. As in traditional calico patterns the forms are strongly outlined in various colors. The palette is muted, almost cautious. The geometry is the simplest imaginable: rectangles in rows and in stacks. Frank was at the beginning of his career in textile design, still finding his own way, and his work is thus overshadowed by other Wiener Werkstätte designers of the time. This, however, would soon change. KW-E

References: Frank, *Arkitektur som symbol* (1995); Persoz, *Traité théorique et pratique* (1846); Völker, *Die Stoffe der Wiener Werkstätte* (1990); Sandberg, in *Dalarnas Hembygdsbok* (1989), p. 59; Musée Oberkampf, *Les Indiennes* (1986).

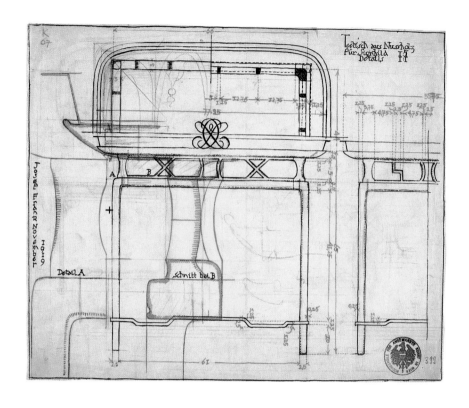

## 13. Drawing for a Tea Table

1919
Ink, pencil on paper
8⅞ x 10⅝ in. (22.5 x 27 cm)

Scale 1:5, details 1:1
Inscription: "JOSEF FRANK NOVEMBER
1919"; "Teetisch aus Nussholz für Signhild"

University of Applied Arts, Vienna
Inv. no. 399

This tea table, designed for Signhild
Sebenius (Frank's sister-in-law, later
Claëson) typifies Frank's ability to create
an independent design by extracting elements from a diversity of cultural sources.
The table is one of the earliest examples
to illustrate his ideal of "organic form."
The pierced apron of the table's base
alludes to its Chinese origins; the owner's
mirror-image monogram recalls similar
monograms from the late seventeenth century which, like the tea-table form itself
(with its removable tray), were known in
Dutch, English, and Scandinavian culture
and are part of their furniture traditions.
CW-D

## 14. "Bolero"

Designed ca. 1920; printed ca. 1925
Linen
Size: 40½ x 50⅝ in. (102.9 x 131.1 cm)
Repeat: 19½ x 8 in. (49 x 21 cm)

Blockprinted for Haus & Garten in Austria

Svenskt Tenn Archive, Stockholm

"Bolero" is related to another Haus & Garten pattern called "Bukovina," after the eastern province north of Transylvania (today divided between Romania and Ukraine). The design consists of gourdlike "sunflowers," one in each repeat unit, with added "ears of rye" like the leaves of a flower stalk. The folkloric impression is strengthened by the bright reds and blues set against a light background. In the Carpathian Mountains men wear richly embroidered vests (*boleros*) that resemble a Spanish bullfighter's garment, with similar patterns.

Before and during the First World War, Josef Frank and Oskar Strnad, his fellow student at the Technische Hochschule, were interested in provincial folk art. Frank may

have found inspiration for this design at the Österreichisches Museum für Volkskunde in Vienna. The museum owned a large collection of textiles from every region of the former Austro-Hungarian empire. In 1917 Frank called a ladderback chair design "Orsova," after a city near the Iron Gate, where the Danube flows through the Carpathian Mountains. KW-E

References: Bossert, *Ornamente der Volkskunst* (1956); Spalt and Czech, *Josef Frank 1885–1967* (1981).

### 15. Side Chair

ca. 1921

Pearwood, bamboo and rattan

33¾ x 17¼ x 19¾ in. (84.5 x 43.8 x 50.2 cm)

Camilla Lundberg, Sweden

Although Frank designed this side chair in Vienna during his tenure at the Kunstge-werbeschule (School of Arts and Crafts), it played an important role in the develop-ment of his career in Sweden. It was made for the Lundberg family home in Djurs-holm, a suburb of Stockholm, which is thought to have been Frank's first commis-sion for a Swedish patron. It may also have been the first work by Frank seen by Estrid Ericson, founder and director of Svenskt Tenn, who during the 1920s, while a guest at Djursholm, admired this chair and became interested in Frank and his work.

The chair displays many of the features that came to characterize Frank's mature work as a furniture designer. As he often did, Frank integrated Western and non-Western sources. A Chinese influence is evident in the use of a woven rattan seat. The thin staves of wood—to be replaced by bamboo in Frank's later work —are placed vertically across the back and enhance the elegant lines of the chair. Vestiges of late-eighteenth and early-nine-teenth-century Viennese furniture can be seen in the slender contours of the stiles, legs, and crest rail. The side chair is remark-

ably lightweight and adheres to a fundamental principle of Frank's design philosophy that furniture should be light to be
moved easily.

The chair was probably made in the furniture workshop of the Kunstgewer-

beschule. Unfortunately no production
records survive from the school workshop,
and the maker is unknown. NS-L

References: Wängberg-Eriksson, "Svenskt Tenn,
Josef Frank och Estrid Ericson" (1985); idem,
"The Interior Designer," in Boman, *Estrid Ericson*

(1989); *Josef Frank inredning* (1994); Wängberg-
Eriksson, *Josef Frank Livsträd* (1994).

**Fig. 15a.** Josef Frank, Armchair, ca. 1925;
mahogany, linen, bamboo; designed for
Haus & Garten in Austria. Private collection, Vienna.

**Fig. 15b.** Josef Frank, Side Chair, ca. 1947;
mahogany, rattan, leather; retailed by
Svenskt Tenn, Stockholm. Model
no. 1179, Svenskt Tenn, Stockholm.

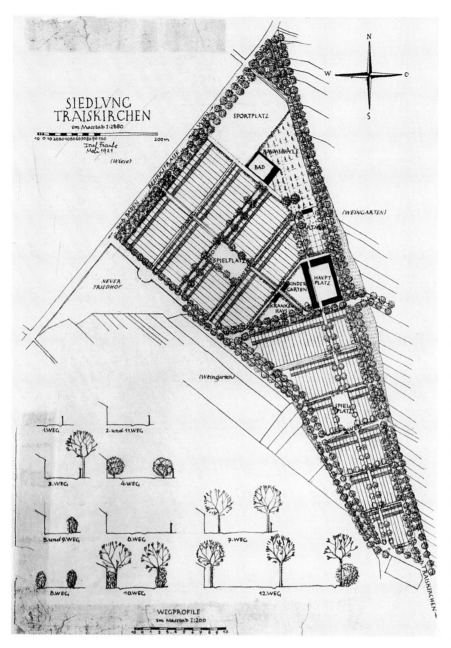

in parallel rows; to the rear of each unit is a long strip of land on which the residents could grow their own food. Both versions include a main square, playgrounds, kindergarten, hospital, public bath, and garden nursery. One of the drawings, dated May 1921, and probably repesenting an earlier version of the project, shows a cross section of the planting scheme Frank intended for the various pathways, while the other includes plans, an elevation, and section of a proposed housing prototype.

The two-story row house is similar to the one Frank designed for another settlement on the Hoffingergasse in Vienna at about the same time. The ground floor contains a small anteroom and a *Wohnküche* (or combination living room and kitchen); upstairs are three small bedrooms. Attached to the house on the street side is a low one-story barn with stalls for small animals.

Frank later published a drawing of a somewhat larger prototype house, also dated 1921, in *Der Neubau*. The plan of the house is similar, with a *Wohnküche* on the first floor, but upstairs there are four rather than three bedrooms and a terrace running the length of the second story on the courtyard side. Unlike the earlier prototype, the barn is separated from the main house and is situated at the far end of the courtyard facing the street. CL

References: *Der Neubau* 6 (February 10, 1924), p. 28; Spalt and Czech, *Josef Frank, 1885–1967* (1981), p. 126; Long, "Josef Frank and the Crisis of Modern Architecture" (1993), pp. 80–81, 277–78.

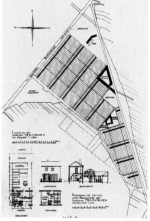

**Fig. 16a.** Housing Settlement in Traiskirchen, Lower Austria, 1921 (project); pencil, pen and ink on tracing paper; site plan, plans, elevation, section of a typical house. Inv. no. 48, Frank-Archiv, Graphische Sammlung Albertina, Vienna.

## 16. Housing Settlement, Traiskirchen, Lower Austria

1921
Pencil, pen and ink on tracing paper
14⅛ x 10 in. (36 x 25.5 cm)

Planting scheme, site plan
Inscription: "Siedlung Traiskirchen im Masstab 1:2880; Wegprofile im Masstab 1:200"; signed "Josef Frank"; dated "Mai 1921"

Frank-Archiv, Graphische Sammlung Albertina, Vienna
Inv. no. 49

This project for an unrealized housing settlement was one in a series Frank designed between 1919 and 1924 in an effort to help alleviate Austria's severe postwar housing

shortage. The circumstances of the commission are unknown, but it was most likely carried out for the *Österreichischer Verband für Siedlungs- und Kleingartenwesen* (Austrian Union of Settlers and Small Gardeners), an umbrella organization of the many grassroots housing cooperatives for which Frank frequently worked as an adviser.

The site for the proposed settlement was a roughly triangular-shaped piece of land on the outskirts of the town of Traiskirchen, some 15 miles south of Vienna. These two drawings depict slightly different versions of the proposed project. Both show a large housing complex with a central public area effectively splitting the development into two distinct zones. The approximately 190 row houses are arranged

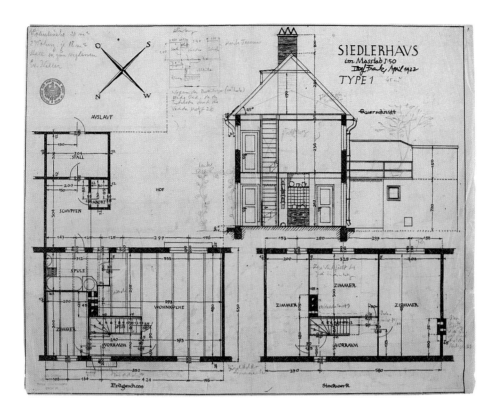

## 17. Model Settlement House Type I

1922 (project)
Pencil, pen and ink on tracing paper
13⅝ x 16⅞ in. (34.5 x 43 cm)

Plans, section
Inscription: "Siedlerhaus Type I im Masstab
1:50"; signed "Josef Frank"; dated "April 1922"

University of Applied Arts, Vienna
Inv. no. 1224

Frank designed this small two-story row house as a prototype for an unknown housing settlement. This drawing, the only extant one of the house, is dated April 1922, suggesting that it may have been intended as a prototype for either the unrealized Rodaun or Stockerau housing settlements, which Frank worked on around this time. The simple structure is similar to the prototype Frank designed for the Traiskirchen Settlement. The entrance is on the left side and leads into a small anteroom. A door on the right side of the anteroom opens into a small combination living room and kitchen (*Wohnküche*) and sink area; off one side of the anteroom is a small bedroom. A narrow central stairway leads up from the living room and kitchen to the second floor, where there are three additional bedrooms. Attached to the rear of the house is a small one-story barn. The main body of the house has a traditional side-gabled roof, while the barn has a flat roof that doubles as a small upstairs terrace and provides access to the hay loft. CL

References: Spalt and Czech, *Josef Frank, 1885–1967* (1981), p. 127; Long, "Josef Frank and the Crisis of Modern Architecture" (1993), p. 280.

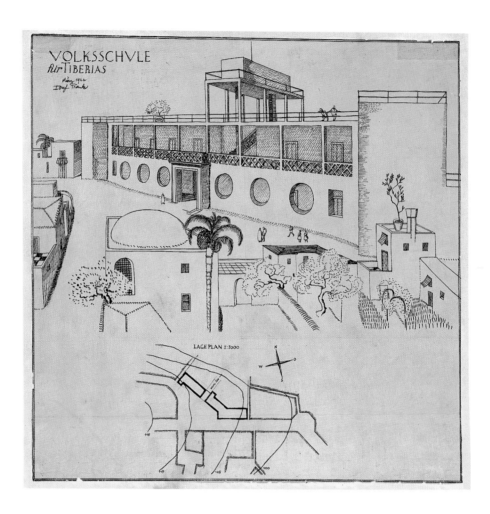

## 18. Elementary School in Tiberias, Palestine

1922 (project)
Pencil, pen and ink on tracing paper
18¼ x 18⅛ in. (46.5 x 46 cm)

Perspective; site plan 1:1000
Inscription: "Volkschule für Tiberias";
"Lageplan 1:1000"; signed "Josef Frank"; dated
"März 1922"

Frank-Archiv, Graphische Sammlung Albertina,
Vienna
Inv. no. 23

Little is known about the circumstances surrounding this unusual project for a school in Palestine. It was mostly likely commissioned by an Austrian Jewish emigré, who may have known Frank or someone in his circle of friends and relatives. This drawing, dated March 1922, is the only surviving record of the project. It includes a perspective sketch of the front elevation and a small site plan, which together allow one to reconstruct Frank's idea at least partially.

The building consists of two irregularly shaped wings set at a slight angle to one other. The longer of the wings has two stories while the shorter one, only a small portion of which is shown in the perspective sketch, is single storied. The plan of the main wing is divided into two longitudinal strips with a gallery running the length of the building on the front side. The second-floor gallery is completely open except for low railing and roof supports, while the groun-floor gallery is partially walled with six large circular and two smaller square openings, which give the structure a vaguely Middle Eastern character. On the rear side of the building off the galleries are presumably classrooms and offices. The main entrance is located in the center of the longer wing and leads to an open stairway linking the building's three levels. The entry portal also serves as a pedestrian passageway connecting the square in the front of the school with the ocean. Like the school in Ortmann that Frank designed the previous year, both of the building's wings have flat roofs which can be used as terraces. The most striking element of the design, aside from the large round openings, is the small roof pavilion, which Frank characteristically has set off to the right of center, a technique he often applied in his works to undermine the sense of monumentality and provide a more complex visual appearance. CL

References: Spalt and Czech, *Josef Frank, 1885–1967* (1981), p. 177; Long, "Josef Frank and the Crisis of Modern Architecture" (1993), pp. 83, 283.

## 19. Main Square for a Housing Settlement in Klosterneuburg, Lower Austria

1923 (project)
Pencil, pen and ink on tracing paper
16¾ x 32½ in. (42.5 x 82.5 cm)

Perspective
Inscription: "Hauptplatz der Siedlung
Klosterneuburg"; signed "Josef Frank"; dated
"Juni 1923"

Frank-Archiv, Graphische Sammlung Albertina,
Vienna
Inv. no. 20

Frank began work on this design for an unbuilt housing project in the town of Klosterneuburg in late 1921 or early 1922. The intended site was a roughly rectangular-shaped piece of land near the Danube, a few miles upstream from Vienna. A site plan published in *Innen-Dekoration* in 1923 shows 118 row houses arranged in five parallel rows running east-west, with several playgrounds and a plant nursery interspersed among the houses. Running perpendicular to the rows of houses are several small pedestrian walkways, creating a grid-like effect.

A drawing for a housing prototype also published in *Innen-Dekoration* shows a three-story row house with a flat roof. The house is similar to Frank's other *Siedlung* houses of the period, with a *Wohnküche* on the ground floor and three bedrooms on the second floor, but there is an additional small third floor room occupying about a third of the roof area; the remainder of the space is taken up by a terrace. Each of the housing units also has a small barn. The barns are separated from the houses by a courtyard and arranged in a continuous line along the street. The scheme is similar to those Frank used for Traiskirchen and several other housing settlements of the early 1920s, but the courtyard is larger, and the complex has a more "modern" appearance, in large part due to Frank's use of flat rather than pitched roofs.

This perspective view shows the center of the complex. To the left of the main square is a community and administrative center; to the right is a school building. The school is particularly noteworthy for its simple, functional design. It is also one of the few early examples of Frank's use of a reinforced concrete frame construction. The regular spacing of the bays gives the build-ing a uniform, symmetrical appearance, unusual in Frank's oeuvre. CL

References: *Innen-Dekoration* 34 (August 1923), p. 338; *Das Kunstblatt* 7 (1924), p. 109; *Der Neubau* 6 (February 10, 1924), p. 26; Spalt and Czech, *Josef Frank, 1885–1967* (1981), pp. 128–29; *Um Bau* 10 (August 1986), pp. 49–51; Long, "Josef Frank and the Crisis of Modern Architecture" (1993), pp. 81–82, 283–84.

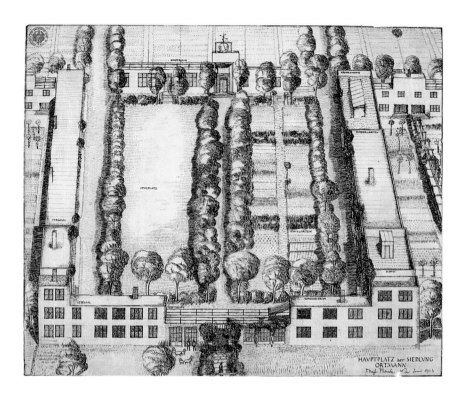

## 20. Main Square for the Ortmann Housing Settlement, Ortmann bei Pernitz, Lower Austria

1923 (project)
Pencil, pen and ink on tracing paper
16⅞ x 16¾ in. (43 x 42.5 cm)

Perspective
Inscription: "Hauptplatz der Siedlung Ortmann"; signed "Josef Frank:"; dated "Wien, Juni 1923"

University of Applied Arts, Vienna
Inv. no. 1243

This unrealized project was to have been the centerpiece of the housing complex Frank designed for Hugo Bunzl's Ortmann paper factory in the late 1910s and early 1920s. Bunzl, for whom Frank had also designed a summer house in Ortmann just prior to the outbreak of World War I, was well-known for his interest in his workers' social welfare, and his many pro-worker projects earned him the nickname "Roter Industrie-Baron" or the Industrial Red Baron. He found a kindred spirit in Frank, who was active in Socialist circles and had

close connections to many in the Austrian Socialist Party leadership.

This drawing, dated June 1923, is the only extant record of the project. It shows a large square framed by buildings on four sides. At the rear (north) side of the square is the already existing *Kinderheim* or preschool, which Frank had designed in 1921. The other three sides are composed of mostly two-story structures and include a gymnasium, reading room, pub, cooperative store, elementary school, kindergarten, and hospital. At the center of the south end adjacent to the pub is a large portal leading into the square. The square itself is bisected by a tree-lined pathway leading from the south portal to the main door of the *Kinderheim*. Also visible in the drawing on either side of the main sqaure complex are proposed row houses similar to those Frank designed for the Klosterneuburg *Siedlung* at about the same time. Like Le Corbusier's projects of the same period, the roofs of the school, kindergarten, pub, and hospital all have low walls or metal railings and are intended to be used as terraces.

Although the project was never realized, several community buildings designed by other architects were later constructed near the *Kinderheim*, roughly approximating Frank's original scheme. CL

References: Spalt and Czech, *Josef Frank, 1885–1967* (1981), p. 119; Long, "Josef Frank and the Crisis of Modern Architecture" (1993), pp. 82–83, 286–87.

PROJEKT
für ein
WOHNHAVS
am
KONGRESSPLATZ

*Josef Frank*
*Dezember 1923*

ANSICHT vom KONGRESSPLATZ

## 21. Municipal Apartment House on Kongressplatz, Vienna

1923 (project)
Pencil, pen and ink on tracing paper
12⅝ x 16½ in. (32 x 42 cm); framed, 20⅞ x
16⅞ in. (53 x 43 cm)

Perspective
Inscription: "Projekt für ein Wohnhaus am
Kongressplatz"; signed "Josef Frank"; dated
"Dezember 1923"

Frank-Archiv, Graphische Sammlung Albertina,
Vienna
Inv. no. 39

This apartment house in Vienna's seventeenth district (now known as the
Wiedenhofer-Hof) was among the earliest
of the series of large housing blocks constructed by the Viennese Socialist government under the auspices of the first "five-
year plan" for housing launched in 1923.
Frank began work on the project in the fall
or early winter of the same year. The site
was a trapezoid-shaped piece of land
bounded on all four sides by streets, with

one side facing a small park. This drawing,
from December 1923, shows an early version
of the project, which differs quite dramatically from Frank's final design. Here Frank
has divided the block into two main sections, linking them with a four-story central
wing. In the final design, however, he opted
for a more traditional scheme, with the
building arranged around the perimeter of
the site. Although Frank greatly simplified
the facade in the later version, the overall
design is similar, with the mass broken up
by regularly spaced white-framed windows
and loggias at the corners. The building
stood out among the city's other housing
projects at the time not only for its uncom-
promisingly modern design, but for its bold
color scheme-warm orange-red walls with
bold white window frames—that earned it
the nickname the "Paprika-Hof."

The apartments, although small—generally 200 square feet or less—were a vast
improvement over the typical prewar tenements in Vienna. Every unit had electricity,
running water, and toilets, and most were

light and well-ventilated. The complex also
provided other facilities, including a cooperative grocery store and a public bath. A
fifth floor was added to the building in
1953, altering its original proportions. CL

References: *Die Wohnhausanlage der Gemeinde Wien*
(1926); *Der Neubau* 6 (10 June 1924), p. 119;
*L'Architecture vivante* (Winter 1926), pl. 42; *Der Tag*
(August 1, 1926), p. 9; *Menorah* 6 (September
1926): facing p. 519; *Der Neubau* 8 (October 10,
1926), pp. 224–26; *Wasmuths Monatshefte für
Baukunst* 10 (1926), pp. 366ff.; *Moderne Bauformen* 26
(May 1927), p. 171; *Wasmuths Monatshefte für
Baukunst* 11 (1927), pp. 381ff.; Taut, *Modern
Architecture* (1929), p. 116; Spalt and Czech, *Josef
Frank, 1885–1967* (1981), pp. 134–37; *Bauwelt* 76
(12 July 1985), pp. 1049–50; Long, "Josef Frank
and the Crisis of Modern Architecture" (1993),
pp. 90–92, 288–89; Achleitner, *Österreichische
Architektur* (1995), pp. 194–95.

## 22. Drop-Front Desk

ca. 1925
Wooden carcass with green paint (re-painted);
brass hardware; interior veneered with Makasar
ebony and cherry wood
43¼ x 31½ x 15¾ in. (110 x 80 x 40 cm)

Made for Haus & Garten in Austria
MAK-Austrian Museum of Applied Arts,
Vienna
Inv. no. H 2286

This drop-front desk appeared in many of
Frank's most important interiors of the
interwar years. It was featured prominently
in 1927, in the living room/bedroom of his
Double House at the Weissenhofsiedlung in
Stuttgart; in 1930 one was included in the
daughter's room in the House for Julius and
Margarete Beer in Vienna; and again, in
1932, it appeared among the furnishings of
the living/dining room in Frank's house for

**Fig. 22a.** Drop-Front Desk, interior view.

the Werkbundsiedlung in Vienna. The
desk's low-maintenance, economical painted
surface made its use ideal in each instance.
The form is a revival of a traditional type
of drop-front secretary, which has its origins in the second half of the eighteenth
century (signaling, in its day, a new kind of
privacy). The strong color of its ultramod-
ern painted surface illustrated Frank's idea
of separating the individual piece of furniture from the white walls of the room
through color contrast. A feeling
of human warmth and security of is
conveyed when the drop-front is open to
reveal its dark wood interior (in stark
contrast to the cool exterior of the desk).
CW-D

References: *Innen-Dekoration* 37 (1926), p. 376; ibid.
42 (1931), p. 393; Boltenstern, *Wiener Möbel* (1934),
p. 43.

### 23. Chest-of-Drawers

ca. 1925

Solid cherry and plywood, cherry veneer; brass hardware

26⅜ x 21⅜ x 13⅝ in. (67 x 54.4 x 34.5 cm)

Made for Haus & Garten in Austria

MAK-Austrian Museum of Applied Arts, Vienna

Inv. no. H 2944

This small, mobile case piece (which had been fitted with casters in an earlier version) is a prime example of Frank's "philosophy of furniture." The design has enough room between the legs and body to avoid an impression of weightiness and to allow the floor and wall to be seen. The carcass is English-inspired. The small, rounded molding (so-called "cock bead molding") used on the body to frame the drawers is quite typical of English design. The drawers, which increase in number and decorative divisions from top to bottom, echo Far-Eastern or English and Flemish cabinets from the seventeenth century. Bombé drawer front sections, which are also found in Flemish cabinetry, are laterally beveled in Frank's model. CW-D

References: *Moderne Bauformen* 28 (1929), p. 81; Boltenstern, *Wiener Möbel* (1934), pp. 18, 93.

**Fig. 23a.** Bedroom, house for A. S. F, Vienna, ca. 1932. From *Innen-Dekoration* 44 (1933).

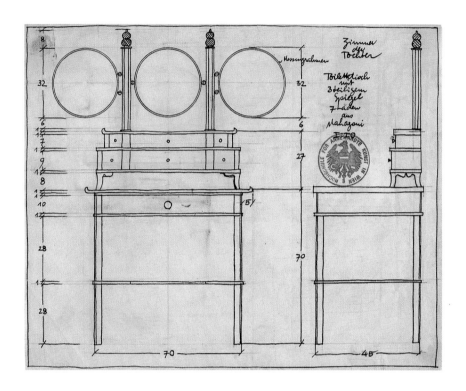

### 24. Drawing for a Dressing Table

ca. 1925
Ink on tracing paper
6¼ x 7⅞ in. (16 x 20 cm)

Inscription: "Zimmer der Tochter Toilettisch mit 3 teiligen Spiegel 7 Laden aus Mahagoni:

University of Applied Arts, Vienna
Inv. no. 403

The dressing table was one of the earliest designs in the Haus & Garten product line. Frank created at least two versions, one with three mirrors (as in this drawing); the other, a single-mirror table. The single-mirror version continued to be made later by Svenskt Tenn and appeared in Frank's installation drawing for the Golden Gate Exhibition in 1939. The piece was created for the "daughter's room," a living room/bedroom in House L. in Vienna. Details of the design are indebted to Chinese furniture, particularly the upturned ends of the horizontal surfaces and the superstructure of the drawers. There is an interesting tension in Frank's design between the traditional form of the table and the more modern character of the mirrors. The side elevation illustrates Frank's predilection for tables and case pieces in two sections, possibly following an English precedent. The dressing table that was executed according to this drawing was made of mahogany with a mirror frame in metal. The shelf element between the legs was concealed behind a gathered, white tulle fabric.

Dressing tables with large mirrors were a relatively common form during this period. The English firm of Heal & Son, which Frank often used for design sources, produced a similar piece, and in France the renowned furniture designer Jacques-Emile Ruhlmann created such tables during the early 1920s for a luxury furniture market. Five years after Frank conceived of this design Ruhlmann introduced his three-mirror version at the Salon des Artistes Décorateurs in Paris. CW-D/NS-L

References: *Innen-Dekoration* 37 (1926), p. 368; Johanssen, *Josef Frank och Svenskt Tenn* (1968); Nationalmuseum, *Josef Frank 1885–1967* (1968); Spalt and Czech, "Josef Frank 1885–1967" (1981); Witt-Dörring, *Neues Wohnen Wiener Innenraumgestaltung* (1980); Wängberg-Eriksson, *Josef Frank Livsträd* (1994).

## 25. Armchair

Designed ca. 1925; this example after 1930
Solid walnut, stained and partly turned
mahogany, beech wood seat frame; original red
leather upholstery, brass upholstery tacks
35¼ x 24 x 26⅝ in. (89.5 x 61 x 67.5 cm); seat
height, 17⅜ in. (44 cm)

Made for Haus & Garten in Austria

Private collection, Vienna

The original earlier version of this armchair
was somewhat smaller (35 x 20¾ x 25⅜ in.);
it was enlarged primarily in the seat width
to make it more comfortable. Here again,
Frank realizes his ideal of an "organically
evolved" form. This design originates with
the tradition of the Windsor chair, whose
influence still lingers in the lateral and rear
apron. For the benefit of greater comfort,
however, the seat, back, and armrests—as
well as the front apron-have been upholstered and a back cushion has been added.
The ornamentation and structuring of the
front apron with tacks are also derived from
English furniture. CW-D

References: *Moderne Bauformen* 27 (1929), p. 81;
Boltenstern, *Wiener Möbel* (1934), p. 14.

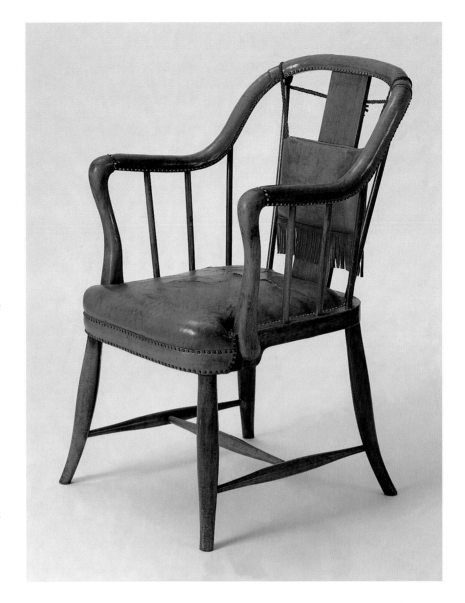

**Fig. 25a.** Both small and large
versions of the armchair.

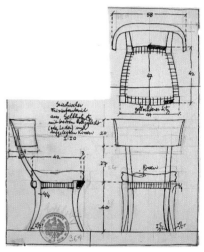

**27. Drawing for Klismos Chair**
ca. 1925
Ink on tracing paper
7½ x 6¼ in. (19 x 16 cm)

Scale 1:10

University of Applied Arts, Vienna
Inv. no. 369

**26. Side Chair**
Designed ca. 1925; this example ca. 1948
Walnut, beech, leather
31½ x 21¾ x 21¼ in. (80 x 55.3 x 54 cm)

Introduced by Haus & Garten, Vienna; currently
retailed by Svenskt Tenn as model no. 300

Svenskt Tenn Archive, Stockholm

Since the eighteenth century the ancient
world has served as a vital source of inspiration for the formulation of a modern
design idiom. During the 1920s, while many
progressive designers looked to the machine
as a design paradigm, others sought inspiration in the classical past. Frank had an acute
understanding of the history of furniture,
and he designed this chair based on the
ancient Greek *klismos* chair. The depth of
Frank's knowledge of ancient furniture is
clear from the three views of the chair illustrated in the drawing. The side view, for
example, shows the seat rail extending
beyond the legs as well as the sloping angle
of the stiles which are features of the *klismos*
form as seen in ancient Greek stele and vase
painting.

Numerous versions of the *klismos*-
inspired form exist within the history of
Western furniture. They were made at the
end of the eighteenth and beginning of the
nineteenth century in France and Prussia.
Frank was not the only twentieth-century
designer to be inspired by the *klismos* form,
which was especially favored in the Nordic
countries and Central Europe. In Sweden,
for example, Carl Malmsten produced a
*klismos*-inspired chair, and the *klismos* form
inspired Finnish-architect Alvar Aalto's earliest furniture designs from the 1920s.
American designers such as T. H.
Robsjohn-Gibbings were also influenced by
ancient Greek furniture.

Side chair no. 300 was introduced by
Frank at Haus & Garten and continues to
be made today by Svenskt Tenn. It is available with an upholstered seat that varies
according to the specifications of the client.
NS-L

References: Richter, *Furniture of the Greeks* (1966);
Spalt and Czech, *Josef Frank 1885–1967* (1981);
Wängberg-Eriksson, *Josef Frank Livsträd* (1994).

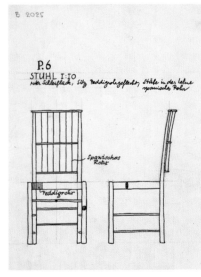

## 28. Chair

ca. 1925
Beechwood, red paint, Spanish reed, bamboo
39⅜ x 17⅜ x 19⅛ in. (100 x 44 x 45.5 cm);
seat height: 16⅞ in. (43 cm)

Made for Haus & Garten in Austria

MAK-Austrian Museum of Applied Arts,
Vienna
Inv. no. H 3137

A lightness of form seems to have been particularly important to Frank in the design of this chair. The orange-red painted surface and the bamboo staves of the chair back are both Chinese-inspired. The actual chair frame is of a single color, creating a visual impression of structural stability. The chair back is of a lighter material (bamboo), giving a feeling of transparency. Frank used the orange-red chair with the green-painted secretary in his Double House for the 1927 Weissenhofsiedlung at Stuttgart. CW-D

References: *Innen-Dekoration* 37 (1926), p. 375; Boltenstern, *Wiener Möbel* (1934), p. 34.

## 29. Drawing for Side Chair

ca. 1925
Ink and pencil on tracing paper
7¼ x 5¾ in. (18.4 x 14.6 cm)

Scale 1:10
Inscription: "roter Schleiflack, Sitz peddi-grohrgeflecht, Stäbe in der Lehne Spanisches Rohr"

Svenskt Tenn Archive, Stockholm

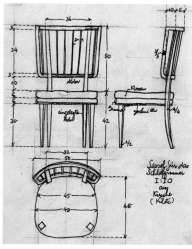

**31. Drawing for Side Chair**

ca. 1925

Ink and pencil on tracing paper

7½ x 4½ in. (19.1 x 11.4 cm)

Scale 1:10
Inscription: "Sessel für das
Schlafzimmer aus Kirsche"

Svenskt Tenn Archive, Stockholm

## 30. Chair

ca. 1925

Mahogany, beechwood seat frame, painted cotton and linen (reupholstered), painted upholstery tacks

31¼ x 20½ x 24¼ in. (79.5 x 52.2 x 61.5 cm); seat height: 16⅞ in. (43 cm)

Made for Haus & Garten in Austria

Private collection, Vienna

The original upholstery of this chair can be seen in a 1933 photograph of the master bedroom of the Steiner House. Clearly the present cushion, which is placed tightly between the front and back legs without the horizontal emphasis of an apron, does not comply with Frank's original intentions, which called for a visible apron to balance the horizontality of the chair back. Only in this way can the upholstered cushion appear to be supported by the mahogany apron. Where Frank failed to insist on a visible wooden apron, as in the same chair model used in the R. L. S. House in the Viennese suburb of Hietzing (*Moderne Bauformen* [1933], p. 362), the wooden structure of the apron is independently covered with fabric, thus achieving the requisite emphasis on the horizontal members. True to his ideological approach to the selection of materials, Frank chose strongly grained woods for the surface decoration of the Steiner bedroom case pieces (palisander for a small dressing table and Swedish birch for a cabinet), while beds and seating furniture are executed in plain, dense woods such as mahogany. CW-D

Reference: *Moderne Bauformen* 30 (1933).

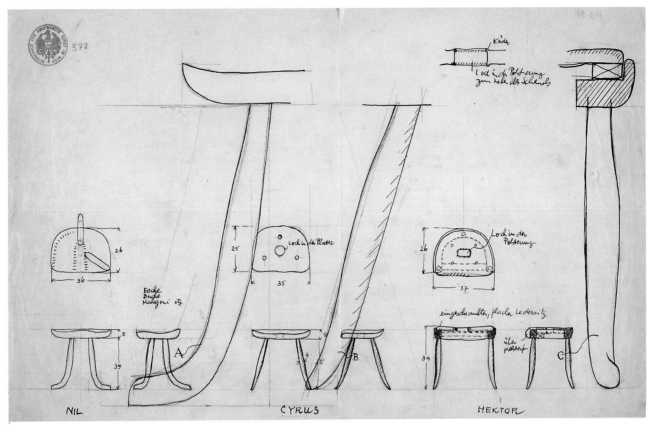

## 32. Drawings for Stools

ca. 1920/25
Ink on tracing paper
9⅞ x 14½ in. (25 x 39.5 cm)

Scale 1:10, details 1:2
Inscription: "Nil, Cyrus, Hektor"

University of Applied Arts, Vienna
Inv. no. 372

Frank worked with variations on the theme of an ancient Egyptian three-legged stool from around 1300 B.C. The original form, a reproduction of which had been available in England in Liberty's sales program since 1884, was introduced into Vienna around 1900 by Adolf Loos, who subsequently reinterpreted it. Around 1925 Frank redesigned this stool replacing all the

sharp-cornered elements with smoothly flowing rounded contours and fitting the stool with a saddle seat and carrying hole in the center. cw-d

References: *Innen-Dekoration* 37 (1926), p. 355; Boltenstern, *Wiener Möbel* (1934), p. 13; Ottillingor, *Adolf Loos* (1994), pp. 124–26.

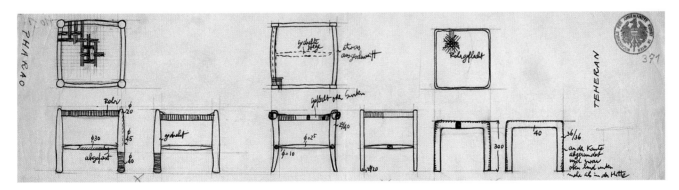

## 33. Drawing for Stools

ca. 1920/25
Ink on tracing paper
4⅜ x 16 in. (11 x 40.5 cm)

Scale 1:10
Inscription: "Pharao, Krösus, Cypern, Teheran"

University of Applied Arts, Vienna
Inv. no. 371

Frank's rejection of the decorative unity of furniture designed en suite was reflected in his equally impassioned battle against standardized furniture. The diverse shapes he developed for his seating furniture are telling evidence of this attitude. His conscious use of historical names for these stools reflects a quest for tradition that was a vital aspect of the development of his working philosophy. cw-d

Reference: Boltenstern, *Wiener Möbel* (1934), p. 13.

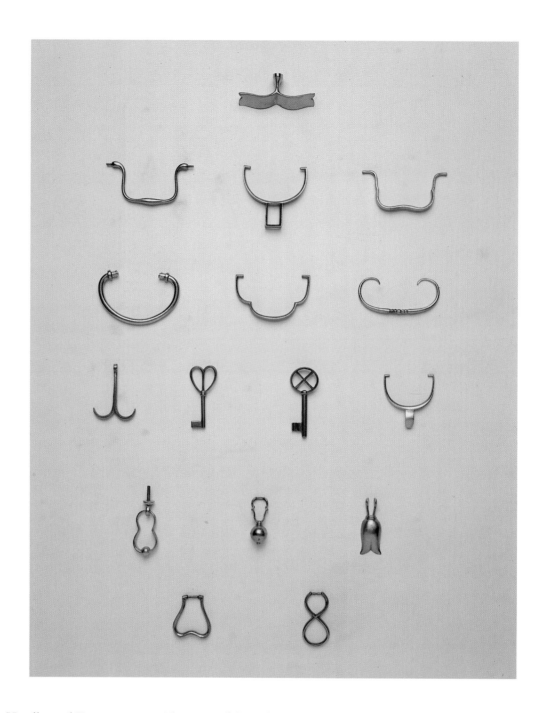

### 34. Drawer Handles and Keys
ca. 1920/30
Cast brass

Made for Haus & Garten by J. T. Kalmar, Vienna

MAK-Austrian Museum of Applied Arts,
Vienna
Inv. no. [Me] 947

This group of drawer handles and keys is part of a broad range of hardware designed by Josef Frank for his furniture. In 1924, at the Jubiläumsausstellung des Wiener Kunstgewerbevereins (Jubilee Exhibition of the Viennese Decorative Arts Society), held at the Austrian Museum for Art and Industry, he exhibited similar drawer handles and keys of his design, made by the Einhorn firm and intended for general sale. To a certain extent they may be traced to a group of mounts created by Hugo Gorge and Frank for the Wiener Werkstätte (WW archive no. M 3091-3111) in 1920. The teardrop-shaped drawer pulls in particular, which have no Austrian predecessors, may have been inspired by English models.

These designs and other recurring details in Frank's work can be found, for example, in the furniture of Ernest Gimson. CW-D

References: Österr. Museum für Kunst und Industrie, *Vienna 1924* (1924), p. 30; "Moderne Möbelbeschläge nach Enwürfen von Architect Dr. Josef Frank . . . Ausgeführt von der Broncewaren-Fabrik Hugo Einhorn" (sales catalogue).

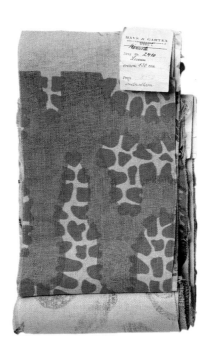

### 35. Haus & Garten Fabric Samplebook
1925–30
Paper and linen
7 x 10 in. (17.8 x 25.4 cm)

Svenskt Tenn Archive, Stockholm

Although Frank most likely brought this
samplebook with him to Stockholm, it
is not known exactly how it became part of
the Svenskt Tenn Archive. It contains a
broad selection of swatches of Frank's
printed fabrics and is important historically
in documenting specific Haus & Garten
designs. Illustrated here are "Tulipan,"
"Koralle," and "Primavera." NS-L

### 36. "Frühling"

Designed ca. 1925–30, printed ca. 1930
Linen
Size: 25⅞ x 13½ in. (65.7 x 34.3 cm)
Repeat: 15 x 18 in. (38 x 46 cm)

Blockprinted for Haus & Garten in Austria

Svenskt Tenn Archive, Stockholm

The repeat of this pattern, a naturalistic depiction of birch branches with leaves and catkins, has been planned to be reproduced alternately, just as bricks are placed in a wall. This explains its oblique direction, upward to the left. Varying the size of the foliage lends rhythm and vigor to the pattern, without which it would have become simply a "surface pattern."

"Frühling" (Spring) belongs to Frank's Haus & Garten period and was printed on different fabrics (both rough, unbleached linen and cotton chintz). Two color schemes are known: purple-red and pale blue on rough, naturally colored linen; and brown and bright green against a light blue background suggestive of a Nordic spring evening flooded with light.

The two printing blocks needed for "Frühling" have been in the Svenskt Tenn Archive since 1987. Carved from pearwood, with details in boxwood, they are visually almost as powerful as the patterned fabric itself. KW-E

Reference: Spalt and Kapfinger, *Josef Frank 1885–1967* (1986).

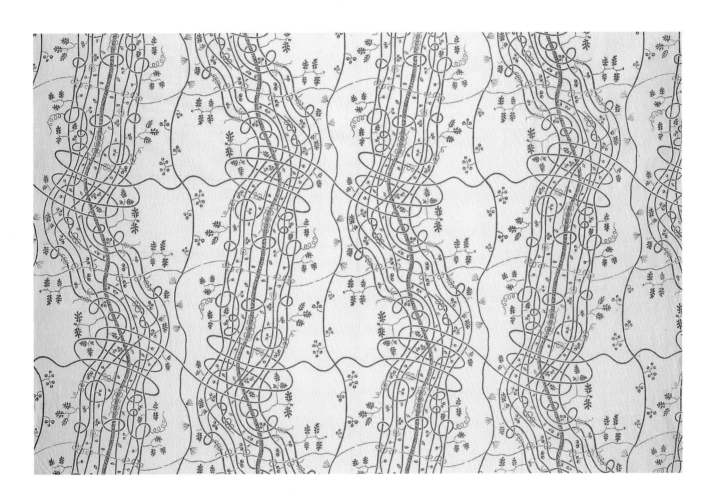

## 37. "Seegras"

Designed ca. 1925–30, printed ca. 1930
Chintzed cotton
Repeat: 14¼ x 10¾ in. (36.5 x 27.5 cm)

Blockprinted for Haus & Garten in Austria

Private collection, Vienna
Example shown: The Victoria & Albert
Museum, London

This pattern, a bold gambit with its great
wavy lines, was produced in the 1920s, a
time of great experimentation for Josef
Frank. In order to print "Seegras," a soft
sea-green monochrome, just a single carved
woodblock was required. Each time the
block was moved over the fabric to the next
position, it was rotated a half-turn before
printing. Another possible printing
sequence involved completing every other
section with the block in one direction and
then rotating it and printing the blank sections.

The design has four inversion centers,
one on each side of the repeat, the most

easily found being those located where the
"lonesome" lines intersect. The bunched
lines of the design wave one way or the
other, like sea grass in the surf, providing a
sense of continuity while at the same time
concealing the geometric repetition. The
bunches of sea grass are held together by
large spirals of thread which form recurring
horizontals. Leaves and tendrils lighten the
composition in a subtle way. KW-E

Reference: Spalt and Kapfinger, *Josef Frank
1885–1967* (1986), p. 28.

### 39. Woodblock for "Mistral"

ca. 1925
Pearwood
15 x 12⅞ in. (38.2 x 32 cm)

MAK-Austrian Museum of Applied Arts, Vienna

Inv. no. T11.481a,b

### 38. "Mistral"

Designed ca. 1920–25, printed ca. 1925–30
Linen and cotton
Size: 27⅛ x 23⅝ in. (69 x 60)
Repeat: 14¼ x 12¼ in. (36 x 31 cm)

Blockprinted for Haus & Garten in Austria

MAK-Austrian Museum of Applied Arts, Vienna

Inv. no. T 11.381, c

The design is named for the Mistral, the seasonal northerly wind of southern France, and indeed the large palmate leaves appear to be blown from below, forming a turbulent flow pattern in which flowers serve as stationary points. The background dots may represent dust swirling in the air, not uncommon when the Mistral is blowing.

The geometry of the pattern is easy to understand: a rectangular grid with uniform rectangles placed vertically. The immobile horizontal rows of figures contrast with the implied meandering motion of the leaves. In addition to yellow and red printed on a natural background, as seen here, the Svenskt Tenn Archive holds two other color combinations: blue and red, and green and red, both of which were printed in Vienna for Haus & Garten.

This pattern may be compared with "Tang" (later renamed "Aristidia") which was designed shortly afterward. Unlike "Mistral," "Tang" is based on a geometric element that is almost impossible to distinguish. In the 1920s Frank was experimenting with a range of different expressive approaches.

The two woodblocks for "Mistral" (one shown), superb pieces of art in themselves, were presumably carved in Vorarlberg in the far western part of Austria, near the Bodensee, a region renowned for its expert wood-carvers. KW-E

Reference: Spalt and Kapfinger, *Josef Frank, 1885–1967* (1986), pp. 7 and 29.

### 40. "Hügel"

Designed, ca. 1925, printed ca. 1930
Cotton; fragment
Size: 55⅛ x 27⅛ in. (140 x 69 cm)
Repeat: H. 15½ in. (37.5 cm)

Blockprinted for Haus & Garten in Austria

MAK-Austrian Museum of Applied Arts,
Vienna
Inv. no. T 11.316

In choosing the word *Hügel* (hill) as a name
for this design, Frank may have been suggesting the Styrian landscape with its
rolling fields. In the pattern the magnified
blades of grass have been organized in long,
slightly bent and irregularly curved rows.
They point rhythmically in different directions as if they were fluttering in spring
breezes. Scattered flowers are vaguely reminiscent of the blue anemone (*Hepatica
nobilis*). "Hügel" is a variation of the design
theme Frank initiated with "Primavera" and
its rows of flowers, but here he has sacrificed richness of detail for an overall simplified scheme. Although it was specified
that the grass, flowers, and butterflies were
to be white, the background could be printed in apple green or, as shown here, sky

blue. Unfortunately only a fragment of the
textile has survived, meaning that the repeat
pattern is no longer known in its entirety.
KW-E

Reference: Spalt and Kapfinger, *Josef Frank
1885–1967* (1986).

### 41. "Sweet"

Designed, ca. 1920–25, printed ca. 1925–30
Rayon
Size: 13⅜ x 98 in. (34 x 249 cm)
Repeat: 15½ x 16¼ in. (39.5 x 41.5 cm)

Blockprinted for Haus & Garten in Austria

MAK-Austrian Museum of Applied Arts,
Vienna
Inv. no. T 11.320

"Sweet," one of Frank's early patterns, was probably designed shortly before Frank and Wlach founded Haus & Garten in 1925. The geometric element is clear and simple, indeed almost conventional. Although there is a historicizing link to "Biedermeier stripes," the stripes are artfully varied with winding vines, including a *Convolvulus* species (bindweed). The flowers and leaves, depicted on a modest scale, are laid out in horizontal rows on thin branches, a device that balances the slender and airy verticals. During Frank's Haus & Garten years, "Sweet" was usually printed on cotton chintz. KW-E

Reference: Spalt and Kapfinger, *Josef Frank 1885–1967* (1986).

## 42. "Karma"

Designed, ca. 1925–30, printed ca. 1930

Linen

Size: 11⅜ x 13 in. (29 x 33 cm)

Repeat: 11¾ x 11 in. (28 x 30 cm)

Blockprinted for Haus & Garten in Austria

Svenskt Tenn Archive, Stockholm

Within each unit of this almost quadratic design, the repeat pattern recurs four times, in two directions, up and down. The colors are the primaries—yellow, blue, and red—plus green. A thick-stemmed vine with large heart-shaped leaves creates a pulsating, wavelike line across the pattern. The name "Karma" is from the Hindu/Buddhist belief in a force generated by our actions tying us to our earthly lives. Here there is a "geometric" calm that never becomes heavy and boring.

When used as drapery with daylight streaming through it, "Karma" is as striking as a sunlit grape arbor, which is how it appears in the interior of Frank's single-family house at the 1932 Vienna Werkbundsiedlung. KW-E

Reference: Gmeiner and Pirhofer, *Der Österreichische Werkbund* (1985), p. 171; Spalt and Kapfinger, *Josef Frank 1885–1967* (1986).

### 43. "Labyrinth"

Designed ca. 1925–30, printed ca. 1930
Linen
Size: 38½ x 49½ in. (97.7 x 125.7 cm)
Repeat: 11¾ x 11¾ in. (30 x 30 cm)

Blockprinted for Haus & Garten in Austria

Svenskt Tenn Archive, Stockholm

This pattern was originally called "Fioretti" (small flowers), after the abundant flower motifs that serve as a background for the sinuous labyrinth. Only two woodblocks were required for the printing, one for the blue, the other for the green dye. Later, during Frank's tenure with Svenskt Tenn, other color combinations were also made.

The pattern is a geometrical tour-de-force. It is designed so that the blocks must each be turned four times during the printing process, a quarter-turn each time. On the fabric sample it is fairly easy to find three four-fold rotational axes around which the blocks were rotated. The ingenious interplay of lines is reminiscent of two tangled skeins of yarn, one thick and one thin, which both entrap and disturb. The calm of the starry background serves as a counterpoint to the tangle of lines.
KW-E

Reference: Spalt and Kapfinger, *Josef Frank 1885–1967* (1986).

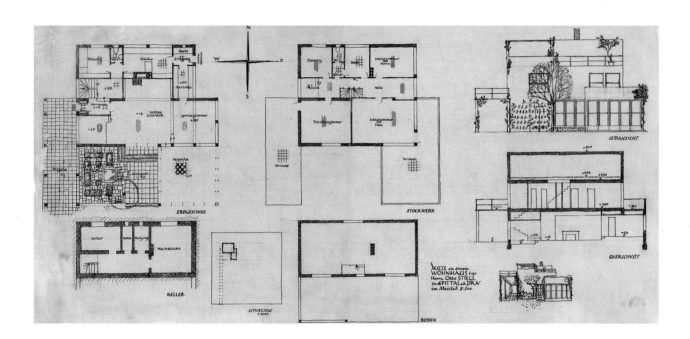

### 44. House for Otto Stiegl in Spittal a.d. Drau, Carintha

ca. 1926 (project)
Pencil, pen and ink on tracing paper
11¾ x 25¼ in. (30 x 64 cm)

Site, plan, perspective, elevation, section, plans
Inscription: "Skizze zu einem Wohnhaus für Herrn Otto Stiegl Spittal a.d. Drau in Masstab 1:00"

Frank-Archiv, Graphische Sammlung Albertina, Vienna
Inv. no. 71
Not in exhibition

Frank evidently designed this project for an unrealized three-story house around 1926. A model of the house was published in *Moderne Bauformen* the following year, and the house bears some resemblance to several of Frank's other works from the same period. Its basic cubic shape is similar to Frank's prewar Scholl House, and the use of pergolas and attached balconies is reminiscent of the Bunzl Summer House. Here Frank has combined the two ideas, employing the balconies and pergola to help break up the building's mass. The overall effect, however, is rather awkward, and the house lacks the lightness that often characterizes Frank's later works.

The general layout of the house, which emphasizes the living areas and their connection with the outdoors, is similar to Frank's earlier residential designs, as is the informality of the plan, which avoids strict axes and symmetry. New, however, are the many changes in level on the ground floor (which Frank has indicated by showing the number of centimeters above or below the ground level for each space), an idea he employed frequently during the late 1920s and early 1930s. CL

References: *Moderne Bauformen* 26 (May 1927), p. 175; Spalt and Czech, *Josef Frank, 1885–1967* (1981), p. 195; Long, "Josef Frank and the Crisis of Modern Architecture" (1993), pp. 112–13, 295–96.

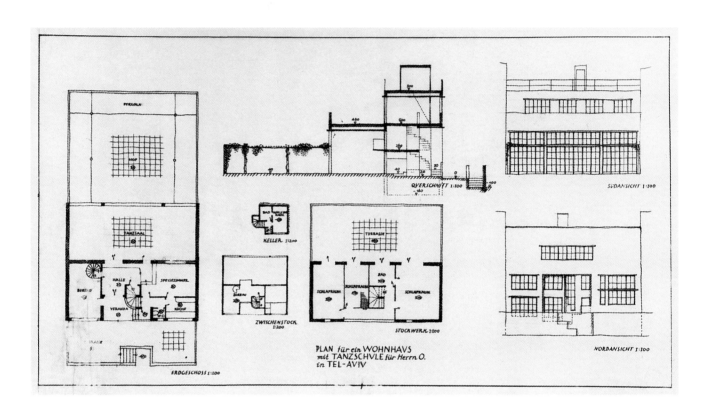

PLAN für ein WOHNHAVS mit TANZSCHVLE für Herrn O. in TEL-AVIV

### 45. House with a Dance School for Mr. Ornstein, Tel Aviv

ca. 1926 (project)
Pencil, pen and ink on tracing paper
14¼ x 24 in. (33.5 x 61 cm)

Plans, section, elevations 1:100; plans 1:200
Inscription: "Plan für ein Wohnhaus mit Tanzschule für Herrn O. in Tel-Aviv"

Frank-Archiv, Graphische Sammlung Albertina, Vienna
Inv. no. 17

Frank evidently designed this two and a half-story combination dwelling and dance school at about the same time as the Stiegl House. The two houses share a number of similiarities, including their blocky massing, the use of balconies and pergolas, and changes in level on the lower floor. The Ornstein House, however, is much more sophisticated in terms of its overall composition and layout. Elaborating further on his notion of employing variations in level to enliven the spatial effects of his interiors, Frank here has placed an entresol (or *Zwischenstock*, as he refers to it on the plan), between the ground floor and the upper level bedrooms. This intermediate level not only serves as the office for the school and an observation area (from the rear, the room overlooks the nearly two-story dance hall), but it also creates a feeling of spatial play and disjuncture, which Frank increasingly emphasized in his work from the mid-1920s on. With its vertical spatial orientation and use of the entresol, the Stiegl House resembles Frank's most important work of the decade, the villa for Julius and Margarete Beer in Vienna. CL

References: *Moderne Bauformen* 26 (May 1927), p. 185; Spalt and Czech, *Josef Frank, 1885–1967* (1981), p. 201, Long, "Josef Frank and the Crisis of Modern Architecture" (1993), p. 296.

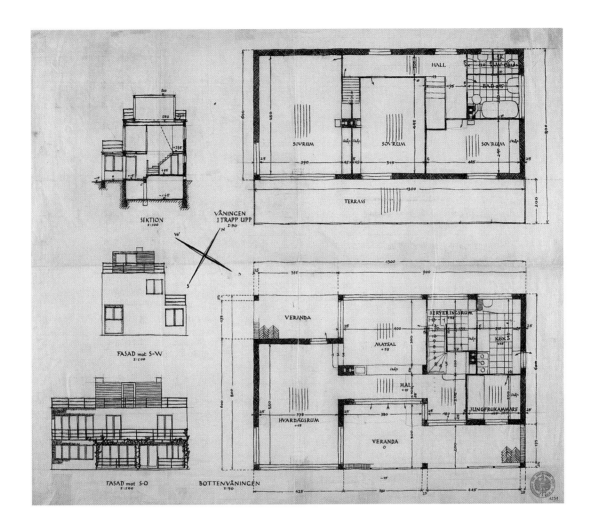

## 46. House for Axel and Signhild Claëson, Falsterbo, Sweden

Rostockervägen 1, Falsterbo, Sweden
ca. 1926
Pencil, pen and ink on tracing paper
17¾ x 20¼ in. (45 x 51.5 cm)

Plans 1:50; Elevations and section 1:100

University of Applied Arts, Vienna
Inv. no. 1231

The Claëson House was the first of a series of summer houses Frank designed for relatives and friends in the small resort town of Falsterbo at the southern tip of Sweden. The Claësons were Frank's brother- and sister-in-law; Signhild Claëson, née Sebenius, was his wife's sister.

Frank evidently began work on the project in the summer of 1924, and over the next two and half years he produced a series of different designs. The earliest extant drawings, dated August 1924, show a flat-roofed, two-story house, rectangular in plan, with a large L-shaped living and dining area, kitchen, and maid's room on the ground floor, and two small bedrooms on the second floor. In a later version, proba-

bly from 1925 or 1926, Frank added a roof terrace and a small wooden structure, which he referred to as a "cabin" or "hut." In one version the "cabin," which has windows on all four sides to provide views of the ocean and surrounding countryside, is shown at the northwest end of the roof; but in the final drawings Frank placed it nearer the midpoint. The chimney on the southern end of the structure is open to create a large fireplace on the terrace so that the Claësons and their guests could enjoy the roof during the long, cool Swedish summer evenings. The lower floors of the Claëson House are similarly arranged to take advantage of the oceanside setting. The second-story bedrooms open out onto terraces on

both sides, while the living and dining areas look out onto a large stepped terrace facing the southwest. Large windows throughout the house create a sense of spaciousness and serve to reduce the distinction between the interior and exterior.

In plan, the Claëson House, which retains the regular layering of floors, is less ambitious than the Stiegl or Ornstein houses. The house's brick masonry walls and unadorned windows recall the Wilbrandtgasse House, but the simple planar masses and its overall horizontal articulation bear closer resemblance to other modernist houses of the mid-1920s, such as Mies van der Rohe's Wolf House in Guben, Germany (1925–27). CL

References: *Moderne Bauformen* 26 (May 1927), p. 182; *Der Baumeister* 26 (March 1928), p. 100; Döcker, *Terrassentyp* (1929), p. 100; Hoffmann, *Neue Villen* (1929), p. 44; *Moderne Bauformen* 28 (1929), p. 44; *Ord och bild* 1 (January 14, 1929), p. 59; *Österreichischer Werkbund* (1929), p. 30; *Studio Yearbook* (1929), pp. 14, 50; *Veckojournalen* 40 (1929), pp. 33–36; Eckstein, *Neue Wohnbauten* (1932), p. 50; Spalt and Czech, *Josef Frank, 1885–1967* (1981), pp. 22–29; Long, "Josef Frank and the Crisis of Modern Architecture" (1993), pp. 109–110, 297–98; Welzig, "Die Wiener Internationalität des Josef Frank" (1994), pp. 118–29.

## 47. House for Axel and Signhild Claeson, Falsterbo, Sweden

Rostockervagen 1, Falsterbo, Sweden
ca. 1926
Ink on tracing paper
14¾ x 17¾ in. (37.5 x 45.1 cm)

View from the southeast

Private collection, Vienna

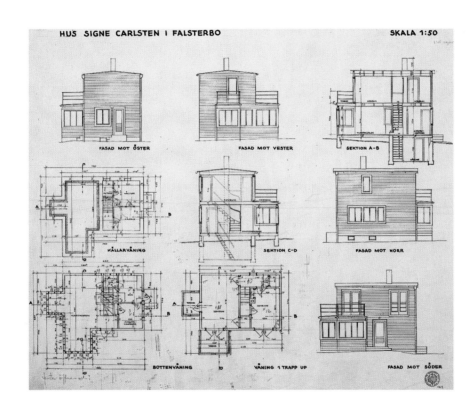

HUS SIGNE CARLSTEN I FALSTERBO      SKALA 1:50

FASAD MOT ÖSTER      FASAD MOT VESTER      SEKTION A-B

KÄLLARVÅNING      SEKTION C-D      FASAD MOT NORR

BOTTENVÅNING      VÅNING 1 TRAPP UP      FASAD MOT SÖDER

## 48. Signe Carlsten House, Falsterbo, Sweden

Fyrvägen, Falsterbo, Sweden
ca. 1927
Pencil, pen and ink on tracing paper
22⅞ x 27½ in. (58 x 70 cm)

Plans, elevations, section 1:50
Inscription: "Hus Signe Carlsten i Falsterbo;
Skala 1:50"

University of Applied Arts, Vienna
Inv. no. 1212

The Carlsten house is similar to the nearby
Claëson house, although somewhat more
modest in scale and materials. The two-
story structure is built of wood and has a
low-pitched side-gabled roof. The interior
plan is also similar to the Claëson house
with a combination living and dining room,
kitchen, and maid's room on the ground
floor and bedrooms on the second floor. CL

References: Eckstein, *Neue Wohnbauten* (1932),
pp. 49–50; Spalt and Czech, *Josef Frank,
1885–1967* (1981), pp. 30–31; Long, "Josef Frank
and the Crisis of Modern Architecture" (1993),
pp. 110–11, 299.

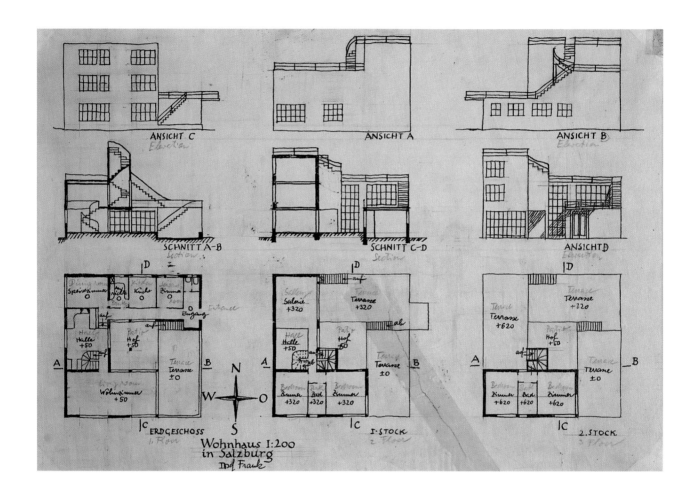

ANSICHT C — Elevation
ANSICHT A
ANSICHT B — Elevation
SCHNITT A–B — Section
SCHNITT C–D — Section
ANSICHT D — Elevation
ERDGESCHOSS — 1. Floor
1. STOCK — 2. Floor
2. STOCK — 3. Floor

Wohnhaus 1:200
in Salzburg
Josef Frank

### 49. House in Salzburg

1926 (project)
Pencil, pen and ink on tracing paper
10¾ x 15 in. (27.3 x 5⅞ cm)

Plan 1:200, sections, and elevations
Inscription: "Wohnhaus in Salzburg"; signed
"Josef Frank"

Private collection, Vienna

This remarkable project is part of a series
of mostly unrealized houses Frank designed
between 1926 and 1930 that explore his
rapidly evolving ideas for forging a new
kind of spatial organization. Although
these projects—which include the House

for Otto Stiegl, House with a Dance
School for Mr. Ornstein, House for
Dagmar Grill, House for Vienna XIX,
Residence for Mr. and Mrs. A. R. G., and
the House for M. S.—display a wide array
of planning ideas, they all focus on the
same basic themes: the use of an architectural promenade (or promenades) to link
the main spaces and connect the
interior with exterior; the breakup of the
regular horizontal layering of floors to
enhance the sense of spatial play; and the
insertion of interior courtyards to open up
the building mass and heighten the impression of variety and complexity. In many
respects these projects all build on Frank's
earlier pre–World War I ideas of linking

together house and garden and of avoiding
conventional axial planning, but the means
he employs are much more ambitious and
sophisticated.

The central focus of the House in
Salzburg is a pair of continuous, spiraling
paths through and around the house. From
the main entrance on the east side, the main
route of penetration leads into a one-story
wing containing the kitchen and other service rooms. From there one may continue
along a hallway and up a small stairway
through the one and half-story hall to the
main living areas. A second pathway leads
up an exterior stairway and across the various terraces to the roof of the three-story
block on the south. One may stop anywhere

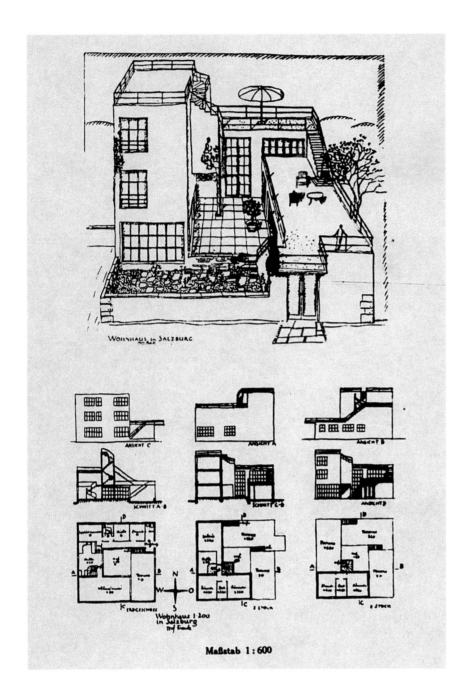

WOHNHAUS in SALZBURG

Maßstab 1 : 600

## 50. Project for a House in Salzburg

1926
Pen on transparent paper
14⅝ x 15⅜ in. (37 x 39 cm)

Elevations, sections, and plans

Professor Friedrich Kurrent, Munich

along the way or continue climbing upward. Each route leads to a changing architectural setting, and each turn or shift offers new spatial sensations.

At first glance the entire ensemble seems rather haphazard, an impression that is enhanced by Frank's seemingly casual and playful freehand drawing technique. In fact, the plan is based on a carefully conceived quadratic scheme composed of various rectangular blocks linked together to form a whole, and Frank has taken extraordinary care to work out the dimensions and positioning of the various spaces and the scheme of fenestration. Underlying the entire conception is a clear and well-thought-out proportional system, which,

despite its rather idiosyncratic guise, is still quite classical in many ways.

Much of the spatial play in the house is based on the sensation of climbing, a technique Frank would explore in a number of other houses of this period, most notably his Beer House, one of the only works of this type he was able to realize. By the early 1930s, however, Frank largely abandoned this vertical emphasis in his designs, and focused instead on using freely arranged or curvilinear walls to engender spatial complexity and diversity. CL

References: *Moderne Bauformen* 26 (May 1927), p. 184; Spalt and Czech, *Josef Frank, 1885–1967* (1981), p. 186; *Lotus International* 29 (1981), pp. 112–13; Long, "Josef Frank and the Crisis of Modern Architecture" (1993), pp. 113–14, 293–94; Welzig, "Die Wiener Internationalität des Josef Frank" (1994), pp. 129–31.

### 51. House for Dagmar Grill in Skärgården, Sweden

ca. 1927 (project)
Pencil, ink on paper
13⅜ x 12⅝ in. (34 x 32 cm)

Perspective

Svenskt Tenn Archive, Stockholm

Frank designed this large five- or six-story house as a fantasy project for Dagmar Grill, his wife's cousin. In its overall conception, the design is similar to the project for a House in Salzburg, which Frank prepared around the same time. Like the Salzburg house, the main body of the structure is based on a quadratic scheme and features a series of blocks of different heights and sizes that spiral up and around a small central courtyard. Here, however, Frank has added projecting balconies on the outside to take advantage of the house's location at water's edge. No interior plans for the house have survived, but the pattern of the fenestration suggests that Frank intended to break up the regular horizontal layering of floors. CL

References: Spalt and Czech, *Josef Frank, 1885–1967* (1981), p. 187; Long, "Josef Frank and the Crisis of Modern Architecture" (1993), p. 301.

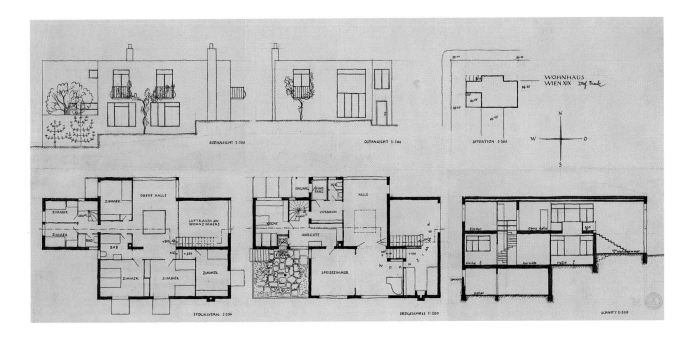

## 52. House in Vienna XIX

ca. 1927 (project)
Pencil, pen and ink on tracing paper
11 x 24 in. (28 x 61 cm)

Elevations, plan, section 1:100/Site plan 1:360
Inscription: "Wohnhaus Wien XIX"; signed
"Josef Frank"

Frank-Archiv, Graphische Sammlung Albertina,
Vienna
Inv. no. 35

Frank evidently designed this two-story house around the same time as the Residence for Mr. and Mrs. A. R. G. The name of the client and the precise location of the proposed site are not known, but the house was evidently intended for a large corner lot in Vienna's nineteenth district, a generally well-to-do area, with numerous large single-family houses. The main entrance of the house is on the north side and opens to an anteroom with an adjacent half-bathroom. On the the east end of the house is a hall with adjoining living and dining area; the northwest corner contains the service areas. The southwest corner of the house is taken up by a small walled courtyard with a second entry leading into the pantry. The upper floor, which includes six bedrooms and a bath, can be reached by either of two stairways—a central spiral staircase or a long, open stairway leading up from the living room. The upper hall overlooks the two-story living room and is pierced by a central light well.

Although rich in the sort of spatial play that was central to Frank's works of this period, this project is much more conventional in terms of its overall layout. The regular horizontal layering of the floors is largely preserved, with the exception of the living room and one of the upstairs bedrooms, which are both raised. The two-story living room and the skylight over the hall, however, would have achieved much the same effect as in Frank's more ambitious plans and at a somewhat lowered cost.
CL

References: Spalt and Czech, *Josef Frank, 1885–1967* (1981), p. 192; Long, "Josef Frank and the Crisis of Modern Architecture" (1993), pp. 345–46.

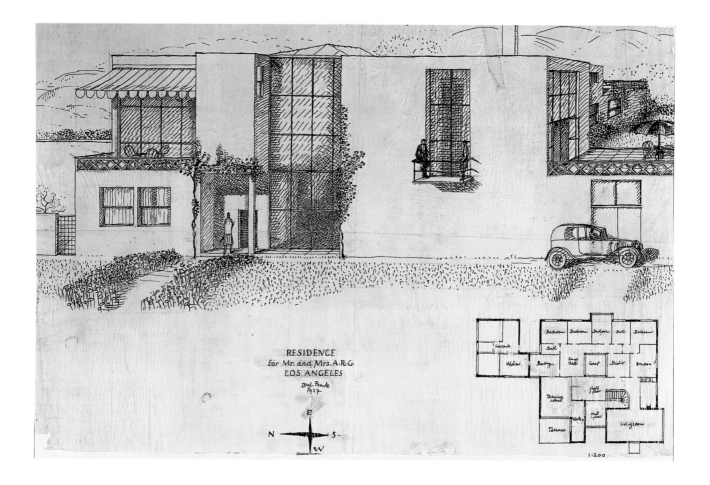

RESIDENCE
for Mr. and Mrs. A. R. G.
LOS ANGELES

Josef Frank
1927

1:200

## 53. Residence for Mr. and Mrs. A. R. G., Los Angeles

1927 (project)
Pencil, pen and ink on tracing paper
17½ x 25⅝ in. (44.5 x 65 cm)

Perspective; plan 1:200
Inscription: "Residence for Mr. and Mrs.
A. R. G. Los Angeles"; signed "Josef Frank";
dated "1927"

Frank-Archiv, Graphische Sammlung Albertina,
Vienna
Inv. no. 28

This project for a large two-story villa is among Frank's most unusual works of the late 1920s. As with many of his unbuilt projects, the house is poorly documented and little is known about the work or the circumstance surrounding its making. This drawing's inscription refers to a Los Angeles client, but an identical drawing with the label "Haus für Wien XIX" ("House for Vienna XIX") was published in *Der Baumeister* in 1928, suggesting that Frank may have had two different prospective clients, or, alternately, that he was seeking a second client after the original one failed to go through with construction.

Only an elevation and a second-floor plan of the project have survived, but they allow a reasonable reconstruction of the house's interior layout. The main body of the house is roughly square, with a projecting servants' wing on the left rear corner. In a rather unconventional move, Frank has placed the main living areas on the second floor, while the ground floor contains the service areas, garage, laundry room, furnace, and so on. The main entrance is under a vine-covered porch and opens into a two-

story glazed hall at the center. On the right side of the hall is a stairway leading to a large second-floor landing. On the second floor, to the left is the dining room and a small breakfast nook; to the right is the living room that opens out onto both a small front balcony and a large terrace above the garage on the far right. The bedrooms and a small studio are located in the rear, and the kitchen and servants' quarters are in a separate small wing on the right rear corner.

In its irregular composition, the plan bears a resemblance to many of Frank's other residential projects of this time. The floor levels, however, are generally uniform throughout, and the main body of the house is broken only by a small light court in the rear. CL

References: *Der Baumeister* 26 (March 1928), p. 98; Grimme, *Das Eigenheim* (1929), p. 25; Spalt and Czech, *Josef Frank, 1885–1967* (1981), p. 185; *Lotus International* 29 (1981), p. 111; *Um Bau* 10 (August 1986), p. 69; Long, "Josef Frank and the Crisis of Modern Architecture" (1993), pp. 111–12, 301–302.

## 54. House for Mr. S. H. B. in Pasadena, California

ca. 1927 (project)
Pencil, pen and ink on tracing paper
12 x 23⅜ in. (30.5 x 59.5 cm)

Perspective, section, plans 1:200
Inscription: "The Residence for Mr. S. H. B. at Pasadena California"; signed "Josef Frank"

Frank-Archiv, Graphische Sammlung Albertina, Vienna
Inv. no. 27

This project for a sprawling house on a hilly site in southern California represents one of Frank's most complex and unusual essays in spatial planning. The original drawing in the Albertina is labeled "Residence for Mr. S.H.B. at Pasadena California," but a nearly identical drawing published in *Moderne Bauformen* in 1927 bears the inscription "The Residence for H.R.S. Esqu. at Pasadena California"; the identity of neither client is known.

The house is situated on a hill sloping up and away from the street. One enters the house at the lowest point at the street and ascends by one of two stairways through a series of spaces of varying heights to the main living areas on the lower floors. To the left of the entrance is the living room; at the rear of the first floor are a dining room, pantry, and small library, each of which is on a different level. (Frank has indicated the exact floor height of each room on the drawings.) The rooms are interconnected with large openings, and each room has access to one of the many terraces. The uppermost floor containing the bedrooms is arranged around a small patio. Here, too,

Frank has broken up the floor level, placing the bedrooms on the left and the large glass-walled study in the rear on a higher level, several feet above the rest of the floor.

In its intricate and unconventional spatial arrangement, the house provides an interesting comparison with Frank's Residence for Mr. and Mrs. A. R. G., which was designed around the same time. Although the two houses share a rather bulky profile, Frank's use of level changes in the S. H. B. House—partially expressed in the massing and the arrangement of the volumes—gives the latter a notably different character, one that is at the same time lighter and more complex. CL

References: *Moderne Bauformen* 26 (May 1927), p. 181; *Lotus International* 29 (1981), p. 113; Long, "Josef Frank and the Crisis of Modern Architecture" (1993), p. 302.

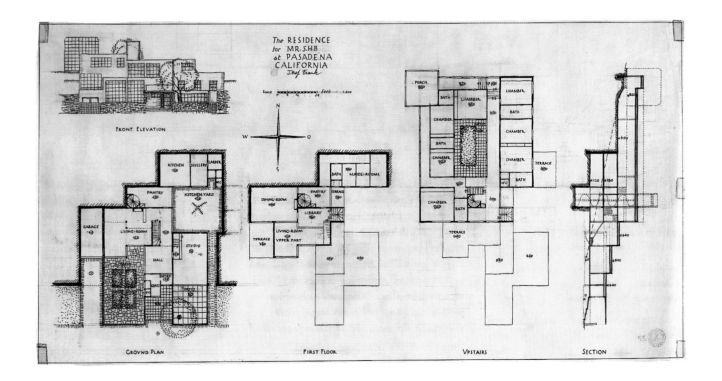

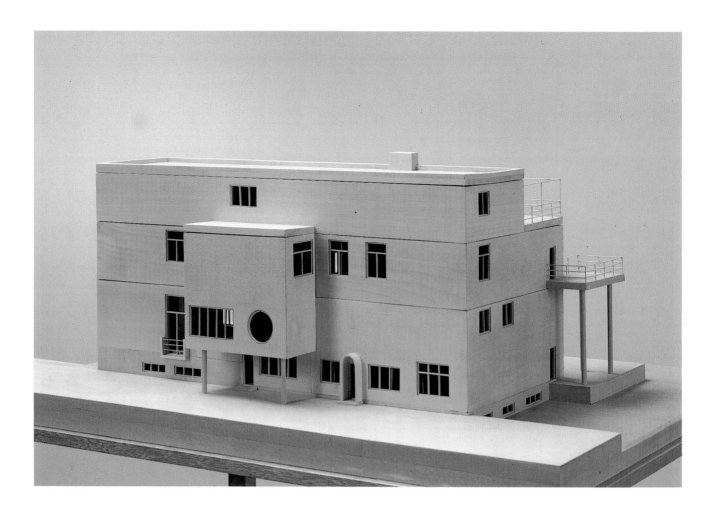

### 57. House for Julius and Margarete Beer (model)

1929–31; model 1975
Linderwood internal walls, Finnish birch plywood
33⅛ x 24⅝ x 12¼ in. (84 x 62.5 x 31 cm)

University of Applied Arts, Vienna

The Beer House was Frank's largest and most important residential commission and the crowning achievement of his spatial planning experiments of the 1920s. Designed for rubber magnate Julius Beer and his wife Margarete, the house also featured one of the most extensive collections of Haus & Garten furnishings and thus provides a particularly good illustration of Frank's ideas of home design.

Frank evidently began work on the house in 1929, although it was not completed until 1931. The site, in the Viennese suburb of Hietzing on the city's southwestern edge, was a narrow trapezoidal lot bounded on the northwest by the Wenzgasse and on the southeast by the Lainerstrasse. Frank positioned the house close to the Wenzgasse, placing it parallel to the street.

The appearance of the house from the street is that of a large rectangle, with a small cubic bay supported by two slender columns extending out from its main body. The fenestration is irregular, clustering around and emphasizing the bay. Viewed from the northeast side, the profile is extremely thin, almost slablike, while the

southwest end, with its stair-step terracing, is reminiscent of Loos's contemporary works, particularly the Moller House (1928). The rear elevation is asymmetrical, its projecting masses expressing the spatial complexities of the house's interiors. In contrast to the front, which is closed and uninviting, the rear is open and lively, with numerous large windows, terraces, and balconies. Several of the larger rear windows originally had retractable awnings. The garden is designed in relation to the house, featuring a sunken patio, various flights of steps, and small retaining walls.

The main entrance is at the center of the street side underneath the bay. It leads into an anteroom. From there, one route leads into the main hall (*Halle*) at the center of the house. A second route leads down a short flight of stairs and into the living room, which in turn is also connected with the hall by a stairway. On the southwest corner, adjacent to the hall, is a large, two-story dining room. Also on the ground floor is a service area with kitchen, pantry, preparation space, and washroom; these are linked to both the dining room and the entrance atrium. A service entrance protected by a shallow concrete porch with a semi-circular roof is located on the right side of the street facade. Heating and storage areas are housed in a basement.

The main body of the house is three-and-a-half stories, with a large entresol positioned between the ground and second stories. The main staircase leads up from the hall to the entresol, past a small library and music room (both of which extend out into the projecting front bay), and from there up to the second floor. The music room is open so that music could be heard throughout the main downstairs rooms. Also housed on the entresol is a servant's living area which is connected to the ground-floor service area by a separate staircase. The second floor has four bedrooms, two-and-a-half baths, a dressing area, breakfast room, and gymnastics room. Three of the four bedrooms open out onto rear balconies. The third floor has three additional bedrooms, one-and-a-half baths, a dressing room, darkroom, and large roof terrace.

In contrast to some of Frank's other interiors of the period, the furnishings were quite sparse, particularly in the public rooms, and despite the numerous large oriental rugs and patterned draperies, the overall feeling was one of luxurious austerity. Especially noteworthy among the interiors were the dining room, with its exquisite inlaid wood floors, built-in cabinets, and ample dining table, and the living room, which featured an attractive, *sachlich* bar and overstuffed couch.

The building was executed in stucco-covered brick masonry and concrete piers, floors, and roof slabs. It has undergone numerous changes over the years, but its main architectonic features have been preserved. CL

References: *Der Baumeister* 29 (August 1931), pp. 316–23; *Moderne Bauformen* 31 (1932), pp. 88–95; *Die Form* 7 (March 15, 1932), p. 76; *Viviendas* 4 (June 1935), pp. 6–15; Sonnek, "Wien: Haus Wenzgasse," in *Paläste und Bürgerhäuser* edited by Wessely (1970), pp. 225–28; Witt-Dörring, *Wiener Innenraumgestaltung* (1981), pp. 33–35; Spalt, ed., *Josef Frank zum 100* (1985), pp. 22–31; Gmeiner and Pirhofer, *Der Österreichische Werkbund* (1985), pp. 118–22; Schezen and Haiko, *Vienna 1850–1930* (1992), pp. 24, 248–51; Long, "Josef Frank and the Crisis of Modern Architecture" (1993), pp. 168–75, 311–12; Welzig, "Die Wiener Internationalität des Josef Frank" (1994), pp. 141–47.

**Fig. 57a.** House for Julius and Margarete Beer, Vienna, 1929–31. University of Applied Arts, Vienna.

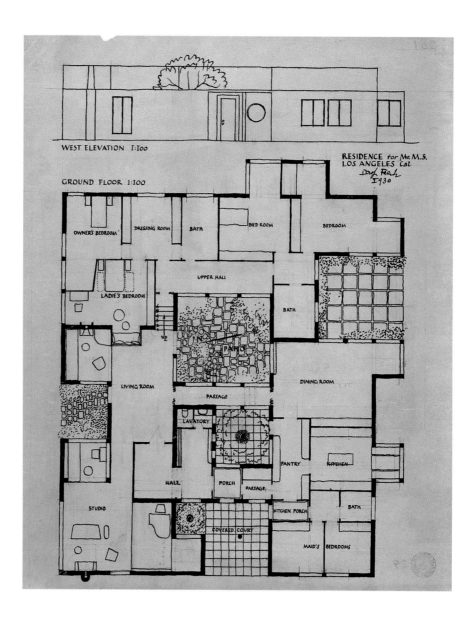

WEST ELEVATION 1:100

GROUND FLOOR 1:100

RESIDENCE for Mr M.S.
LOS ANGELES Cal
Josef Frank
1930

### 58. House for M. S. in Los Angeles, California

1930 (project)
Pencil, pen and ink on paper
14¼ x 11½ in. (36.1 x 29.3 cm)

Elevation, plan 1:100
Inscription: "Residence for Mr. M. S. Los
Angeles Cal"; signed "Josef Frank"; dated
"1930"

Frank-Archiv, Graphische Sammlung Albertina,
Vienna
Inv. 29

Frank prepared three different versions of
this project, all of which were published in
the August 1931 issue of *Der Baumeister* with
Frank's important essay featuring the Beer
House, "Das Haus als Weg und Platz"
(The house as path and place). They were
intended as further illustrations of the
planning principles he discussed in the
piece.

The three schemes are similar, showing
large, single or one-and-a-half story houses
arranged around one or more interior
patios. The earliest of the three projects
(for which the original drawing has not survived) is the most unconventional, with a
long serpentine patio dividing the house
into two wings. The plan also featured
curvilinear walls providing for an unusually
varied arrangement of spaces.

In the second and third schemes shown
here, Frank abandoned the free, irregular
shapes, and reverted to a gridlike plan based
on rectangular spaces. However, he stag-
gered and juxtaposed the rooms, creating in
the process a network of public and private
areas, pathways, and deadends. To further
enhance the rambling feel of the plan,
Frank raised or lowered certain rooms or
portions of the house. This is particularly
true of the third scheme (cat. fig. 58a),
which has spaces on six different levels. CL

References: *Der Baumeister* 29 (August 1931), plate
82/83; Spalt and Czech, *Josef Frank, 1885–1967*
(1981), p. 199; *Lotus International* 29 (1981), p. 113;
Long, "Josef Frank and the Crisis of Modern
Architecture" (1993), pp. 215–16, 314–15; Welzig,
"Die Wiener Internationalität des Josef Frank"
(1994), pp. 208–10.

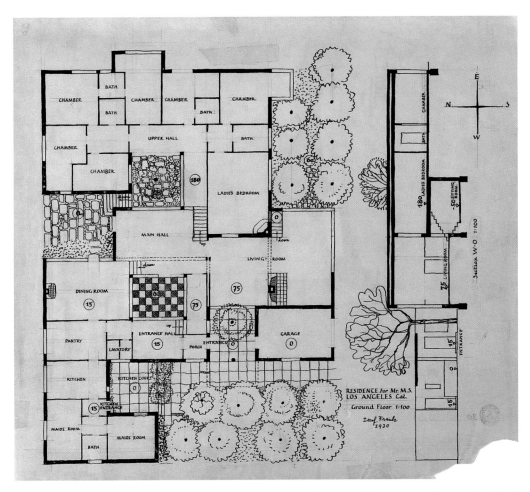

**Fig. 58a.** House for M. S. in Los Angeles, California, 1930; pencil, pen and ink on paper; plan, section. Frank Archiv, Graphische Sammlung Albertina, Vienna, Inv. no. 30.

### 59. "Aralia"

Designed ca. 1928, printed ca. 1947
Linen
Size: 32¾ x 34½ in. (83.2 x 87.6 cm)
Repeat: parallelogram, 28¾ x 32¾ in. (73 x 83 cm)

Screenprinted by Ljungbergs Textiltryck for Svenskt Tenn; currently retailed by Svenskt Tenn, Stockholm

Svenskt Tenn Archive, Stockholm

This bold textile pattern was introduced by Haus & Garten in the late 1920s when the firm was engaged in decorating a villa on the Hohe Warte, a fashionable district in Vienna. "Aralia" was featured in several photographs of Frank's interiors in *Innen-Dekoration* in 1930. This large-leaved design imparted a strikingly new dimension to curtains, wall-hangings, and bedspreads.
A decade later, in 1939, Frank included "Aralia" in his drawing of a "combined bed- and living room" for the Golden Gate Exhibition in San Francisco. And in 1994 "Aralia" was selected for a Swedish postage stamp commemorating 150 years of Swedish design: the Svenska Slöjdföreningen (Swedish Society of Craft and Industrial Design) was founded in 1845 and the Konstfackskolan (School of Arts, Crafts and Design) in 1844.

The large, deeply lobed leaves resemble those of the pattern's namesake, the Aralia, a common houseplant (*Fatsia japonica*), but Frank has employed artistic license in his version. The original wood blocks used for the first printing in Vienna are inscribed with the name "Seerose" (water lily), which is not surprising since the radiating yellowish red flower resembles the yellow water lily.

The thick stem running obliquely upward to the left is entwined in a climbing vine with small flowers. The thin spiral lines, small flowers, and smaller leaves help balance the large, powerful elements of the design. Seventeen woodblocks were needed to print this colorful pattern on fabric; all of them have been preserved and are now in the Svenskt Tenn Archive in Stockholm.
KW-E

References: *Innen-Dekoration* 41 (1930); ibid. 44 (1933); Spalt and Kapfinger, *Josef Frank 1885–1967* (1986).

## 60. Armchair, Model no. A 63F

1929

Beechwood, partly bent and laminated, painted red

37 x 22½ x 19⅝ in. (94 x 57 x 50 cm); seat height: 16¾ in. (42.5 cm)

Executed by Thonet Mundus AG, Vienna

MAK-Austrian Museum of Applied Arts, Vienna

Inv. no. H 2770

In 1929 the Thonet-Mundus firm organized an international competition to encourage the development of a new, modern bentwood chair. It is possible that Frank entered the competition with this model. In the 1920s the bentwood chair began to find its way back into the private domain after having been relegated almost entirely to public areas. Its visual lightness fulfilled the new aesthetic demand for the least obstruction of a given space by furnishings. Here, as in other Frank designs, color plays an important role, lending this piece of furniture a sculptural character and giving the room an atmospheric accent. Thonet offered Frank's design in fourteen different colors. The side-chair version of the armchair design was exhibited for the first time in 1929 in the "Wiener Raumkünstler" exhibition at the Austrian Museum for Art and Industry. The original drawing is preserved in the Svenskt Tenn Archive.   CW-D

References: *Österreichischer Werkbund* (1929), p. 38; Österr. Museum für Kunst und Industrie, *Wiener Raumkünstler* (1929/30), p. 4.

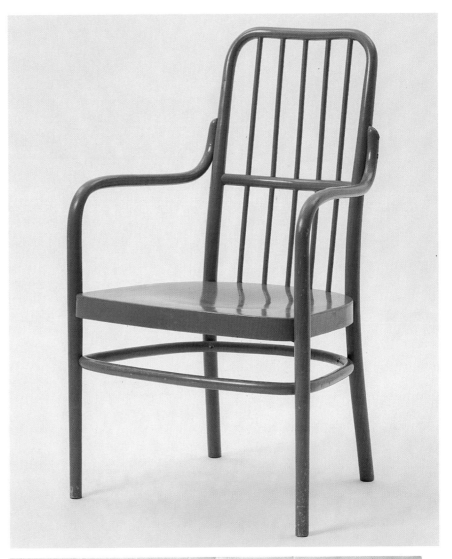

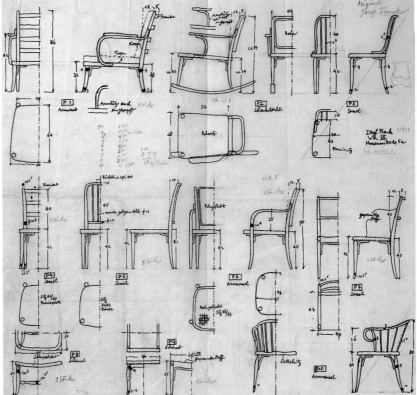

## 61. Drawing for Bentwood Furniture

ca. 1930

Ink and pencil on tracing paper

14¾ x 17⅞ in. (35.7 x 45.4 cm)

Svenskt Tenn Archive, Stockholm

## 62. Cabinet

ca. 1930

Softwood and plywood carcass, printed linen
("Mirakel"; replaced); solid cherry wood base
partially veneered in ash; brass hardware
51⅛ x 39⅜ x 16⅛ in. (130 x 100 x 41 cm)

Made for Haus & Garten, Vienna

Collection Ruth Wilson Kalmar, Vienna

The clearly defined separation of body
and base of the cabinet is similar to cabinets of the sixteenth and seventeenth
centuries, and is not a typical feature of
Viennese case pieces. It is common, however, in English designs, where the use of
textiles for the surface decoration of case
pieces is also known. Both treatments
were important to Frank. The idea of
mobility is underscored in this design by
an emphasis on load-bearing and weighted
elements, expressed here by a hard, heavy
material (wood), which has been fash-
ioned into visual transparency, supporting
a solid block covered in soft material
(fabric). As far as the body itself is concerned, all references to construction—
which Frank declines to consider as a pri-
ority in the design process—are erased by
covering the structure with a nondirec-
tional patterned fabric called "Mirakel," a
pattern Frank created for Haus & Garten.
CW-D

References: *Innen-Dekoration* 44 (1933), p. 185;
ibid., 45 (1934), p. 320.

**Fig. 62a.** The Haus & Garten pat-
tern book opened to a swatch of the
"Mirakel" textile. Svenskt Tenn
Archive, Stockholm.

## 63. Plant Stand

ca. 1930
Tubular iron painted red; aluminum trays
H. 31¼ in. (79.5 cm), Diam. 30⅛ in. (76.5 cm)

Made for Haus & Garten by J. T. Kalmar, Vienna

MAK-Austrian Museum of Applied Arts, Vienna
Inv. no. H 2775

An undated drawing by Josef Frank for a metal plant stand in the Svenskt Tenn Archive shows a three-legged base that is nearly identical to this one. With the most minimal means, Frank is able to convey his idea of unornamented, "organically-evolved" form. The painted surface of the plant stand enhances the decorative aspect of a room. CW-D

## 64. Drawing for Metal Furniture

ca. 1925–30
Ink and pencil on tracing paper
12¾ x 25 in. (32.4 x 63.5 cm)

Svenskt Tenn Archive, Stockholm

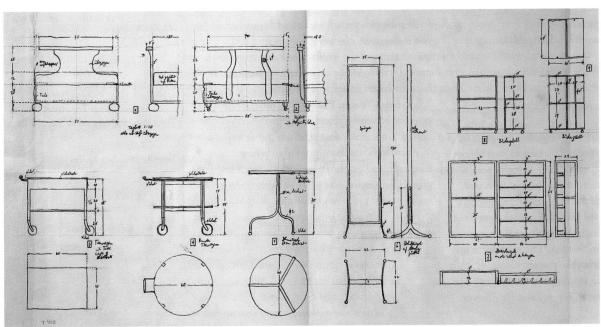

## 68. Sofa

Designed 1934; this example 1995
Linen upholstery
31½ x 110¼ x 55⅛ in. (80 x 280 x 140 cm)

Currently retailed by Svenskt Tenn as "Liljevalchssoffan"; linen upholstery ("Aralia" pattern) screenprinted by Ljungbergs Textiltryck for Svenskt Tenn, Stockholm

Svenskt Tenn, Stockholm

First shown at the 1934 home furnishings exhibition at the Liljevalchs Konsthall in Stockholm, this sofa was the focal point of Svenskt Tenn's installation, which was also Frank's design debut in Stockholm. The sofa epitomized Frank's vision of the modern home as a place of comfort and relaxation. Its scale and proportions—two average-size people reclining side-by-side can rest comfortably—make the design one of the landmark pieces in the history of Western furniture. The arms and back, with their robust curvature, extend far into space and greatly enhance the spatial presence of the piece. Both the sofa and a related armchair, also shown at the 1934 exhibition, were upholstered with one of the tradition-al G. P. & J. Baker textiles, which were often used at Svenskt Tenn. This example, however, is upholstered in the Frank's "Aralia" textile that was introduced in Vienna and later retailed by Svenskt Tenn. NS-L

References: Wängberg-Eriksson, "Svenskt Tenn, Josef Frank och Estrid Ericson" (1985); idem, "The Interior Designer," in Boman, *Estrid Ericson* (1989); idem, *Josef Frank Livsträd* (1994); *Josef Frank inredning* (1994).

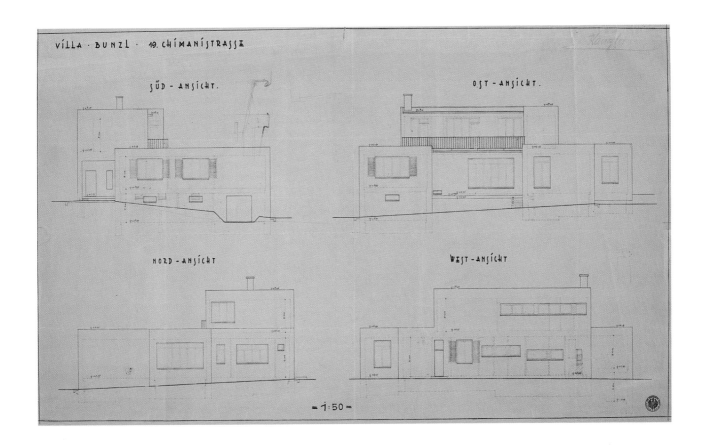

VILLA · BUNZL · 19. CHIMANISTRASSE

SÜD - ANSICHT.

OST - ANSICHT.

NORD - ANSICHT

WEST - ANSICHT

= 1:50 =

### 69. House for Hugo and Olga Bunzl, Vienna XVIII, Chimanistrasse 18

(with Oskar Wlach)

ca. 1935

Pencil, pen and ink on tracing paper

24⅜ x 40⅛ in. (62 x 102 cm)

Elevations 1:50

University of Applied Arts, Vienna

Inv. no. 1220

This house in Vienna's eighteenth district was the second house Frank designed for industrialist Hugo Bunzl and his wife and served as the couple's city residence. Completed just two years before the Anschluss, it was also the last building Frank designed in Austria.

The two-story, asymmetrically planned structure is situated on a wooded site that slopes downward from west to east. It consists of three wings arranged in the form of a U, with the front facade on the south and a courtyard on the east. The main entrance is on the southwest corner and leads into a central hall that faces out onto the courtyard. On the west are the service areas, including the kitchen and servants' rooms, while the one-story wing on the north contains the living room and dining room. The south wing facing the street side houses three small bedrooms and a bath. On the second floor are two additional bedrooms and a second bath. The second floor has been set back to form a small narrow terrace facing east. Although the plan of the house is more conventional than most of Frank's residential designs of the 1930s, his use of subtle spatial shifts and eclectic furnishings nevertheless set if off from the work of the other modernists of the time.

CL

References: *Architectural Review* 83 (April 1938), p. 169; Spalt and Czech, *Josef Frank, 1885–1967* (1981), p. 46–48; Long, "Josef Frank and the Crisis of Modern Architecture" (1993), pp. 212–13, 329–30; Welzig, "Die Wiener Internationalität des Josef Frank" (1994), pp. 210–11.

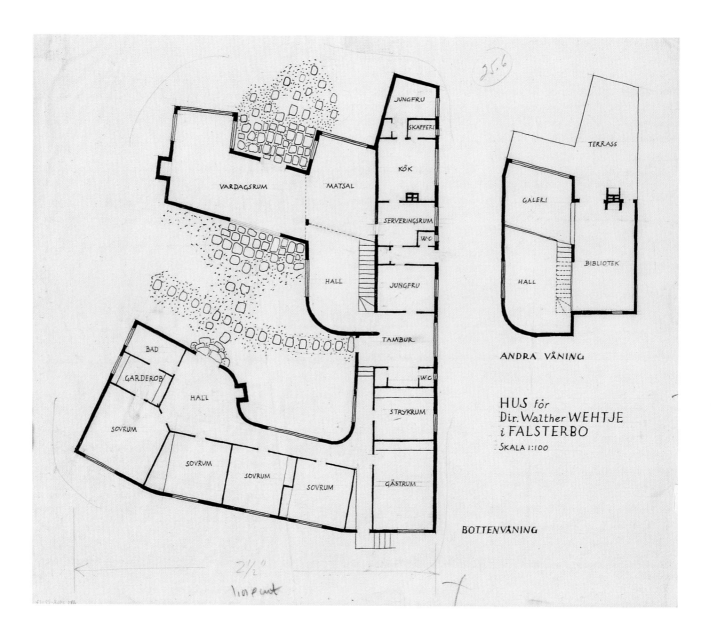

JUNGFRU
SKAFFERI
KÖK
SERVERINGSRUM
W·C
VARDAGSRUM
MATSAL
HALL
JUNGFRU
TAMBUR
W·C
BAD
GARDEROB
HALL
STRYKRUM
SOVRUM
SOVRUM
SOVRUM
SOVRUM
GÄSTRUM

BOTTENVÅNING

TERRASS
GALERI
BIBLIOTEK
HALL

ANDRA VÅNING

HUS för
Dir. Walther WEHTJE
i FALSTERBO
SKALA 1:100

## 70. House for Walther Wehtje in Falsterbo

ca. 1936
Pencil, ink on tracing paper
15 x 17⅜ in. (38 x 44 cm)

Plans 1:100

Swedish Museum of Architecture, Stockholm
Inv. no. 1968-12-17

The Walther Wehtje house was one of the series of summer villas Frank designed in Falsterbo and the last house he built in Sweden. It is among his most ambitious and acomplished executed houses comparable in many respects to his earlier Beer House. Like Beer House it is conceived as a network of paths and zones of repose, but here Frank has confined most of the spatial play to a single uniform level, warping and deforming the orthogonal scheme to heighten the feeling of spatial variety and complexity.

The one-and-a-half-story structure is situated on a sandy, pine-covered rise with views of the Baltic. It is arranged in an irregular U-shaped plan with the main entrance facing south. At the center is a small patio dotted by two mature pine trees. A brief description of the house in *Decorative Art* noted that the site "was small,

hedged in on all sides by other villas—hence the arrangement of the rooms round a secluded central patio . . . which is lit by electric lanterns set in the outer walls. The roof terrace commands an excellent view over the dunes and sea, and makes for a good dance floor on summer nights. This is a summer place, designed to make the most of the short Swedish summer."

The house is divided into two wings: the wing on the north contains the service areas and the living and dining rooms; the wing on the south, the bedrooms and guest rooms. The main entrance is from the patio on the west and leads to a small vestibule. To the left is a curving, two-story-high hall that opens into the main living and dining area. A stairway on one side of the hall leads up to a second-floor gallery and living area and to a large roof terrace. The gallery is open to the hall and has a two-story-high window wall looking out onto the patio. The large living/dining area faces a second patio area on the west side of the house. The other wing of the house containing the bedrooms and two guest rooms is raised several steps higher than the rest of the ground floor and has separate entrances on the east and southwest sides. The rooms are arrayed along a roughly L-shaped hallway with curvilinear walls. The owner's bedroom, on the southwest corner, has a large adjoining dressing room.

The exterior stucco walls were originally painted a pale peach color, which gave the house a light and cheerful appearance, a feeling reflected also by the house's open and airy interior spaces. CL

References: *Studio Yearbook* (1938), p. 20; Spalt and Czech, *Josef Frank, 1885–1967* (1981), pp. 49–51; Long, "Josef Frank and the Crisis of Modern Architecture" (1993), pp. 214–15, 330–32; Welzig, "Die Wiener Internationalität des Josef Frank" (1994), pp. 201–08.

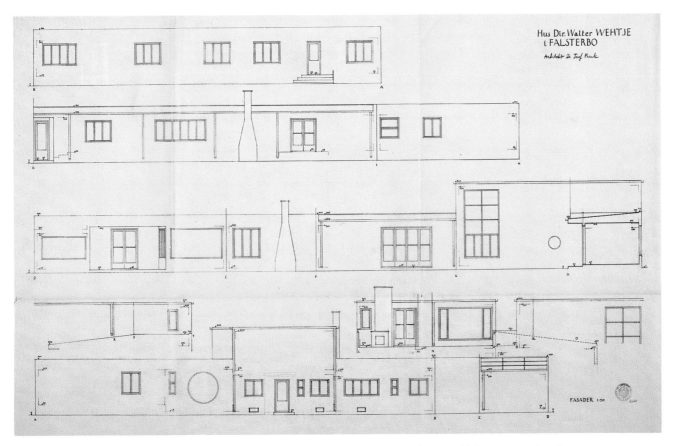

**Fig. 70a.** The Walther Wehtje House in Falsterbo, Sweden, ca. 1936; pencil, pen and ink on paper; elevations 1:50. University of Applied Arts, Vienna, inv. no. 1226.

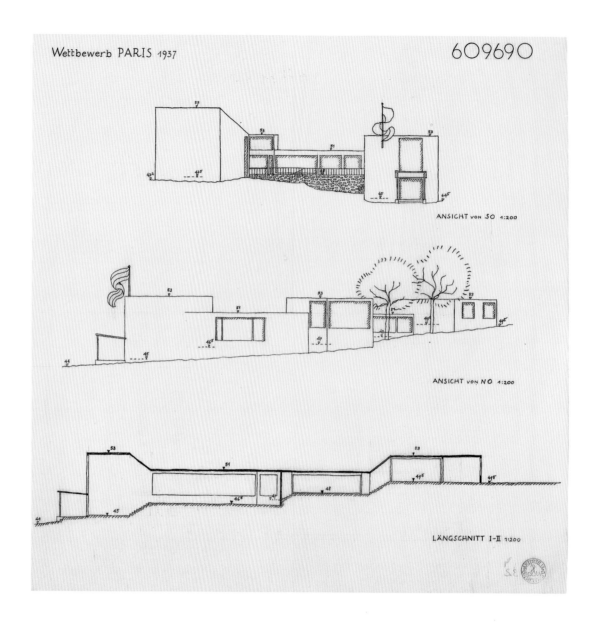

ANSICHT von SO 1:200

ANSICHT von NO 1:200

LÄNGSCHNITT I–II 1:200

## 71. Competition Project for the Austrian Pavilion at the Paris Exposition Internationale

ca. 1936
Pencil, pen and ink on tracing paper
14⅛ x 14⅛ in. (36 x 36 cm)

Perspectives, sections
Inscription: "Wettbewerb Paris 1937"

Frank-Archiv, Graphische Sammlung Albertina, Vienna
Inv. no. 32

Frank entered this project in a competition to design the Austrian Pavilion for the 1937 Paris Exposition Internationale, which was eventually won by Oswald Haerdtl. The long asymmetrically shaped building is situated on a sloping site. No plan for the design has survived, but the elevations suggest that the interior was to have been arranged on a series of different levels and the rooms were to be of various heights.
NS-L

References: Spalt and Czech, *Josef Frank, 1885–1967* (1981), p. 210; Long, "Josef Frank and the Crisis of Modern Architecture" (1993), pp. 216–17, 332; Welzig, "Die Wiener Internationalität des Josef Frank" (1994), p. 213.

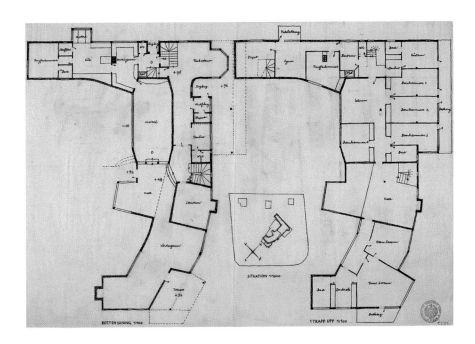

### 72. House for Walther Wehtje in Djursholm, Sweden

1938 (project)
Pencil, pen and ink on tracing paper
14⅛ x 20⅝ in. (36 x 52.5 cm)

Plans 1:100; site plan 1:1000
Inscription: "Residence W. Djursholm, Sweden"; signed "Josef Frank"; dated "1938"

University of Applied Arts, Vienna
Inv. no. 1233

This unrealized project for a house for Walther Wehtje (for whom Frank had designed the beach house in Falsterbo two years before) in many respects marks the culmination of his planning ideas of the 1930s. The sprawling two-and-a-half-story villa was intended for a site in the community of Djursholm, just outside Stockholm. It is arranged in a curving, irregular L-shaped plan. None of the rooms is a regular rectangle, and several have curvilinear walls. The main entrance is on the north and opens into a small atrium. From there the main route leads to a large hall housing the principal staircase to the upstairs. The center of the ground floor is occupied by a large dining room. The northwest wing houses the service areas, kitchen, pantry, and servant's room; the southeastern end, a central hall and living room. As in a num-

ber of Frank's other houses of this period, the ground-floor rooms are placed on several different levels, with short flights of stairs connecting them.

The second floor has a number of bedrooms, a guestroom, an additional servant's room, and several bathrooms. All of the larger bedrooms open onto terraces. The uppermost floor houses a large hall and a sitting room.

No elevations are extant, but the house was probably intended to have had masonry walls covered with stucco and the windows set flush with the walls. CL

References: Spalt and Czech, *Josef Frank, 1885–1967* (1981), p. 52; Long, "Josef Frank and the Crisis of Modern Architecture" (1993), pp. 217–18, 333; Welzig, "Die Wiener Internationalität des Josef Frank" (1994), p. 214.

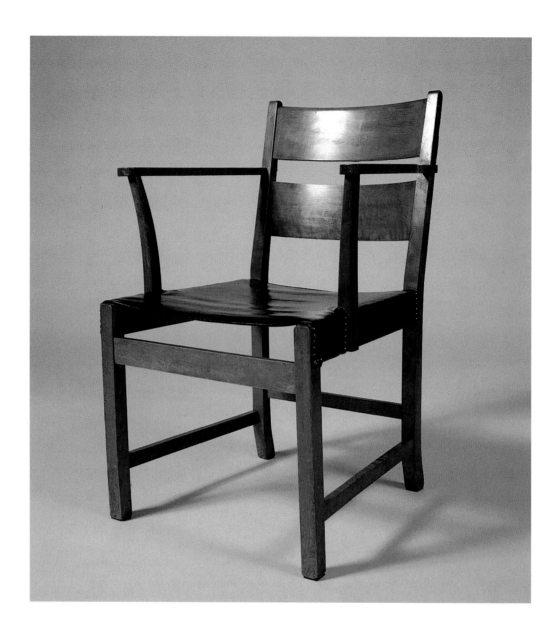

### 73. Armchair

Designed ca. 1936, this example 1951

[Walnut], leather

41½ x 18¼ x 22 in. (105.4 x 46.4 x 55.9 cm)

Retailed by Svenskt Tenn as model no. 542

Western Pennsylvania Conservancy/Fallingwater

Edgar J. Kaufmann is believed to have purchased this armchair for Fallingwater (Bear Run, Pennsylvania; 1937–39), the landmark house by Frank Lloyd Wright, after the 1951 exhibition of Frank's furniture at Kaufmann's Department Store in Pittsburgh. There is an interesting similarity between this chair design and American Arts and Crafts furniture made at the beginning of the twentieth century. Frank softens the rather heavy lines of the chair by giving an

**Fig. 73a.** Frank's armchair at Fallingwater. Western Pennsylvania Conservancy/ Fallingwater.

outward curvature to the vertical supports that join the arms to the seat. The chair was available through Svenskt Tenn with upholstery of different colors, including red, green, and black leather. Svenskt Tenn produced a similar chair with slender vertical members across the back rather than the horizontal cross bars shown here. NS-L

References: Spalt and Czech, *Josef Frank 1885–1967* (1981); Wängberg-Eriksson, "Svenskt Tenn, Josef Frank och Estrid Ericson" (1985); idem, "The Interior Designer," in Boman, *Estrid Ericson* (1989); idem, *Josef Frank Livsträd* (1994); Mathias Boeckl, ed., *Visionäre & Vertriebene: Österreichische Spuren in der modernen amerikanischen Architektur* (1995).

### 74. Stool

Designed 1936; this example ca. 1947–51
Walnut and linen upholstery
H. 15¾ (40 cm), Diam. 23⅝ in. (60 cm)

Currently retailed by Svenskt Tenn as model no.
647; linen upholstery ("Anakreon" with black
background) by Josef Frank

Millesgården, Stockholm

Although designed before the Second
World War, this stool was included among
the furnishings specified by Frank for
the "music room" of Anne's House at
Millesgården. This example of the design
(ca. 1947–51) is particularly noteworthy
because it retains its original upholstery, the
"Anakreon" pattern with a black
background. The upholstered seat thus
made a rather straightforward design a focal
point in one of Frank's most famous interiors. NS-L

Reference: Wängberg-Eriksson, *Josef Frank Livsträd*
(1994).

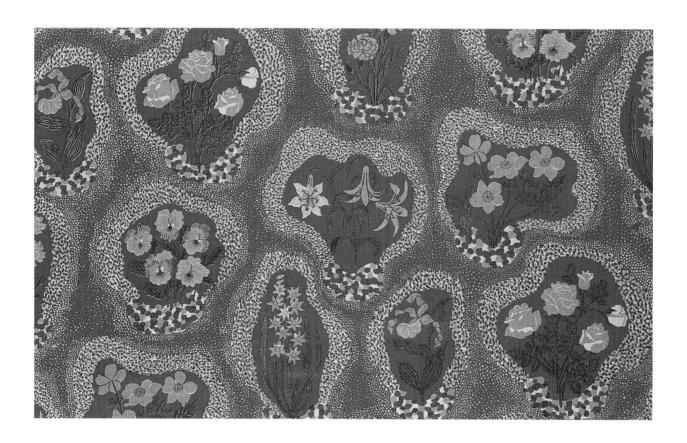

### 75. "Catleya" (*sic*)

Designed ca. 1936, printed ca. 1947
Linen
Size: 35 x 50½ in. (88.9 x 130.8 cm)
Repeat: 29½ x 24 in. (75 x 61 cm)

Screenprinted by Ljungbergs Textiltryck for
Svenskt Tenn; currently retailed by Svenskt Tenn,
Stockholm

Svenskt Tenn Archive, Stockholm

This composition is dominated by medallions outlined in pointillist fashion and enclosing garden flowers in mixed colors. The seven flowers can be identified with some precision, beginning in the center and reading clockwise around it: *Lilium* (center), possibly *Leucolirion*, a Chinese lily; *Anemone* (right of center) of a Mediterranean type; *Cattleya hybrida*, a South American orchid; *Scilla nonscripta*, an English bluebell; *Viola wittrockiana*, a pansy; *Rosa*, a multipetaled rose; and *Dianthus caryophyllus*, a carnation, the flower of Zeus (above the lilies).

"Catleya," as Frank incorrectly spelled it, became the name of this textile. It was printed in three different color schemes: light blue and pink; red and yellow; and brown and yellow. KW-E

Reference: Spalt and Kapfinger, *Josef Frank 1885–1967* (1986).

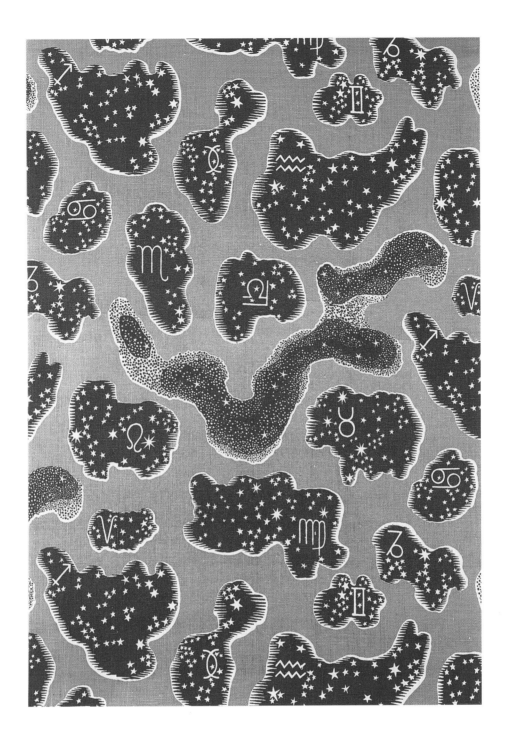

### 76. "Zodiaken"

Designed ca. 1936, printed ca. 1947

Linen

Size: 114½ x 50½ in. (289 x 128.3 cm)

Repeat: 32¼ x 25¼ in. (82 x 64 cm)

Screenprinted by Ljungbergs Textiltryck for Svenskt Tenn

Svenskt Tenn Archive, Stockholm

The constellations of the zodiac and their signs, age-old Babylonian symbols, float like dark blue clouds on a light blue background with a curling Milky Way of hazy star clusters. Above the Milky Way are Pisces, Aquarius, Scorpio, Libra, Sagittarius, and Aries; below the Milky Way are Leo, Taurus, Cancer, Virgo, Gemini, and Capricorn. In some cases the cloud forms are related to the subject of the constellation; the resemblance is perhaps clearest for Pisces, Taurus, and Gemini. For once in Frank's textile compositions the background is flat and undecorated, a design choice that seems warranted by the intricacy of the individual motifs with their small luminous points. KW-E

Reference: Spalt and Kapfinger, *Josef Frank, 1885–1967* (1986).

### 77. "Anakreon"

ca. 1938
Pencil, watercolor, and gouache on paper
37¼ x 54½ in. (94.6 x 138.4 cm)

Svenskt Tenn Archive, Stockholm

A large number of fragments of frescos from the New Palace of Knossos (1600–1400 B.C.) on Crete have been preserved. After extensive restoration most are now in the Archaeological Museum of Iráklion. In the late 1930s Estrid Ericson suggested that Frank use the "blue bird" from the House of the Frescos as the theme of a textile design. On the whole he made few changes in the original composition, adding ivy leaves, flowers, and a bird's nest with speckled eggs and modifying the color scheme

**Fig. 78a.** The bluebird fresco, House of the Frescos, New Palace of Knossos, Crete. From Evans, *Palace of Minos* (1928).

somewhat. He chose olive green to be one of the dominant colors and included saffron crocuses among the flowers. For thousands of years olives and crocuses have been part of the landscape and history of Crete. Ultimately Frank's design came close to his own conception of an ideal textile pattern.

The repeat is large and the choice of geometry (a centered rectangle) creates a rhythmic undulation and upward movement. The pattern's powerful impact is not in the least diminished when the fabric hangs freely in folds as a curtain or drapery where it evokes an almost euphoric feeling of freedom.

Anakreon was a Greek poet who lived during the late archaic period in the decades just prior to 500 B.C. and was widely known in Europe, for his love poems and drinking songs, through late Roman imitations.
KW-E

References: Evans, *Palace of Minos* (1928); Pendlebury, *Palace of Minos, Knossos* (1954).

### 78. "Anakreon"

Designed ca. 1938, printed ca. 1947
Linen, black background
Size: 37¼ x 62¼ in. (95 x 158 cm)
Repeat: 29¼ x 48½ in. (75 x 123 cm)

Printed by Ljungbergs Textiltryck for Svenskt
Tenn; currently retailed by Svenskt Tenn,
Stockholm

Svenskt Tenn, Stockholm

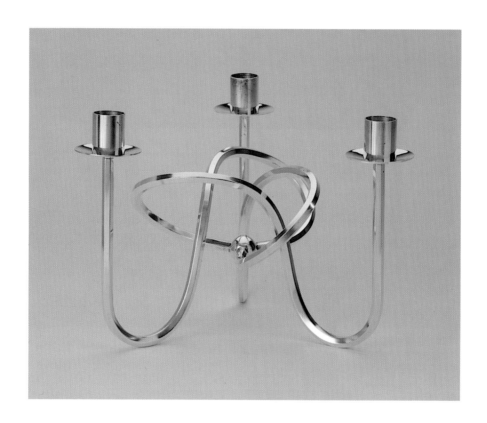

### 81. Three-armed Candlestick

Designed 1938; this example ca. 1950
Silver plated
6¼ x 8¾ x 7¼ in. (15.9 x 22.2 x 18.4 cm)

Currently retailed by Svenskt Tenn

Svenskt Tenn Archive, Stockholm

Candlesticks are integral to domestic interiors in Nordic countries, and over the years Svenskt Tenn has retailed several different types. This three-armed design is thought to have been made by Frank as a symbol of peace and friendship, represented by the continuous line of silver joined by a central knot. NS-L

## 82. Armchair

Designed 1939; this example 1951
Mahogany, linen, cane
31½ x 27½ x 29½ in. (80 x 70 x 75 cm)
Currently retailed by Svenskt Tenn as
model no. 969

Millesgården, Stockholm

This armchair was one of a pair that
figured prominently in the "music room" of
Anne's House, located on the grounds of
Millesgården, home of the Swedish sculp-
tor Carl Milles in a suburb outside
Stockholm. Designing the interiors was one
of the most important commissions for
Svenskt Tenn after the Second World War.

The music room in particular was a
characteristic Frank interior and conveyed
many aspects of his unique design philosophy. A distinct sophistication was combined with a feeling of comfort and relaxation. A typical Frank vocabulary of furni-

**Fig. 82a.** Music room, Anne's House,
Millesgården, ca. 1947–51. Svenskt Tenn
Archive, Stockholm.

ture forms was used, including a fully
upholstered sofa and armchair, small tables,
and a stool. The walls were painted white
and decorative accents achieved through the
furnishings with their colorful and richly
patterned textiles.

Armchair model no. 969 reveals many of
the qualities that are associated with
Swedish Modern design and were evident in
Frank's furniture since his Vienna years. The
overall simplicity and subtle details of the
design evoke an elegance and refinement
further enhanced by the curvature of the
arms and the arm supports. Especially
noteworthy are the caning of the back and
curvature of the splat, devices used by
Frank to break down the overall mass and
reduce the weight of his furniture. The
shape of the splat suggests a lingering influence of Biedermeier furniture in Frank's
work; it is also reminiscent of Haus &
Garten chair backs. NS-L

References: *Josef Frank inredning* (1994); Wängberg-
Eriksson, *Josef Frank Livsträd* (1994).

### 83. Side table

Designed ca. 1939
Marble and walnut
17⅝ x 34⅞ x 17¾ in. (44.8 x 88.6 x 45.1 cm)

Private collection, Sweden

This side table was displayed at the 1939 New York World's Fair, which is widely recognized as being the formal introduction of Swedish Modern design to the United States. The table can be seen in photographs of the installation as well as on the installation drawing. A rare United States Customs stamp, made specifically for the fair, is still attached to the crossbar supporting the marble top. Similar marble side tables were among the furnishings by Frank used in the living room at Tolvekarna, the summer house of Estrid Ericson, in 1942 and in the music room of Anne's House at Millesgården, completed between 1949 and 1951.

Small tables were prominently featured in Frank's interiors. This example typifies the special attention that Frank gave to subtle details of his design. The oval-shaped marble top, for example, has a beveled edge that reduces the overall mass of the form. The table rests on four legs that are circular in cross-section and terminate in a gently protruding foot. Frank has softened the vertical line of the leg with an inward curve approximately ¼ inch from the top. Legs in this shape were used on many other tables by Frank. NS-L

References: Wängberg-Eriksson, *Josef Frank Livsträd* (1994).

**Fig. 83c.** Svenskt Tenn's installation at the 1939 World's Fair in New York. Courtesy, Svenskt Tenn Archive, Stockholm.

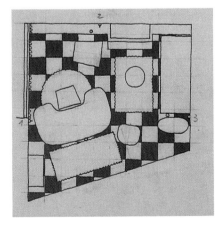

**Fig. 83a.** Installation drawing, New York World's Fair, 1939. Courtesy, Svenskt Tenn Archive, Stockholm.

**Fig. 83b.** Side table (*detail*), showing the U.S. Customs stamp.

## 84. Installation Drawing, Golden Gate Exhibition, San Francisco

1939
Watercolor and pencil on paper
10¼ x 21⅝ in. (26 x 55 cm)

Svenskt Tenn Archive, Stockholm

The 1939 Golden Gate Exhibition at San Francisco included a Svenskt Tenn installation that serves as a summation of Frank's design philosophy during the interwar years. It encompasses the blending of ideas initiated at Haus & Garten in the 1920s and developed at Svenskt Tenn in the 1930s. Historically the exhibition followed the 1939 New York World's Fair that introduced Swedish Modern design to the United States.

Many quintessential designs appear in Frank's drawing of a "combination living- and bed room." The diverse forms range from a dressing table with three mirrors, fully upholstered armchair, small stools and tables, and free-standing floor lamps. The right side of the room has built-in cabinets, which were frequently used by Frank in his Vienna interiors. His choice of a rich palette for this drawing reflects his admiration for color and pattern. The bedroom on the left may be covered in floral wallpaper. Frank had a sophisticated knowledge of

plants, largely acquired through botanical books, which permitted him to make detailed illustrations of different plant forms. The floral theme recurs in the upholstery of the armchair which is clearly based on his "Aralia" textile that was introduced in Vienna. The floor coverings also incorporate floral as well as animal motifs and conform to Frank's belief that small rugs should be spaced throughout a room. A similar animal-shaped floor covering appears in a 1940 drawing for a carpet. NS-L

References: Wängberg-Eriksson, "Svenskt Tenn Josef Frank och Estrid Ericson" (1985); idem, "The Interior Designer," in Boman, *Estrid Ericson* (1989); idem, *Josef Frank Livsträd* (1994).

## 85. Three-armed Floor Lamp

Designed ca. 1939, this example ca. 1940
Steel, brass, leather
H. 59 in. (150 cm)

Currently retailed by Svenskt Tenn as model no.
G2431

Svenskt Tenn Archive, Stockholm

Of the many desk and floor lamps that
Frank designed for Haus & Garten and
Svenskt Tenn, this free-standing floor lamp
is the most accomplished. It was included
in the Svenskt Tenn installation at the 1939
San Francisco exhibition and can be seen in
the installation drawing. Its three arms can
be moved in different directions, the most
striking aspect of the design. These flexible
brass arms and the different color lamp
shades, contrasted with the black and brass
frame, enhance the sculptural quality of the
form. NS-L

Reference: Wängberg-Eriksson, *Josef Frank Livsträd*
(1994).

**86. "Parnassius Apollo"**

ca. 1940
Pencil, watercolor, and gouache on paper
35 x 26⅞ in. (88.9 x 68.3 cm)

Svenskt Tenn Archive, Stockholm

Common ivy (*Hedera helix*), faithfully reproduced by Frank, climbs in soft curves
obliquely and upward throughout this
design. The other plants are the grape
hyacinth and periwinkle (*Vinca minor*). The
Apollo butterfly (*Parnassius Apollo*) gives
the Mediterranean scenery an ethereal lightness, also lending its Latin name to this
pattern. Associated with Mount Parnassus,
which in classical mythology was sacred to
Apollo and Dionysus, this species is widespread in the mountains of Greece.
Another mountain reference is made with
the inclusion of mineral crystals beside the
ivy leaves. The white, red, and black background areas resemble the shapes in frescos
from the Minoan period, especially those

found on Thera (Santorini), a volcanic
island north of Crete. KW-E

Reference: Höckmann, "Theran floral style"
(1980), vol. 1, p. 605.

**87. "Parnassius Apollo"**
Designed ca. 1940, printed ca. 1994
Linen
Repeat: 33½ x 24½ in. (85 x 62 cm)

Screenprinted by Ljungbergs Textiltryck for
Svenskt Tenn; currently retailed by Svenskt Tenn,
Stockholm

Svenskt Tenn, Stockholm

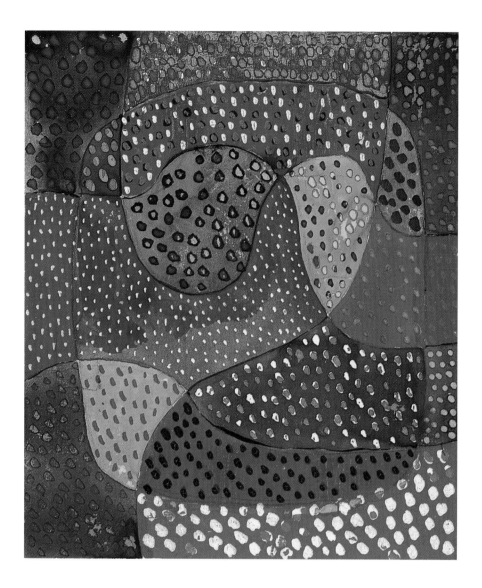

**88. Drawing for Hand-knotted
Carpet**
ca. 1940
Watercolor, gouache and pencil on paper
7⅛ x 6⅜ in. (18.1 x 16.2 cm)

Svenskt Tenn Archive, Stockholm

Frank had little appreciation for the avant-garde art of his time. Clues to his attitude toward it are found in his unpublished 1942 novel about an artist named Lucien Sander who is confronted with the problem of the true/genuine versus illusion/facade. Sander was the founder of a movement called "sublimism," an "ism" invented by Frank with tongue in cheek. The "free" element in contemporary art might have attracted Frank, but not geometric form as an end in itself, nor what was schematic or constructivistic. He rejected authoritarianism in all its guises. His printed textiles were uplifting, almost otherworldly, allowing liberation from the shackles of the room.

Frank took a different approach, however, when designing floor coverings. Here people should recognize terra firma beneath their feet. Frank preferred ornamented surfaces which, he argued, have a calming effect. In his early designs he often used checkerboard tile floors, but in the 1920s he began to develop more complicated floor ornamentation, though without dependence on traditional carpet patterns. His rugs were hand-knotted, using rya or pile techniques, which make a free and bold design possible.

All in all, Frank created some thirty carpet patterns including those shown here. In one (cat. no. 91) blocks of gray and white are sometimes filled with different dotted

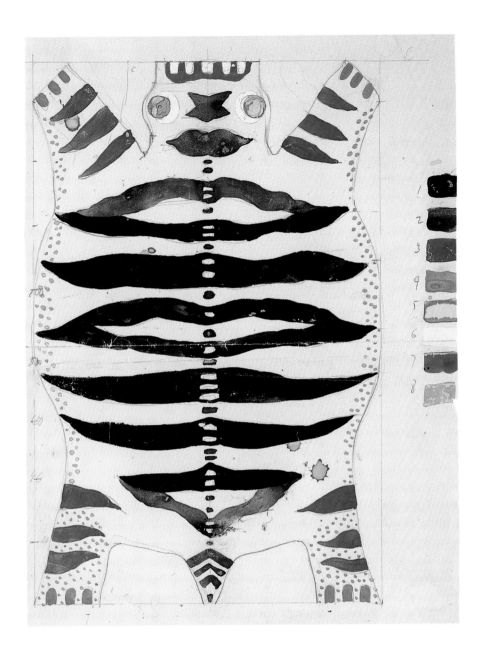

**89. Drawing for Hand-knotted Carpet**
ca. 1940
Watercolor, gouache and pencil on paper
16½ x 11⅞ in. (41.9 x 30.2 cm)

Svenskt Tenn Archive, Stockholm

patterns resembling gravel or concrete and symbols vaguely like Freemason's signs (a blue squiggle at the top like a hieroglyph; a rounded, five-pointed star like that on a footstool found in Tutankhamen's tomb). Another (cat. no. 89) is a zebra-striped animal skin design. Frank had no great love for gamehunting and he designed rugs meant to replace real animal skins, which were relatively common in interior designs in the 1930s. A similar rug can be glimpsed in the 1939 San Francisco combined bedroom/living room.

With its loose, biomorphic central figures, cat. no. 90 is an especially rich composition, a play of colors and dimensions, ornamented with dots and "Tutankhamen" stars. Dominated by red and green, cat. no. 88 is a calmer pattern of curved lines and dotted surfaces. Frank's abstract carpet designs were a pioneering effort and were not fully appreciated when they were first introduced by Svenskt Tenn. Now, however, after more than a half-century, his floor coverings are widely acclaimed. KW-E

Reference: Spalt and Kapfinger, *Josef Frank, 1885–1967* (1986).

**90. Drawing for Hand-knotted Carpet**

ca. 1940
Watercolor, gouache and pencil on paper
11⅜ x 16¼ in. (28.9 x 41.3 cm)

Svenskt Tenn Archive, Stockholm

**91. Drawing for Hand-knotted Carpet**
1938
Watercolor on paper
18⅜ x 16¼ in. (46.7 x 41.3 cm)

Svenskt Tenn Archive, Stockholm

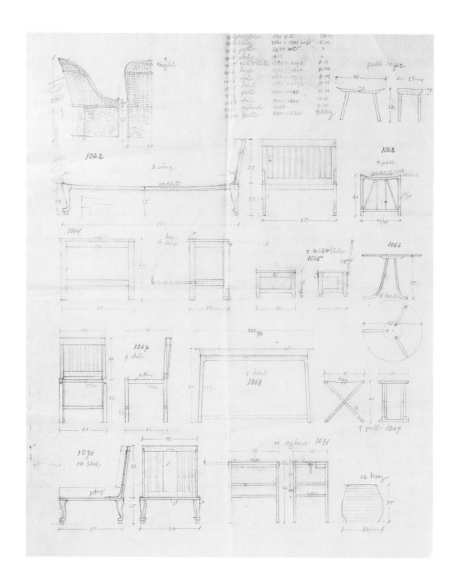

## 92. Drawing for Ancient Chinese and Egyptian Furniture

ca. 1941
Pencil on tracing paper
21⅛ x 16½ in. (53.7 x 41.9 cm)

Svenskt Tenn Archive, Stockholm

Svenskt Tenn played an important educational role in the Swedish design community by organizing exhibitions at its shop on Strandvägen. The spring exhibition in 1941 was devoted to furniture inspired by ancient Chinese and Egyptian furniture. Frank's interest in these sources began in Vienna and persisted throughout his career. At the top of the drawing a key to the designs indicates the name of each piece and gives the date around which the design was created in antiquity and the museum in which a comparable example could be found—the British Museum, London; Metropolitan Museum of Art, New York; Egyptian Museum in Cairo; and an unnamed museum in Peking (Beijing).

The bed (second row in the drawing) is known to have been made for Svenskt Tenn's 1941 exhibition and survives in the Svenskt Tenn collection. Other stools and tables inspired by ancient Egyptian prototypes were also designed by Frank and manufactured for Svenskt Tenn. NS-L

References: Spalt and Czech, *Josef Frank, 1885–1967* (1981); Wängberg-Eriksson, *Josef Frank Livsträd* (1994).

**93. Stool**

Designed ca. 1941, this example ca. 1955
Walnut, leather and brass
14½ x 20 x 16½ in. (36.8 x 50.8 x 41.9 cm)

Currently retailed by Svenskt Tenn as
model no. 1063

Consulate General of Sweden, New York City

This Egyptian-inspired stool appears in Frank's drawing for the 1941 Svenskt Tenn exhibition of ancient Chinese and Egyptian furniture. The form of the stool and its construction bear a striking resemblance to the ancient Egyptian lattice stool, common during the New Kingdom. Egyptian furniture was an important source of inspiration for many designers searching for an appropriate means of expression for modern furniture. English nineteenth-century designers, for example, such as E. W. Godwin, created furniture inspired by these prototypes, and the London retailer, Liberty and Company, sold many Egyptian-inspired designs.

In Vienna Adolf Loos designed small Egyptian-inspired stools before the First World War, and in America such stools are also known, many by anonymous designers.

Svenskt Tenn retailed the stool with a leather or zebra-skin seat. NS-L

References: Killen, *Ancient Egyptian Furniture* (1980); Spalt and Czech, *Josef Frank, 1885–1967* (1981); Wängberg-Eriksson, *Josef Frank Livsträd* (1994).

**94. Stool**

Designed ca. 1941, this example 1966
Mahogany and zebra skin
15¼ x 24 x 15¾ in. (38.7 x 9½ x 40 cm)

Currently retailed by Svenskt Tenn as
model no. 972

Brita and Henning Rydberg, Sweden

This is the second of the Egyptian-inspired stools designed by Frank and retailed at Svenskt Tenn. The round legs are distinctive of certain ancient Egyptian prototypes. It was one of his most successful designs and was acclaimed in Sweden. Its popularity at Svenskt Tenn was perhaps due in part to the appeal of exoticism that was associated with non-Western furniture, particularly ancient Egyptian and African examples. The zebra skin might have been suggested by Estrid Ericson. NS-L

References: Killen, *Ancient Egyptian Furniture* (1980); Wängberg-Eriksson, *Josef Frank Livsträd* (1994).

## 95. "Gröna Fåglar"

Designed 1943–44, printed 1995
Linen
Repeat: 36 x 24¼ in. (91.5 x 61.5 cm)

Screenprinted by Ljungbergs Textiltryck for
Svenskt Tenn; currently retailed by Svenskt Tenn,
Stockholm

Svenskt Tenn, Stockholm

"Gröna Fåglar" (Green Birds) is based on
the Oriental "tree of life," a symbol of the
biological force and survival of species.
In varying forms the tree of life appears
in most cultures. It was a popular motif
in old Persian carpets and Indian cottons
and chintzes. The *palempores* from the Coro-
mandel coast of India were especially magnificent. They were waxed and dyed, then
printed with wood blocks, and finally finished with hand-painting. And in Nordic
mythology Yggdrasil is the tree of the
world.

In "Gröna Fåglar" Frank has tilted the
tree to the left and used the birds to indi-
cate the horizontals. The tree's extensive
root system and trufflelike tubers are
exposed. It is in full bloom but has already
begun to bear fruit at its crown. When the
repeat patterns are joined, the meandering
blue waterways are ingeniously linked.

The green birds have American rather
than Asian sources: a cawing great blue
heron standing on one leg in the stream;
starlings; a spotted "duck" at the foot of
the tree, and a speckled dove sitting above
the ducklike bird. Although he was not aim-
ing at exact reproduction, Frank drew his
birds from a field guide, *The Green Book of
Birds*, which also lent its name to this pattern. KW-E

References: Ashbrook, *The Green Book of Birds*
(1941); Peterson, *Field Guide to the Birds* (1947),
p. 20; Spalt and Kapfinger, *Josef Frank, 1885–1967*
(1986).

## 96 "Rox and Fix"

1943–44

Pencil, watercolor, and gouache on paper
36 x 29⅜ in. (91.4 x 74.6 cm)

Inscription: "Josef Frank, 52 Rindögatan, Stockholm, Sweden"

Svenskt Tenn Archive, Stockholm

In Chinese art the mountain motif is a recurrent one, with the mountains' edges vaporizing into mist. During his years in New York Frank adapted this motif for a powerful, dramatic textile. His design evolved from a loose sketch into a finished pattern of compact mountain peaks of one scale against palmate fig leaves of another. Frank follows an important principle of Chinese painting by incorporating opposites: near and far, mountain and water, high and low, Yin and Yang.

The changing outlines of the mountains makes them seem to recede into the dis-tance. The dots contribute to depth and a feeling of space. The dark figs become muf-fled resting points. The palette is reduced to two colors: dark brown and gray-blue. Here Frank is experimenting with Chinese mannerisms. Chinese artists use a graduated scale of gray in their ink drawings, yet cre-ate the illusion of many colors. The name "Rox & Fix" is a play on the words *rocks* and *figs*. KW-E

## 97. "Rox and Fix"

Designed 1943–44, printed for the first time in
1994
Linen
Repeat: 33 x 24½ in. (84 x 62 cm)

Screenprinted by Ljungbergs Textiltryck for
Svenskt Tenn; currently retailed by Svenskt Tenn,
Stockholm

Svenskt Tenn, Stockholm

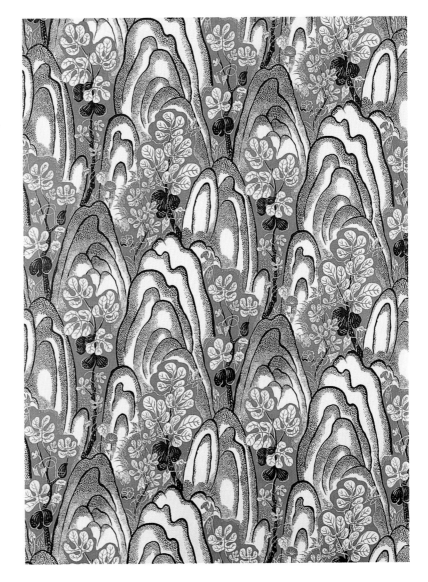

**Fig. 97a.** Shi Tao (1630–1707),
*Landscape*, Qing Dynasty; hanging scroll
in black ink on paper. Cengdu, Sichuan
Provincial Museum.

### 98. "Dehli"

ca. 1943–44

Pencil, watercolor, and gouache on paper
36 x 24⅝ in. (91.4 x 62.6 cm)

Inscription: "Design by Josef Frank exclusively
for...", "Josef Frank"

Svenskt Tenn Archive, Stockholm

Judging from an inscription on the drawing, "Delhi" was probably one of the patterns that Frank offered to the Schumacher's firm while he was living in New York during World War II. The design is a magnificent combination of pale pink and two blue-greens, one dark, the other light. Huge leaves curve protectively over pink umbellate flowers, and pink butterflies flit through the foliage. The plant is "French cotton" (*Calotropis procera*), which is native to tropical Asia and Africa and can reach a height of several yards.

The pattern's impact comes from the refined harmonies of color and the arching interplay of leaves. The contrast in form between the groups of flowers and the curved leaves is strongly emphasized. In this design Frank abandoned his usual "dot device" to divide up the background or soften an outline.

The overall design concept may have been an attempt to adapt to English or American taste, but in any event the size of the pattern must still have seemed rather eccentric, despite William Morris's assertion: "Do not be afraid of large patterns; if properly designed they are more restful to the eye than small ones." For various reasons Frank never managed to establish a permanent contact with Schumacher's, and "Delhi" was first printed by Ljungbergs Textiltryck in Sweden. KW-E

References: Graham, *Tropical Wild Flowers* (1963); Morris, quoted in Thomas, Minguy, and Pommier, *Textile Art* (1985), p. 187.

**99. "Dehli"**
Designed ca. 1943–44, printed ca. 1947
Linen
Size: 35 x 50½ in. (88.9 x 128.3 cm)
Repeat: 30 x 24 in. (76.5 x 61 cm)

Test-printed by Ljungbergs Textiltryck for
Svenskt Tenn

Svenskt Tenn Archive, Stockholm

### 100. "Worry Bird"

Designed 1943–44, printed ca. 1945
Linen
Size: 41 x 33¾ in. (111.8 x 85.7 cm)
Repeat: 31½ x 24¾ in. (80 x 63 cm)

Screenprinted by Silfa, Sweden, for Svenskt Tenn

Svenskt Tenn Archive, Stockholm

The anxious-looking wading bird that Frank has so deftly captured in different poses is reminiscent of the green heron, a species indigenous to the east coast of North America. Despite its name, the bird is more blue than green. When startled it ruffles the tuft on its crown—hence the name "worry bird."

The bird is shown among clumps of reeds in autumnal colors. The plants are organized in irregular rows, an arrangement paralleling that in "Hügel," a textile from some twenty years earlier. The various flowers between the reed beds barely fit into this environment, but they serve to balance the heron's colorful feathers. The meandering light-colored horizontal lines and vertical strokes also help to hold the scene together.

The pattern is based on a repeat of standing rectangles separated by half their height in relation to one another. KW-E

Reference: Peterson, *Field Guide to the Birds* (1947), p. 24.

## 101. "Drinks"

Designed 1943–44, printed ca. 1994
Linen
Repeat: 37¾ x 30 in. (96 x 77 cm)

Screenprinted by Ljungbergs Textiltryck for
Svenskt Tenn; currently retailed by Svenskt Tenn,
Stockholm

Svenskt Tenn, Stockholm

In "Drinks," Frank has gathered our most
common stimulants—coffee, tea, and
cocoa—into an arrangement of starred
clusters like bunches of grapes. Each carefully drawn plant is labeled with its Latin
name in red and black placed beneath it like
a set of scales. The flowers and fruits stand
out sharply against the black background.

"Drinks" is one in a series that also
includes "Poisons" (grapes, hops, and
tobacco) and "Citrus" (lemons, oranges,
and grapefruit). The group is among
Frank's "American" patterns, designed in
New York, 1943–44. KW-E

Reference: Spalt and Kapfinger, *Josef Frank,
1885–1967* (1986).

### 102. "La Plata"

Designed 1943–44, printed ca. 1947
Linen
Repeat: 39½ x 24½ in. (88 x 62 cm)

Screenprinted by Ljungbergs Textiltryck for
Svenskt Tenn; currently retailed by Svenskt Tenn,
Stockholm

Svenskt Tenn Archive, Stockholm

Curving and intersecting vines form a dense
network of pattern elements in varying
sizes. Citrus fruit and dazzling clematis are
primary motifs; an abundance of flowers
and leaf forms in three distinct sizings provides depth. "La Plata" is related to
"Mirakel," a pattern Frank designed twenty
years earlier for Haus & Garten in Vienna,
but "La Plata" has a simpler geometric
plan. In both patterns slender creepers curl
around the vines, to mask their upward
movement.

The name "La Plata" derives from the
Rio de la Plata, a South American river
estuary near Buenos Aires. Frank seems to
have chosen it more for its exotic sound
than anything else. When viewed as pattern
art, this is one of the high points in Frank's
rich and multifaceted production. Tyra
Lundgren, a Swedish artist and designer,
wrote, "It is a fairly long way from printed
textiles of this top class to the others. It is
not just the compositional skill, the fastidi-
ously controlled colors, and the lively
nature of the drawing, but the emanation
of a powerful artistic personality that is
decisive." KW-E

Reference: Lundgren, "Den moderna blommigheten" (1943), p. 92; Spalt and Kapfinger, *Josef
Frank, 1885–1967* (1986).

### 103. "Terrazzo"

Designed 1943–44, printed 1995
Linen
Repeat: 31¾ x 25 in. (80.5 x 63.5 cm)

Screenprinted by Ljungbergs Textiltryck for
Svenskt Tenn; currently retailed by Svenskt Tenn,
Stockholm

Svenskt Tenn, Stockholm

"Terrazzo" is one of the "birthday patterns" that Frank sent from New York to
Estrid Ericson for her fiftieth birthday in
September 1944. Of approximately 200 textile patterns designed by Frank, this is the
only one whose motif is not taken from the
living world. Rather than flowers, birds, or
butterflies, stones of various types provide
color and form. Cut and polished agates, or
chalcedonies, dominate—apple-green
chrysoprase, red carnelian, green heliotrope
flecked with red, among others—but a spi-
ral-shaped mollusk fossil, an ammonite, can
also be identified. The textile's flecked background resembles synthetic stone surfaces.
As was often the case in Frank's later years,
the geometry of the pattern is based on rectangles that together create a centered,
rectangular surface net. For his carpet
patterns Frank often turned to terrace or
mosaic motifs, but their use in fabric design
makes "Terrazzo" unique. KW-E

References: Lundegård, *Stenar i färg* (1961), p. 106;
Spalt and Kapfinger, *Josef Frank, 1885–1967*
(1986).

## 104. "Hawaii"

Designed 1943–44, printed 1995
Linen
Repeat: 74 x 49 in. (188 x 125 cm)

Screenprinted by Ljungbergs Textiltryck for Svenskt Tenn; currently retailed by Svenskt Tenn, Stockholm

Svenskt Tenn, Stockholm

Giving his imagination free rein and without the slightest regard for the genetic imperative of the DNA molecule, Frank has created a colossal tree of life. Widely different species have been "grafted" onto the branches. A "pineapple" resembling a giant melon hangs awkwardly, its threadlike sepal drawn downward. The dark green and pink leaf on the other side of the intertwined stems serves as a counterweight. At the foot of the tree grow botanically correct species such as daisies, lilies of the valley, and wild pansies. From a ground-level branch a mighty tulip pushes upward, and farther up the tree are both the large Oriental flower and mille-fleurs motifs and a swarm of butterflies. In a grand manner, this textile captures a northerner's romantic yearning for exotic places, a yearning that might be satisfied to some extent by incorporating "Hawaii" into an interior. This was Josef Frank's largest pattern; the repeat is over 6 feet in height. KW-E

Reference: Spalt and Kapfinger, *Josef Frank, 1885–1967* (1986).

## 105. "Dixieland"

1943–44
Pencil, watercolor, and gouache on paper
Size: 35¼ x 51½ in. (89.5 x 130.8 cm)
Repeat: 33½ x 48 in. (85 x 122 cm)

Inscription: "JOSEF FRANK, 52 PARK
TERRACE E, 107-1255"

Svenskt Tenn Archive, Stockholm

The word *Dixie* or *Dixieland*, long synonymous with the American South, is
thought to come from the French *dix* (ten),
which appeared on ten-dollar bills from
New Orleans in the mid-nineteenth century. Frank amused himself by drawing a
"global" South. His "Dixieland" is
composed of three distinct parts loosely
representing the Atlantic Ocean, Africa, and
South America. Two huge sunflowers are
located in red Africa, their "suns" filling the
Sahara desert, while the vast Amazonas
region holds watermelons. The ocean, its
waves breaking in white foam along the
coasts, serves as a background for *Nerium
oleander*, a Mediterranean plant that is always
in bloom and now grows profusely in

Florida and the West Indies. The openness
of its leaves and flowers offsets the solidity
of the melon and sunflower forms.
Similarly the intensity of the palette used
for the main elements creates a harmony of
color. KW-E

Reference: Spalt and Kapfinger, *Josef Frank,
1885–1967* (1986).

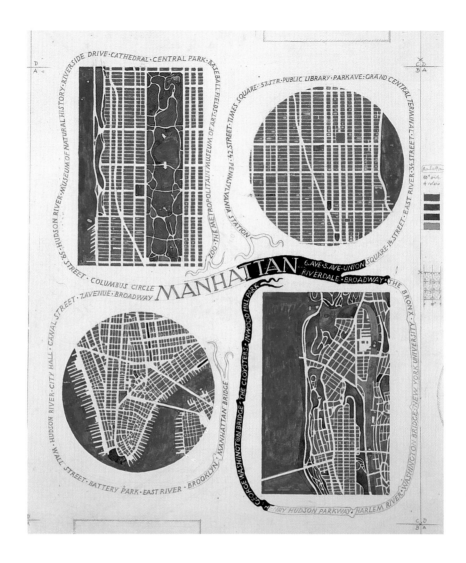

### 106. "Manhattan"

1943–44
Pencil, watercolor, and gouache on board
33½ x 28 in. (85 x 71 cm)

Svenskt Tenn Archive, Stockholm

"Manhattan" reflects Frank's fascination with the city in which he spent the war years. In fact, after returning to Sweden in 1946, he still maintained his New York apartment in case he and his wife Anna decided to return. It was not until 1951 that they finally gave it up.

In his design, Frank used basic forms possessing a modern simplicity—a circle and rectangle—to isolate different parts of Manhattan. The Central Park area and the northern end fit easily into rectangles whereas the southern tip and midtown area from 14th Street to 59th Street are depicted within circles. The black ribbon of text ties the composition together.

In arranging his design Frank made some carefully considered decisions. In the Central Park rectangle he established an

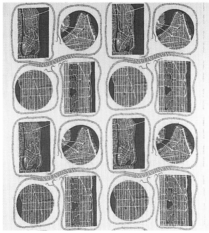

### 107. "Manhattan"

Designed 1943–44, printed ca. 1947
Linen
Repeat: 56¼ x 50 in. (143 x 127 cm)
Size: 118 x 51⅛ in. (300 x 130 cm)

Screenprinted by Ljungsbergs Textiltryck for Svenskt Tenn; currently retailed by Svenskt Tenn, Stockholm

Svenskt Tenn Archive, Stockholm

inner tension by balancing the white streets on red blocks with white winding paths in the green park. The piers at the tip of Manhattan are so densely packed that the outline almost becomes fuzzy, resembling a hair-covered root tip. Unlike the cross streets, the wider avenues are at rhythmically-varying distances from each other, while Broadway, the old Indian path with its oblique course from south to north, breaks the tyranny of the grid. Frank disliked rigid rules of all sorts.

The original drawing is very detailed and meticulously executed and reveals Frank, from a technical point of view, to be a masterful watercolorist, a skill that is apparent in his 1909 thesis drawings of Alberti's Renaissance churches. When Frank returned to Sweden he was commissioned by the Stockholms Enskilda Bank to design a similar pattern based on the map of Stockholm. KW-E

Reference: Spalt and Kapfinger, *Josef Frank, 1885–1967* (1986).

## 108. Table

Designed ca. 1946

Amboyna and walnut

22 x 35 x 38½ in. (56 x 90 x 97.8 cm)

Currently retailed at Svenskt Tenn as model
no. 1057

Private collection, Sweden

A drawing made by Kerstin Österman for
Svenskt Tenn illustrates four tables that
were among Frank's most successful designs:
a round table resting on three legs; an
oblong table on four legs; a square table on
four legs; and this design, with its undulating top resting on a four-legged base. The
contour of the table is unusual for Frank
and is among his most dynamic designs.
Visual interest is heightened by the dichotomy between the strict geometric contours of
the legs and stretcher, and the wavy-edged
top. The design differs from his other
tables, which have simple tops with elegantly shaped legs.

An undulating slab of wood appears in
the work of other designers during the late
1940s and 1950s. Charlotte Perriand, for
example, while working in Japan at the end
of the 1940s, created a table with an irregularly shaped top, and George Nakashima,
the American designer, also used irregularly
shaped slabs of wood for his table tops.
NS-L

References: Spalt and Czech, *Josef Frank,
1885–1967* (1981); Wängberg-Eriksson, *Josef Frank
Livsträd* (1994).

**Fig. 108a.** George Nakashima, Amoeba
Tables, ca. 1951; madrona burl, cherry.
Collection of Mr. and Mrs. George
Nakashima. From Ostergard, *George
Nakashima* (1989).

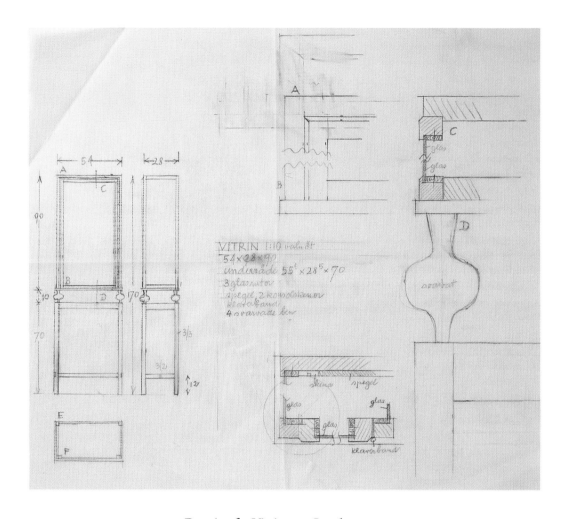

**109. Drawing for Vitrine-on-Stand**
1946
Pencil on tracing paper
8⅞ x 7⅝ in. (22.5 x 19.4 cm)

Svenskt Tenn Archive, Stockholm

The drawing provides the specifications for
the scale and proportions of the cabinet
and the special construction details for the
spindle-shaped feet. NS-L

## 110. Vitrine-on-Stand

Designed 1946; this example ca. 1950
Cherrywood and glass
66⅞ x 35⅜ x 11¾ in. (170 x 90 x 30 cm)

Currently retailed by Svenskt Tenn as model no. 2077

Millesgården, Stockholm

This cabinet is one in a long series of vitrine cabinets that Frank designed, beginning in the early years of his career in Vienna. One of these was a vitrine (also in the exhibition) he created in 1910 for his sister Hedwig. The influence of late-eighteenth- and early-nineteeth-century Neoclassical furniture, which was prominent in that earlier design, has all but disappeared in this later vitrine. Extraneous details have been eliminated, and a subtle but rigorous geometry prevails. In the earlier cabinet the base serves as vitrine, while in this example the base has been reduced to a simple tablelike support on which the vitrine rests its four spindle feet. It is thus gently raised off the base; the effect is one of lightness and visual grace. The relationship of solid to void also heightens visual interest in this vitrine.

Frank designed another vitrine around 1930 in Vienna. It was made of glass and metal and exhibits a geometric rigor and elegant simplicity. Like other case pieces from Frank's Vienna years, it rests on brass legs. NS-L

References: Johansson, *Josef Frank–Tjugo år i Svenskt Tenn* (1952); Nationalmuseum, *Josef Frank* (1968); Wängberg-Eriksson, *Josef Frank Livsträd* (1994).

**Fig. 110a.** Vitrine, ca. 1930. Private collection.

### iii. Dining Chair

Designed ca. 1947; this example ca. 1951
Walnut, rattan, linen upholstery
33½ x 17¾ x 21⅝ in. (85 x 45 x 55 cm)

Currently retailed by Svenskt Tenn as model no.
1165; linen upholstery ("Lyon") by Josef Frank

Millesgården, Stockholm

This is one of Frank's most successful furniture designs. Created shortly after
his 1946 return to Stockholm, it was among
the original furnishings specified for the
music room of Anne's House at
Millesgården. It incorporates many of the
decorative devices that had been introduced
in Vienna. The cane back, subtle curvature
of the stiles and legs, and overall elegance
of the form prevail. Especially interesting is
the arrangement of rattan across the back
which creates a lively rhythmic pattern. The
seat is covered with Frank's printed textile
called "Lyon." NS-L

Reference: Wängberg-Eriksson, *Josef Frank Livsträd*
(1994).

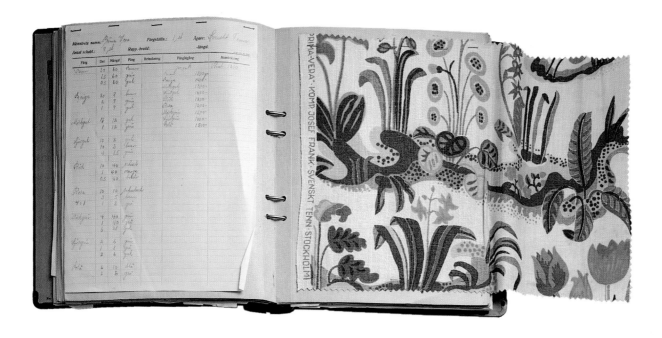

## 112. Erik Ljungberg's textile sample book

ca. 1947–50

12 x 27 in. (30.5 x 68.6 cm)

Svenskt Tenn Archive, Stockholm

The Ljungberg pattern book is open to a sample of "Primavera," one of Josef Frank's most enduring textile designs. Erik Ljungberg, who manufactured camouflage patterns for the Swedish army during the Second World War, established a textile printing business in Gothenburg with his brother Einar in 1942. He concentrated on further developing the film-printing technique that had been invented in America in 1907. By 1946, when Josef Frank returned from the United States and Estrid Ericson was interested in starting to produce Frank's printed textiles in Sweden, the "master printer" Erik Ljungberg was available for work, and since 1947 Ljungbergs Textiltryck, AB in Floda, some twenty miles west of Gothenburg, has printed most of Frank's fabrics for Svenskt Tenn.

"Primavera" has been in production since Frank's Haus & Garten years. As many as thirty-five carved blocks were need-ed for the block printing. Overall nine dif-ferent colors are involved—brown, beige, dark gold, light gold, red, pink, dark green,

## 113. "Primavera"

Designed ca. 1925, printed ca. 1947

Linen

Repeat: 26½ x 30¼ in. (67 x 77 cm)

Screenprinted by Ljungsbergs Textiltryck for Svenskt Tenn; currently retailed by Svenskt Tenn, Stockholm

Svenskt Tenn Archive, Stockholm

light green, and blue—requiring nine dif-ferent stencils for the film printing. Step by step they are moved up over the raw fabric, and the dyes are applied one after the other.

The pattern is very skillfully composed. Most of the spring flowers sprout in hori-zontal bands: tulips, squills, hyacinths, daisies, violets, anemones, and forget-me-nots. With their size and upward thrust the tulips break the bands of flower beds that cut across. The original master is repro-duced in vertical columns which are dis-placed vertically by barely a quarter of the basic repeat so that the resulting surface net is constituted by parallelograms. This cre-ates a slight rise to the left across the entire pattern. The horizontal repetition is much more difficult to detect than the vertical. The name "Primavera" relates to Sandro Botticelli's early Renaissance allegorical painting in which Flora, the goddess of flowers, strews spring's flowers over the fields. In 1909 Josef Frank lived for a time in Florence, working on his doctoral disser-tation on the churches of Renaissance architect Leon Battista Alberti. KW-E

References: *Innen-Dekoration* 44 (1933), p. 203; Rabén, *Det moderna hemmet* (1950), p. 212; Spalt and Kapfinger, *Josef Frank, 1885–1967* (1986).

THE U.N.
headquarters

## 114. United Nations Headquarters, New York

ca. 1947 (project)
Pencil, pen and ink, watercolor on paper
26⅝ x 21⅞ in. (67.5 x 55.5 cm)

Perspective
Inscription: "The U.N. headquarters"

Frank-Archiv, Graphische Sammlung Albertina,
Vienna
Inv. no. 18

This large watercolor is the only surviving documentation for the project. Whether Frank actually intended to submit it to the United Nations Heaquarters competition or merely sought to demonstrate his own ideas is not clear, but the project does provide an interesting glimspe of his own vision of modern architecture at the time.

The main complex was to have consisted of three multistory blocks of various heights linked together by a number of closed bridges. The structure and form of the towers, with their taut glass skins and crisp massing, is expressly "modern"; the shortest of the three is even shown raised on slender *piloti*. But Frank's introduction of complex geometric patterning on the surfaces of the buildings, reminiscent of Josef Hoffmann and Koloman Moser's decorative style just after the turn of the century, served to diminish the hard-edged effect, giving the structures the appearance of large decorated jewel boxes. CL

References: Spalt and Czech, *Josef Frank, 1885–1967* (1981), p. 240; Long, "Josef Frank and the Crisis of Modern Architecture" (1993), pp. 239, 337.

### 115. Additions to the Swedish Parliament Building (Riksdagshuset), Stockholm

ca. 1950 (project)
Perspective
Pencil, watercolor on paper
16 x 22⅞ in. (40.5 x 58 cm)

Swedish Museum of Architecture, Stockholm
Inv. no. 1968-12-20

The existing Swedish Parliament Building was a large nineteenth-century structure framing an open courtyard along the waterfront of Stockholm's old city. Frank proposed to add a twenty-two-story square glass and steel tower connected to one wing of the existing building by a second-story bridge. Although Frank's use of royal blue glass and alternating black and white banding creates a decorative effect similar to his proposal for the United Nations Headquarters complex, the overall effect of the building is more expressly "functional." CL

References: Spalt and Czech, *Josef Frank, 1885–1967* (1981), p. 161; Long, "Josef Frank and the Crisis of Modern Architecture" (1993), p. 347.

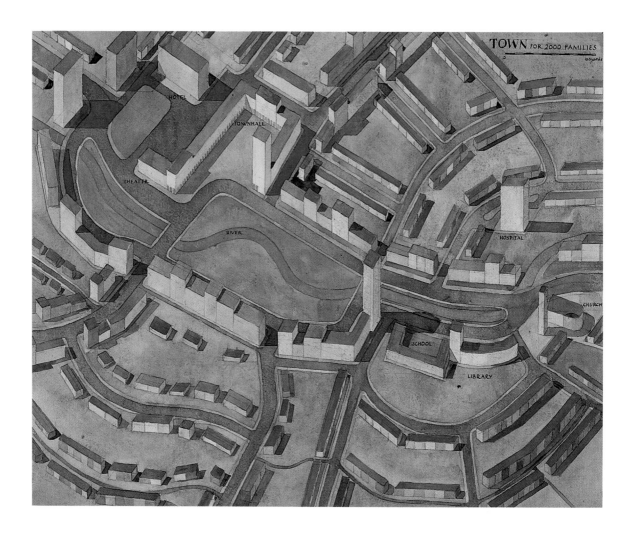

### 116. Town for 2,000 Families

ca. 1950 (project)
Pencil, watercolor on paper
18¼ x 22⅞ in. (46.5 x 58 cm)

Inscription: "Town for 2000 Families"

Swedish Museum of Architecture, Stockholm
Inv. no. 1968-12-07

This project for a small city is one of several urban plans Frank designed in the late 1940s or early 1950s. Here, as in the other proposals, the streets are irregularly arranged, with the larger buildings clustered to form civic and shopping areas. Large green spaces separate the buildings, so that the overall character is reminiscent of Ebenezer Howard's garden city schemes. In many respects, the design also harkens back to Frank's various projects for the Austrian *Siedlerbewegung* (settlers' movement) of the early 1920s. Despite the relatively large scale of the public structures, the emphasis is still on low-density single-family dwellings, with each house provided its own green space. CL

References: Spalt and Czech, *Josef Frank, 1885–1967* (1981), p. 167; Long, "Josef Frank and the Crisis of Modern Architecture" (1993), pp. 237–38, 351.

### 117. Thirteen house designs for Dagmar Grill: House 8

ca. 1950 (project)
Pencil, watercolor on rag paper
17¾ x 19⅞ in. (45 x 50.5 cm)

Perspective

Frank-Archiv, Graphische Sammlung Albertina, Vienna
Inv. no. 104

The thirteen fantasy houses Frank designed for his wife's cousin Dagmar Grill are among his most important late works and are a powerful demonstration of his attempt to find a solution to what he perceived as the banality and sterility of postwar modern architecture. Frank first sketched out the designs in a series of seven letters written to Grill between July 22 and August 15, 1947. He evidently reworked the designs several times over the course of the next half decade. At one point he reproduced all of the houses in india ink on three sheets of tracing paper (see chapter 5, figs. 5-17, 5-18, 5-19). He numbered the houses 1 through 13, changing the original numbering of the houses in the process. (The chronological sequence, as Hermann Czech has shown, is 1, 2, 5, 6, 7, 4, 3, 9, 8, 10, 11, 12, and 13.) Later, probably in the early 1950s, he produced large watercolors of several of the designs, one of which (House 9), he included in his "Accidentism" manifesto published in the Swedish journal *Form* in 1958.

The houses themselves provide a vivid illustration of Frank's notion of making architecture that appears as if it "originated by chance." The first four houses are variations of residences he had designed in Sweden and Austria in the late 1930s, with complex interior plans juxtaposing right-angled and freely formed spaces. House 7, the fifth of the series, however, marks something of a departure. Not only does it include a series of low hipped roofs, but the columns that support the roofs and upper stories are no longer aligned, but rather arranged more or less randomly. In the letter which included the drawing, Frank wrote of the house: "with a roof, but complex (*krångligt*)."

The next two houses, numbers 4 and 3, are based on a rigid rectangular grid within which the plans were developed freely. In House 9, however, which followed, Frank wholly abandoned the cubic scheme, creat-

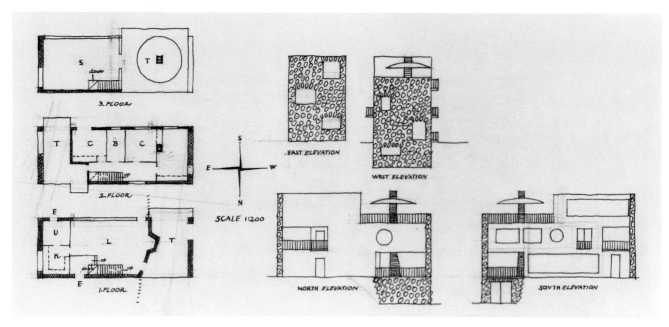

**Fig. 117a.** Thirteen house designs for Dagmar Grill: House 8, ca. 1947 (project); Pencil, pen and ink on tracing paper; Elevations, plans 1:200. Inv. no. 82, Frank-Archiv, Graphische Sammlung Albertina, Vienna.

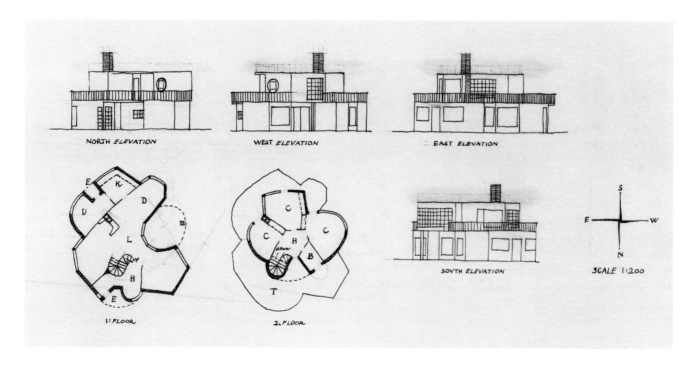

### 118. Thirteen house designs for Dagmar Grill: House 9

ca. 1947 (project)
Pencil, pen and ink on tracing paper
11⅝ x 16½ in. (29.5 x 42 cm)

Elevations, plans 1:200

Frank-Archiv, Graphische Sammlung Albertina,
Vienna
Inv. no. 83

ing two completely different and irregular floor plans, with one superimposed upon the another. Writing to Grill, he noted that this house was "the most complex so far." In the letter, he also came back to a point he first made in his essay on "Das Haus als Weg und Platz" (The house as path and place) about the superiority of irregular spaces to rectangular ones: "When one draws a crooked line, without thinking about it, as a plan, it is still better than the carefully crafted rectangles of a *funkis* [functionalist] architect, is that not so?" With its completely free and unpredictable spaces, House 9 summed up Frank's yearning for architecture that broke completely away from the rationalist spirit of modernism.

For the next house in the series, House 8, Frank again returned to the rectangular grid, but this time he experimented with breaking up the building mass through a number of terraces and further elaborating the facade by using windows of different shapes and sizes, as well as different building materials—field stones, stucco, and poured concrete. He was evidently not

completely satisfied with the effect, for he wrote to Grill that "the house is not very complex, only a little. We can vary it later on." House 10, which followed, is similar to House 8 in most respects, though it includes an atrium at the center.

For the last three houses, numbers 11, 12, and 13, Frank once more renounced the rectangular grid, reverting to completely free plans. House 12 is reminiscent of the prewar Wehtje house. It is based on a more or less linear progression of spaces so that one could pass through the house in a continuous path. The other two houses, however, like House 9, are composed of wholly irregular spaces that seem to follow no discernible order; they also lack any overt sense of spatial sequence or hierarchy, and are thus perhaps the best representation of Frank's "Accidentist" ideas. CL

References: *Form* 54 (1958), p. 162; *Lotus International* 29 (1981), pp 106–16; Long, "Josef Frank and the Crisis of Modern Architecture" (1993), pp. 218–29, 242–45, 338–40.

### 119. Thirteen house designs for Dagmar Grill: House 9
ca. 1950 (project)
Pencil, watercolor on rag paper
11⅝ x 16½ in. (29.5 x 42 cm)

Perspective

Frank-Archiv, Graphische Sammlung Albertina, Vienna
Inv. no. 8

## 120. Six Houses for Dagmar Grill: D-House 4

ca. 1953 (project)
Pencil, watercolor on rag paper
14⅜ x 23¼ in. (36.5 x 59 cm)

Perspective

Frank-Archiv, Graphische Sammlung Albertina,
Vienna
Inv. no. 14

Frank apparently did most of the work on
this series of six houses in the fall or early
winter of 1953, although some of the drawings may predate this time. The designs are
similar in many respects to the thirteen
houses Frank presented in his letters to
Dagmar Grill in 1947, but they are somewhat more straightforward in overall conception and layout and were apparently
conceived as actual plans rather than "fantasy" houses. Most of the houses are
duplexes, with one unit intended for Grill

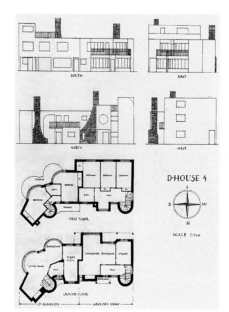

**Fig. 120a.** Six houses for Dagmar Grill:
D-House 4, ca. 1953 (project); pencil, pen
and ink on tracing paper; elevations, plans
1:100. Frank-Archiv, Graphische Sammlung
Albertina, Vienna, Inv. no. 63.

and the other evidently for an acquaintance.
All of the schemes juxtapose more or less
regular, rectangular rooms with unusual,
free-form spaces. The facade treatments
vary considerably, ranging from smooth
pink stucco and rough boulders in concrete
to tile in a black-and-white checkerboard
pattern. CL

References: Spalt and Czech, *Josef Frank,
1885–1967* (1981), pp. 234–37; Long, "Josef
Frank and the Crisis of Modern Architecture"
(1993), pp. 341–44.

**121. Six Houses for Dagmar Grill:
D-House with Checkerboard Parapet**
ca. 1953 (project)
Pencil, watercolor on tracing paper
12⅝ x 20⅛ in. (32 x 51 cm)

Perspective

Frank-Archiv, Graphische Sammlung Albertina,
Vienna
Inv. no. 15

## 122. Chest-of-Drawers

Designed ca. 1950; this example 1951
Walnut and brass
31⅝ x 51 x 17¾ in. (80 x 130 x 45 cm)

Currently retailed by Svenskt Tenn as model no.
2170
Private collection, Stockholm

This chest-of-drawers is one of Frank's
most sophisticated and refined furniture
designs. In it he has again transformed a
traditional furniture form into a highly personal design statement. The exquisitely patterned grain of wood is enhanced by the
brass drawer handles and feet. Case pieces
with brass legs were among his most idiosyncratic designs. They originated in his
Vienna interiors for built-in furniture and
free-standing forms. As with the cabinet-
on-stand Frank used other means of
embellishment to decorate his case pieces;
in fact one of his most successful choices
for surface ornamentation was a floral pattern. NS-L

**Fig. 122a.** Chest-of-drawers, ca. 1950; mahogany and paper; retailed by Svenskt Tenn as
model no. 1050. Private collection, Stockholm.

**123. Side Chair**

Designed ca. 1950, this example 1940
Rattan and cane
32 x 16⅝ x 19½ in. (81.3 x 42.2 x 49.5 cm)

Larsson Korgmakare AB, Stockholm

Frank first designed rattan chairs for Haus & Garten, and they remained an integral part of his production for Svenskt Tenn. Variations of this side chair were prominently displayed at the Svenskt Tenn installation at the 1937 Exposition Internationale in Paris. The chairs were often shown with a small seat cushion. There is an interesting similarity between the configuration of the caning in the back of this chair and of the dining chair for Millesgården. In both examples cane is bent in five oblong-shaped forms across the back and wrapped around the crest rail of the chair. Frank designed many chairs with rattan backs in different configurations. In Vienna they were often inspired by the shapes of Biedermeier chair backs. NS-L

References: Spalt and Czech, *Josef Frank, 1885–1967* (1981); Wängberg-Eriksson, *Josef Frank Livsträd* (1994).

### 124. Teapot

Designed 1952, this example 1952
Pewter and palissander
H. 4½ (11.4 cm), Diam. 9 in. (22.9 cm)

Stamped with Svenskt Tenn trademark
[two angels]

Svenskt Tenn Archive, Stockholm

The idea of a pewter teapot is likely to have come from Estrid Ericson, who founded the Svenskt Tenn shop in the 1920s to revive the tradition of Swedish pewter that dated to the seventeenth century. Björn Trägårdh, Frank's predecessor, produced many pewter designs for Svenskt Tenn in the early 1930s, and Svenskt Tenn continued to retail pewter vases, ornamental boxes, jewelry, and other objects, all sharing an overall simplicity.

The drawing indicates that Frank designed the teapot with a creamer and sugar bowl, and a photograph of the teapot with four accessories appeared in *Konsthantverk och Hemslöjd i Sverige 1930–1940* which featured the best Swedish design of the decade. NS-L

References: Huldt, Hörlén, and Seitz, *Konsthantverk* (1941); Wängberg-Eriksson, *Josef Frank Livsträd* (1994).

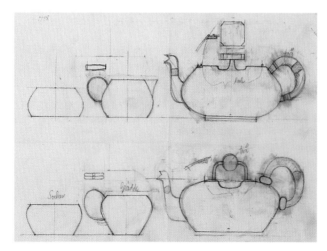

Fig. 124a. Drawing for teapot, creamer, and sugar bowl; pencil on tracing paper. Svenskt Tenn Archive, Stockholm.

Fig. 124b. Tea service, ca. 1935; retailed by Svenskt Tenn, Stockholm. From Huldt, Hörlén, and Seitz, *Konsthantverk* (1941).

### 125. Pair of Candlesticks

Designed ca. 1950; this example ca. 1950
Wood and brass
H. 12¼ in. (31.1 cm), Diam. 5¼ in. (13.3 cm)

Svenskt Tenn Archive, Stockholm

Frank's great admiration for color extended
to small objects, such as these candlesticks.
Their long slender contours are enhanced
by the rich colors he has chosen.  NS-L

## 126. Accessory Box

Designed ca. 1950, this example ca. 1950

4½ x 5⅝ x 4⅝ in. (11.4 x 14.3 x 11.8 cm)

Glass made at Gullaskruf, Sweden; pewter produced at Svenskt Tenn, Stockholm

Svenskt Tenn Archive, Stockholm

This box is typical of designs that Estrid Ericson probably suggested to Frank during his tenure at Svenskt Tenn. A fine sense of proportion and geometric rigor contribute to the success of the design, and its sensuous red color is intensified by the pewter rim.

Little is known about the relationship of Svenskt Tenn to the Swedish glassmakers. The shop today continues to retail different glass products. During the late 1930s the acclaimed French designer René Lalique was featured in a small exhibition at the Svenskt Tenn shop. NS-L

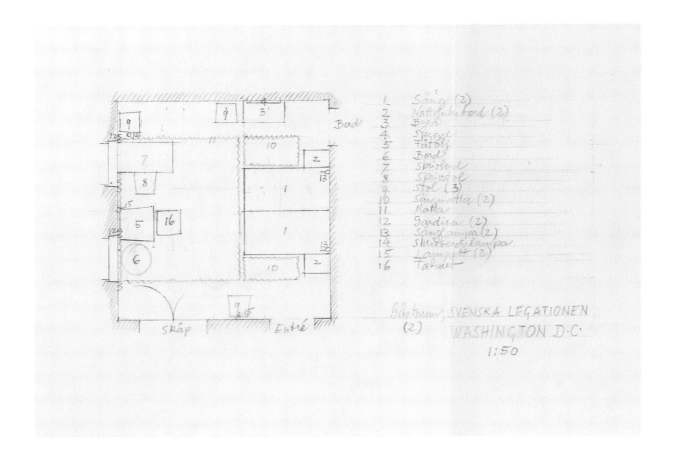

1. Säng (2)
2. Nattdukbord (2)
3. Byrå
4. Spegel
5. Fåtölj
6. Bord
7. Skivbord
8. Spinstol
9. Stol (3)
10. Sängmatta (2)
11. Matta
12. Gardiner (2)
13. Sänglampa (2)
14. Skrivbordslampa
15. Lampett (3)
16. Taburet

Gästrum, SVENSKA LEGATIONEN
(2)     WASHINGTON D·C·
1:50

## 127. Plan for Guest Room, Swedish Embassy, Washington, D.C.

ca. 1955
Pencil and ink on tracing paper
11¾ x 16½ in. (29.9 x 41.9 cm)

Scale 1:50

Svenskt Tenn Archive, Stockholm

**Fig. 127a.** Guest room, Swedish Embassy, Washington, D.C., ca. 1955. Svenskt Tenn Archive, Stockholm.

During the 1950s Svenskt Tenn received many commissions to furnish Swedish embassies and consulates around the world. Frank was responsible for planning these interiors, which featured many of his furniture designs. The guest-room plan shows how Frank laid out each area, carefully specifying the position of each piece. Characteristic Frank/Svenkst Tenn pieces were included in the room, among them the cabinet-on-stand, fully upholstered chair, leather upholstered armchairs and beds. Frank textiles were used for the bed covers and curtains. NS-L

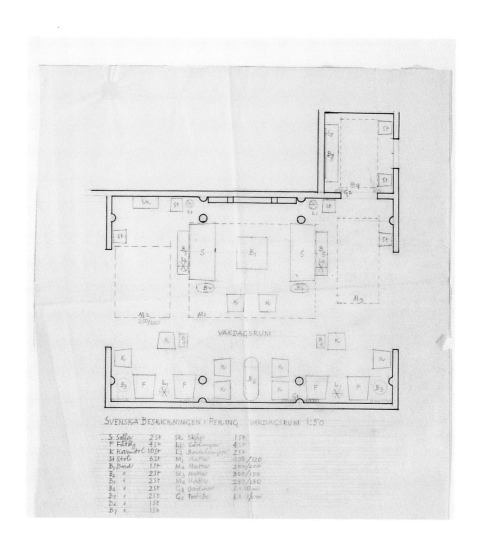

SVENSKA BESKICKNINGEN I PEKING VARDAGSRUM 1:50

| S | Soffa | 2st | Sk | Skåp | 1st |
|---|---|---|---|---|---|
| F | Fatölj | 4st | L₁ | Golvlampor | 4st |
| K | Karmstol | 10st | L₂ | Bordslampor | 2st |
| St | Stol | 6st | M₁ | Mattor | 450/220 |
| B₁ | Bord | 1st | M₂ | Mattor | 250/200 |
| B₂ | " | 2st | M₃ | Mattor | 300/150 |
| B₃ | " | 2st | M₄ | Mattor | 290/130 |
| B₄ | " | 2st | G₁ | Gardiner | L = 10 m |
| B₅ | " | 2st | G₂ | Portiäre | L = 1,6 m |
| B₆ | " | 1st | | | |
| B₇ | " | 1st | | | |

## 128. Plan for Living Room, Swedish Embassy, Peking (Beijing)

ca. 1955
Pencil and ink on tracing paper
12½ x 11¾ in. (31.8 x 29.9 cm)

Scale 1:50

Svenskt Tenn Archive, Stockholm

**Fig. 128a.** Living room, Swedish Embassy (Beijing), ca. 1955. Svenskt Tenn Archive, Stockholm.

Svenskt Tenn designed the interiors of the Swedish embassy in Bejing during the tenure of Dag Hammarskjold. In typical Frank fashion the layout is precise, with each piece carefully specified. Frank, who had been influenced by Chinese design throughout his career, created an interior that skillfully combined traditional aspects of Chinese decor with his own furnishings. The frame around the doorway is among the more authentic details. Tables and fully upholstered sofas were featured in the living room. NS-L

### 129. House with a Large Round Window

mid-1950s (project)
Pencil, watercolor on rag paper
17½ x 23⅝ in. (44.5 x 60 cm)

Perspective

Frank-Archiv, Graphische Sammlung Albertina,
Vienna
Inv. no. 16

This project was one of a number of
similar works Frank designed in the mid-
1950s. Some of the houses were evidently
intended for prospective clients—most
of them friends or acquaintances of
Frank's—but none of the works was realized. This house, like a similar project for a
house with a large round window and a
house with blue walls, is based on cubic
forms of various sizes, which have been juxtaposed to create a complicated play of
shapes and spaces. In terms of planning
and layout, the houses are somewhat more
conventional than either the Thirteen

Houses for Dagmar Grill or the D-Houses,
but they still display Frank's interest in the
composite and the complex. CL

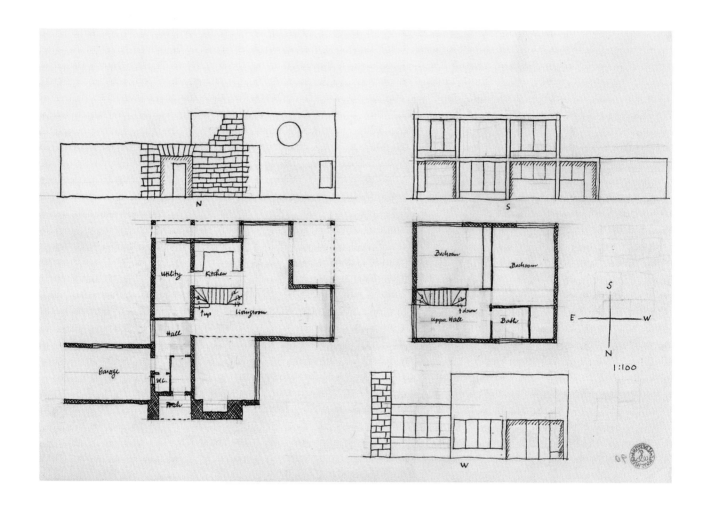

**130. Project: House with a Large Round Window**

mid-1950s (project)
Pencil, pen and ink on tracing paper
11⅝ x 16½ in. (29.5 x 42 cm)

Elevations, plans 1:100

Frank-Archiv, Graphische Sammlung Albertina,
Vienna
Inv. no. 90

It is not clear whether this project represents a variant of the similar design for a house with a round window or a wholly different work. The design also shows some similarities to the house with blue walls which Frank evidently executed about the same time. CL

**131. House with Blue Walls**
Pencil, watercolor on rag paper
12⅝ x 20⅛ in. (32 x 51 cm)

Perspective

Frank-Archiv, Graphische Sammlung Albertina,
Vienna
Inv. no. 7

**132. Double House with Round Windows**
mid-1950s
Pencil, watercolor on paper
16⅛ x 23⅜ in. (41 x 59.5 cm)

Perspective
Inscription: "Dubbelhus, norrsida, 140 kvm"

Swedish Museum of Architecture, Stockholm
Inv. no. 1968-12-04

### 133. Round Stone House

mid-1950s (project)
Pencil, watercolor on rag paper
18¼ x 26¾ in. (46.5.x 68 cm)

Perspective
Frank-Archiv, Graphische Sammlung Albertina,
Vienna
Inv. no. 1

This small two-story house was intended
for a site in Provence, where Frank often
spent time in his later years. In terms of
both plan and materials, it reflects his
desire to experiment with blending the traditional and the new, a preoccupation that
had long been evident in his furniture
designs and shows up strongly in a number
of his residential projects in the mid- to
late 1950s. The house's rough stone walls
recall vernacular Provençal building, while
the reinforced concrete floors, roof, and
columns give the ensemble an unmistakably
modern cast. The layout is conventional in
most respects, but Frank has used the
rounded walls to enliven it. CL

Reference: Spalt and Czech, *Josef Frank,
1885–1967* (1981), pp. 232–33.

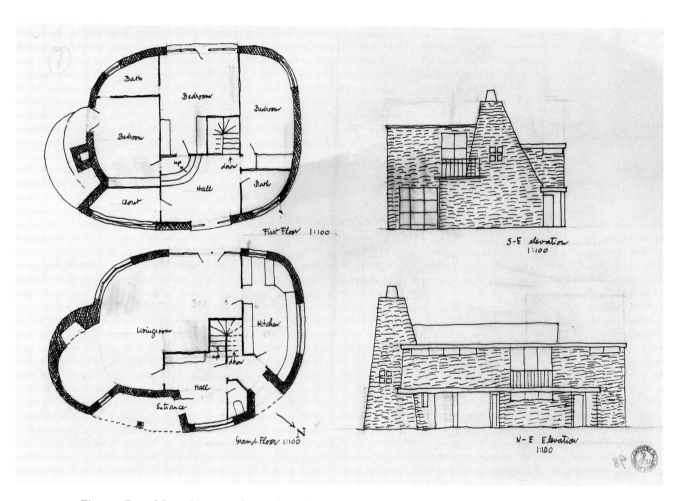

**Fig. 133a.** Round Stone House, mid-1950s (project); pencil, pen and ink on tracing paper; elevations, plans 1:100.
Frank-Archiv, Graphische Sammlung Albertina, Vienna, Inv. no. 98.

## 134. House for Trude Waehner in Southern France

Pencil, watercolor on paper
17⅞ x 24 in. (45.5 x 61 cm)

Perspective

Swedish Museum of Architecture, Stockholm
Inv. no. 1968-12-01

Frank designed this house for his close friend Trude Waehner in the late 1950s. It is among his most remarkable postwar house designs, consisting of a number of seemingly disparate and contradictory elements. The plan of the house, with its irregular spaces, free or curvilinear walls, and changes in level, is typical of Frank's late works. The entrance is under a small porch on the left and leads into a large central living room (*salon*), which is connected to a dining nook and open kitchen. In his usual fashion, Frank has raised the bedroom area above the ground floor; he has also opened up the center of the house to create a spectacular second-story atelier.

Like several of Frank's other works of this time, the Waehner House juxtaposes elements of the old with the new. A round column supporting the front porch emphasizes the entrance in traditional fashion, while at the same time establishing a link with the Mediterranean architecture of the past. Similarly, the house's white stuccoed walls and its roof, which Frank intended to be covered with red tile, are redolent of Provençal vernacular traditions. Yet if the design casts more than a sidelong glance at the architecture of the past, it is by no means a mere historicist exercise. The second-story atelier, with its uniform grid of glass, is unabashedly modern, as is the distribution of its main interior spaces, which are open and free flowing. CL

References: Spalt and Czech, *Josef Frank, 1885–1967* (1981), pp. 230–31; Long, "Josef Frank and the Crisis of Modern Architecture" (1993), pp. 247–49, 356.

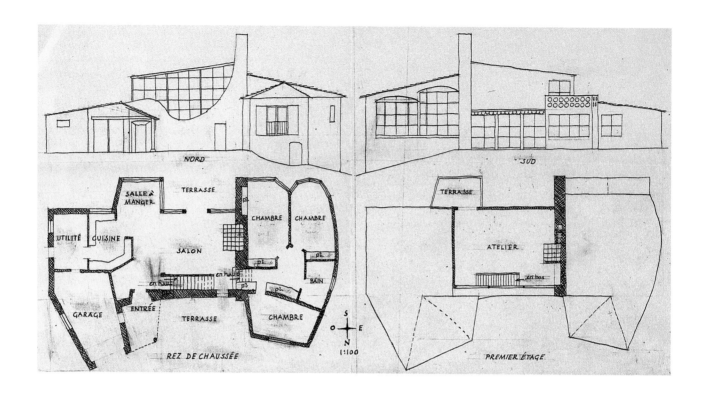

**135. House for Trude Waehner in
Southern France**
Black line print
10¼ x 18¾ in. (26 x 47.5 cm)

Elevations, plans 1:100

Swedish Museum of Architecture, Stockholm
Inv. no. 1968-12-02

# APPENDIX

## Josef Frank: Selected Buildings, Projects, and Interior Designs

Compiled by Christopher Long

**1907**
Competition project for the renovation of the Zedlitzhalle, Vienna

**1910**
Furnishings for the apartment of Karl and Hedwig Tedesco
Vienna III, Untere Viaduktgasse 16

**1911**
Interiors for the Strömberg-Palm Swedish Gymnastics School
Vienna I, Fleischmarkt 1

**1911–12**
Design for an exhibition installation (Room 2)
Winter Exhibition of Arts and Crafts, Österreichisches Museum für Kunst und Industrie, Vienna
(with Hugo Gorge, Viktor Lurje, and Oskar Strnad)

**1912**
Design for a "Living Hall in a Country House"
Spring Exhibition of Austrian Arts and Crafts, Österreichisches Museum für Kunst und Industrie, Vienna

**1912–13**
Interiors for the Museum für Ostasiatische Kunst (Museum of East Asian Art), Cologne
Hansaring 32a/Bremer Strasse (now Adolf-Fischer-Strasse) / Gereonswall

**1913**
Project: Four houses on the Wilbrandtgasse

Furnishings of Frank's own apartment
Vienna IV, Wiedner Hauptstrasse 64

Designs for an exhibition of the Austrian Wallpaper and Linoleum Industries
Österreichisches Museum für Kunst und Industrie, Vienna

**1913–14**
Summer House for Hugo Bunzl
Ortmann bei Pernitz, Lower Austria

House for Dr. Emil and Agnes Scholl
Vienna XVIII, Wilbrandtgasse 3
Villa for Oskar and Hanny Strauss
Vienna XVIII, Wilbrandtgasse 11

**1913–15**
Project: Office building
Vienna I, corner of Am Gestade and Tiefer-Graben
(with Oskar Strnad and Oskar Wlach)

**1919**
Project: "Housing Development with Poured Concrete Buildings"
(with Hugo Fuchs and Franz Zettinig)

**1919–21**
Workers' Housing Project
Ortmann bei Pernitz, Lower Austria

**1920**
Project: Competition for a housing development in Istanbul
(with Oskar Wlach)

Kitchen/living room and bedroom for a worker's home at the exhibition "Einfacher Hausrat"
Österreichisches Museum für Kunst und Industrie

**1921**
Nursery School (*Kinderheim*)
Ortmann bei Pernitz, Lower Austria

Project: Housing settlement in Traiskirchen, Lower Austria

**1921–24**
Hoffingergasse Housing Project
Vienna XII, Hoffingergasse / Frühwirthgasse / Stegmayergasse / Elsniggasse / Sonnergasse / Schneiderhahngasse / Oswaldgasse
(with Erich Faber)

**1922**
Project: Model settlement house, Type I

Project: Settlement house with the smallest possible plan

Project: Expandable settlement house

Project: Settlement for Rodaun

Project: Row house for the Stockerau housing settlement

Project: Housing settlement in St. Veit an der Treisting, Lower Austria

Project: Manager housing in Ortmann, Lower Austria

Project: Elementary School in Tiberias, Palestine

**1922–23**
Project: Housing settlement in Klosterneuburg, Lower Austria

Competition project: Synagogue in Antwerp, Belgium

**1923**
Villa for Dr. Herzberg-Fraenkel
Ortmann bei Pernitz, Lower Austria

General architecture plan for Vienna
(with Peter Behrens, Josef Hoffmann, Adolf Loos, and Oskar Strnad)

"Drawing Room" installation for the exhibition "Modernes Österreichisches Kunsthandwerk"
Österreichisches Museum für Kunst und Industrie, Vienna

Project: Main Square for the Ortmann Housing Settlement
Ortmann bei Pernitz, Lower Austria

Project: Housing block for foremen of the Skoda-Wetzler Company

Sketches for rooms in various settlement houses

**1923–24**
Project: Summer house for Dr. Felix Bunzl in Wattens, Tyrol

Municipal Apartment House on Kongressplatz, Vienna
(Wiedenhofer-Hof Housing Project)
Vienna XVII, Zeilergasse 7–11 / Beringgasse 15 / Liebknechtgasse 10–12 / Pretschgogasse 5
(with Oskar Wlach)

**1924**
Project: Terraced restaurant

Project: Garden pavilion

**1924–25**
Winarsky-Hof Housing Project
Vienna XX, Stromstrasse 36–38/ Vorgartenstrasse / Leystrasse / Pasettistrasse / Kaiserwasserstrasse (now Winarskystrasse)
(with Peter Behrens, Josef Hoffmann, Oskar Strnad, Oskar Wlach)

**1925**
House for Oskar and Hanny Strauss, addition and alterations
Vienna XVIII, Wilbrandtgasse 11

Showroom for Haus & Garten
Vienna I., Bösendorferstrasse 5
(with Oskar Wlach)

**1924–27**
House for Axel and Signhild Claëson
Rostockervägen 1, Falsterbo, Sweden

**1926**
Project: House in Salzburg

Project: Country house with two terraces

Project: Summer house with three terraces

Project: House for Vienna XIII

Project: House for Otto Stiegl in Spittal a.d.
Drau, Carinthia

Project: House with a dance school for
Mr. Ornstein, Tel Aviv

**1926–27**
Double House at the Weissenhofsiedlung
Exhibition
Stuttgart-Weissenhof, Rathenaustrasse 13–15

**1927**
Signe Carlsten House
Fyrvägen 26, Falsterbo, Sweden

Outdoor café at the Austrian Pavilion,
Exposition des Art Décoratifs et Industriels
Modernes, Paris

Furnishing of a model living room for Vienna
municipal housing projects exhibition "Wien
und die Wiener"
Messepalast, Vienna

Exhibition designs for "Kunstschau 1927"
Österreichisches Museum für Kunst und
Industrie, Vienna

Exhibition design for the Österreichisches
Gesellschafts- und Wirtschaftsmuseum
(Austrian Social and Economic Museum)
Vienna I., Rathaus

Project: Reception room for the Vienna City
Hall
Vienna I, Rathaus Platz

Additions and alterations for the house of
Robert and Anna Lang
Vienna XIX, Cobenzlgasse
(with Ernst A. Plischke)

Project: Country house with a terrace
Baden, Lower Austria

Project: House for Dagmar Grill in Skärgården,
Sweden

Project: Residence for Mr. and Mrs. A. R. G.,
Los Angeles / House in Vienna XIX

Project: House for Mr. S. H. B. in Pasadena,
California (also H. R. S. Esq., Pasadena)

Project: Row house settlement in Radhus,
Sweden

**1928**
Stage set for *Captain Brassbound's Conversion* by
George Bernard Shaw, performed at the
Burgtheater in Vienna

Four room apartment for a four- to five-member
family at the exhibition, "Heim und
Technik," Munich, 1928
Furnishings for the villa of H. and M. Blitz,
Vienna
(with Oskar Wlach and Ernst Epstein)

Project: Stucco House in Columbus, Ohio

Apartment house for the City of Vienna
Vienna XIV, Sebastian-Kelch-Gasse 1–3
(with Oskar Wlach and Ernst A. Plischke)

Competition design for the
Reichsforschungssiedlung, Berlin-Haselhorst

**1928–29**
Competition project for an apartment house on
the site of the old Bürgerversorgungshaus
Vienna IX, corner of Währingerstrasse and
Spitalgasse

**1929**
Model row house for the exhibition "Wohnung
und Siedlung" in Linz
(with Alfred Schmid)

Exhibition designs for "Wiener Raumkünstler"
Künstlerhaus, Vienna
(with Oskar Wlach)

**1929–30**
Project: Housing settlement for the City of
Vienna near the Spinnerin am Kreuz
monument
Vienna X, Triester Strasse

**1929–31**
House for Julius and Margarete Beer
Vienna XIII, Wenzgasse 12
(with Oskar Wlach)

**1930**
Facade renovation of the Gustav Carl Lehmann
interior design shop
Hohenzollern Ring 48, Cologne 1, Germany

Tea salon and furnishings at the 1930 Austrian
Werkbund exhibition
Österreichisches Museum für Kunst und
Industrie, Vienna

Furnishings, rose garden, and tea pavilion for the
Karplus House
Vienna XIX, Fürfanggasse 2
(with Oskar Wlach)

Furnishings for the House of Dr. W. B., Vienna
(with Oskar Wlach)

Project: House for M. S. in Los Angeles,
California

Project: Apartment complex on the
Bahnhofsvorplatz, Linz

**1931–32**
Apartment building for the City of Vienna (now
Leopoldine-Glöckel-Hof)
Vienna XII, Steinbauergasse 1–7 /
Gaudenzdorfer Gürtel
(with Oskar Wlach)

Apartment building for the City of Vienna
Vienna XI, Simmeringer Hauptstrasse 142–150
/ Fickeystrasse 8 / Pleischlgasse /
Strachegasse
(with Oskar Wlach)

Plan for the Vienna International Werkbund
Exhibition (final version)
Vienna XIII, Jagdschlossgasse / Veitingergasse /
Woinovichgasse /
Jagicgasse / Engelbrechtweg

House in the International Werkbund
Exhibition
Vienna XIII, Woinovichgasse 32

Project: Single-family house for five persons

Project: Single-family house for six persons

Project: Two-story house for four persons

Furnishings for a villa for A. F. S., Vienna XIII
(with Oskar Wlach)

Furnishings for a house for L. R. S., Vienna XIII
(with Oskar Wlach)

**1934**
Exhibition at Liljevalchs Konsthall, Stockholm
(with Estrid Ericson)

Showrooms for Svenskt Tenn
Strandvägen 5A, Stockholm
(with Estrid Ericson)

**1934–35**
Låftman House (later Croneborg House)
Fyrvägen 15, Falsterbo, Sweden

Seth House (later Thermaenius House)
Fyrvägen 9, Falsterbo, Sweden

**1935–36**
House for Hugo and Olga Bunzl
Vienna XVIII, Chimanistrasse 18
(with Oskar Wlach)

Walther Wehtje House
Rostockervägen 4, Falsterbo, Sweden

**1936**
Project: Austrian Pavilion, Paris Exposition
Internationale, 1937

Project: House for Dir. Bahrke in Falsterbo,
Sweden

**1936–37**
Garden terrace for the Swedish Pavilion, Paris
Exposition Internationale, 1937
(with Estrid Ericson)

**1937**
Haus & Garten Living Room installation in the
Austrian Pavilion, Paris Exposition
Internationale, 1937
(with Oskar Wlach)

**1938**
Project: House for Walter Wehtje in Djursholm,
Sweden

**1939**
Interiors for the Swedish Pavilion at the
New York World's Fair
(with Estrid Ericson)

Furnishings for the Swedish Pavilion at the
Golden Gate Exposition, San Francisco
(with Estrid Ericson)

**1940**
Project: Garden pavilion

**1941–42**
Additions and furnishings for Tolvekarna, Estrid
Ericson's summer house in Tyresö, Sweden
(with Estrid Ericson)

**1942**
Project: Low-cost housing project in the "Gas
House district"
First Avenue / 20th Street / East River Drive /
Avenue C / 14th Street, New York City

Project: New York City slum clearance
First Avenue / 12th Street / Third Avenue /
16th Street, New York City

**1947**
Project: United Nations Headquarters, New
York

**1947–55**
Project: Thirteen house designs for Dagmar
Grill

**1949**
Project: Plan for rebuilding St. Stephen's Square,
Vienna

Furnishings in the exhibition "Svenskt Tenn—
25 år" (Svenskt Tenn 25 Years)
(with Estrid Ericson)

**1950**
Furnishings for the house of Anne Hedmark,
Millesgården
Carl Milles väg 2, Lidingö, Stockholm
(with Estrid Ericson)

**1951**
Competition project for the Kungsträdgården,
Stockholm

Exhibition at Kaufmann's Department Store,
Pittsburgh

**1952**
Design for the exhibition, "Josef Frank—Tjugo
år i Svenskt Tenn" (Josef Frank—Twenty
Years at Svenskt Tenn), Nationalmuseum,
Stockholm
(with Estrid Ericson)

**ca. 1953**
Project: Six houses for Dagmar Grill

**1955**
Project: House with an atelier and courtyard

**ca. 1955**
Plan for a guest room, Swedish Embassy,
Washington, D.C.

Plan for a living room, Swedish Embassy,
Beijing, China

**Undated Buildings and Projects Before 1934**
Project: House in Vienna XVIII

Project: House in Vienna XIX

Project: House with two doors in Vienna XIX

Project: Garden pavilion

**Buildings and Projects After 1946**
Project: Additions to Swedish Parliament building (Riksdagshuset), Stockholm

Project: Horns Department Store

Project: Hotel on a boulevard

Project: Theater for 1,200

Project: Three row-house designs ("Motto:
DBL")

Project: Community of 1,200 families

Project: Town for 2,000 families

Project: Residential district for a city with
20,000 residents

Project: City with 15,000 residents

Pergola and other additions to Trude Waehner's
house, Dieulefit, France

Project: House with a large fireplace

Project: Triple house

Project: House with a large round window

Project: Round stone house

Project: House for Trude Waehner in southern
France

Project: House with blue walls

Project: House at Horslagaregatan 3

Project: House with round rooms

Project: House with a large round window

Project: Double house

Project: Double house with round windows

Project: Double house in Djursholm

Project: Villa for M. Albrée, France

# BIBLIOGRAPHY

Aalto, Alvar. "The Dwelling as a Problem." In *Sketches*. Edited by Göran Schildt. Cambridge, MA: The MIT Press, 1978.

Achleitner, Friedrich. "Der Österreichische Werkbund und seine Beziehungen zum Deutschen Werkbund," *Bauforum* 10 (1977).

_____. "Josef Frank et l'architecture Viennoise de l'entre-deux guerres." In *Vienne 1880–1938: L'Apocalypse Joyeuse*. Edited by Jean Clair. Paris: Centre Pompidou, 1986.

Ahlin, Janne. *Sigurd Lewerentz, Architect, 1885–1975*. Cambridge, MA: The MIT Press, 1987.

Aloi, Roberto. *L'Arrademento Moderno*. Series. (Milan: Hoepli, 1934 and 1939).

Andren, Erik. *Möbelstilurna: den Svenska möbel och inrednings Konstens*. Stockholm: Nordiska Museet, 1981.

Arrhenius, Lilly. *Swedish Design (Svensk heminredning)*. Translated by Albert Read. Stockholm: Vepe Förlag, 1957.

Aschehoug, Elisabeth. "Beauty and Comfort for All." *American Swedish Monthly* (May 1939).

Ashbrook, Frank G. *The Green Book of Birds of America*. Racine, WI: Whitman Publishing Co., 1941.

Attfield, Judy, and Pat Kirkham, eds. *A View from the Interior: Feminism, Women and Design*. London: The Women's Press, 1989.

*Bauten und Entwürfe von Carl König herausgegeben von seinen Schülern*. Vienna: Gerlach & Wiedling, [1910].

Beller, Steven. *Vienna and the Jews, 1867–1938: A Cultural History*. Cambridge, Eng.: Cambridge University Press, 1989.

Benotto. "Frühjahrausstellung im Österreichischen Museum." *Das Interieur* 13 (1912).

Bergquist, Mikael, and Olof Michélsen, eds. *Josef Frank arkitektur*. Stockholm: Arkitekturmuseet, 1994.

Berkeley, George E. *Vienna and Its Jews, 1880–1980s*. Cambridge MA: Abt, 1988.

Björkman-Goldschmidt, Elsa. *Vad sedan hände*. Stockholm: Norstedts, 1964.

Boeckl, Matthias. "Die Mode-Moderne mit dem fabriciertem Stimmungs-Dusel." In *Die verlorenen Moderne*. Exhibition catalogue. Vienna: Österreichische Galerie, 1993.

_____, ed. *Visionäre und Vertriebene: Österreichische Spuren in der modernen amerikanischen Architektur*. Berlin: Ernst und Sohn, 1995.

Boltenstern, Erich. *Wiener Möbel*. Stuttgart: Julius Hoffmann, 1934.

Boman, Monica, ed. *Estrid Ericson: Founder of Svenskt Tenn*. Stockholm: Carlsson Bokforlag, 1989.

_____. *Svenska Möbler, 1890–1990*. Stockholm: Bokförlaget Signum Lund AB, 1991.

Born, Wolfgang. "Ein Haus in Wien-Hietzing." *Innen-Dekoration* 42 (1931).

_____. "Neue Innenräume von Haus & Garten." *Innen-Dekoration* 44 (1933).

Bossert, Hellmuth Th. *Ornamente der Volkskunst*. Tübingen: Ernst Wasmuth, 1956.

Botstein, Leon. *Judentum und Modernität: Essays zur Rolle der Juden in der deutschen und österreichischen Kultur, 1848–1938*. Vienna: Böhlau, 1991.

Brulhart, Armand. "Josef Frank und die CIAM bis zum Bruch, 1928–1929." *Bauwelt* 26 (July 12, 1985).

Carminati, Lio. "Vivere all'aperto." *Cellini* (August 1941).

*Catalogo: Ente Nazionale Piccole Industrie Roma, Esposizione Internazionale di Barcellon, 1929*. Rome: E.N.A.P.I., 1929.

Ciucci, Giorgio. "The Invention of the Modern Movement." *Oppositions* 24 (Spring 1981).

Czech, Hermann. "Josef Frank: The Accidental House, The Thirteen Designs in Letters to Dagmar Grill." *Lotus International* 29 (1980).

_____. "A Mode for the Current Interpretation of Josef Frank." *Architecture and Urbanism* 11 (1991).

*Die Wohnhausanlage der Gemeinde Wien: Wiedenhoferhof im XVII. Bezirk*. Vienna, 1926

Deutscher Werkbund. *Bau und Wohnung* (1927). Exhibition catalogue. Reprint. Stuttgart: Karl Kramer Verlag, 1992.

Döcker, Richard. *Terrassentyp*. Stuttgart: Dr. Fr. Wedekind, 1929.

Doesburg. Théo van. *On European Architecture: Complete Essays from Het Bouwbedrijf 1924–1931*. Translated by Charlotte I. Loeb and Arthur L. Loeb. Basel, Berlin, and Boston: Birkhäuser Verlag, 1990.

Donnelly, Marion C. *Architecture in the Scandinavian Countries*. Cambridge, MA, and London: The MIT Press, 1992.

Dreibholz, Wolfdieter. "Die internationale Werkbundsiedlung, Wien, 1932." *Bauforum* 10, no. 61 (1977).

Droste, Magdalena. *Bauhaus, 1919–1933*. Berlin: Bauhaus-Archiv Museum für Gestaltung and Benedikt Taschen, 1990.

Eckstein, Hans. *Neue Wohnbauten*. Munich: F. Bruckmann, 1932.

Eisler, Max. *Dagobert Peche*. Vienna and Leipzig: Gerlach & Wiedlung, 1925.

_____. "Neu-Wiener Innenräume." *Moderne Bauformen* 26 (1927).

_____. "Neue Bauten und Innenräume von Josef Frank, Oskar Wlach ('Haus und Garten')—Arnold Karplus Wohnhaus auf der Hohen Warte in Wien." *Moderne Bauformen,* 29 (1930).

_____. "Oskar Strnad zum 50. Geburtstag." *Deutsche Kunst und Dekoration* 33 (January 1930).

_____. *Oskar Strnad.* Vienna: Gerlach & Weidling, 1936.

Ericsson, Anne-Marie. *Svenskt 1920—tal konstindustrie och konsthantverk.* Lund, Sweden: Signum, 1984.

Evans, Arthur. *The Palace of Minos at Knossos.* London: Macmillan & Co., 1928.

Fanelli, Giovanni, and Ezio Godoli. *La Vienna di Hoffmann, architetto della qualitá.* Rome: Editori Laterza, 1981.

Fleck, Karola. "Otto Neurath: Eine biographische und systematische Untersuchung." Ph.D. dissertation. Karl-Franzens—Universität Graz, 1979.

Frampton, Kenneth. "Le Corbusier and *L'Esprit nouveau.*" *Oppositions* 15/16 (Winter/Spring 1979).

_____. "Stockholm 1930: Asplund and the Legacy of Funkis." In *Asplund.* Edited by Claes Caldenby and Olof Hulten. New York: Rizzoli, 1986.

_____. "The Other Le Corbusier: Primitive Form and the Linear City, 1929—52." In *Le Corbusier, Architect of the Century.* Hayward Gallery of Art. Exhibition catalogue. London: Arts Council of Great Britain, 1987.

Franciscono, Marcel. *The Founding of the Bauhaus in Weimar: Its Artistic Background and First Conception.* Urbana: University of Illinois Press, 1971.

Frank, Josef. "Über die urspüngliche Gestalt der kirchlichen Bauten des Leone Battista Alberti." Ph.D. dissertation. Technische Hochschule, Vienna, 1910.

_____. "Das neuzeitliche Landhaus." *Innen-Dekoration* 30 (1919).

_____. "Die Einrichtung des Wohnzimmers." *Innen-Dekoration* 30 (1919).

_____. "Der Volkswohnungspalast: Eine Rede zur Grundsteinlegung, die nicht gehalten wurde." *Der Aufbau* 1 (1926).

_____. "Der Gschnas fürs G'müt und der Gschnas als Problem." In *Bau und Wohnung* by the Deutscher Werkbund. Exhibition catalogue. Stuttgart: Akademischer Verlag Dr. Fr. Wedekind & Co., 1927.

_____. "Drei Behauptungen und ihre Folgen." *Die Form* 2 (1927).

_____. "Fassade und Interieur." *Deutsche Kunst und Dekoration* 31 (June 1928).

_____. "Vom neuen Stil: Einige Fragen und Antworten." *Innen-Dekoration* 39 (1928).

_____. "Gespräch über den Werkbund," in *Österreichischer Werkbund 1929.* Vienna: Verlag der Österreichischer Werkbund, 1929.

_____. "Was ist modern?" *Die Form* 5 (August 1, 1930). Reprint. *Der Baumeister* 28 (1930).

_____. *Architektur als Symbol: Elemente deutschen neuen Bauens.* Vienna: Anton Schroll, 1931. Reprint. Vienna: Löcker, 1981.

_____. "Das Haus als Weg und Platz." *Der Baumeister* 29 (1931).

_____. "Zum Formproblem." In *Der gute billige Gegenstand.* Exhibition catalogue. Vienna: Österreichisches Museum für Kunst und Industrie, 1931/32.

_____, ed. *Die internationale Werkbundsiedlung Wien 1932.* Exhibition catalogue. Vienna: Anton Schroll, 1932.

_____. "Rum och inredning." *Form* 30 (1934).

_____. "How to Plan a House." Lecture presented at the New School for Social Research, New York, ca. 1942. Reprint. In *Josef Frank, 1885—1967: Möbel & Geräte & Theoretisches.* Edited by Johannes Spalt. Vienna: Hochschule für angewandte Kunst, 1981.

_____. "Accidentism." *Form* 54 (1958).

_____. "Akzidentismus." *Baukunst und Werkform* 14 (1961).

_____. *Arkitektur som symbol: Element i tyskt Neues Bauen; Oversätlning och efterskrift.* Translated into Swedish by Karin Lindegren. Lund, Sweden: ellerströms, 1995.

_____, Hugo Fuchs, and Franz Zettinig. "Wohnhäuser aus Gussbeton: Ein Vorschlag zur Lösung der Wohnungsfrage." *Der Architekt* 22 (1919).

_____ and Otto Neurath. "Hannes Meyer." *Der Klassenkampf: Sozialistische Politik und Wirtschaft* 3 (1930).

Frank, Philipp. *Einstein: His Life and Times.* New York: Alfred A. Knopf, 1947.

Frei, Bruno. *Jüdisches Elend in Wien.* Vienna: Löwit, 1920.

Galison, Peter. "Aufbau/Bauhaus: Logical Positivism and Architectural Modernism." *Critical Inquiry* 16 (Summer 1990).

Giedion, Sigfried. *Space, Time and Architecture: The Growth of a New Tradition.* Cambridge: Harvard University Press, 1941.

Gmeiner, Astrid, and Gottfried Pirhofer. *Der Österreichische Werkbund: Alternative zur klassischen Moderne in Architektur, Raum- und Produktgestaltung.* Salzburg and Vienna: Residenz Verlag, 1985.

Graham, V. E. *Tropical Wild Flowers.* London: Hulton, 1963.

Green, Christopher. *Léger and Purist Paris.* Exhibition catalogue. London: The Tate Gallery, 1970.

Gregor, Joseph. *Rede auf Oskar Strnad.* Vienna: Herbert Reicher Verlag, 1936.

Greiner, Leopold. "Möbel und Einrichtung der Neuzeit. Arbeiten der Werkstätten 'Haus & Garten'-Wien." *Innen-Dekoration* 37 (1926).

Grimme, Karl M. *Das Eigenheim*. Berlin Stadt- und Landverlag, 1929.

Groth, Hakan. *Neoclassicism in the North: Swedish Furniture and Interiors*. New York: Rizzoli, 1990.

Haerdtl, Carmela. "Una nuova casa di Josef Frank." *Domus* (July 1931).

————. "Una casa privata a Vienna." *Domus* (August 1931).

Hahl-Koch, Jelena, ed. *Arnold Schoenberg-Wassily Kandinsky*. London: Faber and Faber, 1984.

Hahn, Hans, Otto Neurath, and Rudolf Carnap. *Wissenschaftliche Weltauffassung: Der Wiener Kreis*. Vienna: Verein Ernst Mach/Artur Wolf Verlag, 1929.

Hald, Edward. *Swedish Design*. Stockholm: Swedish Institute, 1958.

Hanisch, Ernst. *Der lange Schatten des Staates: Österreichische Gesellschaftsgeschichte im 20. Jahrhundert*. Vienna: Überreuter, 1994.

Harbers, Guido. "'Moderne Linie', Wohnkultur und Stagnation: Abschliessende Randbemerkungen zur Werkbundsiedlung." *Der Baumeister* 30 (October 1932).

Hard af Segerstad, Ulf. *Scandinavian Design*. London: Studio, 1961.

Häring, Hugo. "Bermerkungen zur Werkbundsiedlung Wien-Lainz 1932." *Die Form* (July 15, 1932).

Hautmann, Hans, and Rudolf Hautmann. *Die Gemeindebauten des Roten Wien, 1919–1934*. Vienna: Schönbrunn-Verlag, 1980.

Hayward Gallery of Art, London. *Le Corbusier: architect of the century*. Exhibition catalogue. Edited by Michael Raeburn and Victoria Wilson. London: Arts Council of Great Britain, 1987.

Hilmar, Ernst, ed. *Schoenberg, Arnold: Gedenkausstellung 1974*. Vienna: Universal Edition, 1974.

Hitchcock, Henry-Russell. *Modern Architecture: Romanticism and Reintegration*. New York: Payson & Clark, Ltd., 1929.

———— and Philip Johnson. *The International Style: Architecture Since 1922*. New York: W. W. Norton & Company, 1932.

Höckmann, O. "Theran floral style in relation to that of Crete." In *Thera and the Aegean World*. London, 1980.

Hodin, J. P. *Oskar Kokoschka: The Artist and His Time*. London: Cory, Adams & Mackay, 1966.

Hödl, Klaus. *Als Bettler in die Leopoldstadt: Galizische Juden auf dem Weg nach Wien*. Vienna: Böhlau, 1994.

Hoffmann, Herbert. *Neue Villen*. Stuttgart: Julius Hoffmann, 1929.

Huldt, Åke H., and Eva Benedicks. *Design in Sweden Today*. Stockholm: Swedish Institute, 1948.

————, Mattis Hörlén, and Heribert Seitz. *Konsthantverk och Hemslöjd i Sverige, 1930–1940*. Göteborg: Förlag AB Bokförmedlingen, 1941.

Jara, Cynthia. "Adolf Loos's Raumplan Theory." *Journal of Architectural Education* 48 (February 1995).

Johanssen, Gotthard. *Josef Frank—Tjugo år i Svenskt Tenn*. Exhibition catalogue. Stockholm: Nationalmuseum, 1952.

————. *Josef Frank och Svenskt Tenn*. Exhibition catalogue. Stockholm: Nationalmuseum, 1968.

John, Michael, and Albert Lichtblau. *Schmelztiegel Wien: Einst und Jetzt zur Geschichte und Gegenwart von Zuwanderung und Munderheiten*. Vienna: Böhlau, 1990.

Johnston, William H. *The Austrian Mind: An Intellectual and Social History, 1848–1938*. Berkeley: University of California Press, 1983.

"Josef Frank." *Moderne Bauformen* 26 (1927).

*Josef Frank: inredning*. Exhibition catalogue. Stockholm: Millesgården, 1994.

Kallir, Jane. *Viennese Design and the Wiener Werkstätte*. New York: Galerie St. Etienne/George Braziller, 1986.

Kann, Robert A. *Theodor Gomperz: Ein Gelehrtenleben im Burgertum der Franz Josefs-Zeit*. Vienna: Verl. D. Österr. Akad. Wiss., 1974.

————. "Josef Frank—Siedlungen und Siedlungsprojekte, 1919–1932." *Um Bau* 10 (1986).

Kaufmann, Edgar, Jr. "Scandinavian Design in the USA." *Interiors New York* (1954).

Killen, Geoffrey. *Ancient Egyptian Furniture*. Vol. 1, *4000–1300 B.C.* Warminster, Eng.: Aris & Phillips Ltd., 1980.

Kirsch, Karin. *Die Weissenhofsiedlung: Werkbund Ausstellung "Die Wohnung"—Stuttgart 1927*. Stuttgart: Deutsche Verlags-Anstalt, 1987. *The Weissenhofsiedlung: Experimental Housing Built for the Deutscher Werkbund, Stuttgart, 1927*. Translated by David Britt. New York: Rizzoli, 1987.

Krischanitz, Adolf, and Otto Kapfinger. *Die Wiener Werkbundsiedlung: Dokumentation einer Erneuerung*. Vienna: Compress Verlag, 1985.

Kurrent, Friedrich. "Frank und frei." *Um Bau* 10 (1986).

Lane, Barbara Miller. *Architecture and Politics in Germany, 1918–1945*. Cambridge, MA: Harvard University Press, 1968.

Larsson, Carl. *Lasst Licht hinein: Ein Buch von Wohnzimmern, von Kindern, von Dir, von Blumen, von Allem*. Stockholm and Leipzig: Albert Bonnier, 1911.

Le Corbusier. *Vers une Architecture*. Paris: Editions Georges Crés, 1927. *Towards a New Architecture* (1927). Reprint. Translation. New York: Holt, Rinehart and Winston, 1982.

————. *The Decorative Art of Today*. Translated by James Dummett. Cambridge, MA: The MIT Press, 1987.

————. *Precisions on the Present State of Architecture and City Planning*. Translated by Edith Schreiber. Cambridge, MA: The MIT Press, 1991.

———— and Pierre Jeanneret. *Oeuvre Complète, 1910–1925*. Zurich: Les Editions d'Architecture, 1964.

Leicestershire Museums. *Ernest Gimson and the Cotswold Group of Craftsmen.* Exhibition catalogue (no. 14). Leicester, Eng.: Leicestershire Museums, 1978.

Lethaby, W. R., Alfred H. Powell, and F. L. Griggs. *Ernest Gimson: His Life and Work.* Oxford: Basil Blackwell, 1924.

Levetus, Amelia T. S. "Austrian Architecture and Decoration." *The Studio Year Book, 1913* (London: The Studio, 1913).

———. "The European Influence of the Studio." *The Studio* 105 (1933).

Long, Christopher. "Josef Frank and the Crisis of Modern Architecture." Ph.D. dissertation. University of Texas at Austin, 1993.

Loos, Adolf. *Ins Leere gesprochen.* Paris: Editions Georges Crés, 1921. Reprint. Edited by Adolf Opel. Vienna, Georg Prachner, 1986.

———. *Trotzdem 1900–1930.* Innsbruck: Brenner Verlag, 1931. Reprint. Edited by Adolf Opel. Vienna: Georg Prachner Verlag, 1982.

Lotz, Wilhelm. "Die Wiener Werkbundsiedlung." *Die Form* 7 (July 15, 1932).

Lundegård, Per H. *Stenar i färg.* Stockholm: Almquist & Wiksell, 1961.

Lundgren, Tyra. "Den moderna blommigheten." *Svenska Hem* 4 (1943).

*Machine-Age Exposition Catalogue.* New York: Little Review, 1927.

Marchetti, Maria, ed. *Wien um 1900: Kunst und Kultur.* Vienna and Munich: Christian Brandstätter Verlag, 1985.

Marcuse, Peter. "The Housing Policy of Social Democracy: Determinants and Consequences." In *The Austrian Socialist Experiment: Social Democracy and Austromarxism, 1918–1934.* Edited by Anson Rabinbach. Boulder, Colo., and London: Westview Press, 1985.

Matejka, Viktor. "12 Fragen an Josef Frank." *Bauwelt* 26 (1985).

McFadden, David R., ed. *Scandinavian Modern Design, 1980–1990.* New York: Harry Abrams, 1983.

McLeod, Mary. "Charlotte Perriand: Her First Decade As A Designer." *AA Files* 15 (Summer 1987).

Mendelsohn, Ezra. *The Jews of East Central Europe Between the World Wars.* Bloomington: Indiana University Press, 1983.

"Moderne Möbelbeschläge nach Entwürfen von Architekt Dr. Josef Frank . . . Ausgeführt von der Broncewaren-Fabrik Hugo Einhorn." Sales catalogue. Collection, University of Applied Arts, Vienna: inv. no. 419/2 and 101571–5.

Monk, Ray. *Ludwig Wittgenstein: The Duty of Genius.* New York: Free Press, 1990.

Moravánszky, Ákos. *Die Architektur der Donaumonarchie.* Berlin, Ernst & Sohn, 1988.

Müller, Michael. "Wie Modern was die Avantgarde?" *Um Bau* 10 (August 1986).

Müller-Wulckow, Walter. *Deutsche Baukunst der Gegenwart.* Vol. 10. *Bauten der Arbeit.* Königstein im Taunus and Leipzig: K. R. Langewiesche, 1929.

Musée Oberkampf. *Les Indiennes de la Manufacture Oberkampf de Jouy-en-Josas.* Exhibition catalogue. Jouy-en-Josas: Musée Oberkampf, 1986.

Muthesius. Hermann. *Das englische Haus: Entwicklung, Bedingungen, Anlage, Aufbau, Einrichtung und Innenraum.* 3 vols. Berlin: Ernst Wasmuth, 1904–05. Edited by Dennis Sharp. Translated by Janet Seligman. New York: The English House / Rizzoli, 1979.

Muthesius, Stefan. *Das englische Vorbild: Eine Studie zu den deutschen Reformbewegungen in Architektur, Wohnbau und Kunstgewerbe im späteren 19. Jahrhundert.* Munich: Prestel Verlag, 1979.

Nationalmuseum. *Josef Frank 1885–1967, Minnesutställning.* Exhibition catalogue. (no. 320). Stockholm: Nationalmuseum, 1968.

"Neue Wohnungen von 'Haus und Garten,'" *Innen-Dekoration* 45 (October 1934).

Neurath, Marie, and Robert S. Cohen, eds. *Otto Neurath: Empiricism and Sociology.* Dordrecht, Holland, and Boston: D. Reidel Publishing Company, 1973.

Niedermoser, Otto. *Oskar Strnad, 1879–1935.* Vienna: Bergland Verlag, 1935.

Oechslin, Werner. "*Raumplan* versus *Plan libre.*" *Daidalos* (December 1991).

———. *Stilhülse und Kern: Otto Wagner, Adolf Loos und der evolutionäre Weg zur modernen Architektur.* Berlin: Ernst & Sohn, 1994.

Ornstein, Margit, and Heinrich Löwy, eds. *Josef Popper-Lynkeus: Gespräche.* Vienna: Lowit, 1935.

Ostergard, Derek. *George Nakashima: Full Circle.* New York: Weidenfeld & Nicolson, 1989.

*Österreichischer Werkbund 1929.* Vienna: Verlag der Österreichischer Werkbund, 1929.

Österreichisches Museum für Kunst und Industrie. *Frühjahrsausstellung Österr. Kunstgewerbe verbunden mit einer Ausstellung der k.k. Kunstgewerbeschule Wien.* Exhibition catalogue. Vienna: Österreichisches Museum für Kunst und Industrie, 1912.

———. *Vienna 1924—Wiener Kunstgewerbe—Verein Jubiläumsausstellung.* Exhibition catalogue. Vienna: Österreichisches Museum für Kunst und Industrie, 1924.

———. *Wiener Raumkünstler.* Exhibition catalogue. Vienna: Österreichisches Museum für Kunst und Industrie, 1929/30.

Ottillinger, Eva B. *Adolf Loos—Wohnkonzpte und Möbelentwürfe.* Salzburg and Vienna: Residenz Verlag, 1994.

Palanti, Giancarlo. *Mobili Tipici Moderni.* Milan: Ed. Domus, 1933.

Pauley, Bruce F. *From Prejudice to Persecution: A History of Austrian Anti-Semitism.* Chapel Hill: University of North Carolina Press, 1992.

Pendlebury, J. D. S. *A Handbook to the Palace of Minos, Knossos with Its Dependencies.* London: M. Parrish, 1954.

Persoz, J. *Traité théorigue et pratique de l'impression des tissues.* Paris: Jean François V. Mason, 1846.

Peterson, Roger Tory. *A Field Guide to the Birds.* 2nd ed. Cambridge, MA: Houghton-Mifflin, Riverside Press, 1947.

Pevsner, Nikolaus. *Pioneers of Modern Design from William Morris to Walter Gropius.* New York: Museum of Modern Art, 1949.

Plath, Iona. *The Decorative Arts of Sweden.* New York: Charles Scribner's Sons, 1948.

Platzer, Monika. "Einrichtungshaus 'Haus & Garten,' Josef Frank." Manuscript. University of Vienna, 1986.

Plischke, Ernst A. *Ein Leben mit Architektur.* Vienna, 1989.

Pommer, Richard, and Christian F. Otto, *Weissenhof 1927 and the Modern Movement in Architecture.* Chicago and London: University of Chicago Press, 1991.

Ponti, Gio. "La Casa all'Italiana." *Domus* (January 1928).

———. "Casa di Moda." *Domus* (August 1928).

———. "Verso gli artisti." *Domus* (November 1932).

———. "Espressione e carattere nell'opera di Frank e Wlach." *Domus* (March 1936)

———. "Una abitazione dimonstrativa alla VI Triennale." *Domus* (July 1936).

———. "Novità nelle forniture per la casa." *Domus* (March 1937).

———. "Una villa a tre appartamenti in Milano." *Domus* (March 1937).

Ponti, Lisa Licitra. *Gio Ponti: The Complete Work, 1923–1978.* Cambridge, MA: The MIT Press, 1990.

Popper-Lynkeus, Josef. *Phantasien eines Realisten* (1909). Reprint. Düsseldorf: Erb, 1980.

———. *Das Individuum und die Bewertung menschlicher Existenz.* (1910) Reprint. Dresden: Reissner, 1920.

Posch, Wilfried. "Josef Frank, eine bedeutende Persönlichkeit des österreichischen Kulturliberalismus." *Um Bau* 10 (1986).

Posener, Julius. "Adolf Loos-Der Raumplan." *Arch plus* 53 (1980).

———. "Der Raumplan: Vorläufer und Zeitgenossen von Adolf Loos." In *Adolf Loos, 1870–1933: Raumplan—Wohnungsbau.* Edited by Dietrich Worbs. Berlin: Akademie der Künste, 1984.

Pozzetto, Marco. *Die Schule Otto Wagners, 1894–1912.* Vienna: Anton Schroll, 1980.

———. *Max Fabiani: Ein Architekt der Monarchie.* Vienna: Edition Tusch, 1983.

Prokop, Ursula. *Wien: Aufbruch zur Metropole: Geschäfts- und Wohnhäuser der Innenstadt, 1910 bis 1914.* Vienna, Cologne, and Weimar: Böhlau Verlag, 1994.

Pulzer, Peter. *The Rise of Anti Semitism in Germany and Austria.* Rev. ed. Cambridge, MA: Harvard University Press, 1988.

Rabén, Hans. *Det moderna hemmet.* 3rd ed. Stockholm, Bokförlaget Natur och Kultur, 1950.

Reilly, P. "Report from Sweden." In *Design.* London: Design Council, 1981.

Richter, G. M. A. *The Furniture of the Greeks Etruscans and Romans.* London: Phaidon Press, 1966.

Risselada, Max, ed. *Raumplan Versus Plan Libre: Adolf Loos and Le Corbusier, 1919–1930.* New York: Rizzoli, 1988.

Rukschcio, Burkhardt, and Roland Schachel. *Adolf Loos: Leben und Werk.* Salzburg and Vienna: Residenz Verlag, 1982.

Sandberg, Gösta. In *Dalarnas Hembygdsbok, 1989.* Falun, Sweden: Dalarnas Museum, 1989.

Schezen, Roberto, and Peter Haiko. *Vienna 1850–1930: Architecture* New York, 1992.

Schildt, Göran. *Alvar Aalto: The Decisive Years.* New York: Rizzoli, 1986.

Schweiger, Werner J. *Wiener Werkstätte: Design in Vienna, 1903–1932.* New York: Abbeville Press, 1984.

Sekler, Eduard F. "The Architectural Reaction in Austria." *Journal of the Society of Architectural Historians* 24 (March 1965).

———. *Josef Hoffmann: Das architektonische Werk—Monographie und Werkverzeichnis.* Salzburg and Vienna: Residenz Verlag, 1982. *Josef Hoffmann: The Architectural Work.* Translated by John Maas. Princeton: Princeton University Press, 1985.

Seliger, Maren, and Karl Ucakar. *Wien: Politische Geschichte.* Vol. 2: *1896–1934.* Vienna: Jugend und Volk, 1985.

Sherrill, Sarah B. *Carpets and Rugs of Europe and America.* New York: Abbeville Press, 1995.

Smithson, Alison M., and Peter Smithson. *The Heroic Period of Modern Architecture.* New York: Rizzoli, 1981.

Sonnek, Gerd H. "Wien: Haus Wenzgasse." In *Paläste und Bürgerhäuser in Österreich.* Edited by Christine Wessely. Vienna: Notring der wissenschaftlichen Verbände Österreichs, 1970.

Spalt, Johannes, ed. *Der Architekt Oskar Strnad: Zum hundersten Geburtstag am 26. Oktober 1979.* Exhibition catalogue. Vienna: Hochschule für angewandte Kunst, 1979.

———, ed., *Josef Frank zum 100. Geburtstag am 15. Juli 1985.* Vienna: Hochschule für angewandte Kunst, 1985.

———. "Moderne Weltauffassung und moderne Architektur. *Bauwelt* 26 (July 12, 1985).

——— and Hermann Czech, eds. *Josef Frank, 1885–1967.* Vienna: Hochschule für angewandte Kunst, 1981.

——— and Otto Kapfinger. *Josef Frank 1885–1967, Stoffe, Tapeten, Teppiche.* Vienna: Hochschule für angewandte Kunst, 1986.

Sparke, Penny. "Swedish Modern, Myth and Reality." In *Svensk Form* London: Design Council, 1981.

Stadler, Friedrich, ed. *Arbeiterbildung in der Zwischenkriegszeit: Otto Neurath & Gerd Arntz*. Exhibition catalogue. Vienna and Munich: Österreichisches Gesellschafts- und Wirtschaftsmuseum/Löcker Verlag, 1982.

_____ and Peter Weibel, eds. *Vertreibung der Vernunft: The Cultural Exodus from Austria*. New York: Springer-Verlag, 1995.

Stavenow, Åke, et al., eds. *Swedish Arts and Crafts/Swedish Modern— A Movement Toward Sanity in Design*. Exhibition catalogue. Royal Swedish Commission, New York World's Fair, 1939.

Steinmann, Martin. *CIAM Dokumente 1928–1939*. Basel: Birkhäuser Verlag, 1979.

Stritzler, Nina. "Charlotte Perriand and the Development of the Corbusian Program for *Equipement de l'Habitation*." Master's thesis. The Cooper-Hewitt Museum/Parson's School of Design, New York, 1985.

Strnad, Oskar. "Neue Wege in der Wohnraumeinrichtung." *Innen-Dekoration* 33 (1922).

Strömberg, Martin. "Swedish Modern: svensk lösen i New York." *Svenska Hem i Ord och Bilder* 27 (April 1939).

Stuckenschmidt, H. H. *Schönberg: Leben, Umwelt, Werk*. Mainz: Piper-Schutt, 1984.

"Svenskt Tenn interiör i New York." *Ny Tidskrift för Konstindustri* 13 (March 1940).

"Sweden Offers a New Modern." *House and Garden* 76 (July 1939).

Tabor, Jan. "Die erneuerte Vision. Die Wiener Werkbundsiedlung, 1924–1984." In *Reflexionen und Aphorismen zur österreichischen Architektur*. Edited by Viktor Hufnagl. Vienna: Georg Prachner, 1984.

Tafuri, Manfredo. *Vienna Rosa: La politica residenziale nella Vienna socialista, 1919–1933*. Milan: Electa editrice, 1980.

Taut, Bruno. *Modern Architecture*. London: The Studio / New York: Albert & Charles Boni, Inc., [1929].

Tegethoff, Wolf. "From Obscurity to Maturity: Mies van der Rohe's Breakthrough to Modernism." In *Mies van der Rohe: Critical Essays*. Edited by Franz Schulze. New York: Museum of Modern Art, 1989.

Thomas, Michel, Christine Minguy, and Sophie Pommier. *Textile Art*. Translated by André Marling. Geneva, Switz.: Skira / London, Weidenfeld & Nicolson / New York: Rizzoli, 1985

Torriano, Piero. "L'Arte decorative contemporanea e l'Esposizione di Parigi." *Emporium* (January 1926).

*Traum und Wirklichkeit: Wien 1870–1930*. Exhibition catalogue. Vienna: Österreichische Akademie der Wissenschaften, 1985.

Troy, Nancy. *Modernism and the Decorative Arts: Art Nouveau to Le Corbusier*. New Haven: Yale University Press, 1991.

"Una casa en las proximdades de Viena." *Viviendas* 4 (June 1932).

Ungers, O. M., and Liselotte Ungers, eds. *Documents of Modern Architecture*. Nendeln/Liechtenstein: Kraus Reprint, 1979.

Venturi, Robert. *Complexity and Contradiction in Architecture*. New York: Museum of Modern Art, 1966.

Völker, Angela. *Die Stoffe der Wiener Werkstätte, 1910–1932*. Vienna: Verlag Christian Brandstätter, 1990.

Wagemann, Ines Gesine. *Der Architekt Bruno Möhring, 1863–1929*. Beiträge zur Kunstgeschichte 8. Bonn/Witterslick: Wehle, 1992.

Wängberg-Eriksson, Kristina. "Svenskt Tenn, Josef Frank och Estrid Ericson: En konsthistorisk studie." Master's thesis. University of Stockholm, 1985.

_____. *Josef Frank: Livsträd i krigens skugga*. Lund, Sweden: Signum, 1994.

_____ and R. Jacobsen. *Josef Frank 100 år Svenskt Tenn*. Stockholm, 1985.

Weihsmann, Helmut. *Das Roter Wien: Sozialdemokratische Architektur und Kommunalpolitik, 1919–1934*. Vienna: Promedia, 1985.

Weinzierl, Erika, and Kurt Skalnik. *Österreich 1918–1938: Geschichte der Ersten Republik*. 2 vols. Graz: Styria, 1983.

Weisman, Leslie Kanes. *Discrimination by Design: A Feminist Critique of the Man-Made Environment*. Urbana: University of Illinois Press, 1992.

Weltge-Wortmann, Sigrid. *Bauhaus Textiles: Women Artists and the Weaving Workshop*. London: Thames and Hudson, 1993.

Welzig, Maria. "Die Wiener Internationalität des Josef Frank: Das Werk des Architekten bis 1938," Ph.D. dissertation. University of Vienna, 1994.

"Werkstätten 'Haus & Garten' " in Wien." *Innen-Dekoration* 41 (November 1930).

Westheim, Paul. "Architektur-Entwicklung." *Die Glocke* 10 (1924).

Weston, Richard. *Alvar Aalto*. London: Phaidon, 1995.

Wickman, K., and Monica Boman. "Stockholm, 16 maj 1930." *Form* 2–3 (1980), pp. 24–35.

*Wien 1900: Kunst & Design*, Louisiana Revy [sic], vol. 31, no. 2 (January 1991).

Wigley, Mark. "White Out: Fashioning the Modern." In *Architecture: In Fashion*. Edited by Deborah Fausch. New York: Princeton University Press, 1994.

Wilk, Christopher. *Marcel Breuer: Furniture and Interiors*. New York: Museum of Modern Art, 1981.

Williams, Raymond. *Culture & Society, 1780–1950*. London: Penguin Books, 1958.

Windisch-Graetz, Franz. *Möbel Europas—Romantik-Gotik*. Munich: Klinkhardt & Biermann, 1982.

Witt-Dörring, Christian, Eva Mang , and Karl Mang, eds. *Neues Wohnen: Wiener Innenraumgestaltung 1918–1938.* Exhibition catalogue. Vienna: Österreichisches Museum für angewandte Kunst, 1980.

*Wörterbuch fur Volksschulen* (1926). Reprint. Vienna: Pichler-Tempsky, 1977.

———. *Philosophical Remarks.* Edited by Rush Rhees. Translated by Raymond Hargreaves and Roger White. Chicago: University of Chicago Press, 1975.

———. *Briefe.* Frankfurt: Suhrkamp, 1980.

———. "Lecture B VIII, Lent Term 1931." In *Wittgenstein's Lectures Cambridge 1930–1932.* Edited by Desmond Lee. Chicago: University of Chicago Press, 1982.

Wlach, Oskar. "Zu den Arbeiten von Josef Frank." *Das Interieur* 13 (1912).

Wollin, N. G. *Modern Swedish Decorative Art.* London: Architectural Press, 1931.

———. *Swedish Textiles, 1943–1950.* Leigh-on-Sea, Eng.: F. Lewis, 1952.

Worbs, Dietrich. "Der Raumplan in der Architektur von Adolf Loos." Ph.D. dissertation. Technische Universität Stuttgart, 1981.

———. "Josef Franks Wiener Massenwohnungsbau—ein pragmatischer Versuch." *Bauwelt* 26 (July 12, 1985).

Zahle, E., ed. *Scandinavian Domestic Design.* London: Methuen and Co. Ltd., 1963.

Zweig, Stefan. "Die Monotisierung der Welt." In *Begegnungen mit Menschen, Buchern Stadten.* Vienna/Zurich: Büchern, Städten, 1937.

Zweigbergk, Eva von. "Josef Frank." *Form* 63 (1967).

# INDEX

# Index

# Index

# Index